FLOPS ON 45

THE ONES THAT GOT AWAY

1965 TO 1979

RICHARD LYSONS

INTRODUCTION BY SIMON FRITH

This book is copyright under the Berne Convention. All rights are reserved. Apart from any fair dealing for the purpose of private study, research, criticism or review, as permitted under the Copyright Act, 1956, no part of this publication may be reproduced, stored in a retrieval system, or transmitted, in any form or by any means, electronic, electrical, chemical, mechanical, optical, photocopying, recording or otherwise, without the prior permission of the copyright owner. Enquiries should be sent to the under mentioned address:

EMPIRE PUBLICATIONS
1 Newton St., Manchester M1 1HW
© Richard Lysons 2025

ISBN: 9781915616289

Contents

- INTRODUCTION BY SIMON FRITH. 5
- PREFACE 9
- 1: BEATLE DRIVE .. .. .15
  - George Harrison ..... .15
  - John Lennon ..... .17
  - Paul McCartney ..... .18
  - Ringo Starr ..... .20
- 2: COMEDY TONIGHT ..... .23
  - The Barron Knights ..... .23
  - Billy Connolly ..... .26
  - Freddie And The Dreamers ..... .26
  - The Goodies ..... .28
  - New Vaudeville Band ..... .29
  - The Wurzels ..... .30
- 3: ALL THE FALLEN TEEN ANGELS ..... .32
  - Amen Corner ..... .32
  - The Bay City Rollers ..... .33
  - The Casuals ..... .35
  - Chicory Tip ..... .36
  - The Herd ..... .37
  - Love Affair ..... .38
  - Marmalade ..... .40
  - Slik ..... .42
  - The Tremeloes ..... .43
  - Vanity Fare ..... .46
  - Scott Walker ..... .49
  - The Walker Brothers ..... .51
- 4: MAKING THE MOST OF IT ..... .55
  - Herman's Hermits ..... .55
  - Hot Chocolate ..... .57

  New World .... .61
  Suzi Quatro .... .61
  Racey .... .63
  Smokie .... .64
5: **THE SOUND OF THE UNDERGROUND** .... .66
  Argent .... .66
  Atomic Rooster .... .67
  Bad Company .... .68
  Black Sabbath .... .68
  Eric Clapton .... .69
  Joe Cocker .... .70
  Cream .... .72
  Deep Purple .... .72
  Family .... .73
  Fleetwood Mac .... .74
  Free .... .76
  Genesis .... .77
  Jethro Tull .... .78
  Lindisfarne .... .79
  Medicine Head .... .82
  Nazareth .... .83
  Mike Oldfield .... .85
  Pink Floyd .... .86
  The Pretty Things .... .87
  Procol Harum .... .89
  Status Quo .... .91
  Supertramp .... .93
  Thin Lizzy .... .94
  Traffic .... .95
  Yes .... .96
6: **LADIES' NIGHT** .... .98
  Cilla Black .... .99
  Kate Bush .... .102
  Tina Charles .... .103
  Petula Clark .... .103
  Lynsey de Paul .... .107

	Kiki Dee	110
	Marianne Faithfull	113
	Anita Harris	114
	Mary Hopkin	115
	Linda Lewis	118
	Lulu	120
	Olivia Newton-John	124
	Clodagh Rodgers	129
	Sandie Shaw	131
	Dusty Springfield	136
	Bonnie Tyler	139
7:	THE LONDON BOYS	141
	David Bowie	141
	Dave Clark Five	143
	Darts	146
	Donovan	146
	David Essex	148
	Elton John	151
	The Kinks	154
	Manfred Mann	159
	The Rolling Stones	161
	Small Faces	161
	Squeeze	162
	Cat Stevens	163
	Rod Stewart	166
	The Who	167
	The Yardbirds	168
8:	TALES OF THE BROTHERS GIBB	170
	Andy Gibb	175
9:	SESSION STARS	177
	Blue Mink	177
	Brotherhood Of Man	179
	CCS	182
	White Plains	183
10:	THE REGIONS	185
	Dave Berry	185

Eric Burdon And The Animals... .185
Spencer Davis Group ... .187
Electric Light Orchestra / ELO . .189
Bryan Ferry ... .191
Wayne Fontana ... .191
Geordie ... .192
The Hollies ... .193
Lieutenant Pigeon.. ... .196
The Mindbenders.. ... .197
The Moody Blues .. ... .198
The Move. ... .201
Paper Lace ... .202
Showaddywaddy.... ... .203
Slade.. ... .204
10cc ... .207
The Troggs... .209
Wizzard... ... .211
Roy Wood ... .213

11: LIVERPOOL SUNSET ... .215
Gerry And The Pacemakers ... .215
Liverpool Express .. ... .216
The Real Thing ... .216
The Scaffold... ... .217
The Searchers . ... .221

12: GOOD CLEAN FUN.. ... .226
Tony Christie .. ... .226
Guys 'N' Dolls. ... .227
Engelbert Humperdinck ... .228
Tom Jones ... .230
Matt Monro.... ... .233
The New Seekers ... ... .233
Gilbert O'Sullivan.. ... .236
Pickettywitch... ... .238
Cliff Richard .. ... .239
The Seekers .... .242
The Shadows .. ... .244

Peter Skellern..	.248
Hurricane Smith	.249
13: GLAM	**.251**
Barry Blue	.251
Gary Glitter	.251
The Glitter Band	.253
Steve Harley & Cockney Rebel	.254
Hello	.256
Mott The Hoople	.257
Mud	.258
Roxy Music	.260
Alvin Stardust	.261
The Sweet	.263
T. Rex	.265
14: HARMONY CONSTANT.	**.268**
Arrival	.268
The Fortunes	.269
The Ivy League	.271
The Rockin' Berries	.272
15: MIXED BAG..	**.276**
The Equals	.276
The Foundations	.277
Fox	.278
Hudson Ford	.278
Manfred Mann's Earth Band	.280
McGuinness Flint	.281
John Miles	.282
Mungo Jerry	.283
Don Partridge	.284
The Rubettes	.285
Barry Ryan	.286
Sailor	.289
Crispian St Peters	.291
Peter Sarstedt	.292
Leo Sayer	.292
Steeleye Span	.294

The Strawbs .... .296
The Wombles .... .298
16: CELTIC CONNECTIONS .... .301
Junior Campbell .... .301
Dave Edmunds .... .302
Andy Fairweather Low .... .304
Gallagher and Lyle .... .305
Middle Of The Road .... .306
Pilot .... .307
Gerry Rafferty .... .309
Sensational Alex Harvey Band .... .309
Stealers Wheel .... .310
Them .... .312
17: THE KID'S A PUNK .... .314
Buzzcocks .... .314
The Clash .... .315
Generation X .... .316
The Jam .... .317
Public Image Limited .... .317
Tom Robinson Band .... .318
Sham 69 .... .319
Siouxsie And The Banshees .... .319
The Stranglers .... .320
UK Subs .... .320
X-Ray Spex .... .321
What About Queen? .... .322
AFTERWORD .... .324
SELECT BIBLIOGRAPHY .... .325
ACKNOWLEDGEMENTS .... .329

Introduction

In the music business you were only as good as your last record and it was a highly competitive and well-subscribed game — like snakes and ladders. You rolled the dice, climbed a few steps, but each roll was a gamble where you could easily slide down the snake and end up back where you started.

PAULINE MURRAY[1]

EARLY IN MY CAREER AS A MUSIC JOURNALIST I got the job of writing the 'Single File' page in *Let It Rock*, one of the earliest British rock magazines, published in London between 1972 and 1975. As its Reviews Editor, I knew perfectly well that the magazine was set up to make sense of the emerging genres and ideologies of rock. Album reviews were the ones that mattered, to writers, readers and musicians alike. But I loved writing 'Single File' and reading *Flops On 45* reminds me why.

The simple reason was the flood of free singles — many of which were flops and some of which (flops included) I still have. And this was a particular joy because my love and understanding of popular music had been shaped by singles. As a youngster, I saved my pocket money to buy the 45s I heard on Luxembourg and the BBC's various record request shows. I went to the local electrical goods shop (the only place to sell records in the small market town where I lived), usually to find that they didn't have the record I wanted or, at best, only had a British cover version. An early memory is going in to get Guy Mitchell's 'Singing the Blues' and coming out with Tommy Steele's even chirpier version; my recurring memory is coming out of the shop

---

1. Pauline Murray: *Life's a Gamble. Penetration, The Invisible Girls and Other Stories*, London: Omnibus Press 2023, p.99.

every fortnight with a record I hadn't gone in to buy.

As I got older, read the pop papers and listened to/watched pop programmes, I came to realise that the key question about a single was not whether it was any good but whether it would be a hit. This was the question asked at each moment of its production and promotion and consumption, a question no-one could answer with any confidence or plot with any certainly of success. This remained the case throughout the 1970s, as *Flops On 45* documents. When I first moved to Coventry, in 1972, I still had to buy singles in an electrical goods shop or Boots although, soon enough, new kinds of singles shops emerged: local DJ Pete Waterman's Soul Hole; Virgin Upstairs, a punk hangout managed by Gordon Montgomery, who went on to launch Fopp.

After *Let It Rock* folded I wrote about singles for other music mags. By now I was getting increasing numbers of 12" dance tracks and DIY label releases but the serendipitous logic of the singles market stayed the same. 45s provided transitory entertainment; success (hits) happened randomly; failure, the many records which I dutifully wrote about but no-one else seemed to notice, was equally unpredictable. When I was young I often bought singles that quickly turned out to be unlistenable, however much I hated to admit it; now I praised records which turned to have no sales and ignored to-my-ears characterless records that were soon scampering up the charts. *Flops On 45* is, for me, retrospectively comforting. It shows that the people making, recording and selling singles were equally unable to fathom public taste.

I learned to be a critic on the singles beat. I had continuously to bring into balance aesthetic and commercial judgements. And as an academic trying to make sense of the music industry, I concluded that failure was the most successful product of the creative industries, the thing they did best. But I didn't understand then as I do now what Richard Lysons implies in this book: flops and commercial misjudgements can be celebrated. They mark the limits of record company schemes to manipulate public taste, to ensure success. Everything in the promotional handbook can be in place: star names, advertising budgets, radio play, record shop displays, a spot on a TV or live package show, and still the record stalls at 43.

In the end, though, *Flops On 45* isn't just a fun read about commercial hubris and the vagaries of consumers. It is also a rather moving account of musical comradeship. It pays tribute to the determination and care with which a host of unsung music-makers worked together (with a cheerful knowledge of their likely failure) on the pop hit production line. Composers and lyricists, producers and engineers, arrangers and orchestrators, session musicians and backing singers, with a wealth of professional experience, some of whose names I knew, most of whose names I didn't, worked tirelessly together to make musical offerings that the public would mostly never notice. This seems to me a kind of heroism, a refusal to be brought down by the knowledge that even if a resulting single was a hit, it wouldn't be their names that the public would remember.

Flops On 45 makes an important contribution to popular music history: it honours a forgotten workforce.

Simon Frith
May 2025

Preface

WE HAVE ALL HAD FLOPS IN OUR LIVES: parties with hardly anybody turning up, an inquorate meeting, an art exhibition opening with wine left over, a public event with a tiny audience or a gig with more bodies on stage than those watching. Flops are part of life. In the lives of film directors, concert promoters, pub landlords — to name but three professions, flops can mean financial disaster and/or a ruined reputation.

In the fickle world of popular music, flops can happen to almost anyone. Sometimes these are flops because an artist has alienated fans with their behaviour or the content of a new release. Careful marketing can try to counter this, but often the public can just "decide" that they are tired of a particular artist. Simon Reynolds, when referring to Sparks, described this as: *"the Arc of Fruitless Intensification. This is when artists almost irresistibly find themselves increasing the dosage of whatever it is in their music, lyrics and presentation that makes them unique and stand out from the pack. The thing that starts out as an attraction swiftly becomes an irritant, even a repulsion."*

A hardcore and loyal fanbase can often bring a single into the charts, but then the record may stay for a solitary week because "floating" fans and would-be purchasers have heard or heard about a new record's flaws and simply not bought it. Sometimes a radical change of style or simple retreading of a previous release can result in a flop.

Flops On 45 is an attempt to document the times when established UK chart acts failed to reach the Top Thirty. It is not a list of one-hit wonders nor an attempt to be comprehensive or definitive. These days, thanks to Spotify, YouTube and various streaming services, it is possible to hear pretty much any record. Some of my research and commentary was helped by such services. I had genuinely forgotten what The Sweet's 'Turn It Down' single sounded like. Luckily there is footage of said song on *The Geordie Scene*. I know now why this Chinn-Chapman composition was not a big hit and it was nothing to do with the use of the word "God" in the lyrics as some have claimed. 'Turn It Down' was simply sub-standard and thousands of Sweet fans — and the wider singles-buying public — did not purchase a copy for that reason.

Top of the Pops, Radio One and Radio Luxembourg were crucial to the success of a single. The army of record company pluggers targetted the various producers and disc jockeys, hoping to get their product on the station's playlist, or — as in *Top of the Pops*' case — featured as a new release. The best book about the music "biz" in the early 1970s remains Michael Wale's *Voxpop* (1972). In a dozen or so chapters Wale looks at different roles in the pop industry, interviewing composers, producers, session musicians and so on. The most fascinating chapters concern pluggers and disc jockeys. Significantly, this was researched and written a couple of years before the start of independent local radio in the UK. One *Top of the Pops* appearance — as Sparks realised — could transform a single's fortunes. Without video recorders, BBC i-Player and smart televisions, such television appearances were simply here today and gone tomorrow. Peter Checksfield lists the hundreds of *Top of the Pops* performances that were wiped. Fortunately, some episodes of British programmes such as *Supersonic* and *The Geordie Scene* were preserved, as were a lot of German TV's brilliant *Beat Club* programmes.

In the late 1960s and early 1970s it almost seemed that there was an unwritten rule at the BBC that any popular music programme had to include one or more of the following artists: Cleo Laine, Alan Price, Julie Felix and Labi Siffre. This narrow range of "acceptable" performers gave viewers a very misleading impression of popular music. The television shows that starred Cliff, Cilla, Lulu, Sandie Shaw et al also seemed interchangeable in terms of guests. Most of the above were also regularly on *Top of the Pops*, irrespective of the chart potential or position of their single releases. Peter Checksfield's book is a source of constant fascination, as one counts the sheer number of appearances by such singers on that programme.

Some records were plugged endlessly on both Radio One and

Radio Luxembourg and still did not sell. The phrase "turntable hit" was coined for these releases. *The Guinness Book Of Hit Singles* still brings surprises: Tom Jones's 'Thunderball' peaked at No. 35! The daytime DJs on Radio One had "records *OF* the week" (sic); Tony Blackburn always used to emphasise the word "of". But even many of these singles were flops. However, Blackburn actually *made* some hits, for example Matthew's Southern Comfort's cover of Joni Mitchell's 'Woodstock' reached No. 1 after constant plays by him.

I recall that my purchasing of flops started out at a second-hand record shop in Brook Street in Chester (a few doors down from where the Grey & Pink shop is now) in 1971. The front room of the shop sold mostly singles and a few albums, while the back room (clearly the moneymaker) sold porn. The whole place smelled of cat pee, but that did not put me off. I remember that the owner had another shop in Wrexham. Second-hand singles at this shop started at about 20p and I immediately bought a few Scaffold ones – '2 Day's Monday', 'Goodbat Nightman', 'Thank U Very Much', 'Do You Remember' and, of course, 'Lily The Pink'.

There were also Pop-Ex singles for sale. These were former juke box records with no 'middle' ; these must have been 30p or 40p in the early 1970s. I was not aware of a nostalgia or oldies scene at the time. Andrew Lauder at Liberty/United Artists seemed to be very much on his own when his company reissued old records. A programme on Radio One called *First Gear* was aired while John Peel and *Top Gear* were on holiday and played rock 'n' roll records. There was another radio show called *All Our Yesterplays*. It is hard to imagine this nowadays with the sheer number of oldie and "Gold" stations, and the number of oldies programmes on Radio Two.

These were the days before published pop discographies, *Record Collector* magazine and even the *Guinness Book Of Hit Singles*. I cannot remember hearing or reading the word 'discography' in the early 1970s. Only blues, jazz and rock 'n' roll music was extensively chronicled and such information was not readily available to schoolboys. The *Rock File* series of books predated the *Guinness* books and were exceedingly useful. Strangely enough, there are very few books about hit singles and even fewer about flops. This book, like my previous study of the

Free Trade Hall in Manchester, aims to fill a definite gap in popular music history.

In *Rock File 2*, Simon Frith's essay, 'The Year Of Singles In Britain' is essential and fascinating reading. Looking at the year 1972-1973, he reveals that about two thousand singles were released and only 180 of these were hits. Frith stresses that not all singles were aimed at the pop charts, citing such specialist markets as records specifically for children (such as Disney ones), brass band enthusiasts, train-spotters, "soul freaks", reggae and "hard soul".

I have restricted this book to British artists between 1965 and 1979. The dates span my key years of being interested in pop music. I started a pop scrapbook in 1965 and I was clearly aware of the charts. The year 1979 saw my graduation and other interests started to take up my time – politics, job-hunting and living independently. In some ways this is a secret history of British pop for those years. Much of it was new to me, and I felt that I kept pretty well informed in those days.

Criteria for inclusion is that the acts have to have had at least two Top Thirty hits in the UK charts between 1965 and 1979, before any of their flops are discussed. I have included Australian acts who made records in the UK and those American acts – such as The Walker Brothers and Suzi Quatro – who worked in London with British record companies and musicians. I used the *Guinness Book Of Hit Singles* in various editions. I know that most of the music papers had their own charts, but for the sake of simplicity (and my own sanity) I have not used them.

At the end of the book you will not find a discography or even playlists. There are simply far too many LPs and CDs that I listened to for the research. I can recommend the compilations and reissues on Ace Records, Cherry Red, BGO, Repertoire and Rhino. The three-disc Gold series are excellent value for acts such as Kiki Dee, Lulu, The New Seekers and The Tremeloes. Proceed with caution whenever you see very cheap CD compilations; some artists re-record their old songs, not always successfully. You can make your own playlists and compilations from Spotify as I have done.

Someone asked me what happened to all these artists whose flops outnumbered their hits. Many went into cabaret and nostalgia tours, some opened their own studios but technology has inevitably reduced the need for many of these facilities. Some still have careers in Europe, especially Germany. One musician and producer, Alan Parsons, wisely used some of our more distinctive singers for his various albums. Look carefully at the Alan Parsons Project discography and you will find vocals by the likes of Colin Blunstone, Gary Brooker, Allan Clarke, Dean Ford, Steve Harley, John Miles, David Paton and Terry Sylvester. Clearly, there is life after flops.

Richard Lysons
May 2025

1- Beatle Drive

THE BEATLES, ALONG WITH THEIR RIVALS AND friends, The Rolling Stones, did not have flops in the 1960s. 'Love Me Do' went Top Twenty, 'Please Please Me' reached No. 2 in some charts and after that it was a straight run of chart-toppers starting with 'From Me To You' in 1963 to 'Ballad Of John And Yoko', six years later. The only exception was 'Penny Lane'/'Strawberry Fields Forever' which was kept off No. 1 by Engelbert Humperdinck's 'Release Me'. The irony of the greatest double A-side single of the pop era being outsold by a crooner from Leicester is not lost on rock historians. The year 1967 was very much Humperdinck's year; his three singles were in the charts for a total of 99 weeks. Two of these reached No. 1, the other No. 2.

When The Beatles disbanded, it was assumed that their solo releases would continue the high quality of the group's eight years of recording. In *The Guardian*, Robin Denselow wrote about the initial round of post-group releases in an article called "*Ringo stars*".

GEORGE HARRISON

Initially, George Harrison was the most successful solo Beatle. 'My Sweet Lord' was No.1 on both sides of the Atlantic and its parent triple album, *All Things Must Pass*, sold millions of copies. The album (if we ignore the third disc of jams) was an extremely high quality release with wonderful songs, setting a standard not just for George, but also for his former bandmates. George's follow-up to 'My Sweet Lord', 'Bangla Desh', was one of the first charity singles and reached No. 10 in 1971. Two years later, 'Give Me Love (Give Me Peace On Earth)' also went Top Ten in the UK.

After another 18 month gap, 'Ding Dong' reached No. 38 in 1974. George claims that the words are taken from Lord Tennyson. The single was meant to be seasonal, but I found it tiresome. It reminds me of false jollity at a Christmas party. Roy Carr and Tony Tyler called it: *"meticulously-played emptiness ... a charmless reworking of the traditional peal o' bells."* NME was even harsher: *"I should imagine that some of you have already perused the lyrics of this trite little ballad, as presented in Harrison's ad last week. Repetitive, you may have thought. Blindingly uninspired, you may have murmured to yourself. I have rarely heard a drabber melody, a more vacuous set of lyrics, a cornier production, a more lacklustre vocal or a less inspired song concept ... no other ex-Moptop has ever sunk to these depths.."* In only three years, George's reputation for making quality records was wrecked.

George's next single, 'Dark Horse' was worse; this was the title track of his latest album and the name of Harrison's record label. In *I Me Mine*, George is almost apologetic *"The pity with 'Dark Horse' – the song – was that I hadn't finished the record when I had to go to the States to rehearse the band for the American tour in 1974. So I taught the band the tune and we recorded it 'live' and by that time I had no voice so it's a hoarse (!) version of it, while the other remains unfinished."* This sort of feeble excuse would be unacceptable from even an amateur musician; but coming from a former Beatle and the composer of 'Something', 'Here Comes The Sun' and so many other brilliant recordings, it is unforgivable. 'Dark Horse' did not chart in the UK.

I prefer the follow-up, 'You', which reached No. 38 in 1975. George: *"'You' was written for Phil Spector's wife Ronnie ... I tried to write a Ronette sort of song ... I forgot about it and years later dug the tape out and re-worked it, overdubbed on it and did it myself even though it was recorded in Ronnie's register — a bit high for me."* This is an infectious song, recalling the best parts of *All Things Must Pass* with a great Spector-type production.

The title of 'This Guitar Can't Keep From Crying' clearly echoed George's classic song, 'While My Guitar Gently Weeps'. NME: *"his voice sounds sneering, and the guitar — the tearful one — sounds considerably more muscular than usual ... bit self-absorbed ..."* Chris Ingham was also unconvinced: *"(it) feebly winks back at his other weeping guitar song."*

Worse was to follow for Harrison. Three singles were released from 1976's *Thirty-Three And A Third* album, most notably 'This Song' which was his reaction to the 'My Sweet Lord'/'He's So Fine' plagiarism court case. George himself said: *"I wrote 'This Song' as a bit of light comedy relief – and as a away to exorcize the paranoia about songwriting that had started to build up in me.*" Unfortunately, the song is not funny with self-pitying, rather than witty, lyrics. The video for the song – set inevitably in a court room – is equally humourless. Follow-ups were 'Crackerbox Palace' and a cover of Cole Porter's 'True Love'

'Blow Away', Chris Ingham said, *"perfectly conveys the breezy change of mood required to banish his sporadic blues."* This reached No. 51 in spring 1979. The follow-up was 'Love Comes To Everyone'. *"'Blow Away' did just that, surprisingly. It did show a very un-young sold-out George Harrison but on another level it was a very proficient M.O.R. record, which is what this follow-up is ... nothing new about it. Harrison is turning in terms of durability of his songs into a poor man's Paul McCartney."*

George returned to the British Top Twenty in 1981 with 'All Those Years Ago', his sensitive and moving tribute to John Lennon. Half a dozen years later, he reached No. 2 with his cover of James Ray's 'Got My Mind Set On You'.

George Harrison died in 2001. The *Concert for George* was held at the Royal Albert Hall on the first anniversary of his death. It was recorded and filmed, and is a delightful watch. Suffice to say, none of the above flops were performed by the famous line-up of musicians, all friends of George, brought together by Eric Clapton.

John Lennon

Lennon's first four singles with the Plastic Ono Band were all extraordinary releases, from the Canadian hotel recording of 'Give Peace A Chance' (which reached No. 2), the pain of 'Cold Turkey' with its searing guitar supplied by Eric Clapton, to the powerful Spector productions of 'Instant Karma' and 'Power To The People'. Over half a century later, 'Instant Karma' still sounds incredible. 'Power To The People' was noisier and less effective, but inspired at least one would-be revolutionary on television, a few years later, in the comedy series *Citizen Smith*.

The first two Lennon solo albums, *John Lennon/Plastic Ono Band* and *Imagine* were also produced by Phil Spector. No singles were taken from either album in Britain. 'Imagine' was eventually released as a single in

1975 and reached No. 5. Sadly, the song only reached the top spot in 1980 following Lennon's assassination.

Lennon had only one actual flop in Britain during his lifetime. 'Whatever Gets You Through The Night' was an American No. 1 but struggled to reach No. 36 over here. This collaboration with Elton John is described in the *Virgin Encyclopedia Of Popular Music* as "*a strong rocker*", but I am a little resistant to its charms, as were Roy Carr and Tony Tyler: "*it is catchy, well played, jerky, poppy ... and it could have been recorded by almost anyone*". *Record Mirror* was more positive: "*very uptempo and funky... complete contrast for the man, and it's the best thing he's put out as a single in aeons. Loads of multi-tracking on the vocals whips it all together nicely.*" Elton is featured on piano and backing vocals and, like a lot of his own faster songs such as 'Saturday Night's Alright For Fighting' and 'The Bitch Is Back', it feels more like a characterless impersonation of a rock band. Elton bet Lennon that their single would reach No. 1 in the USA and Lennon promised to appear on stage with Elton if this happened. He did so at Madison Square Garden on November 28th 1974; it was Lennon's last live appearance.

His cover of Ben E. King's 'Stand By Me' in 1975 narrowly avoided being a flop by reaching No. 30. This was followed by Lennon's years at home helping rear his second son, Sean, and he did not release any new product until 1980's *Double Fantasy* album. His assassination in December of that year inevitably brought a surge of record sales and reissues.

Paul McCartney

McCartney was by far the most prolific former Beatle in the 1970s, releasing nine albums of new material, as well as several stand-alone singles in that decade. In 1970 McCartney released his first solo album which contained at least two classics — 'Every Night' and 'Maybe I'm Amazed' — but neither was released as a single at the time. A live version of 'Maybe I'm Amazed' was a hit in spring 1977, taken from the *Wings Over America* album. I cannot help wondering how successful the 1970 studio version would have been if McCartney had released the song as his first solo single. It would have made a logical follow-up to 'Let It Be' and surely would have reached No. 1 leaving his fellow bandmates aghast at his sheer nerve and talent. Paul's first solo single was not released until February of the following year. The *"anaemic"* (according to Chris Ingham) 'Another Day' reached No. 2 early in 1971. This single was never a favourite of mine, sounding weedier than 'Instant Karma', 'It Don't Come Easy' and 'My Sweet Lord'.

The *Ram* album soon followed in May 1971. One of the tracks from *Ram*, 'Back Seat Of My Car' (credited to Paul *and* Linda McCartney) was released as a single in mid-August 1971, three months after the album had appeared. The record stalled at No. 39, *NME* criticised the release of tracks from the McCartneys' latest album for their new single. The reviewer said *"I don't rate this as one of the best tracks (on* Ram*)... it's a ballad that's rich in atmosphere — soothing, flowing, lilting and coloured by engaging harmonies and changing tempos."*

McCartney went on to form Wings and all his recordings for the rest of the decade were released as by either Wings or Paul McCartney and Wings. The core line-up of the group were Paul and Linda McCartney and Denny Laine; a succession of guitarists and drummers came and went.

'Letting Go' was taken from the *Venus And Mars* album as the follow-up to 'Listen To What The Man Said'. I remember the single receiving a lot of radio play at the time. Roy Carr and Tony Tyler called the song: *"one of the few genuinely potent tracks on the album,"* but Chris Ingham disagreed: *"(an) inert sludge-rocker ...an anonymous drone and a disastrous choice for a single."* The record reached No. 41.

Wings' sixth album, *London Town* was issued in February 1978, their first release since the mega-selling 'Mull Of Kintyre' single. Three singles were taken from this album. The first, the rather weedy 'A Little Luck' was another American No.1 and another Top Ten hit in the UK. 'I've Had Enough' was released next; it only reached No. 41. *Record Mirror: "Another band who are capable of producing excellent material, but who are palming us off with sub-standard wares. A weak rocker."* Again, *Billboard* was more positive: *"McCartney's growling vocal and an insistent beat (made the song) a decisive statement in release of pent-up frustrations."* Finally, the title track of *London Town* was released. *Billboard* magazine called it: *"(a) melodic atmospheric ballad."* The song displays many of McCartney's extraordinary strengths as a songwriter: lots of hooks, little touches of brilliance and, of course, a wonderful melody. The single fared even worse than 'I've Had Enough', stalling at No. 60.

The next year, 1979, saw McCartney bounce back with 'Goodnight Tonight', a Top Five hit. Unfortunately, that was his band's musical and commercial peak of that year. There was a new album, *Back To The Egg*, and a single from it, 'Old Siam Sir' reached No. 35; Chris Ingham called the song "*lacklustre and contrived.*" The next single, the double A-side, 'Getting Closer'/'Baby's Request' did as badly as 'London Town'. Ingham again: "*'Getting Closer' is warmed over 'Jet'*", while *Billboard* said: "*an uplifting raker in which McCartney's vocals play off strong guitar, keyboards and drum lines ...*" Ingham calls 'Baby's Request' "*(a) cute Mills Brothers tribute.*" Significantly, this was the final Wings album. McCartney's next release was a second solo album, *McCartney II*, where he was back to doing everything himself, as he had done a decade earlier for his first solo album. *McCartney II* contained two massive British hits, 'Coming Up' and 'Waterfalls'.

Ringo Starr

Unusually for a drummer, Ringo Starr was generally allowed to sing one song on each Beatles' album (apart from *A Hard Day's Night* and *Let It Be*). Songs such as 'Boys', 'Honey Don't', 'Act Naturally', 'What Goes On', 'Yellow Submarine', 'With A Little Help From My Friends', 'Don't Pass Me By' and 'Octopus's Garden'. Whether this was a token gesture or a carefully thought marketing move, doesn't matter, but there was a definite feeling of a rationing of Starr's vocals.

As a solo artist Starr started with two albums: *Sentimental Journey* was exactly that with him attempting standards such as 'Night And Day' with an impressive cast of arrangers. The second, *Beaucoups Of Blues* was a country album from Nashville. Luckily, Starr then released several impressive solo singles at a rate of about one a year. 'It Don't Come Easy' and 'Photograph' still sound good, but clearly have much input from, amongst others, George Harrison. 'Back Off Boogaloo', although reaching No. 2 in 1972, sounds messy and overblown. The *Ringo* album featured all three of his former bandmates on different tracks and it's quite fun, but there is a big difference between one song per album, an occasional hit single and a whole album of Starr singing. His cover of Johnny Burnette's 'You're Sixteen' was enjoyable and the subject matter didn't "feel" uneasy way back in 1974. Harry Nilsson sings backing vocals and Paul performs a kazoo solo. This was Starr's last UK Top Ten hit.

Attempts were made to recreate the magic and success of the *Ringo* album with its follow-up, *Goodnight Vienna* which overflowed with such guest stars as Lennon, Elton John, Billy Preston, Allen Toussaint and Steve Cropper. 'Only You', with Starr's down to earth singalong version the antithesis of the glorious Platters' lead tenor of Tony Williams, scraped into the Top Thirty at No. 28. This marked the end of Starr's 1970s British chart career.

Another track from *Goodnight Vienna*, 'Snookeroo' was penned by Elton John and Bernie Taupin. *Record Mirror*: "*the obvious Elton piano-playing and arrangement makes it more interesting than some of (Ringo's) songs.*" The single was played on Radio One, as was 'Oh My My'. The latter was a three year-old track and had been included on the 1973 *Ringo* album, but not released as a single in the UK until 1976. *Record Mirror*: "*Teapabout sound from Mr Starr that should get a few people on their feet. It's Ringo in a jolly mood with lots of oom pa pa's all over the place ... this joins the pile that should make the charts..*" Maggie Bell also released a version of the song.

Starr continued to release singles to the end of the 1970s. 'A Dose Of Rock 'n' Roll' had an all-star backing group with Dr John on keyboards, Klaus Voorman on bass, the Brecker Brothers on horns and Peter Frampton, who according to *Record World,* added "*some spicy guitar licks*" to the song. The single reached No. 26 in the USA. I remember hearing Starr's cover of Bruce Channel's 'Hey Baby' which was released just five weeks later. Despite the famous musicians and having no less than Atlantic Records legendary Arif Mardin as producer, these were both flops in the UK.

2 – Comedy Tonight

COMEDY AND NOVELTY RECORDS ARE AMONG the hardest singles and albums to have sustaining appeal. Records that were screamingly funny on their first few listens quickly become irritating to the ears.

The Barron Knights

I have been aware of The Barron Knights for 60 years. Both fellow pop stars and their audiences loved the group's clever (and gentle) spoofs. 'Call Up The Groups' was an early favourite with its medley of short parodies of current chart hits, inspired by a similar record in the USA by The Four Preps called 'The Big Draft'. The group has successfully returned to this formula throughout their lengthy career. Successful and enduring parodies and pastiches of popular music are difficult to achieve; Stan Freberg had a few gems, as did The Barron Knights. *"Birth control to Ginger Tom"*, *"There's a dentist in Birmingham"* and *"Christmas Turkey, you can stuff it"* became earworms. These are, respectively, witty adaptations of 'Space Oddity', 'Rivers Of Babylon' and 'Another Brick In The Wall'. They all still make me smile.

The group were accomplished musicians and harmony singers, and this was shown on occasional singles. 'It Was A Very Good Year' was originally written as a solo showcase for Bob Shane of The Kingston Trio. Later the song was covered by both Lonnie Donegan and Frank Sinatra on his *September Of My Years* album. The Barron Knights' version was described by *NME* as having, *"a folksy quality (which) permeates (this) enchanting ballad ... sung mainly in unison with delightful harmonies and absorbing guitar work."* The reviewer admits that although the single has *"charm and appeal"*, its *"lack of gimmicks ... won't enhance their chart chances."* In between the medleys, the Barron Knights recorded several "straight" songs such as this, but none of them were hits.

'Lazy Fat People' was released in March 1967. *NME*: "*This marks a departure from the team's usual send-up discs. Mind you, the lyric is very tongue-in-cheek and it's infused with gimmicks a-plenty. Set at a gallop-pace rhythm.. it's quite different from the boys' usual style.*" Penny Valentine was enthusiastic in *Disc & Music Echo*: "*quite the best Barron Knights have ever made, and how I've hated the others. Pete Townshend wrote it and it really would have made a splendid Who single. As it is, it is a delight, the lyrics are joyous and the odd little quirky noises add charm to an already appealing record. Should be a hit, but perhaps this sort of song really needs The Who, who knows.*" There have been a limited number of covers of Pete Townshend songs. This one works well with its flamenco guitar and witty lyrics.

'Doing What She's Not Supposed To' was reviewed in *NME*: "*A happy-go-lucky bouncer with an easy-going jog-trot beat. It has a cute novelty lyric, but the song isn't startling, and isn't ideal material for them.*" 'Here Come The Bees' was previewed on *Top of the Pops* in October 1967. The song sounds nothing like The Barron Knights and is typical of the British orchestral pop records of the time. The lyrics had lines such as "*The park is full of people holding their hands*", appearing to slightly ridicule flower power. The single received good reviews, but again, failed to chart.

The 1968 Olympic Games in Mexico brought another medley, 'An Olympic Record'. *NME*: "*the boys supplying Olympic lyrics to six well known songs – 'Lazy Sunday', 'I Pretend', 'Delilah', 'Cinderella Rockefella', 'Dream A Little Dream Of Me' and 'Here Comes the Judge'. One of the funniest numbers they ever produced and for my money a hit.*" This release only reached No. 35 and was the start of a nine-year chart absence for the Barron Knights.

When reviewing 'Love And The World Loves You', *NME* explained the group's problem: "*The Barron Knights have made a rod for their own backs with their novelty mickey-taking discs [when] you get a straightforward ballad ... you tend to be a bit disappointed because the group have lost its individuality.. This is an attractive song with a pleasant melody and is appealingly handled by Duke D'mond with harmonic support from the other boys.*"

By 1971, The Barron Knights were signed to Penny Farthing and went back to recording medleys of pop parodies. 'Popumentary '71' concerned itself with Europe (what was then called the Common Market). They put new words to 'Banner Man' (Blue Mink), 'Grandad'

(Clive Dunn) and 'Did You Ever' (Lee Hazlewood and Nancy Sinatra). The B-side saw 'Chirpy Chirpy Cheep Cheep' (Middle Of The Road), 'Resurrection Shuffle' (Ashton, Gardner & Dyke) and 'Knock Three Times' (Dawn). 'Did You Ever' replaced Lee and Nancy with Ted Heath and Harold Wilson, echoing a famous part of impressionist, Mike Yarwood's act. *NME* called it " *a hilarious party record.*" The record buying public disagreed.

'You're All I Need' was released in 1972 and reviewed in *NME*: "*The vocals are close to John Kongos and the guitar is definitely like Bolan's on this straight pop song which should stand a good chance with the boppers.*" The boppers ignored it.

The group's 'The Ballad Of Frank Spencer' in 1974 was a tribute to the character played by Michael Crawford in the BBC1 comedy series *Some Mothers Do 'Ave 'Em*, the creation of writer Raymond Allen. The single has a Johnny Cash type country backing and the singer has a faux American accent. In between the verses there are short "Spencerisms" as so often performed by such impressionists as Mike Yarwood and Lenny Henry. Unfortunately, the single is not actually funny.

The Barron Knights made a successful comeback in 1977 when the group had a Top Ten single with 'Live In Trouble'. *Top of the Pops* appearances revealed the group to now have perms or greying hair, but it was exactly the same formula as their 1960s triumphs. The Barron Knights even had a chart album, *Night Gallery*, which reached No. 15. 'Back In Trouble' followed straight after, in January 1978 and was reviewed in *Record Mirror*: "*Spoofs of 'Bohemian Rhapsody', 'Telephone Man' and 'Space Oddity'! The last mentioned is the best — 'Birth Control to Ginger Tom' etc. Fun. Sure to get a lot of radio plays. Chart material.*" Surprisingly, this release flopped. Perhaps the group should have waited until the next Christmas season.

Christmas 1978 saw 'A Taste Of Aggro' do even better than 'Live In Trouble', reaching No. 3. The following Christmas brought 'Food For Thought', but this single staggered to No. 46. 'Get Down Shep' was a one-joke song, lampooning *Blue Peter* presenter, John Noakes. The song is in a country style and does not stand up to repeated listening. The Barron Knights continued to release records throughout the 1980s and into the 1990s. There have been line-up changes over the years; most of the original line-up have died or retired, but original member Pete Langford remains.

Billy Connolly

It's difficult to believe that Billy Connolly had a No.1 hit single in November 1975 with his parody of Tammy Wynette's 'D.I.V.O.R.C.E.' hit. Her original version had reached No. 12 in the British charts the previous summer. The introduction of independent local radio in Britain in 1972 had significantly challenged BBC Radio One and Two's duopoly of daytime radio. The new stations became incredibly popular in London (Capital Radio), Birmingham (BRMB), Liverpool (Radio City) and Manchester (Piccadilly Radio) and introduced many country records to the British. The following summer, Connolly released another parody of a country song. This was 'No Chance', mimicking J.J. Barrie's 'No Charge' which had reached the UK top spot in April 1976. Connolly's spoof reached No. 26. Both of his hit records seemed amusing at the time, but – like many parodies – have a diminishing impact with repeated listening.

Successful follow-ups were a challenge. 'Isn't It A Shame' was written by songwriting team Phil Coulter and Bill Martin but did not chart. 'In The Brownies' was released in 1979. *Sounds: "If ever there there was a record that deserves the piss taking out of it, it was 'In The Navy'. The Big Yin does it admirably, as ever. The disco beat can fool you for a minute with lines like 'Young man, you're sure to ... (??) blind. if you don't eat up your carrots.."* The single is not very funny.

Freddie And The Dreamers

Freddie Garrity had one of the better singing voices in the early 1960s beat boom; it was clear, tuneful and its slight Mancunian burr prevented any attempt to sound convincingly American. Unfortunately, Garrity generally hid this ability with his group's "comedy" routines and stupid dancing. If you need convincing, listen to 'I Understand' with its clever 'Auld Lang Syne' counterpoint; this single went Top

Five in the winter of 1964/1965. The group's final British chart entry was 'Thou Shalt Not Steal' which scraped in at No. 44. *NME* saw the group copying Ken Dodd's example of a comedy act being serious: "*a lilting, sentimental and smoochy sing-along ballad plus cascading strings*". This John D. Loudermilk song had been a hit for Dick and Dee Dee in the USA and was also covered in the UK by Glenda Collins, one of Joe Meek's artists.

The group's 1966 release 'Playboy' confused Penny Valentine: "*I don't know about this. I somehow feel that dear Freddie with his looning around ... isn't really a contender for the hit parade. This is a strange song. If he really is a 'Playboy' then why is he so wrapped up in the one girl?*" *NME* was more impressed: "*this is a fast-moving item with a storming, driving beat. Organ underlines Freddie's solo, and there's a rasp guitar naggingly incessant rhythm.*"

'Brown And Porters (Meat Exporters)' was released in 1967. Despite the group's comedy image, it is a good performance, featuring a recorder and brass. There is even an acapella part that sounds like a madrigal. *NME*: "*A catchy little jingle of a song, as you would expect from a John Carter/Geoff Stephens number. Actually the lyric isn't as way-out as you might think. Still it is pleasant and cute. Infectiously handled by Freddie with the Dreamers providing fugal-type harmonies. Mid-tempo bouncy but not an obvious hit.*"

'If You've Got A Minute Baby' was compared in *NME* to Gerry Marsden's latest record because both acts had abandoned ballads "*in favour of bright-and-breezy material ... A (Freddie) Garrity composition which grows on you after several spins.*" 'Get Around Downtown Girl' was also reviewed in *NME*: "*Penned by the Greenaway-Cook team, it's a bright happy-go-lucky finger-clicker with a very hummable tune. The group's falsetto harmonies and handclaps are the ideal backcloth to Freddie's partly dual-tracked solo. This is good straightforward uncomplicated pop - catchy and commercial ... it could well restore the group to the chart.*"

By the end of the decade Freddie and the group's bassist Pete Birrell were settled in Southern Television's *Little Big Time* children's programme. Freddie now had longer hair and bushy sideburns, but still acted silly and screamed. They would perform Albert Hammond and Mike Hazlewood's musical *Oliver In The Overworld* during the programme. A hit single resulted – 'Gimme Dat Ding' – but this was by session singers, Tony Burrows and Roger Greenaway as The Pipkins – and Freddie and co missed a chart opportunity.

THE GOODIES

Tim Brooke-Taylor, Graeme Garden and Bill Oddie originally worked together on Radio 2's *I'm Sorry I'll Read That Again*, before appearing in *Broaden Your Mind* on BBC2. *The Goodies* television series started in 1970 and the title and incidental music were always central to the shows. Oddie was a talented musician. Some may remember his wonderful version of 'Ilkley Moor Bah T'At' sung in the style of Joe Cocker. The trio originally recorded for Decca and a *World Of The Goodies* compilation was later released, showing them on their trandem.

However, their major success came with signing to Bradley's Records. In twelve months between December 1974 and December 1975, The Goodies had no less than five Top Thirty UK hit singles. The first, 'The Inbetweenies' had a more popular – and risque – B-side, 'Father Christmas Please Don't Touch Me' sung to the chorus of the 'Battle Hymn Of The Republic'. The follow-up, 'Funky Gibbon', reached No. 4 and featured Dave MacRae (formerly of Matching Mole) on keyboards. The latter's 'funky' clavinet was an integral part of the single but was impossible for anyone in the *Top of the Pops* orchestra to replicate. In the end, MacRae played the instrument for the Goodies' appearances on the programme.

'Bounce' was released in May 1976 and was the last of The Goodies' releases on Bradleys Records. This broke the trio's run of hit singles. MacRae stayed as arranger, but there was new producer – Miki Antony. 'Bounce' is another pastiche of funk, but interspersed with country fiddle and electric guitar. There are odd snippets of different voices – camp, German, French and so on.

The trio moved to Island Records for 'Elizabeth Rules UK'. This is another pastiche; this time Bill Oddie's target is the Philadelphia sound of The Stylistics. He sings in a controlled falsetto about the Queen. There is no sign of the other two Goodies. Next was a disco cover version of Disney's 'M.I.C.K.E.Y. M.O.U.S.E.' Theme, again arranged and produced by Miki Antony.

The Goodies returned to *Top of the Pops* in December 1978 performing 'A Man's Best Friend Is His Duck'. Graeme Garden and Tim Brooke-Taylor are both wearing the huge flat caps and waistcoats from the Black Pudding Bertha days. Garden is singing lead in a faux Northern accent and the song is clearly a spoof of such acts as Brian and Michael. The song is in waltz time and dominated by an accordion. Tim Brooke-Taylor (in his Goodies role as a monarchist) sports a Union Jack waistcoat and gives a posh monologue. Bill Oddie meanwhile is dressed... as a duck. Not the Goodies' finest hour. 'Rastashanty!' is something else. Like a National Lampoon spoof of similar vintage, the song relies on the synonyms, the Wailers (as in Bob Marley's band) and whalers (as in hunting). There is a reggae, beat, dub effects, the sound of seagulls and such lines as *'blubbering in a Babylon'*. Forty-five years on, this is a period piece and no more offensive than 'Dreadlock Holiday'.

THE NEW VAUDEVILLE BAND

'Winchester Cathedral', is a song title that is impossible to separate from the way it is sung – in that ersatz 1920s voice. The Anglophile Americans who had loved such songs as Herman's Hermits' 'Mrs Brown You've Got A Lovely Daughter' also adored this Geoff Stephens' song. The single was recorded by session musicians with a lead vocal by John Carter of The Ivy League. But there was demand from America for the band to make television and live appearances. An early line-up of The Bonzo Dog Doo-Dah Band were asked to if they wanted to become The New Vaudeville Band. All of the Bonzos refused with the exception of trumpeter Bob Kerr who jumped ship and was soon seen on television. The New Vaudeville Band stole a lot of the early Bonzos' stage act – the speech bubbles, Palm Court ephemera and Viv Stanshall's upper class twit persona. "Tristram" became the band's lead singer; he was actually Alan Klein who had been responsible for the songs in the Joe Brown film *What A Crazy World*. There was something contrived about The New Vaudeville Band's appearances on American and European television. They had clearly – like the Bonzos – been aware of The Temperance Seven, but unlike the Bonzos had not put their own unique and creative stamp on their stage act. It's hard to actually put my finger on my reservations, but if you look at the band's television appearances, you will understand what I mean.

Follow-ups, all written or co-written by Geoff Stephens, saw diminishing returns: 'Peek A Boo' reached No. 7, 'Finchley Central' went to No. 11 and 'Green Street Green' staggered to No. 37. Penny Valentine reviewed the latter: "*I'm getting very tired of this Vaudeville Band sound. I'm so woolheaded about it now that I feel I've heard this song a hundred times. All I know is I'm bored by the sound and this lacks any iota of charm.*"

The NVB's 1968 single, 'The Bonnie And Clyde' was reviewed in *NME*: "*Opens like a Whistling Jack Smith disc, but soon breaks into a vocal – with Tristram VII doing his celebrated megaphone routine. It's a catchy little jingle .. and the infectious beat should provide plenty of fun on the dance floor*". It did not bother the charts, perhaps Georgie Fame's chart-topping tribute to the couple was sufficient? 'Dear Rita Hayworth' was released in 1973. *Disc*: "*I've a very soft spot for the N.V. Band — it stretches back to the... days of Winchester Cathedral and other sizeable hits.. So I hope their latest does well. It's a movie-nostalgic job.*"

THE WURZELS

The Wurzels lost their lead singer, Adge Cutler, when he died in a road accident in 1974. The original band had had a Top Fifty entry back in 1967 with 'Drink Up Ze Cider'. In 1976 people felt that changing the words of Melanie's 'Brand New Key' to 'Combine Harvester' was a masterstroke. I suppose that it was the contrast between Ms Safka's earnest bleating voice and the Wurzels' Zummerset accents. I was surprised to discover that the Wurzels' version was a cover of a Brendan Grace chart-topper in Ireland. The Wurzels' rendition reached No.1 in the UK. Follow-ups to comedy records are a challenge. 'I Am A Cider Drinker' was another clever parody using the tune of the Euro-hit 'Una Paloma Blanca' and reached No. 3. Alas, like so many comedy and novelty acts, there followed the inevitable diminishing returns.

'Morning Glory' was the follow-up to 'Cider Drinker' and written by hit songwriting team Guy Fletcher and Doug Flett and was previewed on *The Arrows* television show. It has a plodding pace with brass band and orchestra. A deserved flop. 'Farmer Bill's Cowman' came next in the summer of 1977. It was set to the tune of 'I Was Kaiser Bill's Batman', that irritating whistle-along record from Whistling Jack Smith a decade earlier. The *"ooh arr arr"* began to pall and the new lyrics felt contrived. *"Down on the farm, I don't need no alarm"* The record did not breach the Top Thirty and that was the end of the Wurzels' 1970s chart career.

Perhaps the nadir of The Wurzels' career was 'Give Me England', released in September 1977. *Record Mirror*: *"This is the theme from* Confessions From A Holiday Camp *but comes into the crappy football songs league."*

3 – All The Fallen Teenangels

Amen Corner

Amen Corner hailed from South Wales and were first signed to Decca. They had four consecutive Top Thirty hits, peaking at No. 3 with their cover of the American Breed's 'Bend Me Shape Me'. Amen Corner's interpretation was sublime, using a borrowed riff suggested by singer Andy Fairweather Low. The group moved to be part of Andrew Loog Oldham's Immediate stable where they soon reached No. 1 with yet another cover, this time of an Italian hit, 'If Paradise Is Half As Nice'. Fortunately, Amen Corner's live act was recorded for posterity. The *National Welsh Coast Live Explosion Company* live album was recorded at the Tottenham Royal in spring 1969 and reveals an extremely accomplished live act. The introduction, an instrumental version of 'MacArthur Park', could easily have been mistaken for label-mates, The Nice. The group's organ player Blue Weaver was certainly on par with Keith Emerson, but without the latter's gimmicks. The group next trot non-stop through no less than five soul covers including 'You're My Girl (I Don't Want To Discuss It)' which was also performed by Delaney and Bonnie on their European tour later that year. As the pop equivalent of Cinéma vérité, the album is priceless evidence of a 1960s ballroom gig. Amen Corner then tackle 'Penny Lane' pretty competently before performing four of their hit singles.

'Get Back' was a flop for Amen Corner after their string of hits. This farewell single was released without the group's knowledge and was clearly a last ditch attempt by Immediate boss, Andrew Oldham, to have one final hit before his label imploded. *Record Mirror*: *"Growls of anguish from Beatle lovers, but I found it an exciting hard-pounding treatment with Andy a bit ecstatic in style, occasionally hidden away in the sheer volume, and straining away hard throughout. Good number, energetic treatment – but not their best."* There was a positive review in *NME*: *"Amen adopts a totally different* approach from the famous foursome. It's fast and furious with an underlying guitar theme ... crashing cymbals, rattling tambourines and clanking piano complete the dynamic workout,"* and even a front page advertisement in the same publication. But the single did not bother the charts when it was released in late 1969. Only a few months earlier, The Beatles' original had been No. 1. Amen Corner rearranged the song making it quite funky with Andy Fairweather Low slightly changing the melody of the chorus. Seven years later, Rod Stewart covered 'Get Back' for the soundtrack of *All This And World War Two*. It was just as Rod was going into his mediocre phase and his cover version is predictably dire.

The Bay City Rollers

There seem to be two ways of approaching discussion about the Rollers. The group can be dismissed as *"teenybopper"* fodder and their overwhelmingly female fans patronised and regarded as mindless followers. Radio One disc jockey Johnnie Walker once dismissed the group's records as *"musical garbage"*, but decades later he apologised for his comments.

The other approach to the Rollers' records is more thoughtful; Greg Shaw in *Bomp* magazine even stated that he preferred the Rollers to Bruce Springsteen. Bubblegum music historian Carl Cafarelli has written about the group thoroughly and fairly, citing them as a *"harmless Scottish quintet"* who were touted as *"the next Beatles"* by their management. Cafarelli states that the Rollers were *"an often-underrated, occasionally (if infrequently) terrific power pop group."* If you want to understand the appeal of the Rollers at the height of their popularity, watch the 1975 *Saturday Scene* Awards. Wembley Empire Pool (now Wembley Arena) was full of Rollers fans who had to endure performances by Messrs Glitter and Stardust, as well as Guys 'N' Dolls, The Wombles and worse, before their idols appeared. At the beginning of the show one of the presenters, a young Sally James, sounding like a school teacher in an assembly, tells the audience to be "fair" and give every act equal respect. There was no chance of that happening.

The Rollers first hit the charts in autumn 1971 with their infectious and competent cover of The Gentrys' 'Keep On Dancing'. It reached

No. 9. The record label states: *"produced and directed by Jonathan King"*. King even claims to have sung backing vocals on the recording. The follow-up, 'We Can Make Music', was released the following year and was again masterminded by King. It is not a bad record, despite the *"na-na-na-na-na-na-na"* vocal intro. There is a weedy keyboard, but nice use of strings (arranged by Johnny Arthey). *Record Mirror*: *"It's a perky sing-along and wordless sort of theme at first, then into a neatly commercial sweet-sweet music sort of production."* *NME*: *"the song suffers from being overtly mediocre. This sugar and sweet crap isn't suitable for a 12-year-old."* It flopped.

A few months later, 'We Can Make Music' was followed by 'Manana' which was written and produced by Ken Howard and Alan Blaikley, but still did not succeed, except in Germany. With a drum introduction alongside a tinny synthesiser, the record has a mindless chant reminding me of Dave Dee, Dozy, Beaky, Mick & Tich. Howard and Blaikley's success with the latter and The Herd clearly did not rub off here. 'Saturday Night' was the final single for the Rollers with Nobby Clarke as lead singer. This was the group's best single A-side since 'Keep On Dancing'. *Record Mirror*: *"Another spot-on big commercial production by the Martin-Coulter team. There's a bit of the old fifties rocking style about it in the yi-yi-yi-ing anticipation of the weekend. But it almost stomps along in the seventies (obligatory) style, and anyway the young rolling gentlemen have a big-fan-following. It'll grow on you."* The review was correct in some ways; although *Record Mirror* called it a *"Chart Cert"*, the song was a flop in the UK. However, the track was re-recorded two years later with Les McKeown on lead vocals, and became a huge American hit for the Rollers.

February 1974 saw the Rollers return to the Top Ten with 'Remember'. The group's next eight singles were all Top Five with two chart-toppers in 'Bye Bye Baby' and 'Give A Little Love'. 'It's A Game' was released just as punk was taking off and reached No. 16. This was the Rollers' final Top Thirty entry in Britain. Strangely, at the very same time, their career then began to take off in the USA. The follow-up, 'You Made Me Believe In Magic' stalled at No. 34. It was a complete change of style with strings, brass and almost a Philly/Miami disco beat. *Record Mirror* was blunt: *"This bunch have lost their way."* 'The Way I Feel Tonight' was also condemned by the same paper: *"The *terrors continue to move upmarket with an American-style ballad. Not bad but what a waste of all that publicity."*

'All Of The World Is Falling In Love' was also released in 1978. Naturally, *Record Mirror* reviewed it: *"Another philanthropy special by the looks of it. Slow full ballad with 'Sgt Pepper' trumpet tooting away and standard acapella but from the Tartan lads.."* This was the end of the Rollers' story as far as we are concerned.

THE CASUALS

The Casuals are really only known for their 1968 No. 2 hit, 'Jesamine', co-written under a pseudonym by Marty Wilde. The single is a favourite of Paul Weller who included it on his *Under The Influence* CD compilation. The group can only just be included in this book as the follow-up, 'Toy' reached No. 30. A succession of singles on the Decca label followed and all flopped. The Casuals were based in Rome for a while where they recorded Italian language versions of British hits.

'Fool's Paradise' was the follow-up to 'Toy'. There are gently sung verses and a big singalong chorus with an orchestra. This should have been a hit and would have sounded great on the radio alongside Marmalade's 'Lovin' Things' and Love Affair's 'Everlasting Love'. 'Sunflower Eyes' is even better. The song has piano and strings with earnest vocals and is more excellent late 1960s orchestral pop, sounding to these ears better than the possibly over-familiar 'Jesamine'. There is a lovely chorus: *"sunflower eyes, rainbow skies."* The Casuals' next single, 'Caroline', is something of a hidden gem. Written and produced by Roy Wood, no less, the song features flutes and a prominent piano. The vocals are very like Wood's and the chord changes remind me of 'Blackberry Way' with the words:*"Waiting for Caroline ... Not so easy to compose a line."* This really should have been a hit. The group released two more singles on Decca. 'My Name Is Love' is another big orchestral pop song with strings and brass strongly featured. 'Someday Rock 'N' Roll Lady' was written by the group's keyboard player, Johnny Tebb, and is less impressive. There is bouncy Gilbert O'Sullivan-style piano and slide guitar. The lyrics feel cliched and the chord sequence is somewhat predictable. *Disc & Music Echo* commented: *"Unrecognisable*

Casuals try the Barrelhouse approach ... sung in a funny little Cockney accent."

CHICORY TIP

I clearly remember an early Chicory Tip single entitled 'Excuse Me Baby', a banjo-driven ditty with a 1920s ragtime feel. The group performed the song on *Top of the Pops* in 1970, but it went nowhere. Two years later, thanks to a collaboration with then unknown German producer and writer Giorgio Moroder, Chicory Tip re-emerged. 'Son Of Your Father' was a huge hit, reaching No.1 in the UK in February 1972. The monophonic synthesiser on the record seemed to make all the difference and the riff may have inspired as many bands as Kraftwerk later did. Two soundalikes — 'What's Your Name' and 'Good Grief Christina' — were Top Twenty hits, but interrupted by a couple of flops.

'The Future Is Past' was the follow-up to 'What's Your Name'. The single was performed on *Top of the Pops* in September 1972, but failed to attract much interest. This was heavier than the group's hits and without that characteristic synthesiser. 'Good Grief Christina' saw Chicory Tip return to the charts in early 1973. 'Cigarettes, Women And Wine' was released next. In *Let It Rock* magazine, John Pidgeon commented: *"Chicory Tip sing about their vices in their characteristically banal but previously successful style, demonstrating once again what Mrs Mills would sound like if she swapped her piano for a Moog."* NME were kinder: *"It's a common knowledge within the trade that it's the first 10 seconds and the hook line which dictates whether a record will hit or miss. If that still holds true, then these painted devils are gonna dominate TOTP and BBC1 for the rest of the summer."* Around this time Chicory Tip adopted a glam/superhero image with make-up, masks and Superman tights. They looked ridiculous and uncomfortable. Even at the time, the music press commented that this was an ill-advised change of image. The Sweet seemed to get away with outrageous clothes, but they were better musicians and singers and seemed not to take themselves too seriously.

NME were less kind about 1973's 'I.O.U.': *"Basically manufactured rock 'n' boogie, with the same clumping drums, and a dismal melody line. Basically dreadful."* Record Mirror was more generous: *"This one features some wildish and wooly answering bits, all against some thumping drumming. Add in some off-beat bits of phrasing ... well, it's a foot-stomper first and foremost and it surely must be a chart cert.*" The same paper were merciless about 1974's 'Take Your Time Caroline'. "*This must be the dumbest band in this quadrant of the galaxy. 'Oop- showddywaddying (actually 'doo-dooallyrally') their rancid way around a Rubettes-style verse before ploughing manfully into a pale, lisping chorus straight out of Crispian St Peters, these fellows sure are CRASS...*"

THE HERD

After a run of unsuccessful releases on Parlophone, The Herd signed to Fontana, having caught the eyes and ears of Ken Howard and Alan Blaikley, the team behind Dave Dee, Dozy, Beaky, Mick and Tich. After another unsuccessful single, 'I Can Fly', The Herd had a huge hit with 'From The Underworld', a big production number with dramatic sounds, massed voices and strange lyrics. It was extremely powerful, whatever one thought of the songwriting team of Howard and Blaikley's unashamed gimmicks. 'From The Underworld' reached No. 6 and the group soon had a keen teenage following.

The follow-up, 'Paradise Lost' also used gimmicks including a jazz band introduction that sounded like David Rose's 'Stripper' theme! The rest of the song was totally unconnected with this section and was very much in the same vein as 'Underworld' with more dramatic orchestration and massed vocals. Amongst all this noise was the lead vocals of guitarist Peter Frampton who had a clear and expressive approach. He was also quite handsome and was voted 'The Face Of 1968' by *Rave* magazine. 'Paradise Lost' only reached No. 15, but the group returned to the Top Ten with 'I Don't Want Our Lovin' To Die'. The latter had fewer gimmicks – apart from its unnecessary *basso profundo* vocal introduction – and was uptempo and less pretentious. The single deservedly did better than 'Underworld', reaching one place higher at No. 5.

The Herd's next single was 'Sunshine Cottage', co-written by Frampton and keyboard player Andy Bown who also co-produced the record. There is heavy guitar and definitely no orchestra to be heard. *Record Mirror* concluded: "*Good song idea ... the melody line is sometimes hard* to pick up." In *The History Of Rock*, Barry Lazell described the single as "*a Magical Mystery Tour-influenced psychedelic number, complete with organ and dreamy harmonies.*" Unfortunately, the single flopped and Frampton jumped ship to form Humble Pie with Steve Marriott from The Small Faces, becoming one of the first British "supergroups." Bown also left the group and, after an undistinguished solo career, joined Status Quo where he remains to this day. Frampton, of course, went on after leaving Humble Pie to become a hugely successful solo artist in the USA.

LOVE AFFAIR

Love Affair's cover of 'Everlasting Love' was part of my childhood. It still sounds fresh. Steve Ellis has a soulful voice and makes no attempt to sound black or American. There is a fantastic arrangement by Keith Mansfield with a full orchestra and backing vocals by no less than Madeline Bell, Kiki Dee, Lesley Duncan and one of the Ladybirds. The group's appearance on Germany's *Beat Club* is worth watching. Although they are miming, the group look great with flashing lights, dancers and a clown straight out of Fellini's *La Strada*. This wonderful composition by Mac Gayden and Buzz Cason cannot be ruined by cover versions by the likes of Jamie Cullum or the cast of BBC1's *Casualty*. There was a big fuss at the time when it was revealed that none of the band actually played on the recording.

By late 1969 I was absorbed by pop music. On television, besides *Top of the Pops*, I enjoyed *Lift Off*, *Monster Music Mash*, *Colour Me Pop* (when I was allowed to stay up and watch it) and anything else that presented pop. I had no idea that Love Affair released a final single, 'Baby I Know', with Steve Ellis towards the end of 1969. The single is present on a compilation CD which I have owned for ages and I had to dig it out to listen to it properly. *Record Mirror*: "*Recent events leave Steve Ellis and the boys the one really big scream-creating team. This is a Goodhand-Tait and Cokell song, showcasing Smoky Steve's pop-blues approach. Not instantly their most commercial, but it grows at mid-tempo with spins. Well done arranger Keith Mansfield.*" *NME* liked it: "*A rhythmic ballad with a solid beat makes a perfect showcase for Steve Ellis ... it's the sort of song that grows on you and with Steve turning in his usual gripping performance, coupled with the expansive all-happening sound."*

Steve Ellis said: *"in an attempt to break the mould we recorded a song far removed from the anthem-like previous hits."* With the same songwriter as three of their previous hit singles and the same arranger, 'Baby I Know' is hardly mould-breaking. This is a piano-led song with brass and strings coming in later. For me, the song sounds a bit similar to both 'Angel Of The Morning' and 'The First Cut Is The Deepest'. Ellis then left the group to go solo and continued to work with Keith Mansfield for a while, notably producing the soundtrack to the film, *Loot*. Later he formed the band Ellis with Zoot Money.

Ellis was replaced by August "Gus" Eadon, singer, flautist and keyboardist from Elastic Band whom I remember seeing on *Colour Me Pop*. The new line-up's first single, 'Lincoln County', appeared to have changed little except the lead singer; it was again written by Philip Goodhand Tait and John Cobell, produced by Mike Smith and arranged by Keith Mansfield. *Record Mirror*: *"New singer August Eadon herewith introduced. A throaty sturdy voice, perhaps more powerful and deeper than that of Steve Ellis. A good ... song with a maze of strings and brass behind. No sign of deterioration, glad to say. This is good stuff — full blooded."* *NME* agreed: *"the song is quite catchy and registers quickly — it's got commercialism written all over it."* Around this time Love Affair abbreviated their name to L.A. and went "heavy".

Love Affair later signed to Parlophone and appeared on *Top of the Pops* previewing 'Speak Of Peace, Speak Of Joy' in June 1970. *NME*:*"From a group who want to make a joyful sound, I found this all rather dirgy."* Under a headline of *"Love Affair Revert To Pop"*, the *NME*'s review of 'Wake Me I Am Dreaming' states: *"after a spasm during which Love Affair adopted an uncharacteristic heavy image, the group reverts to its former strictly commercial approach on this, its first single for the EMI firm. This is a very good song indeed ... and since it is a song that grows on you slowly, it's very heavily dependent on Radio 1. It's a solid beat ballad, a showcase for the fruity and expressive tones of Auguste Eadon, framed in a swirling orchestral scoring with choral voices in support ... it's a very pleasant and (after a time) haunting number with a good chance."*

Love Affair staggered on, ending up on the Pye label with yet another Philip Goodhand-Tait song. *NME*: "*I understand that this is a completely new outfit from the original band ... a song with a light feel and an unobtrusive manner. It's definitely not as disturbing as listening to The Sweet.*"

Marmalade

Marmalade (originally The Marmalade) were first known as Dean Ford And The Gaylords! Signed to CBS, the group released a series of singles and their first hit was 'Lovin' Things' in 1968, a superb slab of orchestral pop in the style of Love Affair. A cover of the Beatles' 'Ob La Di Ob La Da' gave Marmalade a No. 1 hit, a song that can become tedious on repeated hearing. After another orchestral pop single, 'Baby Make It Soon', the group signed with Decca Records. Just as they left CBS, Marmalade's cover of the Gibb brothers' 'Butterfly' was released. It failed to reach the charts. *NME*: "*they've taken a delightful descriptive composition by the Gibb brothers and moulded it to their own immaculate harmonic approach. The flowing vocal wafts smoothly along ... framed in a beautiful and highly imaginative Keith Mansfield scoring – with flute, strings and tinkling celeste setting the mood to perfect.*" *Melody Maker* agreed: "*extremely commercial and must surely be a hit. Not one of the group's best offerings.. the Marmalade making a nice professional job of a pretty ballad..*" The single deserved better.

Marmalade's new Decca contract promised the group greater artistic freedom and the first single was the classic 'Reflections Of My Life' which reached No. 3 in the UK and No. 10 in the USA. The song has received millions of plays on American radio. Follow-ups showed the group's versatility; 'Rainbow' was a gentle acoustic song which also reached the third spot. Marmalade's performance on Granada Television's *Doing Their Thing* programme showed a highly accomplished act, bravely and triumphantly covering both Stephen Stills' 'Suite: Judy Blue Eyes' and The Band's 'Cripple Creek' and even performing a Simon and Garfunkel medley. Watching this footage and listening to a lot of the group's recordings made me realise that their lead singer, Dean Ford, was an excellent vocalist and sorely underrated.

In early 1971, guitarist and songwriter Junior Campbell quit Marmalade to study musical arranging, leaving a big void in the group. Luckily, enter stage left guitarist Hugh Nicholson from another

Scottish band, The Poets. The breezy 'Cousin Norman' reached No. 6 and saw a new phase of Marmalade's chart career. The follow-up was 'Back On The Road'. *Record Mirror*: "*it has a strong commercial appeal — a shuffling back-beat, some direct and pacey lyrics and a nice tight feel to the whole thing. Almost a sing-along. Should do very well if not as big as 'Cousin Norman'.*" *NME* praised the song's "*pleasant melody*" and "*the group's golden harmonies.*" This pleasantly simple song wasn't quite as strong as 'Cousin Norman' and reached just No. 35. Next was 'Radancer' which saw the group return to the Top Ten. There was then another line-up change as Hugh Nicholson left to form Blue with Jimmy McCulloch, formerly of Thunderclap Newman. Blue signed with Elton John's Rocket label and eventually had a hit with 'Capture Your Heart' in 1977.

Marmalade moved to EMI with yet another lead guitarist, Mike Japp. This line-up released three singles. The first 'The Wishing Well', a Dean Ford composition, is something of a hidden gem, very much in the style of 'Rainbow'. *Record Mirror*: "*It's a simple sort of opening sound with guitar, gradual build-up of the back-beat and atmosphere, and the persistent commerciality of the record finally registers. It's not one of those instantly saleable ones – but if it gets aired a little, I've no doubt it'll click big.*" The song is not familiar, so I assume that the all-powerful Radio One playlist meeting rejected it. Dean Ford later recorded a heavier version of this excellent song for his solo album with more prominent piano and strings.

The group's second single on EMI was the title track of their new album, *Our House Is Rocking*, and previewed on *Top of the Pops* on November 1st 1973. I can just about remember it from over half a century ago. As the title suggests, this was a heavier song. To these ears, it sounds like a more melodic Quo with better vocals. *Record Mirror*: "*Martial drums ... guitar mixed in and the riff takes over ... some neat harmonic touches which add a fullness to the overall sound. Lyrics come over clearly too.*" Decades later, *Shindig* magazine stated: "*Starting off with a steady march, a guitar soon adds some rapid-fire hammers and pulls, followed by a heavier, Hendrix-like wah-wah pedal groove. A twin-guitar run sweeps in, ushering in Dean Ford and Joe Breen on vocals. Surprisingly, this lively single tanked.*"

The group's third single on EMI, 'Come Back Jo', was reviewed in *Record Mirror*: "*my view is that Dean (Ford) is one of the better group singers to emerge. He has authority, style and flexibility.*" A composition by Dean Ford and guitarist Mike Japp, 'Come Back Jo' has the heavy guitar sound of 'Our House Is Rockin'' but with great vocal harmonies and a brass section reminding me of both 'Lady Madonna' and a Wizzard single. The brass arrangement was by no less than Tony Visconti who also co-produced the song with Alan Harris.

Unfortunately, it seems that there was some sort of split and/or legal wrangle after this and press coverage of 'Original Marmalade' and 'New Marmalade' which is never a good sign. A new line-up (but with the original bass player Graham Knight and drummer Alan Whitehead) emerged in 1976 on the Target label. They had one hit with 'Falling Apart At The Seams'. Later they performed on nostalgia packages and – worse – re-recorded the group's hits from Dean Ford's era. Buyer beware! Ford later moved to the USA and died in 2018.

Slik

Slik were a Scottish group centred on lead singer and guitarist, Midge Ure. Their first hit was originally written by Bill Martin and Phil Coulter for The Bay City Rollers which explains its banal Roller-style chorus. The quasi-religious introduction and verses are more interesting. The follow-up, 'Requiem', repeated the mixture of slow hymn-like intro and verses, again interspersed with banal chorus. It only reached No. 24. I wonder if these two singles influenced Ultravox's 1982 hit 'Hymn' which also featured both religious-themed lyrics and a slow introduction?

Slik's next single, 'The Kid's A Punk', deserves some attention. Most people were first aware of the song by the group's *Top of the Pops* appearance in summer 1976. Finger-clicking Midge Ure is standing under a street lamp, oozing cool street style. He then walks over to his guitar and starts to sing! Later he combs his hair and looks menacingly at the camera. *Record Mirror*: *"A harder, grittier and strained sound from Slik complete with sax break. It should get them away from that former 'pastel' image but oh the song! Common denominator Martin/ Coulter stuff. It's fun to pick out where you've heard the riffs before."* The song was a flop. Slik soon decided to become punks themselves and renamed the group PVC-2. A year later Midge was a member of the Rich Kids alongside former Sex Pistol Glen Matlock.

The Tremeloes

Having parted company with Brian Poole in 1966 and signed to CBS, The Tremeloes first big hit was a lively cover of Cat Stevens' 'Here Comes My Baby', complete with a party atmosphere and general mucking about. Their run of hits included a chart-topper with 'Silence Is Golden', their sensitive cover of a Four Seasons B-side.

Another quiet ballad, 'Be Mine', was clearly designed to appeal to the fans of 'Silence Is Golden'. It was composed by no less than four Italians and features acoustic guitar and close harmonies. I think this is the side of The Tremeloes that I prefer, rather than the rather contrived party sounds on many of their hits. Penny Valentine in *Disc & Music Echo*: "*Here comes another huge smash. On this one they turn up sounding a bit like The Ivy League, drifting from falsetto togetherness to gentle voices on an Italian ballad that will catch on even faster than the others.*" Unfortunately 'Be Mine' stalled at No. 39, but the group soon bounced back with more up-tempo singles. The group sourced several of their singles from Continental hits.

'Once On A Sunday Morning' was originally a Spanish hit titled 'Cuando Sali De Cuba'. Group members Alan Blakley and Chip Hawkes are listed as co-writers. *NME*: "*Characteristic of The Tremeloes' cheerful carefree approach, this is a catchy Spanish number to which the boys themselves have added the English lyrics. There's a brass section, adding depth to the arrangement, handclaps accentuating the beat, background chatter to supply an air of casual informality, and the inevitable la-la chorus. This is easy, undemanding listening. It's straightforward uncomplicated pop with instant commercial appeal. And while it's very much like several other Tremeloes discs, it's bound to be a hit.*" *Record Mirror*'s singles reviewer agreed: "*a direct, catchy, well-sung and commercial record which will sell hugely.*" The single was previewed on *Top of the Pops* on June 19th 1969, but did not enter the charts. The song was no worse really than the group's other "fun" hits, but perhaps the record buyers were getting tired of the same happy formula.

This chart failure clearly led to a change of policy and two later hits, written by group members Alan Blakley and Chip Hawkes, were a great improvement – '(Call Me) Number One' reached No. 2 in late 1969 and 'Me And My Life' peaked at No. 4 early the following year.

In between there was 'By The Way'. *Shindig*: "*A finely-crafted piece boasting gently picked acoustic guitar, gooey Mellotron, triple-tracked harmonic guitar and the group's customarily strong harmony vocals.*" It reached No. 35. All the group's singles from '(Call Me) Number One' onwards were written in-house by Blakley and Hawkes.

Like Marmalade, The Tremeloes had had a showcase in 1970 on Granada Television's *Doing Their Thing*. The programme showed the various facets of the group, some pathetic humour (as heard on those early singles), fine guitar playing from Rick West and a rock 'n' roll medley. Earlier in the set there was a medley of 'Games People Play' (with West on electric sitar) and 'Proud Mary'. The Trems include no fewer than nine of their singles. Here was a group who deserved more than a post-chart life in cabaret.

'Right Wheel, Left Hammer Sham' has a great twin-guitar harmony part. Drummer Dave Munden's vocals are pretty powerful when he sings: "*give it a try*" too. *NME*: "*a very good pop record. It powers along at a fast pace with a strumming beat that's so insistent and demanding it dominates the whole routine.*" Despite an appearance on *Top of the Pops*, the single flopped. 'Hello Buddy' was one of the Trems' better singles. Chris Welch summed it up well in *Melody Maker*: "*A country style song with steel guitar and banjo that makes suitably pleasant listening, and will undoubtedly become a sizeable hit.*" The single was The Tremeloes' final chart entry, reaching No. 32

The follow-up was 'Too Late To Be Saved'; *NME*: "*This newie is fairly strong.. a bouncy number, it features a hard-hitting solo vocal, with all the lads coming together on the constantly repeated title hook. Perfect for the discos; it's one of those songs that grow on you...*" In *Disc*, Penny Valentine, as usual, gave a more considered view: "*Unlike Marmalade, who managed to break through their original image and maintain it, the Trems have always had a hard time whenever they tried to move away from bang, crash, wallop records ... it's rather Marmalade in feel with very soft guitar and vocal work. Even when it breaks into slightly more dogmatic vocal and echo it keeps nice and easy.*" There is strummed acoustic guitar and drummer Dave Munden on lead vocals; later, horns come in. Unfortunately, it actually was too late for this talented group to be saved. This single was the last one that The Tremeloes performed on *Top of the Pops*.

NME reviewed 'I Like It That Way', the group's final release on CBS: "*After the foolish announcement last year that they were going 'heavy', which nearly cost them their careers, the Trems are back doing what brings them money. Pure unadulterated pop. It's very much on the safe and clean side, with an idiotically catchy chorus. But that's the market they've been successful with in the past.*" Spencer Leigh takes up the tale: "*The Tremeloes fell from grace through trying to be a heavy rock group, writing and performing more serious material. They rubbished their previous hits which is never a wise move. When the singles failed, they were left with egg on their face.*" Although apologies were soon made and the group claimed that they were misunderstood, it is probably not a good strategy to condemn one's (once) loyal fans.

The Tremeloes' singles were now on the Epic imprint, and Simon Frith kept reviewing the group's releases in *Let It Rock*: "*The Tremeloes do Elvis on 'Blue Suede Tie' but give him a crude and clanging background that would never have been allowed in Nashville.*" *NME*'s reviewer elaborated: "*the Trems come back with a rock 'n' roll offering. There's a bit of 'Get Back' and a little 'Buddy Holly' with echo vocals, etc. The thing really moves and with a lot of rock-type stuff getting in nowadays, perhaps the Trems'll see some action again.*" Apart from the humourless title, this is quite a good single. Chip Hawkes hints at an Elvis-style vocal without resorting to the approach of Mud's Les Gray.

'Ride On' was reviewed harshly in *NME*: "*What, one asks, are the Trems doing ripping off T. Rex licks? At the end of the record one is still none the wiser, though the '50s-styled piano and harmonies could possibly excite some comment. One aches to give the Trems a good review, but this dreary, crass offering doesn't really leave openings for favourable comment ... E for effort.*" To my ears, there is a bit of Quo in there as well.

The (possibly) ironic record titles continued the following year with 'Make It, Break It'. Frith, again: "*Failed last ditch come-back attempt: the Tremeloes, now known as the Trems — and I still can't remember anything about it.*" *NME* agreed: "*This is the Trems idea of a heavy number, which means there's lots of echo on the vocals, a mix that's three parts bass to one part watery treble, and no tune to speak of.*" The group's next single, 'Do I Love You' isn't too bad. There are acoustic guitars playing in harmony and soft lead vocals. The piano and the song's beat sound a little Gilbert-ish and there is an impressive guitar solo. The words are uninspired: "*I don't wanna die, I don't wanna cry, I don't wanna say goodbye.."

The Tremeloes carried on, adding and losing members. At one point they called themselves Space and released an album on DJM, *Don't Let The Music Die*. In 1983 the group covered the Eurohit, 'Words' and received television coverage, but missed out to F.R. David's original which went to No. 2. Thirty years on, Dave Munden and Alan Blakely are no longer with us and Chip Hawkes' two sons are now in the group.

VANITY FARE

Vanity Fare were first signed to Page One and had three hits. Their first chart appearance was 'I Live For The Sun' in 1968 and reached No. 20. It is a breezy slab of what is now called sunshine pop. There is an energetic performance on Germany's *Beat Club*. Follow-ups were slightly problematic. '(I Remember) Summer Morning' continued the fair weather theme and, despite being previewed on *Top of the Pops*, failed to chart. *NME* called the single: "*a lilting rhythmic ballad ... the lads' delightful vocal blend ... a very pleasant and extremely melodic tune.*" It is a slower and more subtle song and deserved a better fate.

Next was 'Highway Of Dreams', co-written by hit-songwriter John Carter of The Ivy League. *NME*: "*this is a tingling exciting sound ... storms along at a cracking pace with a sort of half-shuffle beat that's not unlike The Beach Boys' surfing rhythm ... there is a hummable tune, a Jerry Lee-type rocking piano ... and a colourful harmonic blend.*" 'Highway Of Dreams' is very commercial and catchy. Again, this failed to chart.

'Early In The Morning' followed in the summer of 1969 and, with its distinctive harpsichord and strange guitar break, stood out in the charts. The song was co-written by Mike Leander who would later write, create and produce hits for Gary Glitter. The group's harmonies were expertly slick; this was Vanity Fare's biggest hit in the UK, reaching No. 8. The single was also a big hit in the USA. The follow-up, 'Hitchin' A Ride', written by songwriting team Mitch Murray and Peter Callender also featured an unusual instrument; in this case a descant recorder. The song had a great melody and a memorable chorus. Although probably better known than 'Early In the Morning',

'Hitchin' A Ride' did not enter the UK Top Ten. Again, this was a huge hit in the USA, selling over a million copies and earning a Gold Disc. The song appealed apparently, to the hitch-hiking youth of that country.

Successful follow-ups were again problematic, despite some interesting releases and Vanity Fare did not bother the UK charts again. Penny Valentine disliked 'Come Tomorrow', the follow-up to 'Hitchin'': *"I am afraid I must express boredom with this new one. It starts with a confusing broken up and falling down opening and the song sounds as though it was written for a barber shop chorale."* To me, 'Come Tomorrow' sounds like 'Early In The Morning Mark II' with the same clomping beat but unfortunately no harpsichord.

'Carolina's Coming Home' was penned by no less than four writers, Rogers Cook and Greenaway, along with John Goodison and Tony Hiller. The group performed the song on *Top of the Pops*. *NME*: *"These lads have developed an exceptionally distinctive vocal blend and this latest effort is again noteworthy for its ear-catching quality. A bright-and-breezy number at a fast pace. I think the material falls just fractionally short of the previous two (hits). However, this could be counter-balanced by the infectious beat."* The single opens with a strong chorus and – unsurprisingly, considering half of the writers – sounds a lot like White Plains. It is catchy but a little predictable. The organ sounds rather weedy, but I like the use of harpsichord in the middle eight.

'Where Did All The Good Times Go' was the first single for the group on DJM, showing Vanity Fare leaving the care of Larry Page and signing with Dick James. This single was not the Ray Davies song which Bowie later revived, but by Buie and Cobb. *NME*: *"For the most part it's Trevor Brice dual-tracking with the other boys coming in only for the chorus ... there's a beautifully scored string section and a wistful oboe solo. It's a pretty ballad with a lilting rhythm and an over-riding air of poignancy. A delightful track, technically immaculate and well performed."*

The follow-up, 'Better By Far' is a hidden gem. It was a Tony Macaulay and John MacLeod composition which several artists had already attempted, notably Long John Baldry and Terry Reid, but none of them entered the British charts. The same writing team had penned 'Let The Heartaches Begin' for Baldry and hits for both The

Foundations and Pickettywitch. 'Better By Far' has a great, majestic chorus and deserved wider audiences. I remember hearing this on the radio back in 1971. It is British orchestral pop at its best and a far, far better song than the likes of 'Let The Heartaches Begin'.

'Our Own Way Of Living' was on DJM. *NME*: "*this is a forceful rhythmic ballad, strongly projected by soloist Trevor Brice, backed up by those rich harmonies which have become something of a Vanity Fare trademark.*" It's more than that; it feels anthemic and over-optimistic "*everyone you meet can be your friend.*" I get worn down by this constant emphasis that this is the age of Aquarius.

'The Big Parade' received a full review in *Disc & Music Echo*: "*With a clip-clop beat, an oom-pah-pah and a sound that reminds me so much of their earlier hits, back come some of Britain's finest popsters with a good Neil Sedaka/Howard Greenfield song. It's tailor-made for the group and Trevor Brice's high-pitched voice even sounds like Sedaka in places. The production employs all sorts of jolly effects, like sousaphone, brass band marching and military snatches that sound like the intro to The Nutcracker Suite.*"

'I'm In Love With The World' sounds ordinary despite its feel-good title and positive intentions. It is dominated by acoustic guitar and has counterpoint singing. Co-written by a then unknown Giorgio Moroder, the song feels like a Eurovision entry from the 1970s, having that upbeat ingredient that Abba admired so much in Blue Mink's recordings. You can sense this on Abba's very first release under their name, 'People In Love'. Both these 'Love' songs are the nadir of Vanity Fare's and Abba's oeuvre. Unfortunately, Vanity Fare's career nose-dived while Abba's rose.

Worse was to come. 'Rock 'n' Roll Is Back' is as bad as its title. It is a pastiche of the rock 'n' roll genre with all the predictable clichés, name-checks and "*dancing shoes*" lyrics. *NME*: "*more likely to delight the fans of the Barron Knights than the Teds. A straight time number, sung in close harmony about the current revival.*"

'Take It, Shake It, Break My Heart' was written by Giorgio Moroder and Pete Bellotte who had previously worked with Chicory Tip. This 1973 single was unremarkable and could have been recorded by anyone. There is a rather leaden synthesiser and orchestral backing. 'Fast Running Out Of The World' was released in March 1974. *Record*

Mirror: *"The team Cook and Greenaway wrote it, which is a fair enough guarantee of sheer commercialism. Recall that Vanity Fare have already hit the charts, and you have a definite guarantee of pulling power. Demonstrating their strength, determined and flexible, which will do it for them again with their string-boosted piece."*

Scott Walker

Scott's solo career started well, despite the banning of his single 'Jackie' by the BBC for its (then) controversial lyrics. This Jacques Brel cover still sold quite well, reaching No. 22, and was included on *Scott 2* which topped the album charts in the UK. The follow-up, 'Joanna' was a safer bet. The song was written by Tony Hatch and Jackie Trent for a film of the same name, but not eventually used because of film industry politics. Luckily the single was still released and went to No. 7. Tony Hatch told Mick Patrick: *"Scott loved the song ... and asked if he could change some of the lyrics. His changes were excellent but he declined to accept a co-writer credit, even though we suggested it. He recorded the song with a wonderful Peter Knight arrangement and you could feel Scott's influence throughout."* A year later, 'Lights Of Cincinnati' was released and reached No. 13. Scott's solo singles career was looking promising.

'I Still See You' was the love theme from the film *The Go-Between*. This was written by Michel Legrand and Hal Sharper and released in October 1971. *Record Mirror* liked it: *"just about the best solo vocal performance of the week.. This ... song ... suits his emotive ballad style very well indeed and the arrangement is suitably sympathetic. Slow moving."* There is a harp and luscious strings in this perfectly competent movie ballad. Scott performed the song on *Top of the Pops* but there was no chart action.

Two years later saw another single, 'The Me I Never Know', written by award-winning songwriters, Don Black and John Barry for the latest film version of *Alice In Wonderland*. It was sung in the film by Fiona Fullerton who played the title role. Once again, *Record Mirror* was enthusiastic, almost repeating themselves: *"the best actual vocal performance of the week ... Scott purrs and phrases and punctuates with intuitive skill. Some of that tortured aura of self-doubt that held up his career shows through. Let's hope he'll promote this one. Hope, too, that it'll be a big seller. Chart Chance."*

This was another very slow ballad and not a good choice for a single.

1973 saw the release of a second single. 'A Woman Left Lonely' was written by Spooner Oldham and Dan Penn and taken from Scott's *Stretch* album, his first for CBS. *Record Mirror*: *"Slow, moody, provocative and persuasive ballad. Scott remains an enigma but also a big balladeer."* Oldham and Penn wrote some memorable songs including 'I'm Your Puppet', 'Cry Like A Baby' and 'Out Of Left Field', but 'A Woman Left Lonely' is not one of them.

'Delta Dawn' was released in 1974. Scott was going through a phase of covering a lot of American country songs. The song was written by Americans Larry Collins and Alex Harvey and had been covered by several American female singers including Bette Midler, Helen Reddy, Loretta Lynn and Tanya Tucker. Tucker's version was produced by Billy Sherrill and went to the top of the American country charts. Amanda Petrusich wrote in *No Regrets — Writings On Scott Walker*: *"Walker is trying his best – 'Delta dawn, what's that flower you have on?' he bellows earnestly, while a choir sings backup – but he also sounds vaguely absurd, all aw-shucks affect and misplaced pomp. Consequently, listening to 'Delta Dawn' feels like being hit in the face with a bowling ball. There is little delicacy."* I find this country song rather ordinary.

The Scott Walker cult continued right up to his death in 2019. Some key events perpetuated this. Julian Cope's compilation, *Fire Escape In The Sky: The Godlike Genius Of Scott Walker* was released in 1981 on Zoo Records. The title of the album was taken from Walker's song 'Big Louise'. This compilation, containing only songs written by the singer, introduced Scott Walker to a new generation. Philips released the compilation, *Scott Walker Sings Jacques Brel*, the same year.

A couple of years later, Scott signed to Virgin Records and released a new album, *Climate Of The Hunter*. In 1990 *Boy Child: The Best Of Scott Walker 1967-1970* was released and, like *Fire Escape In The Sky*, consisted of songs written by Scott himself. Sleeve notes were written by Marc Almond who released his own version of 'Jackie' the following year.

1992 saw Polygram release another compilation, *No Regrets – The Best Of Scott Walker And The Walker Brothers*, which carefully mixed Walker Brothers hits with Scott's better known solo tracks. The album reached No. 4 in the album charts. This is a good place to start if you are new to the "Godlike Genius".

The Walker Brothers

Before anyone asks, allow me to quote from Chris May and Tim Philips' pioneering book, *British Beat*: "*Although The Walker Brothers were Americans, the group was based in England and was a prominent if untypical part of the British Sixties pop world.*"

After two chart-toppers with 'Make It Easy On Yourself' and 'The Sun Ain't Gonna Shine Anymore' and a Top Three hit with 'My Ship Is Coming In', The Walker Brothers seemed unstoppable in the UK. Over half a century later, these three songs still sound marvellous. In his essay, 'The Hollow Men', in the *No Regrets* book, Anthony Reynolds described the way that these masterpieces were made: "*There would be no chance of previewing the huge orchestral arrangements before the recording date. Everyone heard the score played for the first time on the very day it was recorded. A few run-throughs would be indulged, mostly for the engineer's benefit ... but essentially this would be the first and last time such arrangements ... were ever played. The result was a form of widescreen, magisterial surround-sound, even in mono. The songs sounded massive and yet were intricately bejewelled with detail. The vocals were clear, upfront, titanic yet intimate. Such factors were all vital trademarks of The Walkers' sound and identity.*"

The next two Walkers' singles, '(Baby) You Don't Have To Tell Me' and 'Another Tear Falls' did not reach the Top Ten and the perennial diminishing returns factor seemed to come in. As the very biggest acts knew, staying at the top was not easy and The Walker Brothers did not cope well with this. 'Deadlier Than The Male' was released in December 1966. Written by Scott Engel (Walker), the title was taken from Rudyard Kipling's 1911 poem 'Female Of The Species'. The song was used as the theme to the 1967 film, *Deadlier Than The Male*, directed by Ralph Thomas and starring Richard Johnson and Elke Sommer. *NME* called the single: "*dramatic and atmospheric ... Scott solos the glowing and effusive lyric in that deep controlled vibrato ... enhanced by a swelling, palpitating Reg Guest backing with strings and tambourine ... has a sort of James Bond/Goldfinger quality and undoubtedly the film will help to boost it.*" *Record Mirror*'s reviewer was impressed: "*a fair old ballad, constructed on the usual 'massive' lines and with a most compelling orchestral backing. By no means the most immediately commercial from the Walkers, but a hit nevertheless.*" Anthony

Reynolds: "*It was hardly laden with hooks. It's the marine-blue verses that draw the listener in – the chorus is little more than a brief descent over which the excellent title is draped – but the song nevertheless is an understated Walker classic.*" In her essay in *No Regrets — Writings on Scott Walker*, Biba Kopf elaborates: "*over co-writer, record producer and close ally Johnny Franz's appropriate Baroque-Bond spy movie quatsch arrangement, Scott's lead vocal folk-spins wisdom from the banal verses he'd contrived to lend truth to the chorus.*" The single stalled at a surprisingly low No. 34.

Two cover versions followed; Lorraine Ellison's 'Stay With Me Baby' and The Ronettes' 'Walking In The Rain'. Neither of them had been hits in the UK and the Walkers had the chance to do well with such exceptional songs. These singles were excellent renditions, yet both stalled at the same lowly position of No. 26. The reunion of The Walker Brothers in the mid-1970s was a big surprise. Scott, of course had released a series of extraordinary albums, conveniently titled *Scott*, *Scott 2*, *Scott 3* and *Scott 4*. The first three albums featured a mix of Jacques Brel songs, Scott's own compositions and ones by other top songwriters. *Scott 4* featured all songs by Scott and did not chart, neither did the fifth album, *Til The Band Comes In*. After this, there was a long stream of unsuccessful albums of cover versions, including a surprising number of country songs. Only 1969's *Songs From His TV Series* charted, reaching No.7 and staying in the charts for three weeks.

The "brothers" came back strongly in 1976 with their excellent cover of Tom Rush's 'No Regrets' which brought the trio back into the Top Ten for the first time in nearly a decade. Again, follow-ups were a problem. 'Lines' was the title track of the second comeback album and released as a single. *Record Mirror* was merciless: "*Scott bellows and booms through a couple of climaxes on this bug production. But it hasn't got enough catchiness, and what is probably an excellent album track comes out as a slow yawn.*"

'We're All Alone' was a Boz Scaggs composition and a track on his best-selling *Silk Degrees* album. Biba Kopf: "*Of all The Walker Brothers' mid-1970s covers, 'We're All Alone' is the only one you could truly call an extraordinary rendition. Everything about it is perfectly poised, down to the simplicity of the drum part ... with Scott's voice rising agonisingly slowly over its duration to bring the song to a peak of emotion as the iced strings melt beneath him.*"

The single flopped so it must have been frustrating for Scott, John and Gary to see Rita Coolidge have a huge international hit with the song just a few months later.

The Walker Brothers' third and final album for GTO was 1978's *Nite Flights*. As a student journalist at the time I received a review copy of this album. GTO was about the only record label that regularly sent me freebies and this album stood out alongside records by Dean Friedman, Giorgio Moroder and several long-forgotten names. *Nite Flights* is one of the genuinely strangest and original albums that has ever been released by a mainstream pop act. Clearly influenced by Bowie's *Low* and *Heroes* albums, the album is something of a hidden gem, mainly due to the first four tracks, written and sung by Scott.

Record Mirror reviewed 'The Electrician': "*First minute is really something else ... but the eerie atmosphere gets flushed down the bog as the old Walker drone clone syndrome vocals take over at snail's pace.*" That is a bit unfair. The whole track – about torture – is a highly disturbing listen. Scott told *NME*'s Bob Edmands: "*This song 'The Electrician' is about torture in South America. It's about the Americans who are going there with their little black boxes. Americans who train people to torture. One review of it said it was a metaphysical love song. It is a love song. There are two lovers in it discussing the coming of one of these Americans. But that line in it about the lights going low is the idea of lights going low in a prison when they switched on the electric chair.*" Edmands later writes: "*this* Nite Flights *album ... is probably the most surprising release so far this year.*" The writer makes a valid point later in the piece: "*If (Scott Walker) was an accredited New York junkie with a rock band, he'd be taken more seriously than he is as one-third of a bunch of schmaltzy balladeers. Even if those balladeers are no longer schmaltzy or inclined towards balladeering.*" This is part of my fascination with flop singles made by chart acts; sometimes we simply miss their best moments because a playlist panel decide not to include a particular record. Or, more seriously, we just do not regard unsuccessful singles as worth considering.

Ultravox's Midge Ure covered 'No Regrets' in 1982 which reached No. 9, two places lower than The Walker Brothers' version. In the same year, Merseyside duo, White & Torch released a single called 'Parade'. This astonishing lost classic sounded just like The Walker Brothers at their 1960s peak. The singer's baritone voice is uncannily like Scott's and the two singers' combined voices sound just like Scott and John together. 'Parade' must have had radio airplay in 1982 as I would not have heard it otherwise. More recently, 'Parade' was covered by another baritone singer, television talent show star Rhydian on *Waves*, his album of 1980s lost classics. The influence of Scott Walker just keeps going.

4 – Making The Most Of It

IN *WORD* MAGAZINE ROB FITZPATRICK WROTE: "*FOR A time during the early to mid 1970s (Mickie) Most's boast was that never a week went by that he didn't have a record in the Top Ten.*" Chris Spedding (who had a hit on RAK with 'Motorbikin'') told Fitzpatrick about Mickie Most. "*He'd get his hair cut every week or so. He'd sit down and the hairdresser would ask what he had in the charts. One week he was asked and he didn't have anything and he was mortified.*"

Mickie Most was featured in the BBC Radio One series *The Record Producers*. The tie-in book, using transcriptions of the programmes' interviews, gives a fascinating insight into his talent for producing so many hits. He had been making hit singles from the early 1960s; his successes included 'House Of the Rising Sun', 'Sunshine Superman' and 'I'm Into Something Good'. Most set up his own RAK label in 1970 which had a better hits-to-releases ratio than any other for several years. For example, out of the label's first ten single releases, nine were British hits. No other label could hope to match this.

HERMAN'S HERMITS

Between August 1964 and November 1966, Herman's Hermits had an unbroken run of Top Twenty hits, starting with the chart-topping 'I'm Into Something Good'. The group's covers of American hits such as 'Silhouettes' and 'Wonderful World' were interspersed with new compositions by the likes of Graham Gouldman, P.F. Sloan and Steve Barri, and Gerry Goffin and Carole King. 'No Milk Today' was an interesting song by fellow Mancunian, Graham Gouldman, and showed a slightly more contemplative side to the group, but still reached the Top Ten.

The follow-up was another Gouldman song, 'East West', in December 1966. This is a seasonal record, but hardly a sing-a-long

Christmas single despite its waltz time. The lyrics focus on an absent performer, feeling homesick. *Record Mirror*: "*In some ways stronger than 'No Milk Today'. Very gently sung, but with some interesting backing vocal and instrumental sounds and the words are rather appealing. Almost a carol appeal in the middle. Herman clearly follows no established pattern – he just does what he thinks suits him. This one does – for sure.*" Penny Valentine in *Disc* also liked it: "*a very pretty record ... I think, certainly as the production goes, this is the best record the group have made.. A huge hit of course..*" Disappointingly, 'East West' only reached a lowly No. 37. Many years later another Mancunian, Morrissey, covered the song, adding extra verses.

'Museum' was Herman's Hermits' first actual flop. Written by Donovan Leitch, who also was working with Mickie Most, this was one of his many songs about London. He had recorded the song himself during the *Sunshine Superman* sessions early in 1966, but it was left off the actual album. Donovan later re-recorded the song in a jazzier style with Most's session men such as John Paul Jones and probably Big Jim Sullivan on sitar. The Hermits' version is less obviously psychedelic, but still contains the rather surreal lyrics. *NME*: "*The combination of Herman performing a Donovan composition may seem a trifle incongruous at first but it works remarkably well. Herman dual-tracks, while the Hermits supply a rippling guitar backing, handclaps and an infectious toe-tapping beat. The result is a disc unlike anything Herman has done before – and very good.*" Clearly, the fans were not ready to hear their idol sing such lines as: "*There she stood in drag, just a-lookin' cool in astrakhan*"!

The last two years of the 1960s were good for Herman's Hermits in the UK singles charts; in the *History Of Rock*, Stephen Barnard wrote: "*the reason for this revival in fortune lay primarily in the programming of BBC Radio One, which favoured precisely the kind of family pop that the pirate stations avoided playing.*" In 1968 the group achieved four consecutive Top Twenty hits with 'I Can Take Or Leave Your Loving', 'Sleepy Joe', 'Sunshine Girl' and 'Something's Happening'. But, unfortunately, Herman's Hermits' singles were becoming blander. Spring 1969 was even better for the group with 'My Sentimental Friend' reaching No. 2. This was Herman's highest British chart position since 1964's chart-topping 'I'm Into Something Good'. Regular *Top of the Pops* appearances helped and singer Peter Noone (aka Herman) was still visibly and actually youthful – he was only 22 years old at the end of the 1960s.

'Here Comes The Star' was written by Johnny B. Young, a friend of Bee Gee Barry Gibb. Originally called 'The Star', this had been a hit for Ross D. Wyllie in Australia. Herman's Hermits heard the song while touring down under. 'Here Comes The Star' was in the same vein as 'East West', showing a more serious side to the group. The song starts with 'Eleanor Rigby' style strings and Peter Noone declares: "*I am the loneliest man in the world*", quite a shocking line from such a popular public figure. There is a big chorus in what is very much a solo performance. *Record Mirror*: "*This has such an easy commercial chorus that it must be a massive hit ... It's one of those 'show-biz all-is-not-so-easy for the star' sagas with a gentle backing and Herman doing his wistful nostalgia thing.*" Disappointingly, the single stalled at No.33.

Noone's time with the group ended in 1971 by which time they had moved to the RAK label. Significantly, the group recorded two singles penned by Tony Wilson and Erroll Brown of Hot Chocolate. There was the courtly love of 'Lady Barbara' and the reggaefied 'Bet Yer Life I Do'. Noone started his solo career well with his cover of David Bowie's 'Oh You Pretty Thing' reaching No.12 in the summer of 1971, several months before the writer's own version appeared on *Hunky Dory*. This was his only solo hit. Later, he appeared in a production of Gilbert And Sullivan's *Pirates Of Penzance* as well performing on the nostalgia circuit around the world. Now an unbelievable seventy-six years old, Noone is still active.

Hot Chocolate

Hot Chocolate were a phenomenon. They were the only British band to have a British hit single in every year between 1970 and 1984. If one single was a complete flop or a minor hit, generally the follow-up was a huge success. At the heart of the band's success was the distinctive singing, and songwriting, of Erroll Brown. For the first half of the 1970s, Brown wrote with bandmate Tony Wilson until the latter left for an undistinguished solo career. The pair had written hits for other Mickie Most productions, 'Bet Yer Life I Do' and 'Lady Barbara' (in conjunction with Bigazzi and Savio) for Herman's Hermits and 'Think About Your Children' for Mary Hopkin (also with a Margaret Wilson, who I assume was Tony's wife).

Between 1970 and 1979 Hot Chocolate released 23 singles in the UK. Among these there were seven flops which failed to reach the Top Thirty. In *Record Collector* magazine Bill Harry summed up the situation: *"Another interesting aspect of Hot Chocolate's career is their durability. Many artists who have enjoyed a string of hits suddenly find themselves with lower chart placings and eventually vanish from the charts altogether. Once they've had a non-chart record they find it almost impossible to return. Not so with Hot Chocolate. If they have a few flops or a couple of minor hits, they are able to reappear suddenly with a massive hit."*

In the *History Of Rock* Bob Woffinden expanded: *"The group's strategy ran contrary to traditional pop wisdom, which had always maintained that an act should capitalise on a hit single straight away by releasing a follow-up record which stuck closely to the formula of its predecessor; by undertaking live appearances in its wake; and by releasing a hastily-recorded album that numbered the hit among its tracks. Hot Chocolate did none of these. After each hit, the group allowed whatever goodwill had accrued to the band to evaporate; even when a follow-up was forthcoming, it was likely to be in a different vein to its predecessor."*

The group started the 1970s with two strong Top Ten singles, 'Love Is Life' and 'I Believe In Love'. The group's next single, 'Mary Anne', was released in 1972 and was the group's first flop. *Record Mirror*: *"Mickie Most production of substance and style. It's an ear-bending slab, very commercial, with hectic drum-bass beat and the verse ... leads into a most direct chorus. Not the strongest of Chocolate bars in terms of melody, but I'm pretty sure it will do well. Nice restrained arrangement most of the way."* *NME* agreed: *"It could do well if they keep their fingers crossed."* Listening to the unfamiliar 'Mary Anne' while researching this book felt like hearing a brand new release. Even this flop is full of hooks from the refrain; *"I was only dreaming"* to Brown's unmistakeable voice when he sings *"Ooh I love you Mary Anne."*

The follow-up to 'Mary Anne' was 'You'll Always Be A Friend' which reached No. 23 later in the year. 1973 saw the release of 'Brother Louie'. Bob Woffinden: *"In 1973 they (Hot Chocolate) changed tack somewhat. 'Brother Louie' departed from the streamlined pop of earlier releases* and had more in common with the sultry sounds of black American groups. With its realistic treatment of the problems of a mixed race love affair, it reflected those feelings of black consciousness that acts like The Temptations and Marvin Gaye had harnessed to advantage." The single went Top Ten. Later in the year the American band, Stories, reached No. 1 in their homeland with their version of the same song. 'Rumours' was released in the summer of 1973. There is wah-wah guitar, a mournful string arrangement and chatter over a reggae-type beat. On top of all this we hear a mumbled chorus and Erroll Brown's distinctive voice. 'Rumours' flopped in the summer of 1973 despite widespread airplay, peaking at No. 44.

The following year, true to form, Hot Chocolate bounced back with 'Emma' which went to No. 3. Three more flops followed: 'Changing World' is slow with a piano introduction and obscure lyrics: "*Through chocolate eyes I see.*" Brown's voice is double-tracked, an octave apart and more strings come in. Unlike 'Changing World', I can actually remember hearing 'Cheri Babe' on the radio. It was more upbeat and simpler but stalled at No. 31. Every Hot Chocolate single has several hooks and we must remember to acknowledge Most's production skills and the quality of the group's musicians, not least lead guitarist, Harvey Hinsley.

Simon Frith praised 'Blue Night', the group's first single of 1975: "*(it) will be a hit but the group still haven't got the respect they deserve for single-handedly preserving melodrama in British pop.*" With such a distinctive vocalist in Erroll Brown, there was a danger that Hot Chocolate's singles would not have enough variety. *Record Mirror* saw the warning signs: "*Erroll Brown and Hot Chocolate are in imminent danger of falling into one of the easiest traps – repeating themselves. Sure, they've done quite well with singles like 'Emma', but this is practically the same music and phrasing with different words. Very doomy feel to the whole thing, and it's much too samey.*" On the B-side of 'Blue Night' was a track called 'You Sexy Thing', co-written by Erroll Brown and Tony Wilson. Six months later this was released as an A-side.

The departure of Tony Wilson in 1975 did not appear to have any negative effect on Hot Chocolate's hit making. Brown appeared to be no less successful when writing songs on his own. The hits continued. Mickie Most revealed some of the group's approach: "*(other times) their stuff needs quite a bit of work on it, like bass parts and drum patterns, but then they'll come in with another one which'll be just perfect, and won't need anything doing to it.*" On one occasion Most told the group that: "*'I'm going to call your next album Every 1's A Winner' but there wasn't a song with that title at the time. So Errol went away, and then said 'I've been rehearsing that song', and I said 'What song's that?' and he said that after I gave him that title, he wrote a song around it. We were in the studio, so we recorded it, just like that.*"

For most of the rest of the decade Hot Chocolate were on a winning streak with no less than nine consecutive Top Twenty hits. Only 1976's 'Heaven's In The Back Seat Of My Cadillac' interrupted this pattern when it peaked at No. 25. The hits included, of course, 'You Sexy Thing' (No. 2 in 1975) which returned to the Top Ten on two further occasions in 1987 and 1997. The latter was due to its famous inclusion in *The Full Monty* film. 'So You Win Again' did even better, reaching No.1 in the summer of 1977. This was one of the rare occasions when Hot Chocolate used an outside writer. In this case it was Russ Ballard, formerly of Argent. Ballard also wrote, amongst others, Hello's 'New York Groove' and Rainbow's 'Since You've Been Gone' and 'I Surrender'.

Hot Chocolate finished the 1970s with a couple of flops. 'Mindless Boogie' was reviewed in *Record Mirror*: "*Not exactly an experimental Hot Choc record, not exactly a disco Hot Choc record, but it's not quite what we're used to from them. They've started thinking about their songs more than they used to. This is quite aggressive, has a driving thumping beat and is quite possibly a piss take of the whole set-up.*" It went no higher than No. 46.

The title of 1979's 'Going Through The Motions' (No. 53) hinted at a certain cynicism from Erroll Brown and his colleagues about their day job. Actually, the song concerned an unsatisfactory relationship and Erroll tells his partner: "*Your heart isn't in it baby*" and he can feel her love "*flowing away.*" The synthesiser and guitar are heard over an insistent disco beat. Brown's vocals are always passionate and dynamic.

The group's hit-making streak continued until 1984 with half a dozen more Top Twenty singles. Erroll Brown left Hot Chocolate in 1986 and had a solo career of sorts. He died in 2015.

New World

New World were from Australia but were based in the UK. They won ITV's *Opportunity Knocks* although vote-rigging was alleged to be an issue at the time. This folk-lite trio were beaten to the Top Ten by Lynn Anderson with their competing renditions of Joe South's 'Rose Garden'. Lynn Anderson was a one hit wonder in the UK, but New World went on to have three more Top Twenty hits. The most successful of these was 'Tom-Tom Turnaround', the first hit for songwriters Nicky Chinn and Mike Chapman. Chinn and Chapman's genius was to tailor-make appropriate songs for their different acts. New World's successful follow-ups were 'Kara Kara' (peaked at No. 13) and 'Sister Jane' (peaked at No. 6). These singles were steady sellers; in total, these four aforementioned singles were in the charts for 52 weeks.

A surprise blip in New World's run of hits was 'Living Next Door To Alice' in 1972 which I remember hearing repeatedly on the radio, but it did not chart. Just four years later, in 1976, another RAK act, Smokie reached No. 5 with the same song and this benefited from the production skills of the song's writers, Chinn and Chapman.

New World's final appearance in the UK singles charts was 'Rooftop Singing' which reached a lowly No. 50. This MOR singalong was completely different to the trio's earlier rather earnest 'folk' singles. The trio's next release was a version of 'Old Shep'. What were they thinking?

Suzi Quatro

Suzi signed with the RAK label in 1971 and her second release on that label, 'Can The Can', reached No. 1 two years later. This was the first chart-topper for RAK. Five more Top Twenty hits followed in quick succession, including another No. 1 with 'Devil Gate Drive'. Like Slade and Quo, Suzi seemed to have a residency at *Top of the Pops*. Perhaps over-familiarity has diminished the impact of her success. She was the first female bandleader/instrumentalist on *Top of the Pops*; Julie Driscoll, Sonja Kristina et al were lead singers but did not play an instrument. Suzi led the way for Joan Jett, Chrissie Hynde and many

many more.

Record Mirror reviewed 'Your Mama Won't Like Me': "*Funk hits Ms. Quatro on this new single with a much fuller backing sound that stirs things up and sets them down in a very soulful way. There's still Suzi's vocals ripping through the whole thing, but the combined sound is certainly one of the best things she's done.*" There is funky guitar and keyboards and even a brass section and quasi-provocative lyrics: "*I wear my jeans too tight.*" etc. I can see why it stalled at No. 31. I suppose Suzi's fans were getting alienated.

'I Bit Off More Than I Could Chew' broke this run of hits by flopping completely. Simon Frith commented in *Let It Rock*: "*Suzi Quatro, who bored us for so long with her variations on 'Can The Can', has been making a valiant effort to get tougher, brassier, funkier. Why did nobody buy 'I Bit Off More Than I Could Chew'* — *do people prefer her as a plastic leather dolly?*" The song has funky keyboards and a horn section – nothing like the Suzi that people knew and loved. It sounds a little contrived to me.

Mike Chapman told the authors of *The Record Producers*: "*I heard ... 'Tell Me Something Good' by Rufus and I wish I'd never heard that record, because it sounded like the death knell for Suzi Quatro. I came back from America with this wonderful idea to make a record that sounded something like 'Tell Me Something Good', so we wrote a song called 'Your Mama Won't Like Me' – I happen to think that both that one and 'I Bit Off More Than I Could Chew' were two of Suzi's best records, technically. Unfortunately, that sort of music was not as appealing to the public outside America as I thought it was going to be, so Suzi didn't really get off the ground with that musical image, and things started to crumble round our ears. With 'Your Mama', she got the new release spot on* Top of the Pops, *and just when we needed the second* Top of the Pops, *the record stuck at number 31, and then the follow-up 'I Bit Off More Than I Could Chew', just didn't do anything at all.*"

'I May Be Too Young' was reviewed in *Record Mirror*: "*It's back to the rockers for Mrs Q courtesy of Chinn and Chapman, and after the failure of her last attempt at the charts it's probably the best thing she could do. Unfortunately it sounds a bit repetitious after the first four bars, and whilst the public might prefer this to her previous singles, it isn't that exciting.*" *Disc* was equally critical: "*... she's old enough to know how to deliver a dynamic rock composition with the right amount of aggression. Only trouble is we've heard it all before. Suzi Quatro in '75 sounds very much like Suzi Quatro in '73. Two years have passed by, yet* the lady and her well-seasoned songwriters still cling to the same old rock 'n' roll cliches and gimmicks. Even Suzi's staunchest of fans must be getting a trifle tired of Chapman-Chinn formula rock." This single is pseudo-autobiographical with its references to "Suzi" and "Baton Rouge". There is a big chorus and it is more tuneful than the previous two singles.

Suzi was absent from the British singles charts for two long years, returning with 'Tear Me Apart' in spring 1977 which reached No. 27. Next was 'Roxy Roller' which recalls the sound of Suzi's first singles on RAK, with a 'Devil Gate Drive' beat. The single is back to the sound of a rock band with a guitar riff and solo. *Record Mirror*: "*Best single she's put out for a long time. Not so shouty as 'Tear Me Apart', her last effort. Should put her back in the charts.*" Sadly, 'Roxy Roller' didn't do so.

Suzi had her highest chart placing for four years in 1978 when the untypical 'If You Can't Give Me Love' reached No. 4. Again, successful follow-ups were a challenge, but Chinn and Chapman must have realised that the tunefulness of 'If You Can't Give Me Love' was popular. 'The Race Is On' went no higher than No. 43. To me, this sounds more like a song for Smokie. It starts as a slow, piano-led ballad then speeds up into a jaunty sing-a-long with the rest of the band joining in: "*Here we stand like a couple of fools.*" I quite like it.

Even a duet with Smokie's Chris Norman, 'Stumblin' In' – only reached No. 41, despite being, in Chapman's own words, "*a huge hit in America, a number three record.*" 'Stumblin' In' deserved a higher chart placing in Britain – the singers' voices worked well together and the song has a great hook.

Racey

I only include Racey for completists' sake. I did not want to sneer in this book, but may fall into that trap here. Everything about Racey repels me; their outfits on *Top of the Pops* made The Rubettes look like fashion icons. The group's stage act and the pure crassness of their output must make them RAK's weakest signings. 'Lay Your Love On Me' reached No. 3 and 'Some Girls' did even better grasping the No. 2 spot. Later hits, 'Boy Oh Boy' and a revival of Dion's 'Runaround Sue', were less successful. In between were a couple of flops – 'Such

A Night' and 1980's 'Rest Of My Life'. 'Such A Night' has the usual prominent piano and terrible semi-spoken vocals. The chorus is incredibly corny and the refrain: *"I've got a whole lotta loving and living to do"* grates.

Smokie

Smokie were originally billed as Smokey, but Motown's Smokey Robinson soon put a stop to that. They were a proper group from Yorkshire who had been together for many years. After signing with RAK, they had an impressive unbroken run of ten Top Twenty hits starting with 'If You Think You Know How To Love Me' and including 'Don't Play Your Rock 'N' Roll With Me' with its 'His Latest Flame' guitar figure. Smokie released their own version of the New World flop, 'Living Next Door To Alice'. All but one of these (a cover of 'Needles And Pins') were written by their producers Nicky Chinn and Mike Chapman.

Smokie's eleventh hit single, 'Mexican Girl', was their first self-penned A-side (written by lead singer Chris Norman and drummer Pete Spencer) and reached No. 19. It sounded no different to their previous hits. Two more group compositions, 'Do It To Me' and 'Babe It's Up To You', were released as singles. 'Do It To Me' has a simple guitar figure and sounds like one of the group's previous hits, not least because of Chris Norman's unmistakeable voice and the group's harmonies. The weakest part is the song's actual title. *Record Mirror* commented on 'Babe It's Up To You' *"it is instantly memorable. A year's absence doesn't seem to have made much difference. Acoustic-ish chorus and a mock rock chorus. They needed a confident bubblegum return and this is it."* I feel that the song starts gently (like 'Alice'), but is not helped by a cheesy Sir Douglas Quintet-style organ in the chorus. There are also hints of a Euro-pop beat; no wonder that Smokie were — and still are – so popular in Germany. I wonder if the group should have been allowed to write their own A-sides earlier in their chart career.

Smokie had just one more minor hit. At the start of the 1980s, a good cover of the Bobby Vee hit 'Take Good Care Of My Baby', written by Gerry Goffin and Carole King, reached No. 34. Eventually, lead singer Chris Norman left the band and both he and the new line-up of the band would have huge success in Europe and beyond.

Mickie Most and RAK went on to have huge success at the beginning of the 1980s with Kim Wilde and, of course, Hot Chocolate. RAK sold out to EMI in 1983, but was revived as a label five years later. Most died in 2003.

5- The Sound Of The Underground

MOST MAJOR BRITISH ROCK BANDS IN THE LATE 1960s and on throughout the 1970s issued singles. The notable exception, I suppose, was Led Zeppelin. This policy clearly worked as the band had an incredible run of No.1 albums in this country from *Led Zeppelin II* in 1969 right through to *In Through The Out Door* a decade later. Pink Floyd did not release any singles in the UK between 1969 and 1979; again, it seemed to increase the band's album sales in those years, rather than reduce them.

Argent

Formed by former members of The Zombies and The Roulettes and named after keyboard player, Rod Argent, Argent were an unusual rock band to look at; lead singer and guitarist Russ Ballard always wore sunglasses, but unlike fellow shade-wearers, Ian Hunter or latter-day Jeff Lynne, did not seem to have much stage presence. For many people, the focus of the band was its leader, Rod Argent, with his long curly locks and formidable keyboard technique (Rick Wakeman, no less, was an admirer). 'Hold Your Head Up' was a huge hit in 1972, reaching No. 5 and staying in the singles charts for twelve weeks. Follow-ups had mixed fortunes. 'Tragedy' was also from the *All Together Now* album but only reached No. 34.

The anthemic 'God Gave Rock 'n' Roll To You' brought Argent back into the Top Thirty. It was covered later by Kiss. 'It's Only Money (Part 2)' was the follow-up. *Record Mirror*: "*Russ's powerful voice strides through a bass riff and the odd group touch of vocal and it's a repeated phrase that insists on being sung. Almost drug-like in the way this production takes over.*"

'Thunder And Lightning' was released in February 1974. *Record Mirror*: "*A see-saw rhythmic sound before Russ gets at it. Lots of aggression and power ... Brass figures pointing incisive fingers. Great big banks of rolling sound ... Argent reach out and grab one by the scruff of the neck in this kind of mood.. Chart Cert."*

'Man For All Reasons' was released four months later. *Record Mirror*: *"Russ Ballard song with a martial kind of beat and a deliberate build-up in the production. Rather a different style and approach for Argent, yet it comes off well enough. Some of the vocal work is outstandingly laid down. Yet it could sink virtually without trace."* It did.

Russ Ballard left the band in March 1974 and was replaced by two new members, guitarist John Grimaldi and singer/guitarist John Verity.

'Keep On Rollin" was a track on Argent's third album, *All Together Now* but was finally released as a single in November 1974. This was the the first Argent/White composition to be an A-side since 'Hold Your Head Up' and was essentially a showcase for Rod Argent. *Record Mirror*: *"The intro belies the rest of the record; boogie piano all on its own, then suddenly they're all there, bumping and rolling and generally getting it on ... I don't think it's the right single material for Argent."* The song is strangely characterless, but I can imagine its popularity at live concerts. Appropriately, a longer version was featured on the band's live double album, *Encore*.

Atomic Rooster

Atomic Rooster had two Top Twenty hits in 1971; 'Tomorrow Night' reached No.11 and 'The Devil's Answer' did even better, peaking at No. 4. Successful follow-up singles were problematic, especially when the band were joined by Chris Farlowe and the band's music changed. Atomic Rooster were now on Pye's progressive label, Dawn. 'Stand For Me' was panned in *NME*: *"very nondescript and riff-infested. It's a pity Chris Farlowe has fallen to this boring 'progressive' type of music. He was great as an R and B singer, but here he only makes the mess even more confusing."* There is funky piano and wah-wah guitar, soon joined by horns and female backing vocals, sounding nothing like the band's previous material. Then Farlowe – never a singer I particularly liked – starts wailing. The song is rather repetitive and is, of course, nothing like as memorable as the Ben E. King song of the same name. The chorus is uninspiring:

"*Stand by me ... girl I'll set you free.*" The single was taken from the *Made In England* album, the one with the denim (!) cover. It flopped.

'Save Me' was a re-recorded version of the band's older song 'Friday The 13th' and featured on the album *Nice 'N' Greasy*. There are more horns and funky guitar, arranged and produced by keyboardist Vincent Crane and Farlowe shouting again! By now I am pretty sure that Atomic Rooster had alienated the purchasers of both their hit singles and hit albums.

BAD COMPANY

Great things were expected of Bad Company when they were formed in 1974 by two members of Free – Paul Rodgers and Simon Kirke, Mick Ralphs of Mott The Hoople and Boz Burrell formerly of King Crimson. 'Can't Get Enough' was a powerful debut, peaking at No. 15, but helping publicise the band's first (eponymous) album which reached No. 3. Bad Company's second album, *Straight Shooter* was released the following year and also reached No. 3. However, the first single, 'Good Lovin' Gone Bad' stalled just outside the Top Thirty. Basically, it wasn't as good as 'Can't Get Enough'. *Record Mirror*: "*Mick Ralphs penned number for one of the best bands around. Full of driving bass notes and tight drumming – and, of course, those vocals. All the best features of the material used on their last (and first) album here. It's a taster for the album, and a singles chart-hit.*"

Unusually – but deservedly – the second single taken from *Straight Shooter*, 'Feel Like Makin' Love', did better, reaching No. 15. The latter was something of a rock classic; not quite a power ballad, but a subtle "semi-slowie" just right for playing at the end of rock discos. Subsequent Bad Company singles did not trouble the British charts.

BLACK SABBATH

Sabbath reached No. 4 in 1970 with 'Paranoid', the title track of their second album, staying in the singles charts for an impressive eighteen weeks. The album went to No. 1, no doubt helped by the band's appearances on *Top of the Pops*.

'Am I Going Insane (Radio)' was released in 1976. *Record Mirror*: "*From their* Sabotage *album, a surprising single from one of the 'eavy bands. Whilst a lot of singles-from-albums don't work, this one does better than most. Still I can't see it achieving much, but it could be an outside chance.*" Sabotage had reached No. 7 in the album charts in autumn 1975.

Sabbath returned to the UK singles charts after eight long years when 'Never Say Die' reached No. 21 in 1978. 'Hard Road' was the follow-up. *Record Mirror*: "*The usual meat chomping musical morass has been tidied up with (yes) harmonies. This is Sabbath assailing your ears with a truncheon rather than a night stick.*"

ERIC CLAPTON

Clapton had been in the singles charts since 1965's Yardbirds hit 'For Your Love'; the B-side 'Got To Hurry' was a taster of his blues guitar playing. Later, he had hit singles with Cream, Delaney and Bonnie ('Comin' Home') and Derek And The Dominoes. An edited version of 'Layla' was a belated hit two years after the release of the band's double album. The song had appeared on the 1972 *History Of Eric Clapton* compilation and reminded record buyers of this powerful song. I remember people dancing to the song at parties.

Two years later, Clapton made his solo debut in the UK singles charts with his cover of Bob Marley's 'I Shot The Sheriff'. I must have been one of millions who had not heard the original beforehand. The cover version reached a promising No. 9 in 1974. 'Willie And The Hand Jive' was Clapton's next single. *NME*: "*Strictly in the time-honoured tradition of milking a product to the veritable bone comes Son Of 'I Shot The Sheriff' whupped straight offa the astoundingly successful* 461 Ocean Boulevard. *For 'laid-back funky' read 'pallid, sickly bereft of spark'.*" This rather slight song had been written by Johnny Otis in the late 1950s and covered in the UK by Cliff Richard.

Clapton's next single was a cover of the gospel song, 'Swing Low Sweet Chariot' which peaked at No. 19 in 1975. This was to be Clapton's last Top Thirty entry for the rest of the decade. There followed a long series of flops, some of which were "turntable hits".

Bob Dylan's 'Knockin' On Heaven's Door' was from the soundtrack of the *Pat Garrett And Billy The Kid* film. The singer had a cameo part as "Alias". This haunting song reached No. 14 in 1973, returning Dylan to the UK Top Twenty for the first time since 'Lay Lady Lay'. Clinton Heylin calls the song: *"an exercise in splendid simplicity, containing one of the easiest melodies this rarely complex composer ever conjured ... the song had been co-opted by an old friend, Eric Clapton, who inflicted a faux reggae arrangement on it in August 1975. This travesty was a surprising hit in its own right."* Clapton's rendition reached No. 38 in the UK. Apparently, Clapton had played guitar on a session for Jamaican-born Arthur Louis who was recording a reggae version of 'Knockin' On Heaven's Door'. Marc Roberty tells the story: *"He (Clapton) liked it so much he recorded his own version, using the same arrangement. Unfortunately, Arthur Louis released his version a few weeks before Eric's but he received hardly any air play."*

'Lay Down Sally' was co-written by Clapton, Marcy Levy (later known as Marcella Detroit of Shakespear's Sister) and guitarist George Terry and only reached No. 39. In the USA it topped the country charts. Marc Roberty: *"Eric plays some tasty licks in a clearly J.J. Cale influenced skiffle number."* 'Promises', a year later, was more country-style, similar to Don Williams. Roberty called it: *"an inferior rewrite on the melody of 'Lay Down Sally'"*. The single peaked at No. 37.

'Hello Old Friend' was reviewed in *Record Mirror*: *"Enrico's in slightly soulful mood (as in sorrowful, not in disco) and being helped by a gaggle of girlie singers. Could be a smallish hit."* The same publication reviewed 'Carnival': *"The marvellous husky-voiced axeman supremo in fine form on this track from No Reason To Cry."*. I found 'Carnival' a bit laboured and was unsurprised when it flopped.

JOE COCKER

Joe Cocker's chart career had two highlights with the classic chart-toppers 'With A Little Help From My Friends' and 'Up Where We Belong' — in 1968 and 1983 respectively. Cocker's definitive version of Leon Russell's 'Delta Lady' reached No. 10 in 1969. After this there were plenty of flops. Joe's cover of The Box Tops' 'The Letter' was released less than three years after the original and only reached No. 39. This was Cocker's only hit of the 1970s in the UK.

Cocker's first two albums were on Regal Zonophone and both primarily featured cover versions. As he had transformed Ringo's showcase on *Sergeant Pepper*, Cocker did the same with songs such as diverse as 'Bye Bye Blackbird' and 'Do I Still Figure In Your Life'. Leon Russell produced Cocker's eponymous second album. *The Mad Dogs And Englishmen* tour of 1970 became a double live album and a film. Masterminded by Russell, it arguably did more for his own career than Cocker's. Within a year Russell was working with Bob Dylan, George Harrison and Eric Clapton, to name but a few. Cocker's subsequent career was less star-studded and less successful.

Cocker signed to Fly (later Cube) Records and released a series of seven flop singles. This started with a live version of 'Cry Me A River' (from *Mad Dogs And Englishmen*) which was a big hit in the USA. I remember hearing 'Woman To Woman' on Radio One. *NME*: "*this unmelodic ethnic chant laid over a none-too-imaginative boring riff evokes little of the magic that instigated Cocker Power ... this doesn't give the Sheffield Soulman a chance to exercise his vocal prowess. Maybe I expected too much, but then Joe set a very high standard himself.*"

'Put Out The Light' impressed *Record Mirror*: "*Mr Cocker wraps those powerful vocals round this tres up-tempo little number that's got a great bass/drum riff running throughout ... I think this one, full of brass and solid with it, is a good 'un.*" 'You Are So Beautiful' was also reviewed in *Record Mirror*: "*this is Cocker in mellow mood – well, the old raucous vocals are still there but the backing's all down to strings and things.*" This Billy Preston composition was later adopted by The Beach Boys' Dennis Wilson as a solo showcase and crowd-pleaser at the band's late 1970s concerts. I find the song a little one-dimensional and was always puzzled by its popularity.

Cocker's final single on Cube, 'It's All Over Bar The Shoutin'', was taken from his album *Jamaica Say You Will*. *Record Mirror*: "*Great disco record featuring a great girl chorus and a distressingly effective performance from Cocker. Not, however, the stuff that chartbusters are made of.*"

Cocker signed to A&M Records in 1976. 'I Broke Down' was reviewed in *Record Mirror*: "*Joe takes it faster than you think, snarling, gurgling and vibrating as the piano honks and the chick vocalists shout back the responses – Not a hit but Joe's great.*" Cocker then moved to the Asylum label. 'Fun Time' was written and produced by New Orleans' Allen Toussaint.

The follow-up was an unnecessary cover of 'A Whiter Shade Of Pale'. Cocker did not feature in the charts again until his duet for *An Officer And A Gentleman* with Jennifer Warnes in 1983.

CREAM

Despite their instrumental prowess and consistently high standard of material, Cream are not mentioned much these days. The reunion of 2005 reminded us of this extraordinary trio. It was good to see Eric Clapton with his former bandmates, Ginger Baker and Jack Bruce (both now deceased). Cream were definitely a singles act as well as selling huge quantities of albums on both sides of the Atlantic. The band had five Top Thirty singles in the UK, including 'I Feel Free' (No. 11), 'Strange Brew' (No. 17) and 'Badge' (No. 18).

In the middle of this success was 'Anyone For Tennis' which only reached No. 40. Subtitled 'The Savage Seven Theme', this is an oddity in Cream's canon. Released in May 1968, the song was recorded for the band's *Wheels Of Fire* double album, but issued instead as a single four months beforehand. *NME*: "*this is a strangely fascinating disc. It has one of those puzzling enigmatic lyrics, and it's set to a throbbing beat. There's an ear-catching guitar sound going on behind the solo vocal, and the added strings have been exceptionally well moulded to the mood of the disc. It's restrained, almost delicate and gently compelling*". Marc Roberty described it as "*a pleasant, rather whimsical ditty.*" The song uses acoustic guitar, viola, congas and Mellotron.

DEEP PURPLE

Deep Purple's first hit single, 'Black Night', was hugely successful in the UK, reaching No. 2 in 1970 and staying in the charts for an impressive 21 weeks. They were one of the first "heavy" bands to appear on *Top of the Pops*. Like Fleetwood Mac and Jethro Tull, Deep Purple realised that they could attract a new audience if they didn't put their singles on their albums. Many teenagers simply could not afford to buy albums regularly. The guitar riff might have been "borrowed" from a Ricky Nelson single, but 'Strange Kind Of Woman' also reached the

Top Ten. Later in the year the title track of the band's *Fireball* album reached No. 15.

The following spring saw an edit of 'Never Before' released as a single. It was deemed the most commercial track from the band's new *Machine Head* album. Keyboard player Jon Lord: "*a terrific song; wonderful middle eight.*" *NME* was harsh: "*Their strength lies in combining phrases, licks, passages and churning it up and spitting it out as their own. The structure here seems to lack something, but much of their stuff suffers from that.*" It reached No. 35. The album also contained some of Deep Purple's most popular live songs – 'Highway Star', 'Smoke On The Water' and 'Space Truckin''. Any of these would surely have done better as single releases.

In 1973 singer Ian Gillan and bassist Roger Glover both left Deep Purple and were replaced by David Coverdale and Glenn Hughes. Two albums by this Mark III line-up – *Burn* and *Stormbringer* – went Top Ten in Britain but the band never regained the impact of its previous line-up. The single 'Might Just Take Your Life' did not reach the charts. The band, now with a "Mark IV" line-up, split up in 1976. Significantly the band's three chart appearances in the singles charts in 1977 and 1978 were with older material: 'Smoke On The Water' at last reached No. 21 and two E.Ps, *New Live* And *Rare I and II* reached No. 31 and No.45 respectively.

FAMILY

Family were, to use one of their own song titles, a "strange band". They had four Top Thirty hits between 1969 and 1972 and were frequent visitors to *Top of the Pops*, appearing a total of eleven times. I remember feeling slightly unsettled whenever I heard lead singer Roger Chapman's voice. He was an unlikely front man, looking and sounding nothing like such rock gods as Robert Plant, Ian Gillan and Roger Daltrey.

'Today' was released in 1970 and was an unusual choice for a single. We hear acoustic and slide guitars in harmony in a very slow, sleepy and totally uncommercial song. Chapman's vocals are quite restrained, nothing like the "strangled goat" (not my words) that we had heard on the hit singles. I remember hearing the song on Radio

One so, clearly, the station's playlist panel must have liked it. 'Larf And Sing' was taken from the band's next album, *Fearless*, but sank without trace.

The rather disturbing-sounding 'In My Own Time' reached No. 4 in the summer of 1971 and stayed in the charts for thirteen weeks. The single charts in that year were highly eclectic with room for a wide range of genres from progressive rock to bubblegum, reggae and soul music. 'Burlesque' was Family's last chart entry in 1972, reaching No. 13. The follow-up was gentler. I remember 'My Friend The Sun' getting some airplay on Radio One. *NME*: "*From the* Bandstand *album, a change of pace for the group, taking in a light acoustic guitar and vocal track. Roger Chapman's voice is without the usual edge and boosted a couple of octaves. The composition is quite a good one, with an accordion filling the holes.*" The song still sounds good and deserved to do better.

'Boom Bang' was a complete contrast; Simon Frith in *Let It Rock*: "*more aggressive than usual and reveals Roger Chapman sounds even better with a female chorus.*" *Record Mirror* also liked it, praising the song's "*big full sound and, as usual, the group have positively insisted on coming out with something different,*" predicting "*obviously a hit. Chart Cert.*" The single was also reviewed in *NME*: "*a very odd track that wouldn't have seemed out of place in the Eurovision Song Contest ... if it wasn't for Chappo's voice.*" But surely that was the whole point about Family (and later Streetwalkers) — Roger Chapman's vocals were central to the band's sound.

Frith's colleague, John Pidgeon at *Let It Rock* reviewed 'Sweet Desiree': "*Another English band to produce a fine soul single ... raucous, good-humoured club music – all fat brass, chunky guitar and drunk-funk piano*". While *NME* noticed: "*Something of a change for Family with this one, as it's Tony Ashton on lead vocals and not the ace lamb-aper Roger Chapman. The cut hasn't the strength of either 'Burlesque' or 'Boom Bang'*".

FLEETWOOD MAC

Fleetwood Mac were originally billed as "Peter Green's Fleetwood Mac featuring Jeremy Spencer" and featured the contrasting blues styles of these two guitarists. Spencer was something of a white reincarnation of Elmore James, but could replicate many other styles as rock 'n' roll, high school pop, Bo Diddley and Elvis Presley. Green was more original, creating perhaps the most impressive 'white blues' performances of any British musician. Like many of their fellow rock bands, Fleetwood Mac kept their singles separate from their albums. Green's 'Black Magic Woman' (later covered by Santana) and 'Need Your Love So Bad' both reached the Top Forty and still sound striking. Green's voice was bluesy but without trying to sound either black or American. This was a musician who even BB King rated.

The instrumental, 'Albatross', hit No. 1 in early 1969, staying in the charts for twenty weeks. Fleetwood Mac's next two singles – 'Man Of The World' and 'Oh Well' both reached No. 2 in the charts and even the heavier 'The Green Manalishi' went to No. 10.

By 1971 both Peter Green and Jeremy Spencer had left the band and fellow guitarist, Danny Kirwan, was forced into a new role as the front man. 'Dragonfly' was the band's next single. Taken from a poem by W.H. Davies (most famous for *Autobiography Of A Supertramp*) 'Dragonfly' was pleasant enough; Rikky Rooksby: "*a slow shuffling minor key instrumental with wonderfully textured guitar playing. It has shimmering chords and the tune coming down in octaves. Kirwan harmonising with himself as he sings the words ... (he) plays some fine lead, and the rhythm section turns in a sensitive performance perfect for the track.*" *Disc & Music Echo*'s reviewer liked it: "*a guitar-based roll-a-long piece with the same gentle appeal as 'Albatross' without the impact. The two lead guitars playing the instrumental harmony while the vocal harmony has very definite CSNY shades ... very pleasant but not a commercial success.*" *NME* agreed: "*a beautiful record ... A charming and enchanting ballad with a gentle lilt, it has a descriptive lyric that's delightfully harmonised, a cushion of delicate guitar playing and a memorable melody line. Not unlike 'Albatross' with words! Could even make No. 1!*" Despite a *Top of the Pops* appearance, 'Dragonfly' did not bother the charts.

Over the next three years Fleetwood Mac released a series of flops including a rather pointless cover of The Yardbirds' 'For Your Love'. 'Did You Ever Love Me?' was reviewed in *NME*: "*Three counter-pointed instrumental figures back up Christine McVie's voice as she sings about how her love just won't go.*"

There were no chart entries of new material between 'The Green Manalishi' in 1970 and the start of the Buckingham-Nicks era in 1976.

Even the singles taken from *Rumours* were not big hits in the UK with 'Dreams' only reaching No. 24. Unbelievably, the strange title track of *Tusk* was the new line-up's biggest hit of the late 1970s reaching No. 6. Needless to say, by 1977 single sales in the UK were irrelevant to Fleetwood Mac with the massive sales of the *Rumours* album. Recently, after the sad death of Christine McVie, people are looking back at Fleetwood Mac's hitless years in the first half of the 1970s. There is plenty of material to explore on a series of albums such as *Penguin*, *Mystery To Me* and *Heroes Are Hard To Find*.

Free

The first year of the 1970s was a great one for rock hit singles in the UK including Free's first chart entry, 'All Right Now'. This was boosted by the band's memorable appearances on *Top of the Pops*. Free were talented and raw. 'All Right Now' (an edited version which omits the beginning of the guitar solo) sounded exciting at the time, surrounded by so many inoffensive and undemanding pop hits. Alan Clayson: *"The hit song of 1970 was Free's 'All Right Now' which, owing much to the Rolling Stones' 'Honky Tonk Women' of 1969, was an album-enhancing 45 that would pulsate from college jukeboxes along with fare from Humble Pie, Black Sabbath and their ilk, appealing to male consumers recently grown to man's estate."* 'All Right Now' entered the singles charts at the beginning of June and stayed for twelve weeks. At the end of August, Free appeared at the Isle of Wight Festival and an extended version of their hit single was a highlight of the weekend. The band were still relatively young at the time, ranging in age from just eighteen to twenty years old, even though 'All Right Now' was taken from their third album, *Fire And Water*. Both single and album would reach No. 2.

'The Stealer' was an unlikely follow-up to such a massive hit single. It seems that the band insisted on releasing this track whereas label boss, Chris Blackwell, had preferred 'Ride On A Pony'. *NME*: *"It'll soon be up there challenging for No. 1, bound to chalk up enormous sales. Add to this an authoritative and commanding solo vocal plus a repetitive riff melody that sticks in the mind."* 'The Stealer' flopped completely in the UK and scraped to No. 49 in the USA. This slowish rocker feels a bit ordinary to these ears, despite Paul Kossoff's suitably fierce guitar playing. The parent album, *Highway* was released in December 1970 and only reached No. 41.

The piano-led 'My Brother Jake' was another change of style for Free and reached No. 4 in spring 1971. Two more Top Twenty hits followed, but the band's chart career was often disrupted by line-up changes and, sadly, the physical state of guitarist Paul Kossoff. 'Travellin' In Style' was the second single taken from the *Heartbreaker* album and was the follow-up to the hit, 'Wishing Well'. This is a fairly standard country blues song with such evocative lines as *"Well the train I ride, Is leaving the station"*. *NME*: *"features Paul Kossoff ... playing some pleasant country-ish licks, and Paul Rodgers contributing some acoustic rhythm work, plus his usual virtuoso vocal performance. Free have lost some of their old immediacy and impact, and it'll take a much snappier cut than this to give them another hit single."* Despite Paul Rodgers' excellent voice and an impressive guitar solo, I find the song a little dreary. I had not heard this track for several decades and I knew exactly how it went, this must make it either memorable or predictable.

GENESIS

Genesis released a series of unsuccessful singles on Decca in the late 1960s which now command three figure sums among collectors. Once signed to Tony Stratton Smith's Charisma label, the band continued to release unsuccessful singles which also attract high prices. In 1974, 'I Know What I Like' became Genesis's first hit single, reaching No. 21. I seem to remember it having plenty of airplay with its catchy chorus and Peter Gabriel's strange spoken coda: *"Me, I'm just a lawn mower"* etc.

'Counting Out Time' was released in 1974, *NME*: *"The promised tune intended to tide G. fans over until the band tours again next year ... (It is) very nearly interchangeable with (Family's) 'My Friend The Sun' ... There's a dwarf guitar solo. Otherwise, a fairly stock performance with minor embellishments."*

Singles extracted from both *The Lamb Lies Down On Broadway* and *A Trick of the Tail* albums all flopped. *NME* on the latter's title track: *"Beginning sounds like 'Your Mother Should Know' and slides into a beautifully* structured melody, fine words and a superb vocal by Phil Collins ... With or without Gabriel, Genesis remain the best of the classico-rock kind." 'Your Own Special Way' was taken from the *Wind And Wuthering* album, the second one to feature Phil Collins on lead vocals. An acoustic ballad written by Mike Rutherford, it was the band's first single to chart in the USA. It peaked at No. 43 in the UK. Later in 1977 the *Spot The Pigeon* E.P. reached No. 14, the band's first Top Thirty entry for three years.

By 1978 Genesis were a trio and the hits started a-coming. The band's songs became simpler in both lyrical and musical content. 'Follow You, Follow Me' was the band's first Top Ten hit and reached No. 7. *Record Mirror* disliked the follow-up, 'Many Too Many': "*Boring single that never gets off the ground from a band who, despite their usually somnolent effect, have produced a couple of good singles lately. A limp album track which bathes in professionalism, but has such little enthusiasm, it cannot fail to depress.*" I always liked this song; it sounds very American FM radio, but Collins is singing soulfully and it is preferable to these ears to 1980s Genesis or his solo work.

JETHRO TULL

Tull, like other progressive acts such as Fleetwood Mac, Deep Purple and Atomic Rooster, benefited from releasing singles and having the subsequent *Top of the Pops* exposure. I fondly remember Ian Anderson's appearance being often commented upon: his great coat, flute, shaggy hair and "wild" eyes. Ian Anderson and his colleagues widened their audience by performing their Top Ten hits, 'Living In The Past', 'Sweet Dream' and 'The Witch's Promise' on the weekly television pop show. 'Life's A Long Song' was an E.P. and reached No. 11. As the band's music became more ambitious and lengthier, singles were less important.

'Bungle In The Jungle' received a lot of airplay on Radio One and was a Top Twenty hit in the USA. *NME* made it Single Of The Week: "*extracted from the new* War Child *album, Ian Anderson against a backdrop of hard working strings, tasteful acoustic guitar, tasteless electric guitar, flute and similar artefacts explores the metaphor of life as a jungle ... a light attractive single.*" Ian Anderson himself commented: "*It's a rather odd song for Jethro Tull,*

I think. Every so often there are those songs that fall into the conventional pop rock structure — but that style isn't our forte. We're not very good at it because I'm not that kind of singer, and it doesn't come easy to me to do that stuff. But 'Bungle' is one of those songs that was nice to have done. It's got that Jethro Tull ingredient, but it's a little more straight ahead." This was a flop in the UK.

The title track of *Minstrel In The Gallery* was released as a single in summer 1975. The review in *Disc* was headlined *"Roaring Back Into The Charts"* and was lavish in its praise: *"Exquisitely tasteful chunk of relentless rock here, held together by some nicely timed, forceful guitar chords and a typical Tull tune ... All told a remarkably well-constructed song, and an extremely accessible one."* Another flop.

The self-deprecating 'Too Old To Rock 'N' Roll, Too Young To Die', another title track, was released as a single in 1976. Ian Anderson was not yet thirty years old at the time. Nearly half a century later, Anderson — and many others of his contemporaries from the 1970s — are still making music and touring. *Record Mirror* reviewed the single: *"I wouldn't have said this was a typical Tull single, sounding almost like Cat Stevens in some parts before having a very small boogie at the end. Needs a few spins, but it's got an appeal. Don't see it high in the charts though."*

Tull's final Top Thirty entry was the *Ring Out Solstice Bells* E.P. in 1976; it had an attractive picture sleeve and was a pleasant pagan alternative to the usual Christmas songs on the radio. The song later appeared on the *Songs From The Wood* album which was Tull's most successful in the UK since 1973's *A Passion Play*. Clearly, Jethro Tull's charting singles still helped promote album sales. 'The Whistler' was also released as a single from *Songs From The Wood*. Again, there was airplay and television exposure but it flopped.

LINDISFARNE

This Geordie band seemed to have everything; an evocative name that suggested antiquity and regionalism, at least one very talented songwriter, a refreshingly unpretentious image and approach and most importantly, the approval of not only John Peel but also several other Radio One colleagues. In 1971 Lindisfarne recorded no less than nine sessions for Radio One, including five blues songs for *Mike Raven's R&B*

Show. They recorded their first John Peel Concert on June 24th 1971 and later even recorded a theme tune for Peel's programme around the time that he used a BBC announcer to proclaim *"Friday Night Is Boogie Night"*. Lindisfarne covered the Stones' 'Jumpin' Jack Flash' and retitled it 'Dancing Jack Peel'.

Their single, 'Lady Eleanor', was a turntable hit when it was first released in 1971. There seemed to be a lot of "lady" songs around this: 'Lady Rose' (Mungo Jerry), 'Lady D'Arbanville' (Cat Stevens), 'Lady Barbara' (Herman's Hermits), no doubt inspired by the Stones' song of courtly love, 'Lady Jane' on *Aftermath*. Led Zeppelin also featured a "lady" in the first line of 'Stairway To Heaven'. Lindisfarne had an interesting mixture of sad songs, singalongs and pop tunes. 'Meet Me On The Corner' was written by bass player Rod Clements and lead vocals were by Ray Jackson (who had played mandolin on Rod Stewart's 'Maggie May'). The single reached No. 5 meaning useful *Top Of The Pops* appearances. 'Lady Eleanor' was reissued and fared even better, reaching No. 3.

'All Fall Down' came from the band's third album, *Dingly Dell*. Like 'Lady Eleanor', the track had a lead vocal by its writer, Alan Hull. This angry protest song was hardly singalong stuff; *"Councillors, magistrates"* was not an attractive opening line for pop radio. *NME*: *"Quite a pleasant Alan Hull tune from the Geordie lads this time around even though it doesn't sound like an obvious hit."* In *Let It Rock* Simon Frith confessed: *"I've even been neglecting the message of Lindisfarne's eco-political 'All Fall Down', spellbound by Alan Hull's sarcasm."* Record Mirror noted: *"some highly philosophical lyrics all about the way we treat this world of ours and Lindisfarne are in such superb nick these days that it must be a certainty for the singles charts."* It only reached No. 34.

Worse was to come; 'Court In The Act' as well as having its awful pun title, failed to chart. *NME*: *"an intro not unlike Eddie Cochran's 'Summertime Blues', this single has a distinct underlying rock 'n' roll feel. The acoustic guitars and mandolin decorate this rough bottom and the Alan Hull composition is the best thing they've done in some time. The tune is strong and should do very well."* Simon Frith was less impressed: *"Lindisfarne's monotonous 'Court In The Act' (does not) work as a 45 – buy the album."*

Lindisfarne's split in 1973 effectively destroyed their chart career.

In the *NME Encyclopedia Of Rock*, compilers Nick Logan and Bob Woffinden wrote: "*The rapid rise and equally rapid fall of Lindisfarne remains one of the mysteries of British rock.*" Alan Hull and Ray Jackson retained the band's name and brought in extra musicians, while the rest of the original line-up went off to form the folkier Jack The Lad. Lindisfarne's fourth studio album, *Roll On Ruby* produced no hit singles, nor did its follow-up *Happy Daze*. I must confess that I never got to hear either album, not even the singles, respectively 'Taking Care Of Business' and 'Tonight'. *NME* on the former: "*It's an uncompromising jaunty singalong from the new improved Lindisfarne paragenesis, and, while it falls short of the cosmic summit, I kind of like it.*" Simon Frith agreed: "*Special mention for Lindisfarne's 'Taking Care Of Business', THE record of '74 even if you haven't bought it yet.*"

Lindisfarne Mk II soon split and Alan Hull embarked on a brief solo career. The original line-up of Lindisfarne reunited for home town Christmas shows in 1976 at Newcastle City Hall and had a tremendously warm reception. These legendary concerts have continued ever since as the band's line-up changed over the decades.

In 1978 the original line-up signed a new contract with Mercury. There was a Top Ten hit with 'Run For Home' with its rather awkward 'Be My Baby' rhythm. The follow-up, 'Juke Box Gypsy' did not even reach the Top Fifty. *Record Mirror* were unimpressed with the latter: "*Geordie cabaret band jangle their way through a spirited close relation to Lynyrd Skynrd's 'Sweet Home Alabama'. Unlikely to be a hit unless I've underestimated the momentum of 'Run For Home'.*" The band carried on into the next decade, but the scope of this book does not cover these releases. The author saw Lindisfarne's Christmas show two years running in the early 1980s at Manchester Apollo, but felt that the festive atmosphere was a little contrived. There were party hats and the band were joined by a saxophonist who played a Junior Walker song. Half a century on from the original split, Rod Clements leads the latest line-up of Lindisfarne who regularly tour. Alan Hull died in 1995, aged just fifty; Simon Cowe died twenty years later in Canada.

Medicine Head

Medicine Head were signed to John Peel's Dandelion label and released two singles that faded into obscurity – 'His Guiding Hand' and 'Coast To Coast'. Their third release, '(And The) Pictures In The Sky' was a hit reaching No. 22 with the help of a *Top of the Pops* appearance. The band's image and instrumentation was unique – the long-haired singer and guitarist, John Fiddler, also played a bass drum with Peter Hope Evans, an Afro-haired jews harp/harmonica player, alongside him.

Someting of a hiatus followed; Hope Evans left the band and producer Keith Relf (former lead singer of the Yardbirds) briefly joined the band. This line-up released two singles and an album called *Dark Side Of The Moon*. The fact that Pink Floyd were able to use exactly the same title a couple of years later shows that the Medicine Head *Dark Side* album was hardly heard. 'Kum On' was reviewed by Penny Valentine who had now moved to *Sounds*: "*It's a rather dirgy paced number with a lot of vocal echo, overloaded with bongo works, that gains no pace throughout the entire track. Slightly monastic and sinister and Lennon-orientated.*"

Peter Hope Evans rejoined Fiddler to the delight of both their fans and John Peel. 'How Does It Feel' is a great single and I bought it at the time. The band had recorded an early version for a Peel session in August 1972 under the title 'Not Like A Soldier But Like An Old Love Song' – a line from the song. Three weeks later, the same song – now known as 'How Does It Feel' – was recorded for a Bob Harris Radio One session. In *Let It Rock* magazine, Simon Frith wrote "'*How Does It Feel' is the drone as before and their best record yet.*" I have to agree. After the collapse of the Dandelion label, Medicine Head signed with Polydor and had a Top Three hit with 'One And One Is One'. The album of the same name included 'How Does It Feel' so this brilliant song would have been heard by a wider audience. Both songs relied on extra instrumentation, notably producer Tony Ashton's keyboards.

There were two more hits: 'Rising Sun' and 'Slip 'N' Slide'. Both sounded like nothing else in the charts, but again relied on a fuller sound than merely Fiddler and Hope Evans. 'Rising Sun' peaked just outside the Top Ten at No. 11, while 'Slip 'N' Slide' equalled '(And The) Pictures In The Sky's peak at No. 22. For 'Slip 'N' Slide' the band had expanded to a five-piece with Family's Rob Townsend on drums.

'(It's Got To Be) Alright' was the follow-up. *NME*: "*The last Medicine Head single was really good. 'Alright' moves along at a similarly sluggish pace, features a somnambulist bassline and enraptured bedside vocals from John Fiddler. Not quite as interesting, but might make it.*" *Record Mirror*: "*quite down-beat for Med Head ... simple bass line running throughout ... and some slow, breathy vocals. Quite nice actually but whether it's commercial enough is another matter..*"

Unfortunately, Medicine Head were to have no more British hits. Their releases came out on the ill-fated WWA and Barn labels. 'Mama Come Out' was released in November 1974 on WWA. Simon Frith: "*Producer Tony Ashton has been listening to black music. He's at last given Medicine Head's essential monotony just enough shifts of sounds to keep it gripping. For dancing only though.*" In *NME* Nick Kent was also quite impressed: "*Actually this isn't bad. A 'Honky Tonk Women' cow-bell intro is followed by a reggae bass-line and then the sound of someone sitting on an accordion gracefully. A hit.*" Kent, unusually, was wrong about that.

'It's Natural' saw a return to the duo of Fiddler and Hope Evans, reinforced by their next album title *Two Man Band* which had sleeve-notes by John Peel. *Record Mirror*: "*Chooga chooga train rhythm gives away the mode of travelling on this otherwise sparse nonentity.*" The follow-up, 'Me And Suzie Hit The Floor', was another single that would have worked well on the dance floor. There is a distinctive harmonica/guitar unison riff underlied by a tremendous rhythm track dominated by Peter Hope-Evans' jews harp. John Fiddler is still active and making new music as Medicine Head.

NAZARETH

I saw Nazareth just before my sixteenth birthday in 1973. They were performing at Liverpool Stadium, a former boxing venue. The band were at their commercial peak in Britain with two Top Ten singles – 'Broken Down Angel' and 'Bad Bad Boy' just before and after I had seen them. Dan McCafferty was a powerful and charismatic vocalist and guitarist Manny Charlton a versatile and modest player. The band mixed original songs with some excellent and imaginatively chosen cover versions. Nazareth's total reworking of Joni Mitchell's 'This

Flight Tonight' was perhaps their most effective cover and certainly their most successful. It peaked just outside the Top Ten at No. 11 in autumn 1973.

The follow-up, 'Shanghaied In Shanghai' was reviewed in *Record Mirror*: "*This is typically lively Naz stuff, with them belting speed on a chorus line that is very good indeed. Tremendous percussive effects which put the seal on the whole performance. It's a very strong group and they make good records. Guitar figure midway does another short sharp miracle, and really it sounds like a directly commercial performance all round. Chart Cert.*" The single only reached No. 41, but the parent album, *Rampant* went Top Twenty.

Nazareth's version of Boudleaux Bryant's 'Love Hurts' was a powerful single, but a complete flop in Britain when first released in 1974, despite receiving wide airplay and positive reaction. The Americans seemed to know better as the single became a Top Ten hit over there. Originally recorded by The Everly Brothers, there had been a notable version by Gram Parsons and Emmylou Harris. A year later Traffic's former drummer, Jim Capaldi, released an inferior uptempo rendition that reached No. 4 in Britain. Sometimes there is no rhyme or reason – and certainly no justice – when singles fail to reach the charts.

'Hair Of The Dog' was the title track of Nazareth's sixth album. This album flopped in the UK but was a million seller in the US. *Record Mirror*: "*Lots of typical Nazareth trademarks, punchy rhythm and high vocals.*" It is not one of the band's better moments. The rather unattractive lyrics "*.. heartbreaker, soul shaker.. now you're messing with a son of a bitch*", could have discouraged radio producers. Guitarist Manny Charlton's use of Frampton-style mouth tube does not help, either. A musician of his calibre does not need gimmicks.

A powerful cover of Tomorrow's psychedelic classic, 'My White Bicycle' brought Nazareth back into the Top Twenty in 1975. For many younger fans this would have seemed a new song as the original version had not charted in Britain. Nazareth's up and down singles chart career continued. 'Holy Roller' only reached No. 36. *Record Mirror*: "*Extremely good follow-up to 'My White Bicycle' that's much more subtle than a lot of their material. After a couple of spins it really starts to get to you. Nice one.*" I disagree: I find this group composition rather unremarkable. I am not even sure what the song is about. Apart from Charlton's always excellent guitar playing, there is not much else to say. This would be Nazareth's last chart entry for nearly two years.

'Carry Out Feelings' was praised in *NME*: "*Easily their most ingenious single to date. At odds with their usual all-out assault, the song's feel recalls classics by The Hollies. The lyrics are on a level with anything by Graham Gouldman or other pop maestros.. With one song they've eclipsed their greatest hits set.*" 'You're The Violin' was released five months later in June. *Record Mirror*: "*Hmmmm ... solid pounding bass hook and Dan's tea-strainer vocals add up to a superb song – but one that sounds to me to be much more at home on an album ... Naz need much more of a stormer, possibly in the same way that Queen can always pull one out of the can for a single. Might be a small hit, but it doesn't really take off.*"

'I Don't Want To Go On Without You' was released in November 1976. *Record Mirror*: "*Unusual Nazareth single. Slow, tortuous with cruising guitar. Not bad but no hit.*" 'Somebody To Roll' was released in January 1977. *Record Mirror* again: "*Interesting piece of surrealistic guitar and controlled style, but not their best. A bit spacy for chart consumption.*" 'Gone Dead Train' was released in January 1978. *Record Mirror*: "*Wam bam rock. Old Danny Whitten number to be found on Crazy Horse's first L.P. This interpretation is only very average.*" The single reached No. 49.

MIKE OLDFIELD

People tend to forget that Mike Oldfield was a John Peel favourite at the start of his solo career. Peel's thoughts on *Tubular Bells* were even quoted by Virgin Records in their first advertisements (including the tasteless Virgin Releases, one picturing a naked pregnant woman): "*Well, I've been introducing* Top Gear *for nearly six years now but I think that it is certainly one of the most impressive LPs I have had the chance to play on the radio. A really remarkable record from Mike Oldfield.*" A short excerpt from the album was released as a single after its use in the film, *The Exorcist*. In the US, the single was even sub-titled 'Theme From The Exorcist' where it went Top Ten. In the UK the single halted at No. 31.

Oldfield's next two singles were aimed at the Christmas market. A double A-side of a brisk instrumental version of the carol, 'In Dulci

Jubilo' was paired with 'On Horseback', a clever mix of Olde English narration and a catchy chorus. This reached No.4 in 1975. A year later, Oldfield revived an old folk tune entitled 'Portsmouth' which recalled his inclusion of 'The Sailor's Hornpipe' on the *Tubular Bells* album. 'Portsmouth' went one place higher, reaching No. 3.

'William Tell Overture' was released in February 1977 and was hyped up in an advertisement: *"The new single from the more whimsical side of Mike Oldfield. You clog-danced to 'In Dulci Jubilo'. You crashed through the ceiling to 'Portsmouth'. Now hear 'William Tell' by Mike Oldfield. It'll shake you to the core."* Actually Oldfield's version of the last movement of Rossini's *William Tell Overture* was a much slower arrangement to the composer's original. It flopped.

November 1977's 'Cuckoo Song' was billed as Mike Oldfield with Les Pennin, who had worked on the *Ommadawn* album and whose virtuoso recorder playing had been heard on 'In Dulci Jubilo' and 'Portsmouth' (I had always assumed that Oldfield had played every note of these). 'Cuckoo Song' was written by Micahel Praetorious (1571-1621). *Record Mirror*: *"Another festive contender from the* Tubular Bells *camp. Certain to get airplay, certain to be a hit."* Nothing – as you will discover by reading this book – is certain in the UK singles charts. Another flop.

PINK FLOYD

Pink Floyd had two hit singles in the first half of 1967; 'Arnold Layne' reached No. 20 and its follow-up, 'See Emily Play', hit the Top Ten reaching No. 6. Their third single, 'Apples And Oranges' was described in *NME* as *"the most psychedelic single the Pink Floyd have come up with. The vocal rises in octaves as it progresses until it's roaring into the heights. And behind the falsetto harmonies there's a perpetual growling, shuddering noise coupled with a reverberating organ resonance. Although much of the track is way-out, there's a catchy and repetitive chorus which should prove a reliable sales gimmick."* It was the band's final recording with the increasingly unreliable Syd Barrett.

'It Would Be So Nice' was released on April 12th 1968, less than a week after Barrett officially left the band. The song features composer Richard Wright on lead vocals and multi-tracked keyboards. *Record Mirror*: *"sounds like a very big hit to me. Just about everything thrown into the* backing arrangement ... and the song is good, in every way. Nice rolling sound, plenty of surprises and a compact production from Norman Smith. Actually, I think it's the best they've yet produced. Chart Certainty."

NME reviewed the next single 'Point Me At The Sky' at length: "*After an unexpected subdued ballad-type opening, The Pink Floyd brings out all its various psychedelic gimmicks – muffled echo vocals, reverberating twangs, jet stream effects and sundry oscillations and distortions. The overall effect is quite shattering — a positive wall of conflicting sounds, among which you can pick a walloping beat and a commercially catchy riff phrase. There are also several tempo breaks when the routine assumes an air of almost pastoral tranquillity. Apart from the excessive volume, I found it intriguing and absorbing, quite the best Floyd single to be issued for some time.*" This was the band's third consecutive flop and their last single for eleven years. The failure of this single persuaded the band to stop releasing singles in the UK altogether. Floyd were joining bands such as Led Zeppelin who simply did not issue singles in the UK. 'Money' from the *Dark Side Of The Moon* album was released as a single in the US and went Top Twenty. Over a decade later, Pink Floyd released 'Another Brick In The Wall (Part 2)' from their 1979 album, *The Wall*, and had the Christmas No.1 that year.

THE PRETTY THINGS

I must confess that I cannot remember anything of the music of The Pretty Things when growing up in the 1960s. If I remember, it was the band members' hair that was most mentioned and their ironic name. This band were definitely *not* pretty. Various factors raised the band's profile in the next decade; their signing to Led Zeppelin's Swansong record label and David Bowie's covers of 'Rosalyn' and 'Don't Bring Me Down' on his *Pin-Ups* album. The Pretties had three Top Thirty hits on Fontana – 'Don't Bring Me Down', 'Honey I Need', and 'Cry To Me' before a series of flops.

'Come See Me' was reviewed by Penny Valentine: "*There's a filthy guitar on this song ... It has an ugly arrangement and the great moving sound on it is rather wasted.*" *NME* was more enthusiastic: "*A real wildie, this! Opens with startling drum tattoo, and breaks into hypnotic and incessant stamp beat. Phil May sings the repetitive lyric in spirited style, with shouts of encouragement from the others plus some grating rasp guitar and crazy piano work. All the time, there's a storming insidious beat. Virtually no melody which may well prevent it from climbing high in the chart, but it gets right down to the guts of r-and-b."*

NME also reviewed 'A House In The Country': *"Not so wild as most of the boys' discs, but still drives along with a thumping beat. A Ray Davies composition with one of his more novel and lighthearted lyrics. An absorbing twangy guitar sound supporting the soloist with the other lads joining in on the title phrase. Bouncy and quite tuneful."* Record Mirror: *"A Ray Davies song but the treatment is a long way from Kink sounds. Rather growled lead voice, with strident guitar figures. All at a handsome mid-tempo beat. Lyrics are rather good. Should be a hit, probably a sizeable one."*

'Progress' was also reviewed in *Record Mirror*: *"This one should do well enough. Big brassy backing over a slow moving vocal opening, then the whole thing sort of erupts into a wild swinging climax. One of the Things' strongest in terms of commercial tug."* This is quite an authentic stomper with an unusual pronunciation of the song's title.

'Defecting Grey' was the band's first release on EMI's Columbia label in November 1967. Penny Valentine enthused: *"The Pretty Things very cleverly have managed to make the transition between blues and freak-out. Now they come up with 'Defecting Grey' which is a faintly, ugly, clever thing done in an extremely competent way."* Record Mirror: *"Change of sound and style for the group.. But I draw your attention to the mood-switching and the sheer power later on. Could either flop out or click big."* Over forty years later Lenny Helsing wrote in *Shindig*: *"a complex cacophony of noise that bombards the listener, gentle, then violent, with a mesh of distortions, and an invidious low-emitting drone. Mellotron and sitar ever so slightly diffuse the sense of disquiet, while waltzing, high-as-a-kite vocal intimations float on top. 'Sitting alone on an empty bench, Mirrored above in the sky, sky, sky.' As a single it was peerless, both blatantly challenging and sonically schizophrenic."* Helsing compares 'Defecting Grey' to 'Strawberry Fields Forever' and 'See Emily Play', claiming that the former makes the other two records seem *"relatively benign"*.

February 1968 saw the release of 'Talking About The Good Times', perhaps my favourite Pretty Things single. *Record Mirror*: *"There's a quieter approach from the Pretties these days. I prefer it and there is a lot of know-how put into this strong song, specially in the backing sounds ... it must be in with fair chances. Slightly over-complex though."*

Despite being produced by Norman 'Hurricane' Smith, none of The Pretty Things' singles on Columbia and later, Harvest, reached the charts. A compilation on Harvest's Heritage imprint of *Singles A's & B's* alerted me to 'Defecting Grey' and 'Talking About The Good Times' and many more. I admit to be truly astonished by what I had heard. In the sleeve notes to the album, Paul Cox writes that the band's 1970 single, 'Good Mr Square' "*sounded as if it could have come from the Beatles' Abbey Road.*" It was even recorded in the same building. The single's parent album, *Parachute* was *Rolling Stone* magazine's LP Of The Year, but was overlooked in the UK. The Pretties deserve rediscovering; perhaps Noel Gallagher could name drop them in one of his interviews?

PROCOL HARUM

Procol Harum are often branded one-hit wonders because of the sheer popularity and ubiquity of their multi-million selling 'A Whiter Shade Of Pale', but its follow-up, 'Homburg' also went Top Ten in 1967. The following year, 'Quite Rightly So' staggered for one week to No. 50. The single was taken from the band's *Shine On Brightly* album. *Record Mirror*: "*sounds dead right to me to create the hat-trick of biggies. Great moody sounds, yet every thing crystal-clear, with fine organ sounds. Distinctive.*" *Disc & Music Echo*: "*This will grow on you ... the production is fine and solid and determined. It is truly professional stuff.*"

Procol's next single, 'A Salty Dog' was a year later again; this was also the title track of their third album. Naturally there is a *Beat Club* appearance on German television. In *Melody Maker*, even Chris Welch was uncharacteristically serious, "*Their finest hour. Procol have given us more than a successor to 'A Whiter Shade Of Pale', they have given us one of the greatest pop singles to emerge in recent years. The tune is beautiful, the arrangement brilliant, the performance perfect ... sung by Gary Brooker with every ounce of feeling he can summon, it is the kind of contribution to music pop can be justly proud of. As the strings move from climax to climax so every listener with the slightest sensitivity will be moved.*" Unbelievably, 'A Salty Dog' stalled at No. 44. This is one flop that you must get to hear.

'A Whiter Shade Of Pale' returned to the charts in 1972 when it was reissued on the Fly label, reaching No. 13 and staying in the charts for three months. The B-side featured 'Homburg' and 'A Salty Dog' so the latter would have found a larger audience than on its original release. The band's first and third albums were reissued by Fly in the Doubleback series along with ones by Tyrannosaurus Rex and Joe Cocker. Meanwhile, the current line-up of the band had recorded a live album in Canada with the Edmonton Symphony Orchestra which was a million seller in the USA. A compelling live version of 'Conquistador' reached No. 22 and there were a few more flops – 'Robert's Box', 'Souvenir Of London' and 'Nothing But The Truth'.

'Robert's Box' was reviewed in *NME*: "*It starts out vaguely Traffic-ish, with a multiplicity of congas and a curiously empty sound, then relapses into a more predictable Harum sound. I don't see many people being killed in the rush to buy it, but it could sell a few more copies of the* Grand Hotel *album.*" This was the problem for bands like Procol Harum; despite several line-up changes, the band's sound was basically Gary Brooker's rather mournful voice singing Keith Reid's unusual lyrics over layers of keyboards and guitars.

'Souvenir Of London' was banned by most radio stations. Lyricist Keith Reid had a pencil inscribed with 'A Souvenir Of London' and then wrote the song's lyrics about VD! It seems that singer/pianist Gary Brooker wrote the song as an "*affectionate tribute to London's former cockney buskers*" who he used to see outside an Underground station. Neither single helped their parent album, *Grand Hotel* reach the British charts.

'Nothing But The Truth' was reviewed by John Peel in *Sounds*: "*It's all meaty positive stuff with some fine drummery. There's a latent power, too, something like a huge engine cruising. Often the impression of restrained power is more exciting than the vulgar demonstration of that power. Such is the case here. There is an orchestra on the strength, too, but it never intrudes as the side builds with subtlety and energy. A fine single!*" Record Mirror: "*Trouble with having made a true pop classic, 'A Whiter Shade Of Pale', is that it's nigh impossible to match it, let alone beat it. This isn't in the same class but it's better than most. Jangling up-tempo piano boosts the intro; lyrics are good, optimistic, none too easy to sing, I'd say. But a big consistent sound which fires the whole thing.*"

The next single 'Pandora's Box' was a surprise hit, reaching No. 16 in autumn 1975. The song had the best facets of the band – a haunting melody, Gary Brooker's soulful voice and archetypal Keith Reid lyrics that were just as indecipherable as ever. There followed three more singles. 'The Final Thrust' was also taken from the Procol's *Ninth* album as a follow-up to 'Pandora's Box'. There is some rather unattractive staccato piano and guitar and a bland singalong chorus that has a touch of both Victoria Wood and Lynsey de Paul.

'As Strong As Samson' was a track from 1974's *Exotic Birds And Fruit* album but was released in an edited version as a single in January 1976. It was worth the wait. This is one of the band's hidden gems with a memorable opening line: *"Psychiatrists and lawyers destroying mankind"*. The hook at the end of the chorus: *"Weakest man, be strong as Samson/ When you're being held to ransom"* is just wonderful. 1977's 'Wizard Man' was Procol Harum's last single of the 1970s before splitting up and an unexceptional finale for such a talented band. The song is rather ordinary with a predictable melody and plodding beat.

STATUS QUO

Quo's singles success started well in 1968 with 'Pictures Of Matchstick Men' reaching the Top Ten. The follow-up, 'Black Veils Of Melancholy' was described in *NME* as *"[an] unnecessarily gloomy title and difficulty in comprehending the lyrics ... the sound is as tingling and electrifying as their first hit – complete with wowing organ and quivery twangs."* But *Disc & Music Echo*'s reviewer disagreed: *"I should think this, being a much better record (than 'Matchstick Men') should do very well indeed. It reminds me of a lot of things – sort of Vanilla Fudge crossed with 'Hey Joe' ... sounds like a hit."* Described in *Shindig* as *"that 'difficult' follow-up single"*, the magazine's writer continued: *"not only does 'Black Veils Of Melancholy' ape its hit predecessor a little too closely for comfort, the Quo scuppered its chances of success by appearing in a demonstration outside 10, Downing Street in opposition to the British government's dismantling of Radio Caroline in April. The Beeb duly blacklisted the single."* The poppier 'Ice In The Sun', co-written by Marty Wilde, saw Quo return to the Top Ten.

'Make Me Stay A Little Bit Longer' was released in January 1969. *Disc & Music Echo*: *"It has hints of 'Ice In The Sun' and is a fast, odd, coming-down series of notes. Of tune, I could find little, which always disconcerts me."*

NME: "*all the familiar ingredients are here — the strident guitar recorded with an excess of top, the strumming and contagious beat, the underlying organ and the spirited vocal. Maybe the song isn't as strong as their previous hits — but the vigorous and energetic rhythms coupled with the vibrant and enthusiastic approach should carry it.*"

Quo's third chart entry, 'Are You Growing Tired Of My Love' staggered to No. 46 later in the year. This was Rick Parfitt's first lead vocal on a single and a particular favourite of Pye's John Schroeder, who produced it: "*(It) still is a very strong song both lyrically and melodically and has hit written all over it.*" *NME*: "*it's an excellent record ... the best Quo have ever done. Opens quietly with the air of moodiness heightened by clanking piano and deep-throated cellos. Then it breaks into the melodic chorus — a beautiful melody. The strings backing is imaginative, the harmonies are colourful and the beat is solid enough for dancing. Very good — a hint of the Bee Gees about it.*"

The band covered The Everly Brothers' 'The Price Of Love'; *NME* said it was "*worth reviving.. It was always a good song*". Chris Welch in *Melody Maker* added: "*A fine repeat version of the old Everly Brothers hit. They do their best to match the soul of Don and Phil's vocal and the backing is solid without getting too messy in any attempt to update the sound. Not a hit I would have thought unless there is a whole generation who haven't heard the original.*" Despite front page advertising in some music papers, the single was not a hit. The track introduced road crew member, Bob Young, on harmonica who would become a useful co-writer in the band. Bryan Ferry had a hit with the song in 1976 when it was the lead track on his *Extended Play* release. The Quo would have to wait until 1970 for their next hit which was 'Down The Dustpipe'. This moved closer to the band's later successful "boogie" sound and again featured Young's blues harp.

'Tune To The Music' followed — *NME*: "*Sounds like 'Down The Dustpipe' at 78rpm until Mike Rossi's half asleep vocal comes in to squash the illusion, but also to confirm the impression that all the poor man's Canned Heat have done is speed up the tempo and basically rejig the formula that secured them their last hit. Apart from the uplift of the guitars break, drones along in tedium.*"

Quo, of course, went on to a triumphant sequence of Top Twenty hit singles on Vertigo from 'Paper Plane' in 1973 onwards. Using The Doors' 'Roadhouse Blues' (which they covered on the *Piledriver* album) as a blueprint, their sound stayed pretty much the same until the atypical acoustic 'Living On An Island' in late 1979. As far as successful reinventions go, Status Quo are up there with Marc Bolan and The Bee Gees. Only the single, 'Accident Prone', broke the hit pattern in 1978, reaching no higher than No. 36. *Record Mirror*: *"and onandonandon. Unmistakeably earthy, unmistakeably Quo. A version on a theme. Rather amusing. A hit."* Quo bounced back nearly a year later with 'Whatever You Want', their biggest self-penned UK hit for five years! Despite the death of Rick Parfitt in 2016, Francis Rossi and Andy Bown continue to keep the band going.

SUPERTRAMP

I suppose Supertramp were ahead of their time in one respect; there was a shocking photograph of a woman's heavily tattooed breasts on their second album's front cover, illustrating its title, *Indelibly Stamped*! This was pre-dating, by several decades, an age when such sights are frequently seen on magazine front covers and Channel 4's *Naked Attraction*. In 1975 the record company's faith finally paid off with 'Dreamer' becoming the band's first hit single and its parent album, *Crime Of The Century*, was even more successful, peaking at No. 4.

Roger Hodgson's vocals and the band's electric piano are something of a Marmite matter. Such distinctive stylistic vocal features, think of Steve Harley and Marc Bolan, can become wearing for even loyal audiences. Luckily, Supertramp had more than one lead singer and there was some variation in approach on the albums. Follow-ups to 'Dreamer' were a challenge. The next album, *Crisis? What Crisis?*, was less successful than *Crime Of The Century* and provided no hit singles with either 'Lady' or 'Ain't Nobody But Me'. 'Lady' is archetypal Supertramp; the electric piano and Roger Hodgson's voice are there, but it is an average song and a little predictable.

The album, *Even In The Quietest Moments*, was released in 1977. 'Give A Little Bit' just scraped into the Top Thirty at No. 29. Another single from the album, 'Babaji', was supposedly in honour of Mahavatar Babaji. *Record Mirror*: *"A pleasant enough ditty to me ... seems like their last single didn't make the charts so maybe this won't either."* Correct.

After a gap of over a year, Supertramp returned with the radio-friendly 'The Logical Song' and 'Breakfast In America' (the latter the title track of the new album). Both were Top Ten hits, but a third single taken from the album, 'Goodbye Stranger' went no higher than No. 57. A Rick Davies composition, the writer sings lead on the verses with Roger Hodgson taking the lead on the choruses. *Billboard* said *"it's one of the best executed trade-offs between (Rick) Davies and (Roger) Hodgson vocals."* Hodgson would leave the band in late 1982. Predictably, neither Hodgson nor his old band went on to great success.

THIN LIZZY

Thin Lizzy's first hit single was the band's adaptation of the traditional 'Whisky In The Jar'. This was dominated by Eric Bell's memorable guitar part. There is a story that the band plugged the song on BBC1's *The Basil Brush Show*. The next three years saw a series of flops before 'The Boys Are Back In Town' brought the band back to the Top Ten. In *Let It Rock*, Simon Frith reviewed the follow-up to 'Whisky In The Jar', 'Randolph's Tango': *"Thin Lizzy confuse their excellent singer with Randolph's Tango — a cluttered tune that isn't a tango."* Record Mirror's response was mixed: *"there is something a bit repetitious about the melody ... the la-la-la-lah bits come off infectiously well, so does some that lead guitar work and the persistent drumming."*

This was followed by 'The Rocker', taken from the band's second album, *Vagabonds Of The Western World*. *Record Mirror*: *"Though more of an album than single-selling team, Lizzy did some market research on this one ... four songs were sent out to be sampled by deejays and fans. Ninety per cent asked said 'The Rocker' was the one. It does just that."* This song was one of the very few from the band's Decca days to remain in their repertoire later in the 1970s. 'The Rocker' is the final track on the 1978 album, *Live And Dangerous*.

'Little Darlin'' was released in April 1974. *Record Mirror*: *"They get a big fat sound, belying the shortage of personnel, and rasp on amiably and urgently. All pretty much on the same level, but that's fair enough."* This was Lizzy's final release on Decca Records.

The band signed to the Vertigo label, possibly hoping that the label could help their fortunes as it had done so with Status Quo.

'Philomena' followed in October. Simon Frith in *Let It Rock* wrote: "*Away from the commercial depths there is good pop about. Thin Lizzy are back with 'Philomena' – still Irish, still stately.*" *NME* elaborated: "*When all the singles sound either like impressions of The Glitter Band or processed Philly cheese, something as moderately entertaining as this can find itself elevated to Single Of The Week by reason of its simple honesty. The playing is rumbustious, the guitar riff lodges firm in the memory, and there are words about wild ravers and the wind in the trees that somehow recall John Leyton. (It's sung in impeccable Irish, so more than that I couldn't say.)*"

'Rosalie' was released in June 1975. Simon Frith was unimpressed: "*their rather messy version of Bob Seger's (song)*", while *Record Mirror* were more positive: "*There's a good guitar line there, although it's slightly reminiscent of the Stones at some time or other. Probably won't do a bundle in the charts, but it's quite a respectable attempt.*" 'Wild One' was taken from the *Fighting* album and was the last of Lizzy's series of flops. *Record Mirror*: "*As a sample of what's to be found on this Thin Lizzy's album this is reasonably accurate, but as I don't reckon the album's much cop, I can't say much for this either, except that it's Lizzy well below their bes*t."

After the success of 'The Boys Are Back In Town', the title track of Lizzy's hit album, 'Jailbreak' stalled at No. 31, but now the band were on a roll. The *Jailbreak* album peaked at No. 10 but stayed in the charts for an impressive 50 weeks. The band then released a series of Top Thirty hit singles starting with 'Don't Believe A Word' right through to 'Sarah' at the end of the decade. Phil Lynott died in 1986.

TRAFFIC

Like so many rock bands, Traffic's career fell into several different phases. In 1967 they were definitely a psychedelic band; 'Paper Sun' was a great single, mixing sitar, Steve Winwood's soulful voice and a great riff and chorus. The follow-up, 'Hole In My Shoe', was a Dave Mason song and plagued the band for many years. When I saw them on their 1974 tour in Manchester, a heckler shouted out 'Hole In My Shoe' (even though Mason had left the band several years earlier). This was followed by some Mancunian wit shouting "*hole in my arse*" (sic). Winwood was not amused.

Traffic's third single was the title song of the film, *Here We Go Round The Mulberry Bush*, a teen comedy based on a novel by Hunter Davies. It reached No. 8. 'No Face, No Name, No Number' was the band's fourth single. *NME*: "*A complete contrast from any of Traffic's previous singles – and a really beautiful ballad. It's haunting, reflective heart-searching and plaintive ... the scoring is beautiful – employing ripples of harpsichord, glowing cellos and violins, solo flute and background music ... not as commercial as their best two but should do well.*" It peaked at a disappointing No. 40.

Dave Mason's 'Feelin' Alright' was his first lead vocal for a Traffic single since 'Hole In My Shoe'. *NME*: "*Basically it's a nagging insistent blues ... rattling piano and torrid sax – plus a vocal that gets down to the very foundations of r-and-b ... it generates a wholly convincing atmosphere of moodiness.*" Penny Valentine: "*it's been well worth waiting so long. A truly fantastic record ... it has a big tight production by Jimmy Miller. Great piano lurches in strongly and there's a wild, sudden and totally unexpected sax break. It is a long record, very, very American sounding and probably the best thing they've ever done.*" Joe Cocker recorded a memorable cover version.

When I saw Traffic in concert, they were previewing songs from their forthcoming album, *When The Eagle Flies*. One of these was 'Walking In The Wind', dominated by Rosko Gee's repetitive bass guitar pattern. There are keyboards and, inevitably, Winwood's unique, plaintive voice. This longish track (just under seven minutes) was split in two for single release. Listening to it again – after a gap of several decades – makes me feel it could have been a hit. In *NME* Nick Kent wrote: "*Traffic are no way a singles band and this almost hesitant riff sounds remarkably out of place in 45 rpm form. Still worthy of attention if only to witness how Stevie Winwood masterfully disguises the dire poetics of Capaldi's lyrics with his inspired vocalese.*" Hmm. Jim Capaldi's lyrics are not *that* bad; and certainly better than dozens of his peers.

Yes

Yes had released singles in the UK in the early 1970s but none of them were hits. At the same time, of course, their albums sold very well with two chart-toppers, *Tales From Topographic Oceans* and *Going For The One* among an unbroken run of studio albums in the Top Ten throughout the decade.

Yes belatedly entered the UK singles chart in 1977 with 'Wondrous Stories' which reached No. 7, staying in the charts for an impressive nine weeks. I even remember the song being played as one of the "slowies" at a student disco. The title track of the band's eighth studio album, *Going For The One*, was the follow-up and reached No. 24 and lasted just three weeks in the charts. Such activity tends to make chart experts presume that this is caused by a loyal fanbase. This – two decades later – led to a series of singles entering the charts at No. 1 and then quickly disappearing.

'Going For The One' concluded Yes's 1970s entries in the British Top Thirty. The follow-up, 'Don't Kill The Whale', a taster for their new *Tormato* album, entered the charts at No. 36 and immediately disappeared, clearly an even more obvious example of a loyal fanbase. Even by Yes's standards, the lyrics of 'Whale' are embarrassing: *"I'm asked to justify, killing our last heaven beast"*. The official Yes website describes it as: *"an unusually direct song for the group with its topical message."* There are a few rock songs about the plight of whales, but this is probably the worst.

It seems that the British public did not bother to purchase singles by Yes. Even 1983's 'Owner Of A Lonely Heart' – an American chart-topper – did not rise higher than No. 28 in the UK. Again, the parent album, *90125*, was a steady seller.

6 – Ladies' Night

NONE OF THE BIG BRITISH FEMALE POP STARS of the 1960s — Cilla, Petula Clark, Lulu, Sandie or Dusty — went on to have much singles success in the 1970s. This was despite these singers' continuing ubiquity on British television. All of the above continued to appear time after time on *Top of the Pops*, as well as having either their own television series or one-off showcases. Cilla reinvented herself as a television star, using McCartney's 'Step Inside Love' as the theme tune to her first series. Younger or new faces such as Mary Hopkin and Clodagh Rodgers were now having hits, often using their real name. At the same time, female singer songwriters from the USA and Canada such as Melanie, Joni Mitchell and Carole King were having huge success on both sides of the Atlantic, presenting a more natural and arguably more sincere approach. Compare the front cover of Carole King's 1971 *Tapestry* album and her image with those of Lulu and Dusty of the same era. More importantly, these new American singers wrote, or co-wrote, their own songs and hit singles. We would have to wait for Lynsey De Paul and, more successfully, Joan Armatrading and Kate Bush, for this to happen in the UK. (I am excluding such British singer-songwriters as Sandy Denny and Vashti Bunyan here.) A cursory glance at the British music press for the years studied in this book — 1965 to 1979 — reveals a great deal of old-fashioned language. Female singers are invariably described as "girls" and there is much mention of their looks. However, female singers in those days did not have to wear skimpy costumes or "connect" with their fans. The (overwhelmingly) male journalists had great respect for the big names and genuinely seemed to "care" about these singers' chart fortunes.

CILLA BLACK

In Cilla's autobiography, there is a useful discography compiled by Stephen Munns. Unusually, this artist's highest British chart positions are included so flopspotting (sic) is made easier. I admire this rare level of honesty. Books by many pop stars tend to gloss over when their records flopped in a sentence or two, or simply do not mention or acknowledge them at all.

Having hit the top spot with both 'Anyone Who Had A Heart' and 'You're My World' in 1964, Cilla had a virtually unbroken series of Top Thirty hits right up to the end of the decade. 1968's 'Where Is Tomorrow' peaked at No. 39, despite being featured as a new release on *Top of the Pops*. The song is a very slow ballad with such lines as *"silent is the night"* sounding very old-fashioned even for its time. Then, of course, we are blasted with a characteristic Cilla-style big chorus early on.

Strangely, two of Cilla's best known songs were never A-sides in the UK. 'I Can Sing A Rainbow' was first sung by Peggy Lee in the film *Pete Kelly's Blues* in 1955. The song (which I had always associated with Cilla) was featured on her second album, *Cilla Sings A Rainbow*. The only rendition of the song to enter the UK charts was by The Dells who used it in a medley with 'Love Is Blue' in 1969. Stan Kelly's 'Liverpool Lullaby' — as in *"Ooh you are a mucky kid"* — had first been sung by folk acts Three City Four and the Ian Campbell Folk Group. Cilla's version was buried on the B-side of her 1969 single, 'Conversations'. I am sure this recording could have been a big hit on its own. Audiences loved her rendition of the song.

Cilla finished the 1960s with John Cameron's sublime 'If I Thought You'd Ever Change Your Mind'. The song was originally recorded by Edwards Hand in 1969 which was produced by George Martin and arranged by Cameron. Cilla's version keeps the same arrangement complete with the unmistakeable cor anglais introduction. Decades later, Agnetha Faltskog (formerly of Abba) also recorded a version. If Cilla had continued to record songs of this quality, perhaps her chart successes would have continued.

In 1970 Cilla's cover of 'Child Of Mine', a Goffin and King song from Carole King's *Writer* album failed to reach the charts. This piano-led ballad sounded pretty close to the original and was previewed on *Top of the Pops*. Admittedly, this was not one of this writing duo's strongest songs, the melody feeling predictable and dragging a little. George Martin's strings arrive in the second verse and Cilla's voice gets louder in the middle eight. *NME*: *"a delicate Goffin-King ballad. Opens quietly then gradually builds as George Martin's brilliant arrangement swells to a crescendo and finally tapers off charmingly. In addition to the brazenly sentimental words, there is a repetitive hook based on the title phrase which registers in the mind. I'm sure it's destined to be another fairly big one for Cilla ... very nice indeed."*

Cilla's final big hit was 'Something Tells Me (Something Is Gonna Happen Tonight)' in 1971. This – like 'Step Inside Love' – was used as a theme to her BBC television series. She continued to appear on *Top of the Pops*, long after her entries in the singles charts. March 1972 saw Cilla preview 'The World I Wish For'. *NME*: *"People who go for Cilla will probably be pleased with its up-tempo Greenaway-Cook straight pop song. On this particular tune she reminds me very much of Sandie Shaw circa 1965."* Nine months later, she returned to the programme plugging 'You You You'; neither single bothered the charts.

Cilla parted company with producer George Martin in early 1973 after the *Day By Day With Cilla* album. David Mackay was brought in to attempt to update Cilla's music, aiming to move her away from power ballads to soft rock. 'Baby We Can't Go Wrong' was released in January 1974. *Record Mirror*: *"her first single in more than a year ... signature tune for her new TV series. So ... it's a hit ... it's a gentle sort of love song, with the full Black-type power held back ... usually it creeps up all guile and secrecy after a quiet-sung verse. This is Cilla in a comfortable, happy mood and the arrangement is splendid. As a theme it's as good as her former one, 'Something Tells Me', though less explosive."* This was Cilla's first chart entry in over three years but only reached No. 36.

June 1974 saw the release of Cilla's sensitive cover of the late Jim Croce's 'I'll Have To Say I Love You In A Song', but unfortunately, no-one bought it. Four months later, she released 'He Was A Writer'. *Record Mirror*: *"Cilla has definitely settled for more mature songs recently and this is quite emotional in parts. After a couple of listens the chorus tends to stay with you, and Cilla is popular enough to guarantee a couple of listens."* This is one of Cilla's better singles with a clever storyline about working in a bookstore and meeting a writer. The song and performance are quite a departure for her, showing a far more subtle side.

The following year saw Cilla singing the title theme to the film *Alfie Darling*. The song was written by Alan Price who also starred in the film as the eponymous hero. Despite a lush string arrangement and delicate Spanish guitar, both the song and Cilla's performance are rather ordinary. The film was universally panned. The song and film were unworthy successors to Cilla's performance of Bacharach and David's 'Alfie' and Michael Caine's masterful acting in the original 1966 film.

A year later, a new single, 'I'll Take A Tango' was slammed in *Record Mirror*: *"if you are expecting neo-tango music and a funny lyric, forget it. The whole thing's dirgy and Cilla croaks her way through it, sounding as if she's doing a bad impersonation of Melanie."* Cilla performed the song on an episode of *Seaside Special*. The words are execrable: *"Down in my soul, I hate rock 'n' roll."*

The flops continued and disappeared without trace: 'Little Things Mean A Lot' had been a No. 1 hit for Kitty Kallen in 1954. Cilla: *"To coincide with the launch of my eighth Cilla series in 1976, I made a new EMI single. For this I turned to one of my favourite golden oldies – the first time I'd ever done this in my twelve-year recording career."* This writer must confess that he had never encountered Miss Kallen or her rather ordinary 1950s ballad. Cilla's version has awful keyboards including a very unattractive bass sound.

'Easy In Your Company' was the theme song for the ITV series, *Cilla's World Of Comedy*. Written and co-produced by former Manfred, Mike Vickers, this was yet another mediocre song despite a funky bass intro. Cilla's 1977 single, 'I Wanted To Call It Off' seemed to be completely unconnected with that year's music. Sung in a high register, the song seemed to be pushing a more sensual side to her. Cilla performed the single on *Top of the Pops* in a long pink ballgown on a dais surrounded by mystified youngsters.

'Silly Boy' was enthusiastically introduced by Tony Blackburn in 1978 on *Top of the Pops*, saying that even though Cilla's records have always been of a high standard, that *"this one is an exception."* In fact, it is probably her worst single of the 1970s, a weedy disco beat with lines like *"you come on like a movie star"* Cilla deserved better songs than 'Silly Boy'. The following decades saw Cilla become a television presenter with *Blind Date* and *Surprise Surprise*.

KATE BUSH

The story of Kate's career has been told many times. Her debut single, 'Wuthering Heights' was unique. She simply did not sound like anyone else. Kate's first appearance on *Top of the Pops* reveals a confused audience, not quite believing what they were seeing and hearing. The single soon reached No. 1, staying there for four weeks. The gentler 'Man With A Child In His Eyes' also went Top Ten and showed a less melodramatic approach. Kate's first album, *The Kick Inside*, included both singles and peaked at No. 3, staying in the album charts for an impressive 70 weeks.

Kate's first flop, the third single of her career, 'Hammer Horror' is rarely mentioned, staggering to No. 44 in late 1978. Kate conceived of the song after watching *Man Of A Thousand Faces*, a biopic of Lon Chaney starring James Cagney. *Record Mirror*: *"Kate keeps up the formula and doesn't upset the fans. Sounds like Joni Mitchell popping tabs with the LSO. Quirky, offbeat and all that stuff. Also a minor hit and an annoying twinge in the arse."* This is not one of Kate's better singles and the promo video with Kate's hair crimped and plunging neckline feels worrying close to self-parody or a performance by television impressionist Faith Brown. The song is omitted from Kate's 1986 *The Whole Story* compilation. The incredible success of 'Wuthering Heights' and its parent album must have put pressure from EMI to make a quick follow-up. The *Lionheart* album was released less than nine months after *The Kick Inside*, in time for the Christmas market. The follow-up single to 'Hammer Horror', 'Wow', was released in the following spring and was easier on the ear, reaching No. 14. This single coincided with Kate's only British tour to date. The *Lionheart* album peaked at No. 6 and dropped out of the charts while *The Kick Inside* was still selling.

Tina Charles

I have a vague recollection of a teenage Tina Charles performing an impressive rendition of 'River Deep Mountain High' on *The Two Ronnies* television programme in the early 1970s. Her first chart entry was as the uncredited lead singer on 5000 Volts' 'I'm On Fire' in autumn 1975. She reappeared in 1976 and reached the top spot with her first hit single, 'I Love To Love (But My Baby Just Loves To Dance)', the beginning of a highly successful partnership with Biddu. As we will see throughout this book, having a huge hit, especially a chart-topper, at the beginning of an artist's chart career can only mean one thing. To paraphrase Yazz, the only way is down. Tina's next chart entry was the less impressive 'Love Me Like I Love You' which peaked at No. 31. Her two next releases of 1976: 'Dance Little Lady Dance' and 'Dr Love', both went Top Ten. After this we sadly saw a slow decline.

'Fallin' In Love In Summertime' was released in summer 1977, the follow-up to the 'Rendezvous' hit and was dubbed *"Tinabopper"* in *Record Mirror*. The single flopped, but Tina soon returned to the charts with a medley of 'Love Bug' and the Searchers' 1963 chart-topper, 'Sweets For My Sweet'. Tina's version of 'I'll Go Where The Music Takes Me' seemed a little pointless. Jimmy James had had a Top Thirty hit with the song only two years earlier and Tina's version peaked four places lower at an unimpressive No. 27. This was her final hit of the 1970s.

'Making All The Right Moves' was promoted on *Top of the Pops* in September 1978. *Record Mirror*: *"Tina moves away from the realm of endless production and into the total antithesis – insufficient attention. A song with commercial potential but which won't even raise a second glance with the lacklustre treatment dealt by both arrangers and Mama Charles herself."* Clearly the magic Tina/Biddu partnership had grown stale.

Petula Clark

Pet Clark has had an extraordinary career, spanning over seven decades and going through very different phases. Her first single, a version of

'The Little Shoemaker', was released in 1954 and a successful career in France followed. Pet signed with Pye Records in the late 1950's and had a British chart-topper with 'Sailor' in 1961.

'Downtown' marked the start of a fantastic run of collaborations with Tony Hatch and reached No. 2 in the UK and No. 1 in the USA in 1964. Strangely, some follow-up singles did not even reach the Top Forty. 'You Better Come Home' and 'Round Every Corner' both went no higher than the upper 40s. 'Round Every Corner' was a little repetitive and lacked the charm of Pet's bigger hits. 'A Sign Of The Times' did even worse, managing just one week at No. 49 in April 1966. *Record Mirror*: *"Another Tony Hatch song for Pet, with brassy introduction leading into a thumping beat. Fast-paced and sung with great clarity and style. Already a hit in the States and good enough to click big here. Catchy little tune."*

'Who Am I' was the follow-up to 'I Couldn't Live Without Your Love'. The latter had reached No. 6, boosted by Pet's three performances of the single on *Top of the Pops*. 'Who Am I' was yet another song by Tony Hatch and Jackie Trent and featured a harpsichord. Despite being a flop in the UK, the song became the standard opening number for Pet's concerts.

'Colour My World' flopped in the UK. *Record Mirror*: *"Not her most commercial but it does have a grow-on-you appeal. Usual excellent chorus bit, easy to remember. Fine-swinging big-band backing. Must be a big hit."* In the USA *Billboard* magazine had liked it: *"Chalk up another chart-topper in this intriguing Hatch-Trent rhythm number featuring the popular Indian sitar sound and exceptional Clark vocal work."* The single reached No. 16 in the *Billboard* charts.

Pet's partnership with Tony Hatch was extraordinarily productive. His songs were consistently impressive and there seems to be no rhyme or reason why some were flops so soon after massive hits like 'Downtown' and 'My Love'. The majority of the songs were varied enough and Pet's voice was always easy on the ear. Perhaps she was over-exposed and like fellow Pye artists, The Kinks, The Searchers and Sandie Shaw, she had simply too many singles released each year.

In the liner notes to an Ace Songwriters collection, called *Colour My World — The Songs of Tony Hatch*, Hatch is surprisingly ungenerous when discussing his lyricists; *"Collaboration makes absolutely no difference. I always knew which way a song would go, no matter who I was writing it with. The only difference is collaborating on lyrics can save time – lyric writing can be quite time consuming. I used to have the title and idea running before the other lyric writer came in."*

Pet occasionally broke her habit of recording Hatch songs for her singles. In 1967 her version of Charlie Chaplin's 'This Is My Song' – from the soundtrack of *Countess Of Hong Kong* – reached No.1 in Britain, just pipping Harry Secombe's version to the top spot. Just hearing the opening bars of either rendition brings memories of 1967 flooding back. As Bob Stanley, among others, has commented, that year in chart terms was as much the Summer of the Ballad as it was the Summer of Love. If we added together the combined singles sales in that year of Engelbert, Tom, Anita Harris, Pet, Harry Secombe et al, it would number millions.

'The Cat In The Window' was composed by Gary Bonner and Alan Gordon who had written hits for The Turtles. This song was not one of their strongest compositions and something of an inconsequential single for Pet. She continued to record for the Pye label, but the hits became less frequent. 'The Other Man's Grass Is Always Greener' was her last Top Twenty hit. 1968 saw just one single 'Kiss Me Goodbye', written by Barry Mason and Les Reed, stay in the Top Fifty for a solitary week – at No. 50. *Record Mirror*: *"Another change of style for Pet and to be truthful I'm not so keen on this song because it takes too long to 'warm up'. But then the chorus starts and that really is commercial. A mite patchy, then, is the summing up. But well sung, of course."* Tony Hatch produced this single and was apparently not offended by Pet using another writing team, saying that it gave him "breathing space" to come up with new material himself. In Andrea Kon's biography of Petula, Hatch was quoted as stating: *"Pet's successes always radiated sunshine and this one didn't."*

She released two more singles written by Tony Hatch and Jackie Trent. 1968's 'Don't Give Up' sounds rather ordinary and predictable to my ears. Even the title and some of the words (eg *"love will be yours in the end"*) sound a bit obvious. However, in *Disc & Music Echo*, Penny Valentine felt that 'Don't Give Up' was: *"as good as all the others"* but, despite a *Top of the Pops* appearance, the single flopped. 1969's 'Look At Mine' is better with a lively opening and country-styled guitar, but also did not reach the charts. 'No One Better Than You' was released in the last months of the 1960s. *Record Mirror*: *"A Clive Westlake song – Barrel-organ-y opening and then Pet operates on a chugging beat ballad. It's a happy sound, production and style. The chorus is directly commercial, even if it takes time to start properly."*

Pet had now parted company with her long-term hit-making team. This always struck me as puzzling; her partnership with Tony Hatch and (often) Jackie Trent was the nearest that a British singer got to matching Dionne Warwick's work with Burt Bacharach and Hal David. Pet had no chart appearances in 1969 and 1970 whatsoever. Her version of 'Happy Heart' lost out to Andy Williams who reached No. 19 with his superior interpretation. Pet had returned to acting in 1968 when she starred in *Finian's Rainbow* alongside Fred Astaire and Tommy Steele. A year later, she appeared in the musical version of *Goodbye Mr Chips* with Peter O'Toole in the title role. The latter film had a score by Leslie Bricusse, even though Tony Hatch and Jackie Trent had written a rival title song. There were copyright problems, leading to the Hatch/Trent song not being used.

'The Song Of My Life' was released in early 1971. This French melody had English lyrics written by Jack Fishman. *Disc & Music Echo*: *"Petula Clark is almost drowned in the lushness of the strings ... but somehow manages to hold her own. Some life, I say, if that's its song — but it'll sell a bonfire in France!"* In the UK, 'The Song Of My Life' reached No. 41, slipped out of the charts and reappeared, peaking at No. 32.

'The World Song' was co-written by Pet and previewed on *Top of the Pops* in September 1971. This was the era for worthy songs, as this one appears to be. The song moves from someone arranging a local gathering to a *"world party"* (I wonder if Karl Wallinger ever heard this?) with lumpen lines such as *"maybe we could hear the voices of China, sharing a harmony with Carolina"*.

Pet's last hit of the 1970s was her rendition of 'I Don't Know How To Love Him' from the rock musical *Jesus Christ Superstar*. There was a crowded market of versions of this Lloyd Webber/Rice song including the original by Yvonne Elliman (as Mary Magdalene) from the 1971 original double album. Yvonne's version was featured on a four track maxi-single of songs from the musical, but still fared no better than

Pet's cover. Both records reached a lowly No. 47.

A year later, Pet was back in the *Top of the Pops* studio performing 'The Wedding Song (There Is Love)' which was written by Paul Stookey, the tall one in Peter, Paul and Mary. The words remind me of those Christian posters of the time which often had a woodland scene accompanied by some empty statement. Stookey's song speaks of *"the union of your spirit"* and *"woman draws her life from men and gives it back again"*. This song is apparently very popular at weddings. I would hate to hear it at such an occasion.

Pet's move to Polydor Records did not help her chart fortunes. She was still a massive international star and had her own television series on BBC1 between 1972 and 1974. She continued to record, perform and tour. At the beginning of the 1980s, Pet starred as Maria in a stage revival of *The Sound Of Music*. More recently, she narrated and presented an excellent BBC4 programme on French chanson.

Lynsey de Paul

Lynsey de Paul was a multi-talented singer, songwriter, orchestrator, producer, artist and cartoonist. She had already written and co-written hits for other artists, before appearing in 1972 with the infectious 'Sugar Me' which was originally written for Peter Noone. Lynsey often wrote with Barry Green (later Barry Blue). She was the first British female singer songwriter to have hits with her own compositions in the singles charts. Lynsey was also the first female songwriter to win an Ivor Novello award for Best Contemporary Pop Song for her third hit, 'Won't Somebody Dance With Me'.

There is a paucity of intelligent critical writing about Lynsey, but Simon Frith wrote in *Let It Rock*: *"Lynsey's skills are pop skills. She's got no artistic pretensions, she's content enough to construct pop songs. She builds them around the unique character of her voice, which is very sweet, very pure, but thin, lacking any range of power. Her pop song-writing skill is remarkable, certainly the most impressive that's ever come from an English girl ... her problem is that this skill is part of a tradition that has never regarded women as anything other than pretty faces. She's compelled to go on the defensive, to adopt a pose of self-deprecating jokiness (similar to that of Gilbert O'Sullivan, another uneasy MAM artist)."*

The follow-up to 'Sugar Me', 'Getting A Drag', had reached the Top Twenty, but the next release, 'All Night', failed to chart, despite a *Top of the Pops* appearance. *Record Mirror*: *"She's got a 'feel' for the right approach in pop, and there's that element of sauciness about her songs which come over well. This one is a persuasive intriguing sort of performance which registered instantly with me."* I tend to disagree; 'All Night' is sort of funky with uncharacteristic electric piano and a prominent bass guitar. It feels like one of Victoria Wood's lesser songs. The line, *"Won't you stay inside my parlour?"* just didn't work in an age of David Bowie, Lou Reed and gang. *NME*: *"If Gilbert O'Sullivan can go heavy then so can Lynsey de Paul. Her production is excellent, and the various keyboards interlock beautifully. However, her irritating little girl delivery and the lameness of the song trivialise the record."*

Over the next four years Lynsey would have singles released on three different record labels. This seemed to affect her career, creating a sort of "yo-yo" effect with her chart placings. She had reached No. 14 with the wistful 'Won't Somebody Dance With Me', but this was her final release on Gordon Mills' MAM label, leaving Gilbert O'Sullivan to be their principal hit maker.

Next was a solitary release on Warners – 'Ooh I Do' – which peaked at No. 25. Perhaps Lynsey de Paul's disadvantage was that her attractive looks tended to dominate the (largely) male-written reviews of her records. These were different times. Even in serious rock monthly magazines, reviewers fell into this trap. *Let It Rock*'s John Pidgeon said: *"Lynsey, looking and sounding as though candy floss wouldn't melt in her mouth, is kidding that she's a teenager in love on 'Ooh I Do'."*

Later in 1974, Lynsey had signed to Don Arden's Jet Records, having been introduced to him by her friend, Roy Wood. She had her second Top Ten hit with 'No Honestly', the theme tune to a TV comedy series starring real-life couple John Alderton and Pauline Collins. This cheerful single stayed in the charts for an impressive twelve weeks and won Lynsey her second Ivor Novello award. The follow-up, 'My Man And Me' only reached No. 40. *Record Mirror*: *"a very slow, dreamy number — very romantic. It's got a pretty haunting melody, that should make the charts without any difficulty."* A flawless solo performance on *The Old Grey Whistle Test* showed Lynsey at her best. It seems that she had a less than happy spell on Jet Records. I remember hearing her on a Radio 4 Roger Cook radio documentary about Don Arden. There were *"legal wrangles"* once Lynsey tried to leave Arden's management and record companies. This affected her mental and physical health.

Confusingly, *Record Mirror* reviewed 'Rhythm And Blue Jean Baby' twice: *"Lynsey's bit of thumpalong candyfloss whimsy may be lightweight but in a mixed age group setting it has just the right happy beat and straight pop gaiety."* The second review added: *"Easy toe-tapper.. But lightweight really, it's all too simple ... an indistinctive up-tempo song that could have been made by anyone and it's a waste of her talent."* This was a complete flop.

'Hug And Squeeze' was released in October 1975. *Record Mirror* commented on Lynsey's apparent anti-feminist image. Songs with titles like 'Hug And Squeeze' were inevitably misunderstood. The reviewer stated: *"this very whimsical number about bodily contact. Slow and easy ... with Ms de Paul at her dreamiest. But too laid-back methinks."*

'Love Bomb' was also a Jet release. *NME* was scathing: *"she managed to tone down the ooey-dewey eyed, wouldn't-you-like-to-get-me-into-the-sack, jailbait squeak of her previous product. Yeah, Lynsey the producer has done a fine job on this single. She's even managed to include a blend of strings and horns that comes halfway to sounding like a Marvin Gaye track. Although the tune is pleasant, the lyrics are just plain silly."*

In 1977 Lynsey was representing the UK in the Eurovision Song Contest with 'Rock Bottom', a duet with Mike Moran. You may remember the duo's twin grand pianos, rather than the ploddingly average quality of the song. Lynsey was now was on the Polydor label. 'Rock Bottom' reached Number 19 and that was the end of her UK chart career. 'You Give Me Those Feelings' was released in the summer of 1977. *Record Mirror*: *"As part of the pop establishment, she shouldn't have a lot of trouble getting this one over. It's a chunky MOR song with a surprisingly gutsy guitar break. A bit over blown I thought, but subtlety seems to be an out-moded quality."*

'Hollywood Romance' was inspired by Lynsey's move to California in the late 1970s where she lived with the actor, James Coburn. The single was chosen by Dave Lee Travis as his Record of the Week on his BBC Radio One daily show. *Record Mirror* was a little patronising: *"ol' peroxide locks, De Paul is set for a comeback. Sounds like a rip-off of Maria Muldaur."* 'Hollywood Romance' is another list song and has a great rhythm with a busy arrangement by producer Rupert Holmes, making it probably the best sounding Lynsey de Paul single. She sings: "*We'll dance in the dark, sing in the rain*" and the whole song is full of quotes and references to film titles. There are lovely backing vocals and a sax solo. This should have been a hit.

One of Lynsey's final releases of the decade was 1979's 'Tigers And Fireflies'. The single supposedly concerned two of her former managers, Gordon Mills and Don Arden and Lynsey's experiences of being cheated and lied to with dazzling promises. The song was originally called 'False Friends And Fireflies'. We hear jungle noises and the lyrics are full of metaphors and catchphrases: "*They took me to a garden of Eden*", "*out of the frying pan into the fire*" and a hook of "*telling me lies, I couldn't see their disguise.*"

Lynsey died in 2014, but before that she had been an active member of the council of BASCA, the British Association of Songwriters, Composers and Authors, defending the interests of songwriters, no doubt inspired by her experiences on the MAM and Jet labels. In retrospect, all the fuss made about Lynsey wanting to produce her own songs seems strange in this age of so many "powerful" women in pop music. Lynsey really was a pioneer and is still under-appreciated. She hardly gets a mention in books about women in rock and pop and, as Carly Simon experienced in the USA, critics lazily focused on her looks and choice of partner.

Kiki Dee

Kiki (like so many British female singers, she had changed her more "ordinary" name – Pauline Matthews) had been performing since the early 1960s. There is a great photograph of her singing as a teenager in her home town of Bradford. She made a series of unsuccessful records for several labels including Philips and even Motown, where Kiki was the first British artist to be signed. I always liked her clear white soul voice, as good as Dusty's in many people's minds. She was signed to Elton's Rocket Records label and had her first hit in 1973 with 'Amoureuse', a translation of a French ballad which had a magnificent melody.

'Hard Luck Story' was the follow-up. *Record Mirror*: "*this one is so strong and funky and foolproof and dynamic that Kiki seems sure to make it bigger than 'Amoureuse'. The tightness of the backing is matched by the free-and-easy style of Kiki but the end product just has to be described as funky.*" It would be easy for me, half a century later, to highlight the poor predictions of contemporary reviewers, but this was deemed a "Chart Cert" in *Record Mirror*. I cannot remember hearing this single at the time.

Kiki's next release, 'I've Got The Music In Me' continued to show the brasher side to Kiki's voice and reached No. 19. By now the singles were being released as the Kiki Dee Band – not always a good sign for a solo performer.

Follow-ups were problematic; a competent treatment of Nancy Wilson's 1964 American hit '(You Don't Know) How Glad I Am' came next. I was familiar with the song already, or rather my elder sister's rendition of it, on family holiday car trips. Nancy's version must have been played on Radio Caroline for it to be so well known in the UK without actually charting. Kiki had first covered this Jimmy Williams and Larry Harrison composition way back in 1964 where it had an arrangement by Les Reed. Kiki's 1975 version was produced by Gus Dudgeon, no less. It was faster than Wilson's rolling ballad approach and did not have anything like the power, reaching No. 33. *Record Mirror*: "*the arrangement, though quite funky, doesn't do the song any favours, and Kiki's voice is so far back in the mix that her efforts are virtually wasted.*" This was the beginning of a twelve month chart "drought" for Kiki.

'Once A Fool' was written by Dennis Lambert and Brian Potter and previewed on *Top of the Pops* in January 1976, after being buried in the pre-Christmas rush. *Record Mirror*: "*ideally suited to both Kiki and the American market, but less likely, I'd think, to do well here. It's a mid-tempo number, laden with strings and brass and featuring a great bit of sax towards the end. Kiki makes a good job of the vocal, but she might still have a struggle to get a hit with it here.*" I feel that the song is mediocre, despite the writers' record of penning hits for, among others, The Four Tops, Glen Campbell and Tavares. Kiki's wonderful voice enhances this rather simple and dull composition.

Kiki Dee will be forever associated with Elton John and their duet, 'Don't Go Breaking My Heart' which topped the UK charts for six weeks in the hot summer of 1976. The song, written as usual by Elton and Bernie Taupin, but under the pseudonyms of Anne Orson and Carte Blanche, was a clever pastiche of a Motown/Stax duet and far more appealing to these ears than Elton's rockers and most of his ballads. For me, the song stands up there with 'Philadelphia Freedom' as one of his finest 1970s singles. An amusing video of the pair miming the song in a recording studio was shown on *Top of the Pops*. Kiki's dungarees became something of a fashion item and, unlike her duet partner, she had great hair! Her voice was clear, uncontrived and appealing. Unexpectedly, such television and radio exposure raised Kiki's profile and her next single 'Loving And Free' as a double A-side with a revived 'Amoureuse' brought her back to the Top Twenty.

'First Thing In The Morning' had a racy title and was previewed on *Top of the Pops* in February 1977. The orchestra was arranged by Gene Page who worked a lot with Barry White's lush recordings. *Record Mirror*: *"not as instant as 'Loving And Free' but after a few plays it will get to you."* This single halted at a disappointing No. 32.

'Night Hours' was one of Kiki's own compositions and co-produced by Elton and Clive Franks. Despite yet another *Top of the Pops* appearance in April 1977, the single surprisingly did nothing. *Record Mirror*'s reviewer was clearly someone with the *Flops On 45* antennae: *"Kiki's singles at the moment seem to be a hit or miss affair. This one I'd say is the latter – a nice sound, but not really catchy enough to make it big."*

Lorraine Ellison did not chart in the UK with her deep soul classic, 'Stay With Me Baby'. There have been plenty of attempts to cover it. The Walkers Brothers reached No. 26 with their rendition in 1966 and a dozen years later, David Essex reached No. 46 with his cover version. Kiki released her own rendition just six months after Essex's single. *Record Mirror*: *"For once Kiki gets a chance to work out her tremendous voice. Always blurred before by lousy production or dumb material, she elevates this classic as high as it's ever been, scaling the sonic peaks with a style and confidence that makes her almost alien to the Kiki Dee of old."* I agree; it is the best version apart from Ellison's original and deserved to be a massive hit. Sometimes there is no justice in the recording world.

'One Jump Ahead Of The Storm' appeared in January 1979 and was in the same "funky-rock" style of 'I've Got The Music In Me', but not as strong a song and feels unsuited to Kiki's impeccable voice. The song was attempted by Eric Clapton a few years later for his *Behind The Sun* album sessions, but never released.

Marianne Faithfull

Marianne's story is well known. She was the convent girl from Reading who had a hit with a Stones song, 'As Tears Go By'. There is something timeless about that record; the rather plodding arrangement and Marianne singing "*This is the evening of the day.*" The follow-up, 'Blowin' In The Wind' did not chart. Peter, Paul and Mary had already had a No. 13 hit in the UK with this Bob Dylan song, so it was an odd choice of a follow-up single for Marianne. 1965 brought her three Top Ten hits, Jackie de Shannon's 'Come And Stay With Me', John D. Loudermilk's 'This Little Bird' and the French translation, 'Summer Nights'.

Covering Paul McCartney's solo showcase, 'Yesterday' put Marianne in a crowded market. She had performed the song on Granada TV's *The Music Of Lennon McCartney*, but Matt Monro had the biggest hit in the UK with it, reaching No. 8. Marianne's version struggled to No. 36. After this we have the inevitable diminishing returns with a succession of flops. 'Tomorrow's Calling' was the first — *NME*: "*The wispy quivering tones ... in this contemplative mid-tempo song with a delicate folksy feel. Colourful backing of acoustic guitar ..., and strings coming in later. Has an olde-world feel, which may be a slight handicap.*"

'Counting' was by Bob Lind of 'Elusive Butterfly' fame. *NME*: "*one of those perpetual motion type of songs in which Bob Lind specialises, it's set slightly under medium pace with a colourful backing of strings, guitar, throbbing drums and bells. Lind's lyric is as fascinating as ever, though Marianne's delivery is none too clear because of the high register.*" *Record Mirror*'s reviewer also had reservations: "*An even smaller-voiced Marianne with guitar backing and a dull thumping sort of beat ... full of good words, and it has a grow-on-you appeal. Even so, there's something rather odd about it all.*" 'Counting' did not chart.

Next was an ill-advised Ronettes cover, 'Is This What I Get For Loving You Baby'. Marianne's delicate voice just did not have the power or technique to handle such a challenging song which got to a lowly No. 43. Marianne's tempestuous (and very public) private life was beginning to affect her recording career.

In the 1970s Marianne had some success in Ireland as a country singer and she finished the decade with Island Records. Her version of Shel Silverstein's 'Ballad Of Lucy Jordan' revealed a much rougher voice and peaked at No. 48. *Record Mirror: "This old Dr Hook song has certainly been given a new treatment here. The vocals are still fairly countryish but the instrumentation isn't. It's synthesised and choppy. And yet the song still sounds smooth. Her voice though is not as smooth as it used to be ... the years have taken their toll and funnily it does the song good."*

ANITA HARRIS

Anita has been overlooked by pop historians. I remember that she appeared in a couple of Carry On films, *Follow That Camel* and as a nurse in *Carry On Doctor*. Her one woman show at Talk Of The Town was televised and showed Anita's extraordinary versatility, changing costumes and styles at breakneck speed. She reached No. 6 in 1967 with the Tom Springfield song, 'Just Loving You'. In a year of several best-selling ballads, notably 'Release Me', 'The Last Waltz' and 'This Is My Song', 'Just Loving You' stayed in the charts for an amazing 26 weeks. Such success would have made follow-ups a challenge.

The follow-up 'Playground' only reached No. 46. In *Disc & Music Echo*, Penny Valentine wrote: *"a brave record for Anita Harris to have made ... this isn't a song that hits you instantly ... echoey emptiness and then widens into a big production sound."* Co-written by Anita and producer Mike Margolis, there is something very engaging about 'Playground'. The verses sound exciting and the chorus is almost a Northern soul stomper. By 1968 Anita was back in safe territory; 'Anniversary Waltz' was predicted by Penny Valentine to be a chart-topper, but it stalled at No. 21. Anita's version of 'Dream A Little Dream Of Me' lost out to Mama Cass (who reached No. 11.) Penny Valentine also reviewed 1969's 'Loving You': *"There's a saying about a tried and tested formula and obviously that's exactly what the people behind Anita Harris think. And so back to format she goes after a couple of brave but, sadly unsuccessful, ventures away from the 'Just Lovin' You' field. Her fans will love her clean treatment of this old song, and she does it very well. It's not honestly my kind of record, and I found the backing a bit disconcerting if they're really trying to break the mums' market again."* Later, Anita focussed on children's television including a series called *Anita In Jumbleland* and variety.

A 1972 release, 'Genesis', was reviewed in *NME*, *"With her manager Mike Margolis, (Anita) wrote this bouncy number which is virtually a contemporary spiritual. Anita handles it in rhythmic uplifting style, supported by a spirited gospel choir. It's also a catchy little tune with a commercial hook, and it might just sneak into the charts if the Radio 1 boys will give it a break."*

Mary Hopkin

Mary had charmed millions of viewers week after week on ITV's *Opportunity Knocks* in 1968. The story goes that fashion model Twiggy saw her on the programme and recommended Mary to Paul McCartney. I imagine that thousands of teenage girls around that time in Britain played fingerstyle guitar and could sing folk songs in a Joan Baez-style. Mary was just the best. Even on the *Opportunity Knocks All-Winners Show*, she stuck to her version of 'Turn! Turn! Turn!' playing her new guitar, given to her — as she told Hughie Green — by George Harrison. Among the showbiz glitter of the prime time ITV talent show, Mary's voice rang out, making the combination of the words from Ecclesiastes and Pete Seeger's tune arguably more powerful than previous versions by the composer, The Byrds and so many others. The performance was flawless. The song was relegated to the B-side of 'Those Were The Days' (which McCartney produced), but still would have been heard by millions of people at home and on jukeboxes.

Apple Records made Mary an international star with a British chart topper with 'Those Were The Days'. Despite three other Top Ten hits, including her Eurovision runner up, 'Knock Knock Who's There', Mary was not happy with her career. In his autobiography, Tony Visconti relates how Mary told him that Apple saw her as just *"a pop star ... they make me record rubbish ... I won Opportunity Knocks as a folk singer for seven weeks in a row and that's what I am."* Tony and Mary discussed making an acoustic album and they agreed to use Ralph McTell and Dave Cousins with Danny Thompson on bass. This was real folk royalty.

Visconti continues: *"Before we were allowed to make a folk album Mary was asked to do another pop single for Apple. I had found a beautiful song called 'Let My Name Be Sorrow'. The song was pure art, a kind of Chopinesque piece, not the bland song that Apple was expecting. Mary defiantly recorded the song as a gesture of 'I'm going to do it my way.'"* NME: *"a quiet 'down' kind of number with an Olde Englishe feel, convincing melancholy, and backed up by a heavenly choir."* Unfortunately, the single only reached No. 46; perhaps it was too slow and classy for daytime radio play. The song was written by French songwriters and there is a version by Francoise Hardy that was released around the same time.

Mary's folk album, *Earth Song Ocean Song*, has a charming quality half a century on; Visconti describes it as *"one of the most gratifying albums I ever made"*. The single that was taken from the album was 'Water, Paper And Clay'. In the sleeve notes to the CD reissue, Mary explains: *"I was so enchanted by that. It has the quality of an anthem. I liked the fact that I didn't quite understand the lyrics. I liked the mystery. I played the harmonium. I couldn't play and pump the pedals at the same time so Danny (Thompson) and Ralph (McTell) are on their knees pumping the pedals."* Record Mirror: *"An album track, but nevertheless in with a very strong chances as a hit single. ... Back to the roots, in a way, for Mary – a folksy piece with that crystal clear voice doing a good job. The finale with chorus is splendid."* NME agreed: *"this new single has a profound folk flavour ... there's a cheery sing-along taking place in the catchy chorus."* But the reviewer clearly had a crystal ball: *"I hope Mary doesn't lapse into semi-obscurity as a result of her decision to opt out of the mainstream. And there's still enough of a commercial element about this song to put her in with a pretty good chance of success."*

Mary's album included Ralph McTell's classic 'Streets Of London'. At the time, no-one in Britain had had a hit single with the song, despite its ubiquity. 'Streets Of London' was buried on McTell's *Spiral Staircase* album. The Johnstons had released a bouncy treatment in 1970 on Transatlantic with lots of harpsichord. When Mary's album was released, I remember a Radio One D.J. saying that the album's single should have been 'Streets Of London'. I agree; Mary's rendition could easily have been a hit as it was such a pure and appealing performance. Mary herself plays guitar on the track.

Here was a song surely crying out to be a hit single. Sheet music sales of McTell's standard would have been in their thousands and it was regularly sung in school assemblies, youth clubs, churches and folk clubs throughout the land. Readers need to remember that this was one of the main ways songs were shared in the past. Song sheets in the early 1970s cost just 20p, a lot cheaper than singles. Ralph McTell himself had a No. 2 hit in 1974 with a re-recorded version of 'Streets Of London', once he had signed to Reprise. Over 50 years later, this folk classic still resonates. There was a version in 2017 with McTell and Annie Lennox in aid of the Crisis charity.

Mary left Apple Records and recorded 'Mary Had A Baby' for Regal Zonophone in late 1972. Previously recorded by Joan Baez, as 'Virgin Mary (Had A Boy)', the song was a beautiful and stark Christmas hymn. At the same time, Mary herself was pregnant with her first child. *Record Mirror*: *"The traditional air from the Mr and Mrs Visconti team. Glory be to the newborn King, etc with a gentle, rippling backing. Mary sings with her customary clarity and style, and it's all rather Christmassy. Chart chance."* Despite press adverts and some airplay, the song was a flop. If Mary had released this single a few years earlier, it could have been a huge seasonal hit.

'If You Love Me' appeared in 1976 on her husband, Tony Visconti's, Good Earth label. There was an appearance on *Top of the Pops*, Mary's first for nearly six years, and a promo video filmed around Trafalgar Square. A translation of 'Hymne A L'Amour' which was written by Edith Piaf and Marguerite Monmet, 'If You Love Me' had been a hit for Kay Starr in the USA in 1954. Mary's version was dominated by an accordion and closer in style to her debut single, 'Those Were The Days', than her more recent folk rock material. Surprisingly, the single reached No. 32 which suggests that, with a stronger promotional campaign, it could have been a bigger hit. *Record Mirror*: *"Super song, but Piaf sang it with so much guts and Mary doesn't have that same fire."*

A year later we heard Mary's backing vocals on David Bowie's 'Sound And Vision' which was produced by Visconti. You can clearly hear Mary's unmistakeable voice during the song's introduction, *"doo-doo-ing"*! She also appeared in the *King Of Elfland's Daughter*, the project written by ex-Steeleye Span's Bob Johnson and Peter Knight. More recently Mary has released new material, often written by herself, usually in conjunction with her son, Morgan Visconti.

LINDA LEWIS

Linda Lewis was first and foremost a singer-songwriter. An early appearance on *The Old Grey Whistle Test*, in the days when *Melody Maker*'s Richard Williams was the presenter, saw her performing 'What Are You Asking For'. This was a sublime and unaffected performance with Linda accompanying herself on acoustic guitar. Her death in 2023 reminded people of that extraordinary voice. She recorded for a number of record labels and was a regular "name" in the music press. Linda first appeared on *Top of the Pops* in June 1973, performing her self-penned first hit, 'Rock – A – Doodle-Doo' and playing an electric guitar (a rare sight in those day for female performers). The single reached an encouraging No. 15, staying in the charts for eleven weeks.

Two follow-ups on the Raft label, 'Play Around' and 'Sideway Shuffle', were also both written by Linda. 'Play Around' had a positive review in *Record Mirror*: *"this has an interesting, persuasive riff to start it off, some good backing sounds, and Linda doing her soft-then-explosive vocal thing. She gets a big-voiced scene going with an assured backing group. A return to the charts."* *Record Mirror* also reviewed 'Sideway Shuffle': *"this is ... specially created to become a single, not whipped from the nearest album. Linda has this sweet little voice, but she swings a bit (vocally) and this is a stutter-rhythm production that gets through from the off! It shuffles all right – into the top fifty, wouldn't be surprised"* Both singles missed the charts and Linda moved to Bell, at the time, a label with a very high success rate for hit singles.

'(Remember The Days Of) The Old Schoolyard' was composed by Linda's friend, Cat Stevens. *Record Mirror*: *"The beat is very catchy and added to that those amazing vocal talents of Linda's and you've got a record that should more than equal her success of 'Rock-A-Doodle-Doo'. Great song."* The single received plenty of airplay, but unusually for a release on Bell, was not a hit. Cat's own version in 1977 only reached No. 44.

When Bell morphed into the Arista label, Linda continued to release singles and her revival of Betty Everett's 'It's In His Kiss' reached No. 6. Again, follow-ups were problematic including the self-penned 'Rock And Roller Coaster'. *Record Mirror*: *"Rush re-release record taken from Linda's* Not A Girl Anymore *album, this kicks off with a soul/reggae intro, and then rolls along with Linda's voice. Not a disco sound like 'It's In His Kiss', but a nice sound all the same.*

Linda's cover of the Van McCoy song 'Baby I'm Yours' peaked at No. 33 and was followed by half a dozen more singles. Two are worth mentioning. 'This Time I'll Be Sweeter' was reviewed in *Record Mirror*: *"Tender, almost Diana Ross-type slowie gives Linda her best offering for ages with this slowed-up piece of soul. Good range, of course, and it'll be interesting to see if it catches the nation's imagination."*

'Moon And I' was an updated version of Yum Yum's song, 'The Sun Whose Rays' from Gilbert and Sullivan's operetta, *The Mikado*. The song now had new lyrics by Miller and Rost with an arrangement by Jimmy Horowitz and production by Linda's then husband, Jim Cregan. The single was previewed on *Top of the Pops* and Linda gave a wonderful live performance. *Record Mirror*: *"Waxing Of The Week. Perfect single, faultless in every way. Quivering vocals and orchestral backing that could seduce a bronze statue to tears. 5 stars."* Another flop.

'Winter Wonderland' was released for the Christmas market in 1976. This had been popularised by Darlene Love on *Phil Spector's Christmas Album*. *Record Mirror*: *"My, how Christmas brings out the worst in everyone. Jim Cregan produces lovely Linda out of a vale of strings. A bit slow to get going too."* 1977 saw Linda cover another Cat Stevens song – 'Bonfire' – taken from his *Izitso* album. Neither of these releases reached the charts.

Two years later Linda returned to *Top of the Pops*. This time she performed her version of 'I'd Be Surprisingly Good For You', a song from *Evita* by Andrew Lloyd Webber and Tim Rice. There had already been three hits taken from this musical; two were from the original album — Julie Covington's 'Don't Cry For Me Argentina' and Barbara Dickson's 'Another Suitcase, Another Hall'. David Essex had then had a big hit with his version of 'Oh What A Circus' in 1978. The song Linda covered has a great melody and is taken at a faster pace than Covington's original version on the *Evita* album. Linda was now signed to Ariola and the single was produced and arranged by Mike Batt, the Womblemeister himself, but still only reached No. 40.

'Jamaica Highway' was also released in 1979. *Record Mirror*: "*She's got a really nice voice, has Linda. What she really needs is a song to match it. What's the point of having such an impressive range if she can't let rip with it? No song has done her justice since 'It's In His Kiss'. She just sounds like another singer here — a sad pity.*"

LULU

Lulu's singles career was erratic. She released records on seven different labels over fifteen years having started her chart career in her mid-teens reaching No. 7 in 1964 with her cover of 'Shout'. 'Tell Me Like It Is' was released in 1965; the music director was Mike Leander. It flopped but a couple of hits followed 'Shout: Leave A Little Love' reached No. 8, 'Try To Understand' peaked somewhat lower at No. 25. This was Lulu's final hit on Decca.

'Call Me' was a Tony Hatch song also recorded by both Petula Clark and Chris Montez. *NME*: "*a cracker of a disc ... handled with a maturity which belies her years. She varies between the seductively tender and the gustily vibrant ... the backing alternates from a gentle Latin-American rhythm to a driving stamp beat ... I reckon it's the best disc Lulu has made.*" None of these versions were British hits.

'What A Wonderful Feeling' was a 1966 collaboration with Alan Price who wrote, arranged and produced it. *NME*: "*Lulu's in effervescent form as she bubbles through the catchy lyric and Alan Price stamps his unmistakeable personality on the backing, besides joining the gal in a few vocal passages. A real blues-chaser*". *Disc & Music Echo*: "*For a long time now Lulu has been looking for the right song and the right style to get her back in the chart. Now with the help of Mr Alan Price, she has found it. A certainty to slam into the chart. A great swinging sound on a tune that everyone will be singing walking home in the early hours. Lulu sounds totally at ease, very happy. A surprise for everyone and a great one at that.*" It was a disappointing flop.

By 1967 Lulu had signed with EMI's Columbia imprint and had a more successful run of hits, produced by Mickie Most. These started with a strong cover of Neil Diamond's 'The Boat That I Row' in the spring. Lulu's film theme, 'To Sir With Love' went to No. 1 in the US but was relegated to the B-side of 'Let's Pretend' over here. She appeared in the film as one of Sidney Poitier's pupils, alongside Judy Geeson. Lulu told Johnny Black: "*I felt Mickie Most was making me into a female Herman's Hermits. So there was always a lot of push and pull between us, where I wanted to release 'Morning Dew' or 'To Love Somebody' but he wanted 'The Boat That I Row' or 'I'm A Tiger'.*"

'Love Loves To Love Love' was not one of Lulu's better recordings and was a comparative flop, peaking at No. 32. The song will be familiar to viewers of *Top of the Pops* repeats as it was on one of the few surviving episodes from the 1960s. In her memoir, *I Don't Want To Fight*, Lulu is quite blunt about her situation: "*My own recording career seemed to be stuck in a rut. Mickie Most had turned me into a pure pop singer and it wasn't the only sort of music I wanted to be credited with. Given the choice, I wanted to go back to my first love – the rhythm and blues songs of my childhood.*"

In 1969 Lulu represented the UK in Eurovision; 'Boom Bang-A-Bang' was a joint winner and reached No. 2. Time and again, a singer's Eurovision entry was one of their weaker songs; I cite 'Puppet On A String', 'Congratulations', 'Knock, Knock, Who's There', 'Jack In A Box' and 'Long Live Love' as further evidence.

Lulu: "*When my contract with Mickie expired I didn't renew it. It was time to move on. Jerry Wexler of Atlantic Records in America was quick to sign me. He thought I had a soulful voice ... I was tremendously flattered.*"

Great things were expected when Lulu recorded at Muscle Shoals Studios. Disappointingly, she writes only a couple of paragraphs about these times in her memoir. The first single released, 'Oh Me Oh My', was excellent but only reached No. 47. *Record Mirror*: "*Link up with Messrs Wexler, Dowd and Mardin has really done Lulu a power of good. Moodily slow opening, sort of half-spoken, with crisp attack and then, indeed, a load of soul. Maybe isn't instantly commercial, songwise, but by golly. Lovely performance.*" The song was covered three years later by Aretha Franklin, working with the same production team. Clearly, Aretha had heard, and was impressed by, the original recording. Lulu definitely knew the song's strength; she performed it on BBC1's *Seaside Special* seven years later.

'Hum A Song' was billed as Lulu with The Dixie Flyers. *NME*: "*It's a thoroughly infectious and bubbling routine based upon a simple phrase that nags away at the brain ... Lulu's in sparkling form.*" Penny Valentine: "*I was rather surprised that Lulu's first single from Atlantic didn't do better and I can only *hope that someone wakes up soon and realises what good stuff she is doing out in those studios. This is a sneaky little piece with a tinkling opening which falls over itself. Really fast, crisp stuff on the verse and rolling guitar, organ and tambourine on the chorus."* Record buyers must have thought otherwise.

'Got To Believe In Love' raised a fair point for *NME*'s reviewer: *"From the point of view of the British market Lulu hasn't had a very happy time since joining the Atco label. Could it be that her material is geared more to the American scene than to British tastes?"* The writer added: *"this is a blatantly commercial disc which I'm sure will find mass appeal. The beat is contagious and forceful and Lu's poppy personality styling is egged on by swinging organ and a bustling backing ... cute and catchy."* Disc & Music Echo also expressed concern: *"for Lulu this (is) probably THE test record for the lass who's had little success with her ventures in the American recording studios. It's difficult to know exactly why the past few singles have failed and even more difficult to know whether this will succeed. It's bouncy enough with guitars, organ and tambourine among the busy backing instruments and the whole thing has the same sort of feel as 'The Boat That I Row'. Lu double tracks her vocals and puts a lot of hard work and if this had been released 12 months earlier I'd have said instant hit. Now I have the horrible feeling it's dated. I hope not ... it would be awful to see her fade away just because of the wrong songs."* Despite being produced by Tom Dowd and a *Top of the Pops* appearance, this single flopped.

'Everybody Clap' was previewed on *Top of the Pops* with an all-star backing band including husband Maurice Gibb, Les Harvey on guitar and, unbelievably, Led Zeppelin's John Bonham drumming; Lulu was surrounded by her family and friends. *NME* was quite sympathetic: *"she's had the greatest difficulty in making her presence felt in the Chart here. The poor girl is probably wondering what on earth she has to do to make the British fans cough up! I feel that this latest offering should have a more universal appeal. It's catchy ... and extremely danceable. There's an irresistible bounce beat, a sing-along hook chorus and a rich sound to the backing ... Lu's sparkling personality shines through. Penned by her husband and brother, Messrs (Maurice) Gibb and (Billy) Lawrie, it gives her a fighting chance of a disc comeback."*

The follow-up, 'Even If I Could Change' was reviewed in *NME*: *"Lulu is a great little talent, but she needs another Mickie Most to guide her recording career. On this, her latest outing, she sings well, but then she always does. However, both song and stereotyped arrangement come off the conveyor belt, and do little to enhance her reputation."*

Lulu summed up her time on Atlantic: *"We did two albums together, New Routes and Melody Fair, both of which were well received in the States. Sadly this success didn't translate to the UK. Some people said I alienated myself from the British public by becoming too 'American' in style. Perhaps that's true. More likely I couldn't shake the 'pop star' label that had been attached to me."*

Lulu eventually made a comeback in 1974 with her cover of David Bowie's 'The Man Who Sold The World' which featured Bowie on saxophone and backing vocals. The single reached a healthy No. 3. Another "man", 'The Man With The Golden Gun', was the theme song to the new James Bond film. *Record Mirror*: *"Most James Bond songs have a very distinctive feel to them, due both to tradition and John Barry, and this is no exception. I don't think it ranks amongst her best work, but it should get an awful lot of exposure."* *NME* agreed: *"It's full of sinister brass interjections and all the mystery, intrigue and excitement of a stale meat pie."* I cannot remember hearing this single on the radio and it remains one of the worst, and worst-selling, Bond themes.

1975's 'Take Your Mama For A Ride' was released on the Chelsea label. *Record Mirror*: *"After the quick demise of Lulu's last offering, 'The Man With The Golden Gun', it's a very definite change of direction and sound with this one. Uptempo song, with quite a funky beat ... it's not too bad. Not sure if it's chart material."* This one peaked at No. 37. 'Heaven And Earth And The Stars' was released later that year. *Record Mirror*: *"There are a lot of influences at work here, for during the course of the song Lulu sounds like everyone from Barbra Streisand to Kiki Dee to Gladys Knight. It's a very mature, attractive interpretation of an attractive song, but maybe it's all just a little too low key to do much as a single."* Lulu: *"At that stage I was being produced by Wes Farrell ... (who) also produced David Cassidy ... We made some great records, which didn't quite make it, perhaps because the record label didn't have enough faith."*

'Your Love Is Everywhere' was written by Peter Shelley and Paul Gurvitz who also respectively produced and arranged the single. Lulu was now briefly on the GTO label. She performed the song on *Top of the Pops*. *Record Mirror* called it *"funky and repetitive."* Lulu finished the decade with two releases on Elton John's Rocket Record Company label. The first was 'Don't Take Love For Granted', written by Neil Harrison. This quality soul ballad has very slow verses and prominent strings. The chorus's female backing vocals sound like the Gibb brothers, coincidentally! The inferior follow-up, 'I Love To Boogie' wasn't the Marc Bolan song, but co-written by Mick Stubbs of the British rock band, Home. This white funk track reminds me of Hot Chocolate's style, but does not really go anywhere. Lulu performed the song on television in a glittery catsuit and seemed to be trying a little too hard to be raunchy. Both singles sank without trace. If Lulu was signed to Elton John's label, surely she should have had first pick of his own songs. Two of Elton's compositions songs were included on Lulu's 1978 album, *Don't Take Love For Granted*, but neither released as A-sides. She deserved better.

One can hardly accuse Lulu of being inactive during the fifteen years covered in this book. She had half a dozen Top Ten hits during this time and three more Top Thirty hits amongst over two dozen single releases. We must not forget Lulu's age, or rather her youth. She was not even sixteen when 'Shout' hit the charts in 1964. At the end of the 1970s, Lulu was just 31 years old. In the last 30 years, Lulu has had something of a revival and, more importantly, a reassessment. As well as her chart-topping duet with Take That of Dan Hartman's 'Relight My Fire', she has appeared at the Electric Proms and was featured in Mike Figgis's film, *Red, White & Blues*.

Olivia Newton-John

Olivia was born in Cambridge and her family emigrated to Australia when she was just four years old. She returned to Britain in the mid-1960s and was involved in *Toomorrow*, an extraordinary flop of its own which involved an album and film. Olivia's recording career is complicated by its twists and turns. Even at the time of her recent sad death, journalists tended to underestimate her strong singing voice. If you require convincing, listen to the climax of her collaboration with ELO on their 1980 chart-topper, 'Xanadu'. That final high note is produced by pure technique.

Signed to the Pye International label, Olivia's first hit was a cover of Dylan's 'If Not For You' which many people already knew from its appearance on George Harrison's album, *All Things Must Pass*. The follow-up was a masterful version of Lesley Duncan's 'Love Song'. Elton John also covered this song on his *Tumbleweed Connection* album as a duet with the composer. As well as having a beautiful subtle melody, 'Love Song' features a delightful repeated piano figure. Olivia's version is faultless and I am surprised that it flopped. *Record Mirror*: "*a very important follow-up … it's another performance job requiring uncommon skill in getting the point across. There's a breathless romantic feel to it all and a very clever arrangement, full of simplicity and unusual effects. Olivia sings very well indeed.*" *NME* agreed: "*an appealing romantic ballad … soothing and relaxing … not so commercial as 'If Not For You'.*" .

Olivia's lively cover of George Harrison's 'What Is Life' (also from *All Things Must Pass*) reached No. 16. The follow-up 'Just A Little Too Much', written by Johnny Burnette, had been a British hit for Ricky Nelson in 1959. Taken from her *Olivia* album and arranged and produced by Bruce Welch and John Farrar, the single was a flop, despite a *Top of the Pops* appearance in August 1972. This was an uptempo country song and dominated by piano; the guitar solo is far inferior to James Burton's performance on Nelson's version. Olivia soon bounced back with a cover of John Denver's 'Take Me Home Country Roads' which went to No. 15.

Her penultimate single for Pye was 'Let Me Be There'. *Record Mirror*: "*it's just right for Olivia, with the touch of the C and W feel in the backing and chorus. Male voices, including from the bass area, push it along in a gently relaxed style. Thing is that Olivia is always popular and if this song doesn't exactly extend her, it's very commercial.*" The single flopped in the UK, but surprised everyone by becoming first a country hit and then Olivia's first Top Ten single in the US. Written by former Shadow bassist John Rostill, 'Let Me Be There' sounded like an authentic Nashville hit with a singalong chorus as if the composer had been listening to 'Take Me Home Country Roads'. Olivia won a Grammy for Best Female Country Vocalist. This was the start of a highly successful partnership with producer John Farrar who had been part of the trio Marvin, Welch and Farrar with Hank and Bruce out of the Shadows.

Olivia's Eurovision entry for the UK was her final single on the Pye label in 1974. 'Long Live Love' is not the worst ever British Eurovision entry (there are too many competitors for that dubious accolade), but is probably her weakest single. The phrase "*Sally Army band*" always grated with me. There was that "oom-pah" beat echoing the sound of Cliff Richard's 1968 Eurovision entry, 'Congratulations'. Both Olivia's song and dress seemed old-fashioned alongside the winning performance by Abba, as television critic Clive James pointed out in his review in *The Observer*. The Swedish quartet raised the standards for contest entries, but also laid the foundations for other less talented groups such as Brotherhood Of Man Mark II and Buck's Fizz.

A change of label came later in 1974 and Olivia's first single on EMI was 'If You Love Me (Let Me Know)' also written by John Rostill. *Record Mirror*: "*It's perky enough to suit Olivia's jaunty voice — puts her in the upper register, and there's a brassiness about the backing which punctuates the whole thing. Touch of double tracking on the chorus.*" Again, the single did nothing in the UK but was huge in the US. 'I Honestly Love You' was Olivia's only UK hit for three years, but her American success continued. In 1974 she won three Grammies, two of which were for the Best Female Country vocalist. There was something of a backlash in Nashville about Olivia winning country music awards with some resignations from the Country Music Association. Sadly, John Rostill did not live to see Olivia's huge successes in the US with his songs. In November 1973 he died in sad and mysterious circumstances in his home recording studio in Radlett. His body was discovered by his songwriting partner and friend, Bruce Welch.

By now Olivia had split up with Bruce Welch and moved to the US. She continued to work with John Farrar who wrote three singles for her: 'Have You Never Been Mellow', 'Something Better To Do' and 'Don't Stop Believin''. An accomplished songwriter, Farrar clearly knew what sort of songs to write for Olivia's range and tone. 'Have You Never Been Mellow' was the title track of her album. *Record Mirror* was optimistic: "*This record's already doing incredible things in the American charts, and there shouldn't be any problem repeating the success here. Pretty song and arrangement, with Livvy doing some breathy vocals. Should be a huge hit.*" There clearly was a problem in the UK as the single went to the top of the *Billboard* charts in the USA and crossed over to the country charts, too. Over here the disc did nothing.

In between the Farrar hits in the US, Olivia recorded John Denver's

'Follow Me' for her next single which she previewed on *Top of the Pops*. *Record Mirror*: *"Very country camp-fire styled song ... beautifully sung by Livvy. It's not, however, her most commercial offering. At first I couldn't decide whether or not I liked the hillbilly flavoured banjo scudding about in the background, but after hearings I've concluded that I don't."* The single was another UK flop.

'Something Better To Do' in 1975 was taken from Olivia's *Clearly Love* album. *Record Mirror* provides thorough analysis: *"The flavour of this is very much Bette Midler meets Lynsey De Paul. The arrangement is Lynsey-ish all chic and lady-like, while the chorus is exactly Bette Midler's brand of camp. For all that, the record's still unmistakeable Olivia and even if she's not around to promote it, it should put her back in the charts."*

Olivia's next single was 'Come On Over', a strong country-flavoured composition by Barry and Robin Gibb and deserved to be a hit. *Record Mirror*: *"it's a ballad that she sings perfectly. Husky vocals soaring into crystal clear notes. Although there's nothing to fault on the production, I just wonder if it isn't a bit slow for mass appeal."*

The advertisement for 'Don't Stop Believin'' said *"Hear It And Believe It"*. *Record Mirror* was unimpressed: *"Rather tedious baby-soft quasi-ballad from the gal who's grabbing them in the States. She sings it superbly, but that ain't enough."* There is steel guitar, picked acoustic guitar and strings, but it is an unmemorable song. The single reached No.1 in the American Easy Listening chart.

'Every Face Tells A Story' was originally written for Cliff Richard and was the title track of his 1977 album. Award-winning lyricist Don Black later wrote new non-gospel words to the song and Olivia recorded it. *Record Mirror*: *"Her strongest for a long time. Beautifully produced. A big hit if the radio is kind to it."* Olivia had now had half a dozen flops in a row in the UK.

Don Black was also a co-writer of 'Sam', along with Hank Marvin of The Shadows and the ubiquitous John Farrar. This simple ditty became Olivia's first British hit for three years and her first Top Ten single in the UK since 'Banks Of The Ohio'. In his fascinating memoir, *The Sanest Guy In The Room*, lyricist Don Black tells the story behind the song: *"When we were living in Los Angeles I got to know John Farrar, who was one of the guitarists with Cliff Richard's Shadows. He and Hank Marvin had come up with a gorgeous tune. John's wife, Pat, had just had a baby they called*

Sam. That's where I came in. The tune needed a one-word title, and the name Sam sang beautifully on that note. Pat Farrar's best friend was Olivia Newton-John. She heard the song, loved it and recorded it. It went to number one in America's easy listening chart." There seemed to be no logic to Olivia's hits and misses in the UK.

'Making A Good Thing Better' was written by Pete "Eighteen With A Bullet" Wingfield; *Record Mirror*: "*File under sex. But Livvy isn't the blatant sell, more of a latter-day Doris Day. This is pretty but not as good as 'Sam'. I don't know why she doesn't record better songs. With her voice she could handle something a bit stronger.*" Wingfield wrote some excellent ballads on his own first album, *Breakfast Special* such as 'Lovin' As You Want To Be', 'Hold Me Closer' and 'Anytime'. Any one of these three songs would have suited Olivia.

'Please Mr Please' had been co-written by John Rostill and Bruce Welch. Although I can hear harpsichord and flute on the record, this rather MOR song seems to be more faux Americana with its references to Kentucky whisky, a jukebox, Nashville and dimes. Olivia is pleading someone not to play song "*B17*" on the jukebox. This single feels a little too contrived to sound like a country record to these ears.

Farrar would eventually go on to provide two extra songs for the film version of the musical *Grease* where Olivia starred alongside John Travolta. These songs – 'You're the One That I Want' and 'Hopelessly Devoted To You' — are now so closely associated with the musical that audiences for stage productions expect to hear the songs included. The extraordinary success of Olivia's songs from the film, the two chart-topping duets with Travolta and her solo 'Hopelessly Devoted To You', revived her career in the UK.

Later in 1978 Olivia reached No. 4 with yet another Farrar song, 'A Little More Love'. I bought a copy at the time. This was a dramatic change of style and an excellent song, production and performance. *Record World* had commented: "*more rock-oriented than (Olivia's) past pop efforts, and with a song as good as this one the transition should be a pleasing one.*" Unfortunately this "transition" would lead to the dreadful 'Physical' a few years later.

Olivia finished this extraordinary decade with, unbelievably, two more flops. 'Totally Hot' was another Farrar song and the title track of her tenth studio album. This is a slightly funky track with Olivia using a lower, and slightly aggressive, register in her voice. Both the song and the performance are unconvincing; lines like *"gimme what you got, ready or not"* feel cliched. This was followed by 'Deeper Than The Night', a song written by Tom Snow and Johnny Varstand. *Record World*: *"features a wailing guitar line and a strong beat."* Again, it is not one of Olivia's better singles with prominent piano and "funky" guitar and bass. I find it rather ordinary with a less than convincing chorus.

CLODAGH RODGERS

Hailing from County Down in Northern Ireland, Clodagh signed with Decca Records as a teenager. She had been releasing singles since 1962. American songwriter Kenny Young saw her perform on BBC2's *Colour Me Pop* and wanted to work with Clodagh. Her chart debut was in 1969 with Young's 'Come Back And Shake Me' which reached No. 3. Follow-ups, 'Goodnight Midnight' and 'Biljo', both written by Young, also went Top Twenty.

The girl group fanzine, *That Will Never Happen Again* described 'Everybody Go Home (The Party Is Over)' as *"unjustly neglected ... a gem with superb arrangement courtesy of Artie Butler."* There is electric piano and big brass come in. Clodagh goes straight into the chorus and title hook. In contrast the verses are gentle with acoustic guitar and a change of tempo. Despite being a Kenny Young composition and production, the single only reached No. 47 and Clodagh would be absent from the charts for nearly a year.

'Wolf', another Kenny Young song, was released in 1970; *Disc & Music Echo*: *"this absolute smasher of a single ... Quite the best thing Clodagh's done so far."* Clodagh performed the song on *Top of the Pops* and *The Des O'Connor Show*. 'Wolf' is rather creepy, as if Little Red Riding Hood has been transported to the USA with lines like *"I carry my basket"* and *"a stranger lurks behind me."* Alas, the single did not chart.

Clodagh's comeback was her Eurovision entry, 'Jack In The Box', firmly in the tradition of 'Puppet On A String', which went to No. 4. The follow-up, 'Lady Love Bug' staggered to No. 28, and that was the end of her British chart career. Interestingly, the B-side to 'Lady

Love Bug' was a cover of 'Stand By Your Man'. Four years later, the power of airplay on local commercial radio in the UK made Tammy Wynette's original version a chart-topper.

Both 'It's Different Now' and 'You Are My Music', sank without trace despite being previewed on *Top of the Pops* in 1972. 'It's Different Now' was written by Clive Westlake who had penned 'I Close My Eyes' for Dusty Springfield. This is a slow, serious ballad with lines such as "*I used to think when I fall in love.*" Clodagh also performed the song on *The Two Ronnies* television show. 'You Are My Music' is another slow, piano-led ballad, but the chorus is a little predictable and the whole song is unremarkable.

The follow-up, 'Carolina Days' was much better and perhaps Clodagh's finest single. I love the warm melody with the understated steel guitar in support. *Record Mirror*: "*Junior Campbell wrote this latest hymn of praise to an American state, and Clodagh is, vocally, in such good nick that it could well restore her to the charts. Nice Keith Mansfield arrangement helps her out, too. And there's purring personality in the way Miss R. sings out.*" There is footage of Clodagh performing the song on *The Mike and Bernie Winters Show* on ITV.

There appeared to be a pattern here; Clodagh's singles charted if Kenny Young had written and/or produced them. Young is rarely mentioned in pop histories. Before his work with Clodagh, he had co-written 'Under The Boardwalk' and written 'Captain Of Your Ship' for Reparata and The Delrons. Later he founded both Fox and Yellow Dog.

Clodagh performed 1974's 'Get It Together' at a show at the London Palladium where she excelled herself with a challenging song. *Record Mirror*: "*A poignant and philosophical big ole ballad with a pretty strong chorus hook. Big blasts from orchestral backing punctuate the production, also sharp interjection from backing singers. Mood varies from the frenzied to the gentle.*" Most of Clodagh's last few singles for RCA were arranged and produced by Keith Mansfield.

Later in the year, Clodagh covered Carly Simon's 'That's The Way I've Always Heard It Should Be', quite a challenging song with its cynical view of marriage and family life. Carly wrote the music, while her friend Jacob Brackman wrote the lyrics. *Record Mirror* explained the problem with Clodagh's chart career: "*Strange thing is that Clodagh had hits with her lesser singles, doesn't get 'em with the really good ones. This one ... is a first rate one which presumably is the final kiss of death. Still, Clodagh sings it beautifully, softly, womanly. And coolly, if you get the gist.*"

After just one release on the Pye label, Clodagh moved to Polydor where she worked with songwriting team, Guy Fletcher and Doug Flett, who had penned hits for many artists. 'Save Me' was better than some of Clodagh's slower ballads, but despite an appearance on *Top of the Pops* in January 1977, the single flopped. Clodagh retired and was able to look back on a highly successful career. She died in 2025, after three years of illness.

SANDIE SHAW

Sandie Shaw does not always get the recognition as some of her peers, despite the efforts of Steven Morrissey. His essay about the girl from Dagenham in *That Will Never Happen Again*'s double 'All British Girls' issue is worth reading. Sandie's second release, a Bacharach-David song, 'There's Always Something There To Remind Me', topped the charts in autumn 1964. Like Cilla Black, she had covered a Dionne Warwick American hit. Soon, Sandie was working with her own songwriter, Chris Andrews, and hitting the charts with 'Girl Don't Come' and 'Long Live Love', the latter also reaching No. 1. In her memoir, *The World At My Feet*, Sandie gives some insight into her working relationship with Andrews: "*Chris's unhappy first marriage, my fumbling attempts at romance, our successes and our tragedies would usually lead to yet another song. We relived our lives in verse, chorus, verse, chorus, middle eight and out.*" She also credits the crucial role of arranger, Kenny Woodman, and vividly describes a typical recording session.

'Run' was Sandie's first single not to reach the Top Thirty, breaking her run of hits. The song starts with howling wind and spooky strings. Penny Valentine: "*Not one of Sandie's best this, in fact one of her worst, which is a shame because she is singing much better these days ... A foul backing and a rather inconsequential song. Sandie deserves a really good song she can get to grips with and this certainly isn't it.*" To modern ears, it sounds like Sandie is describing fleeing from either a stalker or gaslighter. This single reached No. 32. Morrissey disagreed with Penny Valentine; he saw the failure of 'Run' as "*sinful in view of its great charm.*" There is an irritating emphasis in the song on the wrong words, bringing to mind the Manic Street Preachers' 'Design For Life'.

The follow-up 'Think Sometimes About Me' was an orchestral ballad. Penny Valentine again: "*Hurrah. There I was having a go at Chris Andrews for always writing the same sort of heavy-fisted song for Sandie to fight her way through when he turns up with this. A soft, waltzy song ... Sandie sings with a lovely subtlety, often understating on the lyrics. A nice relaxed performance, a big, big hit and a real winner chorus.*" I agree that the song has a lovely tune. This also reached No. 32.

The *Top of the Pops* producers seemed to like Sandie. She previewed no fewer than seven of her singles on that programme between 1968 and 1972 which did not trouble the charts. This beats both Cilla and Lulu. 'I Don't Need Anything' was Sandie's first single not to be written by Chris Andrews since 'There's Always Something There To Remind Me'. The composers were Vance and Pockriss who had also written 'Itsy Bitsy Teeny Weenie...' and 'Catch A Falling Star'. We hear dramatic strings and a big chorus, more like one of Cilla Black's early offerings. This rather strident song did even worse than its two predecessors, only reaching No. 50. Morrissey called it "*lame*". *Record Mirror*: "*a cover version of the Verdelle Smith number, and a much inferior one, too. Song is a dramatic slow builder with good lyrical content.*" I find the lyrics a little too melodramatic: "*all of my life, I walked alone.*"

Just two months later, Sandie's Eurovision entry 'Puppet On A String' was released. These were the days when British entries for the song contest were taken fairly seriously. Written by Bill Martin and Phil Coulter, 'Puppet' not only won the 1967 contest, but also was a British No. 1 for three weeks. In her memoir, Sandie is scathing about the song: "*I hated it from the very first oompah to the final bang on the big bass drum. I was instinctively repelled by its sexist drivel and cuckoo-clock tune.*" The follow-up, 'Tonight In Tokyo', was written by the same team of Martin and Coulter and reached No. 21.

'Don't Run Away' was previewed on *Top of the Pops* in April 1968. This was almost a Northern soul stomper. *NME*: "*a sparkling performance! This is her most commercial disc for many months, and full credit to composer Chris*

Andrews for abandoning the calypso style with which he was being typecast. *It's an effervescent, vibrant, disc full of life and buoyancy. Sandie bubbles merrily through the happy lyric, encased in an enveloping backing of punchy brass, soaring strings, vigorous beat and girl group. And while the Tamla influence is very evident, it isn't overdone. It's clearly designed for the top half of the chart. A real blues-chaser!"* Record Mirror was less keen: *"Not Sandie's best, alas! Big band backing ... mind you, it's well performed ... but I just feel it lacks instant commercial appeal. And of course, it will make the charts."* This disc was the first complete flop of Sandie's career, but worse was to come.

'Show Me', another Chris Andrews song, was released in June 1968 and is dominated by honky-tonk piano. Sandie's voice alternates between posh and awful faux-Cockney; the latter wouldn't have been out of place in a Lionel Bart musical. *NME* said: *"it's a Chris Andrews number but quite different from his usual output. Opens with a chorus on pub-type honky-tonk piano which quickly establishes the sing along mood. Then in comes Sandie at her most vital and sparkling and then she breaks into Cockney dialect in one chorus. The backing is brash, rollicking and in the vaudeville tradition. Catchy tune, a strong chart contender."* This single went nowhere. Luckily, *Top of the Pops* viewers were spared this abomination. A few months later even *NME* called it *"a dismal flop."*

The follow-up, 'Together', was a competent cover of a Harry Nilsson song. *NME: "it's a song that doesn't have immediate impact, if only because it's more complex and substantial than her recent discs. Sandie's interpretation is mature and expressive ... rather an unusual number for someone who's slightly out of Chart favour."* Penny Valentine also commented on Sandie's chart fortunes: *"turns out to be rather a wise move after a few chart disappointments of late ... If this isn't a hit I shall not only be surprised but staggered."* Record Mirror was also positive: *"I think it's one of the best she's done ... only hope it proves commercial."* Another flop.

Just six weeks later, Sandie's version of 'Those Were The Days' was released, in direct competition with Mary Hopkin's recording on Apple. She even performed the song on *Top of the Pops* as Mary was allegedly "unavailable" one week. Mary's version shot to No. 1 and stayed there for six weeks. Sandie's version sank. The other side of Sandie's single was 'Make It Go', an execrable cod-calypso Chris Andrews composition. What on earth were Pye thinking?

'Monsieur Dupont' was Sandie's last Top Forty hit for nearly fifteen years, reaching No. 6. I know many regard this as lightweight European dross (Morrissey especially hated it), but hearing the song brings back happy memories for me. The follow-up, 'Think It All Over' has an oompah band and reached No. 42; *NME*: *"this reverts to the sparkling calypso-flavoured items in which Chris Andrews specialises. This has a jaunty martial flavour, with a fruity brass and trilling flutes – plus an immensely catchy la-la chorus"*. This single feels predictable and irritating.

Sandie's next single, 'Heaven Knows I'm Missing Him Now' did not chart, despite being previewed on *Top of the Pops*. The song's title was, of course, cleverly altered by Morrissey for the Smiths' single 'Heaven Knows I'm Miserable Now'. Unfortunately, that is where the resemblance ends; Sandie's song is a lightweight, poppy song and has nothing in common with The Smiths' morose classic. *NME*: *"it's a finger-clicking happy-go-lucky number ... quite catchy ... but Sandie is one of those girls who can't automatically rely on a Chart entry and I suspect this is going to need a great deal of radio exposure if it is to succeed."*

Sandie ended the decade with an unlikely album, *Reviewing The Situation* with cover versions of songs by Lionel Bart (the title track was from *Oliver!*), Dylan, Donovan, John Sebastian and The Bee Gees. Unbelievably, the final track was her take on the Stones' 'Sympathy For The Devil'. No singles were released from the album which was ignored by both the public and reviewers.

'By Tomorrow' was Sandie's first single release of the 1970s. This was another change of style with an almost funky piano. *NME* titled the review *"Sandie Deserves A Chance"* but we already knew that the record buying public can be merciless. The review continues: *"A rhythmic ballad with an appealing lyric that is sensitively and expressively handled ... her delightful interpretation is enhanced by a girl group ... has a strange haunting quality ... Only trouble is that with Sandie absent from the Chart so long she'll need tremendous exploitation if it is to succeed."* *Record Mirror* was also impressed: *"this today-sounding opus. Most erratic, hurrying song which for me comes off completely. Most impressive phrasing here and there too which makes it give surprise context. Alas it could miss out."* Another flop.

'Wight Is Wight' was a French song with English lyrics. I remember hearing this on Radio One in the summer of 1970. Here was a tribute to the Isle Of Wight pop festival with a memorable second line, "*Dylan is delight*", referring to the 1969 festival's headliner. Penny Valentine liked it: "*I must say she's improved tremendously. Here her voice is crystal light and leaping as she flies across the lyrics. All very summery stuff. Maybe just a little too feather weight for our charts.*" Unfortunately this reviewer was right.

Early 1971 saw Sandie lose out again in a cover version battle. This time it was for Joe South's catchy song, 'Rose Garden'. American Lynn Anderson reached No. 3 in Britain with her version while *Opportunity Knocks* winners New World, an Australian trio signed to Mickie Most's RAK label, were a dozen places behind at No. 15 with their rendition. By this time, I imagine that Sandie and her record label would have been satisfied with even a lowly Top Forty chart placing.

Later in the year 'Show Your Face' was released. The single was a composition by session bassist Herbie Flowers and Dougie Wright and previewed on *Top of the Pops* in June. *NME*: "*this is one of the most commercial numbers Sandie has recorded for ages ... set to a thumping beat, with an attractive guitar figure behind her vocal, it has an intelligent lyric that's superbly handled ... most absorbing. Seems to me that Sandie's a bit out of favour, both with the public and the DJs at the moment so its potential is only minimal.*" *Record Mirror*: "*She makes darned good records and this ... song is full of plaintive yearning ... She sings with great clarity and style – very much a performance song and I think it's good enough to click. Whether it will be lucky enough, what with plugs etc., is another guess.*" It is quite a soulful, even spiritual, song with lines: "*the power and the glory, just an old fashioned story ... Jesus to guide us.*"

'Where Did They Go' is dominated by banjo, honky tonk piano, oompah tuba and strings and is a ragtime pastiche. *Record Mirror* said: "*A beautiful song with a chugging back beat – and it's with real pleasure that I predict an instant return to the charts for Sandie. A little-girl voice, building chorus line. The arrangement is just right and the performance ... well certainly one of her best ever. Just give it a play. Great stuff.*" The song was previously recorded by Peggy Lee.

Sandie's final single on Pye was her version of 'Father And Son', another cover taken from Cat Stevens' *Tea For The Tillerman* album. An unlikely song for a woman to cover, Sandie changes the gender of some of some of the song's pronouns. The "father" sections are far too low for Sandie's voice, but during the "son" bits Sandie's higher register is more expressive and successful. *NME* was blunt: "*Sandie has failed to come up with a hit in a while. She's back with a glossy image, singing in the cabaret-type formula. Here she performs a passable interpretation. The main flaw lies in the big production. It's a bit too dramatic.*"

Dusty Springfield

Dusty had a No. 4 hit with her debut solo single, 'I Only Want To Be With You'. The song was perennially popular in the UK. The Bay City Rollers also reached No. 4 with it a dozen years later, as did The Tourists – featuring Annie Lennox – in 1979. A decade later a Stock, Aitken and Waterman production with Page 3 model, Samantha Fox went to No. 16.

Dusty's chart career, in hindsight, possibly reflected the singer's own inner angst; there were highs – 1966's 'You Don't Have To Say You Love Me' was a chart-topper – and lows such as 'Your Hurting Kind Of Love' which scraped to No. 37 in early 1965. *NME* reviewed the latter: "*Faster and more forceful than 'Losing You' ... a shuffle-rhythm rockaballad with soaring strings and compulsive beat. Features Dusty's usual heartfelt styling and powerful projection, with occasional extemporisation on the basic theme, and unobtrusive chanting girls. Melodically, it is not of the best from the Ivor Raymonde/Mike Hawker team. But the excellent performance and colourful scoring will carry it high.*" The latter was a solitary blip in a tremendous run of powerful singles and Top Twenty hits from 1963 to 1967. Dusty's soulful and powerful voice was by far the best amongst her British peers. She had excellent songs from the teams of Goffin and King, Bacharach and David and deserved success.

Her 1967 single 'What's It Gonna Be' was reviewed in *NME*: "*Wonderful. A tremendous driving number which Dusty alternately belts and souls her way through, building the drama with each second until the power packed ending ... If there's a drawback, it's that Dusty's on a soul kick here and she doesn't seem to do quite as well in the charts with these numbers.*" Sometimes flops have a second life as Lucy O'Brien explains: "*Success often comes in unlikely quarters ... Although 'What It's Gonna Be' flopped, it was picked up by collectors on the Northern soul scene ... it became a Northern cult hit, featured regularly on the playlist at the Torch in Stoke-on-Trent. Due to its unavailability, 'What's It Gonna*

Be' was heavily bootlegged until Philips reissued it in 1974."

1968's 'I Will Come To You' was written by Clive Westlake who had previously written Dusty's striking hit, 'I Close My Eyes And Count To Ten'. *NME*: *"It's a rhythmic ballad that drives along at a forceful pace with a massive and enveloping orchestral backing. Dusty's in great form particularly in the pulsating chorus ... the verse is something of a throwaway, melodically, but the chorus is both catchy and quick to register."* Penny Valentine also enthused: *"If you thought the lady had reached her zenith with 'Close Your Eyes', you'd be wrong. This is better ... a huge, huge smash if I ever heard one."* Even with a *Top of the Pops* appearance, the single inexplicably flopped.

Despite the excellence of her *Dusty In Memphis* album, her British audience appeared to be getting smaller. 1968's 'Son Of A Preacher Man' was Dusty's final solo Top Ten hit. There were no hits during most of 1969 except 'Am I The Same Girl' which reached No. 43 in the autumn. *Melody Maker*: *"Not the usual Dusty sound at all. This is her little girl voice rather than the belter ... It's a soul ballad which sticks easily in the memory and has a great little band jumping behind her as well as the usual good girls. The song grows on you and it should be an undoubted hit."* *NME*'s reviewer was also impressed: *"Beautiful performance by Dusty in this vocal version of 'Soulful Strut'. Despite the snappy beat, she handles the lyric in subdued and controlled style and displays previously unrevealed vocal dexterity as she soars into high register. It's a sparkling routine which swings smoothly along with just the vaguest hint of bossa nova in the rhythm. Dusty's backed by the usual girl group plus pungent brass and rattling tambourine. I have nothing but praise for Dusty's work-out here. Although it may not be as instantly commercial as some of her singles."* A version of the song by Swing Out Sister would reach No. 21 in 1992.

Dusty's revival of The Rascals' 'How Can I Be Sure' received a thumbs-up in *NME*: *"A beautiful haunting ballad warmly and sensitively handled by Dusty ... it deserves to succeed."* It reached no higher than No. 36. Just two years later, a very similar rendition by David Cassidy topped the British charts. 'How Can I Be Sure' was Dusty's last chart entry for nine years.

The title of the follow-up, 'Brand New Me' sounded ambiguous: did Dusty need to reinvent herself? *NME*: *"It's a swinger – a slow sophisticated rolling swing at the outset as Dusty, supported by smooth chanting from the girl group brings her inherent jazz feel to play. Then it erupts into a powerhouse* swing in the chorus, as that spine-tingling Philadelphia sound comes scorching in - soaring strings, attacking brass and the girls singing along with Dusty."

'Yesterday When I Was Young' had become something of a standard; first released in 1964 with French lyrics by Charles Aznavour, the song's English lyrics were by Herbert Kretzmer. Roy Clark had had a big American country hit with the song in 1969. By 1972 *Billboard* magazine revealed that at least 90 versions had been recorded. Dusty's rendition was panned in *Disc*: "*I've always disliked this song, but Dusty nearly manages to pull the whole thing off. The obstacle that prevented her was the fact that the orchestra is much too lavish and dominating. Instead of complementing her performance, Dusty has to fight it. Unfortunately, thumbs down for this one.*" The song failed to chart.

Dusty moved to the US and largely disappeared from the British public's view yet Philips continued to release her records. 'Who Gets Your Love' was reviewed in NME: "*it's immaculately performed, with special high marks to the piano and guitar players. A very soulful record indeed, and if Dusty steers well clear of mums-and-dads-type material, she'll get some long due overdue credit as one of Britain's longest-serving dues-paying soul singers.*" Record Mirror: "*it's Dusty going full pelt with her American mates. It's soul-filled and pleading, and quite lovely, but it may not be instantly commercial. Fact is that she outstrips most girls and does it apparently effortlessly. She's quite remarkable.*" August 1973 saw the release of 'Learn To Say Goodbye' — Record Mirror: "*this is vintage Dusty, a new American-produced Dusty. And it's great. Just great.*" Without television appearances and airplay on Radio One, there was little chance of these singles reaching the charts in Britain.

Dusty's records were then released on Mercury and she even had her name as the catalogue number. 'Love Like Yours' (DUSTY 1) was followed by 'That's The Kind Of Love I've Got For You' (DUSTY 2). These singles seemed to disappear without trace. Dusty made a rare appearance on *Top of the Pops* in 1979 performing 'I'm Coming Home Again' which was co-written by Carole Bayer Sager. Was the title deliberate to acknowledge that she had spent much of the 1970s in the US? 'Baby Blue' (DUSTY 4) was released in 1979. The single was written by the Buggles team of Geoff Downes, Trevor Horn and Bruce Wooley. According to Horn, the song's "*rough demo ... was a prototype Buggles record*" with a drum machine and special effects. He felt that *"the Dusty track was bland and pedestrian by comparison."* 'Baby Blue' became Dusty's first chart entry in the UK for nine long years, but only reached No. 61.

The Pet Shop Boys revived Dusty's career in the late 1980s with their duet 'What Have I Done To Deserve This' reaching No. 2. It was wonderful to hear her again on the radio; the song was a perfect vehicle for her voice and, unlike so many comebacks, she maintained her dignity and integrity. This led to such solo hits as 'Nothing Has Been Proved' and 'In Private' before Dusty's untimely death in 1999.

BONNIE TYLER

Bonnie, like Mary Hopkin, hailed from Wales but that is where their similarity finished. The former Gaynor Hopkins' voice was seen as "raspy" and she sounded older than her mid-twenties when 'Lost In France' entered the charts in October 1976. The song was written by Ronnie Scott and Steve Wolfe who had discovered Bonnie singing in clubs around Swansea. This team were responsible for nearly all her singles in the 1970s. There was a slight dip with 'More Than A Lover' which peaked at No. 27 and a single called 'Heaven' which flopped. *Record Mirror* reviewed the latter: *"Sultry Welsh maiden takes it a bit slow this time and creates less impact than her previous big ones."* But Bonnie bounced back with 'It's A Heartache' which reached No. 4 and went Top Ten in the American country charts.

In early 1979 Bonnie returned with her cover of Tom Petty's song, 'Louisiana Rain' from his *Damn The Torpedoes* album. The song begins: *"Well, it was out in California."* (a long, long way from Swansea). She performed the song on *Top of the Pops* but the single flopped. Listening to the two versions side by side basically makes Petty's original sound even better. Her last chart entry of the 1970s was 'Married Men' from the soundtrack of the film, *The World Is Full Of Married Men*. The single reached No. 35.

The 1980s were a better decade for Bonnie whose own personal wish was to work with Jim Steinman. She must have heard Meat Loaf's *Bat Out Of Hell* album and marvelled at Steinman's powerful songs. Eventually, Bonnie had her very own Steinman classic, 'Total

Eclipse Of The Heart' which reached No. 1 in March 1983, after a chart absence of nearly four years.

7 – The London Boys

David Bowie

After a series of unsuccessful singles on Decca, Bowie finally hit the charts in 1969 with 'Space Oddity' which nicely coincided with the general excitement after the first American moon landing. It reached No. 5 but was followed by three flops, namely 'The Prettiest Star', 'Memory Of A Free Festival' and 'Holy Holy'.

'The Prettiest Star' was released in March 1970. On this single producer Tony Visconti brought together his two star performers – David Bowie and Marc Bolan. The latter provided lead guitar to Bowie's song. Peter Doggett: *"The problem was not the notes, but the ambience, which left Bolan's guitar as the sonic focus of the track, with an edginess that grated against the voice and rhythm section."* Just three years later, Bowie revived the track for his *Aladdin Sane* album. This time the song was faster and Mick Ronson played the guitar solo. Peter Doggett comments that 'The Prettiest Star' was *"rumoured to have sold no more than 1000 copies"*, quoting the Dame: *"I think a lot of people were expecting another 'Space Oddity'."*

'Memory Of A Free Festival' concerned the Growth Summer Festival And Free Concert in Beckenham and had first appeared on Bowie's second album (later renamed *Space Oddity*). Penny Valentine: *"If this isn't ignored by TV and radio like his last single, it could do almost as well as 'Space Oddity'. It has that same overpowering quality which makes me think David is back at his best with a thundering backing. It starts with harmonies and this flows nicely between Bowie's plaintive voice and ferocious guitar and strings."* *NME* added: *"A rather unexpected follow-up in that it is a complete contrast to 'Space Oddity'. A thoroughly charming and wholly fascinating little song. Set to a relaxed, jog-along rhythm with a wowing guitar packing out the melody line behind David's subdued and sensitive vocal ... the melody is haunting and hummable."*

'Holy Holy' was released in January 1971 and featured Blue Mink as session musicians. *NME*: *"rather a strange little piece ... owing to the peculiar timbre of David's voice, I had to strain to catch what it was all about — because the throbbing beat and heavy backing tend to submerge him at times ... the resulting sound is oddly fascinating ... The rhythm is compelling and there's something strangely haunting about the melody. It could grow on you too — if Radio 1 gives it a reasonable chance."* Disc & Music Echo agreed: *"'Holy Holy' is a strange title and the song is black and half-evil with a highly discordant melody and words that cannot be heard above the mysterious shivery backing. Totally uncommercial and unlikely to be played."* Doggett sees it as *"a private message to his wife, signalling devotion within the acceptance of an open marriage."* It has never been reissued.

Bowie then signed to the RCA label and 'Changes' was released just before Christmas in 1971; this was the opening track on his *Hunky Dory* album. Record Mirror: *"Tremendous single in every way, but David's more into an album thing, commercially speaking ... this is a most earnest bit of pop with fine lyrics."* This was Bowie's last flop for many years. 'Starman' reached No. 10 in 1972 and was the beginning of a thirty-year long, virtually unbroken chart career. Fifteen singles went Top Thirty and even a reissue of the 'Laughing Gnome' reached No. 6.

In the late 1970s it seemed that Bowie fans did not like purchasing two singles from the same album; so 'Golden Years' (from *Station To Station*) went Top Ten, while 'TVC 15' staggered to No. 33. With an intro borrowed from the Yardbirds' 'Good Morning Little Schoolgirl', this single was a much simpler composition and performance than 'Golden Years'.

The same happened with the *Low* album; the first single 'Sound And Vision' was Bowie's highest chart placing for a new song since 'Rebel Rebel', reaching No. 3 (a reissue of 'Space Oddity' had topped the charts in 1975). The follow-up, 'Be My Wife' was his first single since 'Changes' not to chart in the UK. Record Mirror liked it: *"Best cut from his* Low *LP. Mysterious lyrics sounding like his vocal style back in the old days. The song is very reminiscent of vintage Bowie."* Again, Doggett's analysis is helpful: *"this was not a marriage proposal but a confession of living outside and beyond, of restless movement and an empty heart."*

The title track of the *"Heroes"* album reached No. 24 in the autumn of 1977 and its follow-up, 'Beauty And The Beast' staggered to No. 39 the following January. The latter was an odd choice for both album-opener and extracted single. Peter Doggett wrote: *"an uproarious celebration of man and machine – beauty and the beast"* and noted the two voices Bowie uses: *"one calm Bowie (low voice) juxtaposed against one hysterical Bowie (high voice) ... over a lumbering musical vehicle that was not funk, not rock, not disco, but some futuristic combination of them all."*

Clearly, a lesson should have been learned there for someone at RCA. But exactly the same thing happened with the two singles extracted from the next album, *Scary Monsters And Super Creeps*. Despite his "drag" performance on *Top of the Pops* of 'Boys Keep Swinging', the single went to No. 7; the follow-up, 'DJ' only just scraped into the Top Thirty, peaking at No. 29.

Dave Clark Five

The Dave Clark Five's extraordinary success in the US led to the group focussing on their American career, arguably at the expense of their British fans. The group released more records in America and for a while they rivalled The Beatles over there. Consequently, the DC5's chart record in the UK was erratic. They reached No. 1 with 'Glad All Over', the second spot with 'Bits And Pieces' and No. 10 with 'Can't You See That She's Mine'. Follow-ups did not reach the Top Twenty until 1965's 'Come Home', followed by 'Catch Us If You Can' which went Top Five. This was also the British title of their film, directed by a young John Boorman.

In his essential study, *Call Up The Groups!* Alan Clayson described the DC5's strategy: *"Although they scrupulously plugged their singles on British TV, this was only market research for the States. Flops at home could be recouped abroad for more negotiable tracks."*

'Over And Over' was a Stateside No. 1, but staggered to No. 45 in the UK. *NME*: *"(a) contagious bouncer featuring Mike Smith dual-tracking with harmony support plus walloping drums and underlying rasping sax. Also a harmonious interlude. The cute chorus is extremely catchy and it's rather like a beaty sing-along. Each stanza is prefaced by introductory vocal gimmicks reminiscent of 'Catch Us If You Can' – in fact, its major fault is that it compares too closely with Dave's former hit."*

'Try Too Hard' was an appropriate title for the group's first real British flop, coming after a run of a dozen chart entries. *NME*: "*Clanking piano and guitar open, but suddenly a swinging beat with drums and guttural sax. This one really moves, and has great atmosphere. It's Dave's best for some time, and it doesn't deserve the cold shoulder.*" The British record buyers clearly disagreed. Other flops followed: 'Look Before You Leap' was reviewed in *NME*: "*I thought Dave Clark's last disc 'Try Too Hard' deserved hit status, but it didn't quite make it and this one isn't quite as good ... it's fiery, vibrant stuff with Mike Smith taking the lead in this bright and breezy finger-snapper, aided by honking sax, organ and some pretty wild drum-thumps and cymbal crashes by Dave. Ought to register, but alas, probably won't.*" It reached No. 50.

'Tabitha Twitchit' was the next single; *NME*: "*it has all the necessary ingredients – a cute title and an appealing lyric to match, a chorus you can join in on, a storming rhythm with that characteristic Clark stomp beat, shrieking brass and organ. A Les Reed/Barry Mason number, it's happy-go-lucky and good fun.*" *Disc & Music Echo* were less impressed: "*It's ... gimmicky, but I just can't see who would buy it.*" Alan Clayson was also scathing: "*they also touched their musical nadir with 1966's appalling 'Tabitha Twitchit' with its vulgar recycling of the 'Glad All Over' hook.*"

The British flops continued. *NME* reviewed 'Nineteen Days': "*closer to the authentic r-and-b idiom than most of the Five's discs. It has a 'move-on' type of lyric – very repetitive (but insistent rather than monotonous) with falsetto chanting supporting Mike Smith's vigorous vocal ... Already a U.S. hit it could get a small touch here.*"

The DC5 unexpectedly reached the No. 2 position in the UK in 1967 with 'Everybody Knows', an M.O.R. ballad written by Les Reed and Barry Mason. This was the group's highest chart position over here for three years. Unusually, the lead singer on this single was guitarist, Lennie Davidson, not keyboardist Mike Smith. The group seemed to avoid psychedelia altogether and this song had more in common with other clients of Reed and Mason such as Engelbert Humperdinck and Tom Jones.

'Live In The Sky' was the follow-up to 'The Red Balloon' and had brass arranged by Keith Mansfield. This singalong used crowd noises from a Wembley football match but scraped to No. 39. 1969's 'The Mulberry Tree', I feel, was the group's very worst moment. *NME* seemed oblivious to the song's faults: "*It's a happy-go-lucky bouncer with an irresistible poppy beat and with attacking brass adding fire and urgency to the backing ... there's a captivating Caribbean flavour supplying additional sparkle."* At the time cod-Jamaican voices were seemingly acceptable in British culture; The Beatles recorded 'Ob La Di Ob La Da' and there is even a line in 'Bungalow Bill' where Lennon puts on a Caribbean accent. An early version of 'The Long And Winding Road' has a 'humorous' West Indian lilt. 'The Mulberry Tree' just seems incredibly dated and stereotyped.

'Put A Little Love In Your Heart' was released in autumn 1969. This Jackie de Shannon song was a Top Five hit for the composer in the US. The DC5's cover version was described by *NME* as *"extremely strong"*. *Record Mirror*: *"Shouldn't really be any problems with this one. It's a direct-action mid-tempo beater – the lyrics are pretty predictable, but there are building-up ingredients which make it a commercial bet. Mostly a group vocal, some of the usual pounding basic beat and nothing too ambitious."* It stalled at No. 31.

'Julia' was the follow-up to the DC5's last big hit, 'Everybody Get Together', which had reached No. 8. *NME*: *"a powerful soul flecked ballad. It's intensely and convincingly emoted by Mike Smith with chanting support from the other boys that's almost choral in texture. Fine performance."* I cannot remember ever hearing this at the time. A cover of Jerry Keller's 1959 British chart-topper, 'Here Comes Summer', gained some airplay when it was released in summer 1970. *NME* called it : *"[a] bright happy-go-lucky treatment of a poppy toe-tapper."* The single peaked at No. 44. Another rock 'n' rock medley, 'More Good Old Rock 'N' Roll', combined segments from no fewer than eight songs, following the same pattern as the group's 'Good Old Rock 'N' Roll' hit of 1969 and reached No. 34. Apart from a reissue of 'Glad All Over' in 1993, this concluded the group's British chart career in the singles charts.

The DC5 continued to release singles. Neil Young's 'Southern Man' was an unusual choice. *NME*: *"A Neil Young composition ... But Dave has changed all that ... it's now become a frantic raver ... a punch packed vocal by Mike Smith plus a piledriving backing emphasised by bongos and tambourine ... the lengthy instrumental play-out has to he heard to be believed ... Dave has transformed it into a viable commercial proposition."* *Disc & Music Echo* were also enthusiastic: *"Dave and the lads have really gone to town and approached* the song seriously and sympathetically. It's by far their most ambitious single ever and, apart from a slightly chaotic ending, it works. Freaky guitar sets the mood and Mike Smith is in his finest hoarse voice."

'Won't You Be My Lady' was written by Dave Clark and Mike Smith and previewed on *Top of the Pops*. *NME*: "*it's a hard-hitting punch-packed rocker*" and, to my mind, something of a hidden gem, being far, far better than most of the DC5's singles with a striking guitar riff. More singles were released as Dave Clark and Friends with Mike Smith remaining as lead vocalist.

DARTS

The British doo-wop act Darts emerged in the Summer of Punk from the ashes of Rocky Sharpe And The Razors with their energetic medley of 'Daddy Cool' and 'The Girl Can't Help It' which reached No. 6. The band featured no fewer than four lead singers. 1978 was Darts' peak year with three consecutive No. 2 hits with 'Come Back My Love', 'Boy From New York City' and 'It's Raining'. Darts clocked up more than forty weeks in the British singles charts that year with their fourth single of 1978, 'Don't Let It Fade Away', reaching No. 18, but still staying in the charts for eleven weeks. 1979 brought two more Top Ten hits with 'Get It' and 'Duke Of Earl'.

Darts' third single release of 1979 was a change of style. 'Can't Get Enough Of Your Love' was written by drummer John Dummer and produced by Roy Wood. With its electric sitar, the song had a 1960's vibe. *Record Mirror*: "*An unusual and untypical choice for Darts ... Rita Ray sounding almost Spectorish ... fails to inject the necessary life into things to maintain interest. Darts don't have flops so what can I say?*" This single only reached No. 43, but worse was yet to come. A revival of Jackie Wilson's 'Reet Petite' did not even make the Top Fifty.

DONOVAN

Donovan is a real survivor, even though his current appearance seems bizarre (shoulder length grey hair) and his anecdotes about the 1960s, Beatles, Dylan, the Maharishi, Swinging London and so on all have him in the central role as catalyst!

'Josie' is omitted from many of Donovan's singles listings; the track had first appeared on his debut album, *What's Bin Did, What's Bin Hid* in 1965. The song was released as a stop-gap single in early 1966 as legal difficulties made Donovan unable to release new product. *NME*: "*A simple little ditty, as uncomplicated as 'Colours' and, in many respects, rather similar. The lyric is thoroughly engaging, with Don at his most colourfully descriptive, though I thought the melody could have been a bit more substantial. Features some splendid guitar work and maintains a steady mid-tempo.*" This release was ignored by record-buyers who must have known that 'Josie' was an old track.

Donovan had already recorded 'Sunshine Superman'. This early psychedelic classic had reached the top of the charts in the US in the summer of 1966 long before a British audience could purchase it. Finally, the single was released in the UK at the end of the year and reached No. 2. The song still sounds original and interesting, totally unlike anything else released at the time.

After a series of contrasting and original hit singles such as 'Mellow Yellow', 'Jennifer Juniper' and 'Hurdy Gurdy Man', Donovan started the 1970s by being moved to Pye's progressive label, Dawn, alongside the likes of Mungo Jerry. He teamed up with a band called Open Road for an album. 'Riki Tiki Tavi' received good airplay on Radio One. *Record Mirror*: "*this is pure, plain unvarnished Donovan doing his fast-talking, fast-phrasing bit. The basic rhythm just shuffles along and by the mid-waymark it is just about irresistible. Lyrics seem pretty harmless until one concentrates a bit – quite meaningful.*" *NME*: "*a cute and gimmicky chorus hook, even though Don attempts to tie it into a philosophic wordly-wise verse are somewhat contrived. There's a naggy insistence about the the beat and the backing which has an exotic jungle flavour blended with a touch of Caribbean magic ... this one pounds at the brain incessantly..*"

A few months later Donovan previewed his next single on *Top of the Pops*. Titled 'Celia Of The Seals', it was a tribute to fashion model and animal rights campaigner, Celia Hammond. *NME*: "*Dedicated by Donovan to the cause of wild-life preservation, it is an enthralling and exquisite piece that shows Don in his true light – that of a contemporary bard. But bearing in mind that his last single didn't make the grade, I'm wondering if this packs the necessary punch to appeal to the masses."*

Throughout the 1970s Donovan continued to release singles. There was a reunion with Mickie Most and I remember hearing some singles on the radio, notably 'Cosmic Wheels' and 'Maria Magenta'. *NME* on 'Maria Magenta': *"My God, Donovan can sound really gormless when he puts his back into it. Mar-i-a Ma-gen-ta (pause) you are the one."* I feel that audiences began to tire of Donovan's idiosyncratic voice on disc, even if his television and live appearances remained popular. 'I Like You' was also taken from the *Cosmic Wheels* album; *NME*: *"this particular track doesn't really leap off the turntable at you. It's Mr Leitch being fey and romantic again, but with some nice production touches."* *NME* also reviewed 'Sailing Home': *"In an ever-changing world ... you can always rely on (Donovan) to come up with records like this – mellowed-back and laid-out guitar, quivering voice and string interventions."* That is an apt description and summary of Mr. Leitch.

DAVID ESSEX

1973 was a breakthrough year for David Essex; he was highly successful in a London musical (*Godspell*), a British film (*That'll Be The Day*) and with his recording career at CBS. His extraordinary sounding single, 'Rock On', reached No. 3 and its parent album of the same name went to No. 7. At this point Essex wrote his own songs, skilfully arranged and produced by Jeff Wayne. The follow-up single, 'Lamplight' sounded rather like Leon Russell's 'Tightrope' and reached No. 7.

However, the next single, 'America' went no higher than No. 32. Essex: *"It was released in May 1974, and although it charted, it never made the top ten in the UK, probably because the lyric was too personal."* Record Mirror: *"with a moody show-type opening, voices and rasping instrumentation, this one gets off to obvious-hit status from the first bars. David's voice sounds echoey, and it's got a finger-clicking* West Side Story *sort of presentation. The production is ambitious but not overdone."* *NME* were crueller: *"Jerky, echoey vocals as in 'Rock On'. Same spare instrumentation, and prominent humming from a group of people who were understandably thoroughly bored. Essex's observations about America seem limited to the fact that when his plane landed in Phoenix, the sun was shining. The song is no relation to L. Bernstein or P. Simon."* In his entertaining memoir, *Charmed Life*, Essex explains the success of the 'America' single in France: *"where the song became the biggest foreign hit ever ... I asked a French record executive what could be the reason. He told me his theory – the chorus of America goes 'America, America – ca ca' and 'ca ca' is apparently the French equivalent of poo poo. This obviously appealed to the xenophobic French."*

After this temporary blip, Essex's next single, 'Gonna Make You A Star', was a chart-topper and he was on a roll. There were three more Top Ten hits including another No. 1 with 'Hold Me Close'. Unlike the majority of the other teen pop stars of the 1970s such as David Cassidy, Donny Osmond and The Bay City Rollers, we must remember that Essex wrote his own songs. These – as 'Rock On' had displayed – were not conventional ditties, but showed some originality, wit and taste. With Jeff Wayne as producer and arranger and first class session musicians such as Herbie Flowers, Essex brought a new sound to the UK singles charts. Sometimes, as 'America' showed, it was a little hit and miss in both artistic and commercial terms, but worse was to come.

After three Top Ten albums, Essex's fourth album, a live double set called *On Tour*, staggered to No. 51 for one week. Clearly all the teenage girls who flocked to his concerts did not want to hear a recording of the tour in the comfort of their own home. Essex's next studio album, *Out On The Street*, went no higher than No. 31. The first two singles taken from the album, 'City Lights' and 'Coming Home', both peaked at No. 24. The final single from *Out On The Street* was 'Ooh Love'. This release did not deserve to chart. The song starts slowly with heavy breathing and a semi-spoken vocal. The lyrics are dire: *"Ooh love a love a love"*. Essex: *"I think this (lack of success for 'Ooh Love') probably created a little tension between Jeff and me, and although we remained good friends ... I was looking to produce myself."*

This series of flops was only ended by Essex's rendition of 'Oh What A Circus' from the Andrew Lloyd Webber and Tim Rice musical, *Evita*. The single went to No. 3 in the summer of 1978. Essex had not appeared on the original 1977 *Evita* album which had provided hits for Julie Covington and Barbara Dickson. This new recording on his new label, Mercury, saw Essex grow a beard in readiness for playing the part of Che Guevara in the West End production of the musical.

Essex bravely attempted to cover Lorraine Ellison's deep soul classic 'Stay With Me Baby' from 1966. The Walker Brothers' version had reached No. 26 in 1967. Essex did not even get as high as that; his version crept to No. 45. *Record Mirror*: *"Essex blasts his vocal chords out but the orchestral climaxes just aren't powerful enough."* I feel that Essex makes a valiant attempt but simply does not have the technique to master such a challenging song.

CBS released 'Brave New World' which *Record Mirror* called: *"yet another track ... from* War Of The Worlds. *This one is better on the shorter version. Again the production is somewhat excessive, but it will probably do equally well as the other singles from the album."* Unfortunately, 'Brave New World' rose no higher than No. 55, whereas Justin Hayward's 'Forever Autumn' had gone Top Five earlier in the year and 'Eve Of The War' peaked at No. 38. Sometimes, taking a series of singles from a hit album can be counter-productive.

'Goodbye First Love' was performed on *Top of the Pops* in November 1978. The reviewer in *Record Mirror* was not impressed: *"What a load of old cobblers. I'm not above a bit of sentimental romance but this is soaking wet ... I've never really thought much of his voice, but this ballad doesn't tax his voice as much as some of the other rock stuff he's attempted."* Mike Batt is credited as producer and arranger, but this was not the Womblemeister's most successful collaboration with Essex. Four years later, Batt would write and produce the Christmas hit, 'A Winter's Tale', Essex's biggest single for many years.

Both the 'Oh What A Circus' and 'Goodbye First Love' singles were included on Essex's album, *Imperial Wizard*. The album's title track was issued as a single in spring 1979. The label credit said "produced and arranged by David Essex with Christopher Neil". Neil was an experienced singer, writer and producer, responsible for hits by Paul Nicholas and Marshall Hain. Essex, again: *"The single 'Imperial Wizard' was prevented from being a top ten hit, I believe, by a snowstorm that held up the chart returns for two weeks. Standing still at number thirty-one meant it lost its momentum."*

The real reason I feel for the single's lack of success is that, compared with Essex's singles with Jeff Wayne on CBS, 'Imperial Wizard' was simply not of the same standard. Surely most people know that an imperial wizard is a rank in the Ku Klux Klan? The picture sleeve illustration suggests that Essex (and probably neither Christopher Neil nor the record company) did not appear to know this. The song is an acquired taste, a military drum beat, electric harpsichord and an anti-war theme. We hear Essex sing: *"Free the people"* and *"send your generals to the front"*. The line, *"Hungary is hungry and the people are broke"* is less forgivable.

There was worse to come; 'World' was released on United Artists. *Record Mirror*: *"From the Alpha Omega 'musical revelation'. An over-produced, increasingly typical slice of melodrama from a guy I actually quite liked in his lower rent, greasier days."* 1979's '20 Flights Up' was written by Essex and produced and arranged by Mike Batt. The single has a big orchestra and is all about New York. It did nothing. The following year – outside the scope of this book – saw Essex return to the Top Ten with 'Silver Dream Machine' from the film *Silver Dream Racer*. Whatever one thinks of David Essex, he is a true survivor. He has succeeded across the entertainment world and still has a large fan base.

ELTON JOHN

The former Reginald Dwight has been releasing music since the late 1960s. 'Your Song' was his first British hit single way back in 1971 and the first of umpteen hit records over an amazing seven decades. The follow-up, 'Friends' from the soundtrack of the film of the same name, was a flop. *Record Mirror*: *"Good plaintive heart-tugging stuff, just with piano at first. The opening segment takes time to register, but gradually the orchestral arrangement builds up pressure and Elton indulges in some fanciful but intuitive phrasing ... Hit status guaranteed ... probably up there in the top five."*

Over the next five years the hits kept on coming with such classics as 'Rocket Man', 'Goodbye Yellow Brick Road' and 'Don't Let The Sun Go Down On Me'. Only the release of the single, 'Grow Some Funk Of Your Own' in January 1976 broke Elton's run of successful hits in the UK, despite much radio play. Taken from the *Rock Of The Westies* album, this dreary rocker is full of clichés, and is one of the rare occasions when guitarist Davey Johnstone gets a co-writing credit alongside the John-Taupin team. Unexpectedly, the song is guitar-led in the style of 'Saturday Night's Alright For Fighting' and 'The Bitch Is Back'. For me these are the least convincing and appealing parts of Elton's canon. *Record Mirror*: "*this isn't so much funk as an E.J. stomper. Catchy repetitive riff that builds to a driving climax at the end. Power driver of a number, but perhaps better for live performances than as a big chart buster.*" In his memoir, Elton said: "*It was almost a relief when the second single from Rock Of The Westies, 'Grow Some Funk Of Your Own', wasn't a huge hit … I'd never really set out to have hit singles. I was an album artist, who made records like* Tumbleweed Connection *and* Madman Across the Water, *and I'd inadvertently become this huge singles machine, having smash after smash, none of which had been intentionally written to be hit singles.*" Hmmm. Elton's best-selling singles undoubtedly helped his album sales and vice versa. Huge singles machines require a huge network of pluggers. Often, as this book hopes to show, even an artist's finest releases do not become hits. At other times, there is clear evidence that the record buying public lose interest in an artist if their singles are too predictable.

When 'Don't Go Breaking My Heart' reached No. 1 in the summer of 1976, Elton's former label, DJM, sneakily released 'Bennie And The Jets' as an A-side. This was a track from 1973's *Goodbye Yellow Brick Road* album and had been a chart-topper in the US in 1974. I must confess that I never really 'got' 'Bennie And The Jets'. The words, usually an important part of Elton's recordings, were hard to understand. The song's 'live' feel apparently came from overdubbed sounds from both a 1972 Elton concert and Jimi Hendrix's 1970 Isle Of Wight Festival appearance. *Record Mirror* clearly thought differently to me: "*Possibly Reg's greatest hour as he puts Ziggy et al into perspective with this live masterpiece. You all know it, you will buy it and it'll be a monster.*" This single wasn't "live" and only reached No. 34.

In the late 1970s Elton John had reached something of a crossroads. He simply could not sell any more records with each release. At one point he, alone, was responsible for a huge percentage of record sales in the American record industry. So, inevitably, sales levelled off and eventually decreased.

'Ego' was an unusual one-off; the song had been written during the *Blue Moves* sessions. Elton explains: "*just something I had lying around and I wanted to release it for a long time. Unfortunately the time wasn't right. It's* been disappointing ... it's about the silliness of rock stars." *Record Mirror*: "An odd choice of single but maybe it grows on you. I found all the tempo changes too confusing, they spoilt the continuity and it's not really worthy of him." *NME*'s reviewer thought differently: "*The barbed message is delivered against a clipped, tense quasi-tango beat, which momentarily lapses into neo-psychedelic first-person narratives, before regaining vitriolic momentum. Powerful stuff ... I reckon it's E.J's finest-ever recorded statement.*" 'Ego' also reached No. 34.

Elton told Radio One D.J. Andy Peebles: "*I did some stuff with Thom Bell with whom I've always wanted to do separate singles and I wanted to work with because of The Stylistics. I went to Seattle to record and it all went fantastically well, and then I heard the mixes and I shelved it for a year because it was too saccharine and then decided to put out a maxi single in England. It was very strange, because there was one record called 'Are You Ready For Love' which was actually the A-side here.*" This was Elton's lowest chart placing since 'Your Song' in 1971, reaching only No. 42. A remix of the single reached No.1 in Britain in 2003.

Worse was to come with the *Victim Of Love* album and single, a disastrous collaboration with Pete Bellotte, a friend from Elton's days in Hamburg with Bluesology. Elton only supplied vocals and made no keyboard or composing contribution. The first single from the album was a disco version of 'Johnny B. Goode'. A performance of this can be seen on an Australian television show. Words fail me at this point. The title track was released as a single in September 1979. *Record Mirror*: "*Begins like 129 other disco records, but grows out of that, becoming in adulthood a moody, moaning thing, yet catchy with Elt's vocals ... the main feature, 'specially on the rocking chorus*".

It would take a few more years – and records – before Elton made a proper comeback. There were further flops in the early 1980s. 'Blue Eyes' (with lyrics by Gary Osborne) saw Elton return to the UK Top Ten in 1982 for the first time since 'Song For Guy' in 1978. The following year saw a full reunion with lyricist Bernie Taupin and further Top Ten entries. I think we all – including Elton and Bernie – knew that this made both common and artistic sense.

The Kinks

The Kinks, like their labelmates The Searchers and The Rockin' Berries, were not always well-served by Pye Records. The group's hits included three chart-toppers and eleven Top Ten singles. This put The Kinks only below The Beatles and the Stones in terms of British pop groups. Unfortunately, The Kinks' albums' fortunes were regularly undermined by releases on the budget Marble Arch label. Some of their finest albums of the 1960s – *Village Green Preservation Society* and *Arthur (Or The Decline And Fall Of The British Empire)* simply did not chart.

'Wonderboy' broke the group's run of Top Twenty hit singles, stalling at No. 36. *Record Mirror*: "*no specific change in the overall sound ... not necessarily their best: but then they set exceptionally high standards. Philosophy-pop.*" In *NME* Derek Johnson went into greater depth and detail: "*Ray Davies has an incredible flair for writing lyrics of a beautifully descriptive nature – he always gets straight to the point, combining simplicity of thought with a penchant for the more colourful and pleasurable things in life. And his dislike of complex, enigmatic words is again evident in this charming philosophic song. What's more, the tune is as catchy as anything he has written – harmonious and lilting with The Kinks providing a continuous la-la accompaniment to his solo vocal. The beat flows along at a relaxed, easy-going pace, and there's an ear-catching rippling backing. This is a very good pop record indeed – and, if anything, I rate it even more commercial than 'Autumn Almanac' or 'Waterloo Sunset'. Deserves to be big – and it will be!*"

The wistful 'Days' saw The Kinks return to the Top Twenty, but worse was to come. 'Plastic Man' reached No. 31 and the next two singles – both from the recently released *Arthur* album – flopped. 'Drivin'' was previewed on *Top of the Pops* in June 1969. Reviews were mixed — *Record Mirror*: "*Obviously a big hit and in with chances for the 'smash'.*" *NME* were more perceptive: "*The Kinks improve with each release but their popularity seems to diminish accordingly. Maybe their style is out of favour and if that is the case then this record won't stop the trend. It's a 'plum in the voice' story in song, given that familiar dated sound which the group had become noted for. From the quality and production angle, it deserves to be a hit but I can't be too hopeful.*"

'Shangri-La' was released three months later. *Record Mirror*: "*Must be a hit, could be very big. Splendid production.*" *NME* were also enthusiastic: "*opens quietly with Ray Davies singing to a backing of rippling guitars and muted horns. Then this lengthy track breaks into tempo and from then on builds steadily to a shattering climax when all hell breaks loose in the scoring. It's bound to catch the disc buyers' imagination.*" Alas, one of the Kinks' finest performances was not a hit, nor was its parent album, *Arthur*. Two decades later, The Mock Turtles covered 'Shangri-La' as the title track of a Kinks tribute album on Imaginary Records. This new version may have reached a wider audience than The Kinks' original did.

'Victoria' was the third track from *Arthur* to be released as a single. *Melody Maker*: "*this stands a very good chance (with its) overall sound, which is very commercial.*" *NME*: "*It's a good gutsy pop disc. Not as catchy as many of the Kinks' offerings ... not a big hit.*" *Record Mirror*: "*One never knows, does one, about how The Kinks will sell these days. But this is from 'the opera' Arthur and is a substantial change of style.*" It crept to No. 33, two places below 'Plastic Man''s highest position.

After all those flops, The Kinks' last two years at Pye were brighter; 'Lola' went to No. 2 in the summer of 1970 and 'Apeman' reached No. 5 at the start of the next year. A maxi-single was released with songs from the group's soundtrack to the 1971 Hywel Bennett film, *Percy*. The lead track was 'God's Children'. *NME* called it: "*a bouncy singalong number with a jangling backing and happy sound.*"

The Kinks then signed to RCA. *Muswell Hillbillies* was a great album title but produced no hit singles. The next release was the ambitious double, *Everybody's In Showbiz, Everybody's A Star*. One disc was new songs, the second a recording of the band's Carnegie Hall concert. By now The Kinks were an impressive live act, enhanced by The Mike Cotton Sound horn section and female backing singers. The band had their only hit single for RCA with 'Supersonic Rocket Ship' which reached No. 16. Successful follow-ups were problematic. 'Celluloid Heroes' (whose opening lines provided the album's title) was universally praised. *Sounds* called it: "*a fine, fine track from The Kinks' fine album.*" *Melody Maker* was even keener: "*Curtains up on the greatest rock single ever told,*" and *NME* agreed: "*one of the best Ray Davies songs in recent years. Highly melodic and well-worded.*" Simon Frith was equally enthusiastic in

Let It Rock: *"Ray Davies' beautiful string of Women's Own Hollywood clichés is good value as by far the best track from a double album."* 'Celluloid Heroes' is an outstanding song with a wonderful melody and nostalgic lyrics about film stars.

Martin C. Strong: *"The remainder of the 70s saw The Kinks become bogged down in ill-advised concept albums and self-parody although while the band were virtually ignored in the UK, they still had a sizeable following in America."* Over the next four years the band would release four more albums, often linked to stage productions. None of these were successful in the UK, neither were any of the singles taken from them.

Simon Frith panned 'Sitting In The Midday Sun' which was released in the summer of 1973: *"too lazy, even for an exceptionally good summer."* *Record Mirror* was more impressed: *"Languid stuff. It's easy going summery rock with some talkative guitar moments and adds up to a form of good-time music ... strong contender for the Top Ten."* *NME* was less convinced: *"One of those lightweight singles The Kinks put out when they're waiting for Ray Davies to come up with something truly remarkable. It's an adequately pleasant little summer song."*

Ray Davies' "problem" was that he had set The Kinks such a high standard of single releases in the 1960s that the future would inevitably be disappointing. There was considerable pressure on him as lead singer and main songwriter. Most of Davies' 1960s contemporaries either worked in a team – Lennon and McCartney, Jagger and Richard, Steve Marriott and Ronnie Lane – or shared the spotlight as Pete Townshend and Roger Daltrey did in The Who.

'Sweet Lady Genevieve', released in September 1973, received mixed reviews — *Melody Maker*: *"I hope this is the hit it richly deserves to be."* and *NME*: *"Quite nicely performed with some attractive harmonica and National guitar, and Ray sounds great, but the song ain't much cop.."*

The next single, 'Mirror Of Love', received a mixed review from Simon Frith: *"Meanwhile, Ray Davies seems to have opted out of the chart chase altogether. 'Mirror Of Love' is archetypal Kinks – a sado-masochistic love song, echoes of both steel bands and tea dances, their best record since 'Lola'. But it's also arrogantly eccentric and sloppy, certainly not easy listening."* *Melody Maker* described the single: *"With an alcoholic off-beat and amusing lyrics."* In *NME* a young Chrissie Hynd (sic) wrote: *"Yet another Kinks single that positively reeks of white trousers and loafers, Raymond Douglas Davies is the only songwriter who can write such personal material (and he is always very personal) and never get embarrassing. One of the true romantics of our time."* Hynde and Davies would have a relationship a few years later.

'Holiday Romance' was the follow-up in October 1974 and was reviewed in *Melody Maker*: *"Raymond Douglas Davies returns, at last, to the three minute narrative form of the classic Kinks singles, and confirms that he's far from lost his cosmic vision. Could this be a hit of impressive proportions? One hopes so."* Simon Frith was blunt: *"The Kinks, meanwhile, don't have any fans anymore. 'Holiday Romance' was given good reviews everywhere, but I've never even heard it."* Apart from in *NME* where Nick Kent was less keen: *"And still they descend into the quagmire ... unbearably twee and altogether tiresome."*

For 1975's 'Ducks On The Wall', *Melody Maker*'s reviewer made an easy quip: *"Kinks come back with a lame duck."* 'You Can't Stop The Music' was released only a month later and was reviewed in *Record Mirror*: *"The closing track on The Kinks new* Soap Opera *album, the single is more in the mould of Kinks records — good lyrics and a commercial sound. Bouncy feel all the way through, and a sound that you quickly find yourself humming to."*

NME's reviewer was frustrated with 1976's 'No More Looking Back', an unfortunate title for a band with such a wonderful legacy: *"What's with Raymond Douglas? The man who wrote so many enduring singles seems to be unable to clear his mind of musical clutter ... Bring back Shel Talmy. It's urgent!"* This was The Kinks' final single for RCA and their eighth flop in a row.

Later in the year the band signed with Arista and released nine singles in the next three years. 'Sleepwalker' was the first release and also the title track of the album. *NME*: *"Set to a backdrop highly reminiscent of the hallowed back-'em-up-shut-'em-down riffing of Phase 12 Kinks ... the main squeeze is that The Kinks are making good records again."* Melody Maker disagreed: *"Kinks fans/lovers of 'Waterloo Sunset' won't find 'Sleepwalker' very satisfactory ... this isn't quite the leap back to form which was hoped for."* I find the song rather ordinary and predictable; these are not words that one would usually associate with The Kinks.

'Juke Box Music' was released in June 1977. *NME*: *"'It's only juke-box music,' sings the astute Raymond Douglas Davies with one eye cocked on single sales, but not this one methinks."* While *Record Mirror* stated: *"From the murky depths of Muswell Hill comes another success, the single reeks of the early 1970s, but it's still appealing as Ray Davies hisses through the song. Masterful.*" I find nothing masterful about this. There are far better songs written about pop music; just two immediately spring to mind: The Raspberries' 'Overnite Sensation' and the Pet Shop Boys' 'Hit Music'.

'Father Christmas' was released in November 1977. The days when Christmas singles with the actual word in their title – Mud, Slade, Wizzard, even Gilbert O'Sullivan – were long over, so it was curious to see such an original songwriter as Ray Davies pen such a song. *NME*: "*successful Xmas songs are more about mood than specifics, but as this is an anti-Christmas single it's fine. How the mighty have fallen.*" This also feels unsatisfactory, almost like an expensive demo. 1977's punk explosion produced a lot of cynicism and anger, but this just sounds weak and contrived.

The following year, 1978, brought three more singles, 'A Rock 'N' Roll Fantasy', 'Live Life' and 'Black Messiah', spaced two months apart. 'A Rock 'N' Roll Fantasy' is a good song with a great melody and the vocals and instruments feel lush and but the words are unimpressive. 'Live Life' is political with references to the IRA and "*social unrest*", "*crooked politicians*" and "*unemployment queues*". This is from the author of 'Dead End Street'. "*You've gotta live life for yourself.*" *NME*: "*not quite at their best but it's great to hear from them again.*"

'Black Messiah' was slated in *Melody Maker* where the reviewer compared The Kinks to other "*old and irrelevant*" bands such as Slade and The Moody Blues. If the song is meant to be satirical or radical, it fails lamentably. *Melody Maker* comments that Ray Davies' "*Linguaphone Rasta accent feel(s) uncomfortable without the wit and invention of 10cc's 'Dreadlock Holiday'.*" I am not sure about the last comment. I was always uneasy about 'Dreadlock Holiday'.

As The Kinks repeatedly failed to reach the British charts, more and more attention had been given to the huge legacy of past Kinks songs. David Bowie had already covered 'Where Have All the Good Times Gone' on *Pin-Ups* in 1973 and The Jam had a Top Thirty hit with 'David Watts' in 1978. The following year The Pretenders covered 'Stop Your Sobbing' for their first single and later recorded a brilliant version of 'I Go To Sleep'. In the USA Van Halen released a cover of 'You Really Got Me' as their debut single. Slowly, The Kinks became an arena attraction in the States and even had chart albums over there. Meanwhile, back in the UK the band's new releases were continually ignored.

'(I Wish I Could Fly Like) Superman' also attempts political commentary. There is almost a disco beat. 'Moving Pictures' is no better. *Melody Maker* comments positively on the song's *"amiable, proficient shuffle"* but (correctly) criticises the weak lyrics such as *"Life is only a moving picture."* It feels like Ray Davies has been listening to Blondie's 'Heart Of Glass'.

'Pressure' was the final Kinks' single of the 1970s. It is at least exciting, but sounds too much like so many new wave songs of that time, veering close to parody. *Melody Maker*: *"'Pressure' has been whipped off the album and works well as a single. Rowdy, rousing and instantly accessible,"* suggesting that Ray Davies *"might have jotted it down after heavy exposure to The Clash and Ramones."*

Eventually, after no less than a dozen flop singles in a row on Arista, the band struck lucky with the thirteenth, the wonderfully nostalgic and tuneful 'Come Dancing' which reached No. 12 in late summer 1983. It was good to see The Kinks back in the charts. This was, however, their final UK Top Twenty hit.

Manfred Mann

After Paul Jones quit Manfred Mann in 1966, the group signed with the Fontana label and carried on having hit singles. Manfred Mann Mark II beat several other artists to have the hit version of Dylan's 'Just Like A Woman' (from his *Blonde On Blonde* album). The hits continued with 'Semi-Detached Suburban Mr James' and 'Ha Ha Said the Clown' by Tony Hazzard. The next single, a virtually instrumental version of Tommy Roe's American hit 'Sweet Pea', fared badly. The original's words were unimportant so we were missing nothing. *NME*'s review cites the group's *"instrumental prowess and technique"* with *"walloping tympani (underlining) flute and organ"* and *"vibes solo"*. 'Sweet Pea' staggered to Number 36 in May 1967. The band did not trouble the charts until the start of the next year.

'So Long Dad' was Manfred Mann's first major flop. A Randy Newman composition, it was one of the writer's many dark humour songs. Newman was not unknown in Britain; he had penned Cilla's 'I've Been Wrong Before', Gene Pitney's 'Just One Smile' and Alan Price's 'Simon Smith And His Dancing Bear'. *Disc & Music* Echo: "*I had to listen to this a few times. Unlike most Randy Newman songs it didn't have a very definite form – it tends to wander ... Crazy bar room piano honks away with mournful brass and Mike D'Abo sings with feeling ... A rather odd song ... It does not strike me as a gigantic hit.*"

Perhaps 'So Long Dad''s subject matter alienated purchasers. In *Call Up The Groups*, Alan Clayson said, "*the group only missed once when 'So Long Dad', with its lengthy melody line, faltered outside the Top Fifty.*" Singer Mike D'Abo had a similar tenor voice (but with less range and power) to Harry Nilsson who covered the song on his 1970 album, *Nilsson Sings Newman*. There is a fair amount of surviving video footage of Manfred Mann Mark II, mostly from Germany's *Beat Club*. For 'So Long Dad', D'Abo plays to the camera, using hand gestures and body language to help convey the song's subject matter. The rest of the band generally seem less enthusiastic. Tom McGuinness (now on guitar) is grinning, while both Mike Hugg and Manfred look detached, they are probably thinking about their next advertisement jingle project, and bassist Klaus Voorman (yes, the *Revolver* album cover artist and future Plastic Ono Band member) looks uncomfortable.

Manfred Mann's No. 1 hit with Dylan's 'Mighty Quinn' was followed by another flop. The 'Theme From *Up The Junction*' was released in February 1968 and was not strictly the official follow-up to 'Quinn' as it was a film theme. This was a few months after Traffic's Top Ten success with their own film theme to *Here We Go Round The Mulberry Bush*. Manfred's film theme was perhaps too subtle for *Top of the Pops* and Radio One; the verses were slow and thoughtful and the song's chorus was hardly a sing-a-long. *NME*: "*it's a brilliantly descriptive piece, conjuring up mental visions of the sordid, squalid location of the movie. Features some wonderfully sensitive harmonies ... set to a backing of clanking piano, tambourine, twangs and a solid beat. The melody is simple and quick to register with the title phrase constantly repeated. I'm told that this isn't intended as a follow-up to 'Quinn' but with the group's current popularity it could well catch on.*" Record

Mirror's reviewer agreed: *"There are some strong ideas here, and a treatment that is very, very imaginative. It's both exciting and wistful."*

THE ROLLING STONES

Like The Beatles, the Stones did not have actual flops. After the band had left Decca, their former record company released a series of compilation albums without the Stones' consent. These started with *Stone Age* in 1971. The band issued a series of statements and press advertisements condemning the release and disassociating themselves from the album. These album releases continued with *Gimme Shelter* (1971), *Milestones* (1972), *Rock 'N' Rolling Stones* (1972) and *No Stone Unturned* (1973). Decca released an old track, 'Sad Day', from the latter album. The track had previously only been available as the B-side of the American release of '19th Nervous Breakdown' in 1966. This is not one of the Stones' better songs, even for a B-side, having that slightly echoey sound of Andrew Oldham's productions. Simon Frith wrote in *Let It Rock*: *"I'm glad nobody bought The Rolling Stones' awful 'Sad Day' — Decca didn't deserve to make anything from it."* Unsurprisingly, 'Sad Day' did not chart in the UK.

A sixth unauthorised album, *Metamorphosis*, was released by Decca in 1975. A track from the album, 'Out Of Time', was released as a single. This rendition was originally a demo and features Mick Jagger's lead vocals with the orchestration and backing vocals used on Chris Farlowe's No. 1 cover version in 1966. The Stones had originally released the song on their 1966 *Aftermath* album where the unmistakeable riff had been played on marimbas. This version reached No. 45.

SMALL FACES

Including the Small Faces' 'Afterglow Of My Love' in this book is a bit of a cheat. It originally appeared on the band's 1968 album, *Ogden's Nut Gone Flake*, but was released as a single, without Small Faces' permission, just as they broke up in March 1969. *NME*: *"this is as intense and soulful an interpretation as you could wish to find. Steve really pours his heart out and he's backed by an incredible pulverising sound comprising walloping drums, that swirling organ, crashing cymbals, twangy guitars and thundering beat."* Brian Hogg also loved it: *"a brilliantly powerful song, combining their early urgency with a new mature loudness."* Despite its excellence – I rate it up there with 'All Or Nothing' and 'Tin Soldier', 'Afterglow' only reached No. 36. A few years later, Flo & Eddie (aka Mark Volman and Howard Kaylan of The Turtles) covered the song on their second album. On the same album they included a version of Ray Davies' 'Days'. Clearly, these two exponents of fine American pop had the utmost respect for their British counterparts. A few years earlier, Davies had produced The Turtles' album, *Turtle Soup*.

SQUEEZE

Squeeze arrived for most people in the spring of 1978 with 'Take Me I'm Yours'. I clearly remember hearing it as a student and being entranced by both the song's lyrics (*"'I came across the desert"*) and the band's unusual sound with pounding keyboards and dual lead singers, an octave apart. It reached No. 19. Two decades later, I saw lead singer/guitarist Glenn Tilbrook perform the song solo at Manchester University's Academy 3. Somehow, Tilbrook played both the repetitive keyboard pattern *and* the lead guitar interspersions simultaneously.

The follow-up, 'Bang Bang', was less popular. Glenn Tilbrook told Jim Drury: *"I think the song's rubbish. Like all novelty songs, it had its moments. I think we thought it tremendously funny at the time but I have to say I don't laugh anymore."* It crawled to No. 49.

'Goodbye Girl' was the first single released from the *Cool For Cats* album and reviewed in *Record Mirror*: *"Opens with a drum sound that is evocative of 'Take Me I'm Yours'. Great production, good song but rather bland and British ... A grower."* Jim Drury, author of *Squeeze Song By Song*: *"I'd always considered 'Goodbye Girl' as being a hit single. I was amazed when I looked it up and found it only got to No. 63 in the charts."* Chris Difford: *"It was the first single off (the) album and our last release was 'Bang Bang' which was another miserable failure. We gave the illusion that we were massive everywhere and had all these hit singles, but it was a mirage."* Glenn Tilbrook: *"It had a jolly tune, which later to my horror someone pointed out sounded like* The Muppets *theme tune. And I have to agree with them."* Again, the song featured the classic Squeeze sound of the two vocalists singing an octave apart with Glenn Tilbrook the high voice and Chris Difford the low one.

The second and third singles taken from *Cool For Cats* were the title track (sung by Difford) and the classic 'Up The Junction' (sung by Tilbrook); both reached No. 2 in the UK. Releasing the right singles in the right order was and still is, of course, an art. Clearly, this was something that no-one at A&M Records had learned.

CAT STEVENS

The former Steve Georgiou has had three distinctive parts to his musical career: Deram days, Island life and, most recently, after conversion to Islam, his re-emergence as Yusuf Islam. I remember hearing 'Matthew And Son' as a child and finding it quite haunting. His early days on Deram saw releases produced by Mike Hurst with four Top Thirty hit singles. 'Matthew And Son' reached No.2. 'Kitty' only reached No. 47 in late 1967 and was his last chart entry of the decade. *NME*: *"much of his success has been due to the unique quality of his compositions, plus their brilliant arrangements and expert production. This is another superbly produced disc — so much so that the vigorous, all-happening scoring creates just as much impact as the singer. It's a pretty good performance by Cat who handles the lyric with greater authority and expression than in any of his previous singles – indicating that, as an artist, he is maturing all the time."*

Cat's final three singles on Deram are rarely heard, but all deserve attention. 'Lovely City (When Do You Laugh?)' was released in early 1968 and recently described in *Shindig* as having *"galloping Buddy Holly rhythms and snaking fuzz guitar"*. *Record Mirror* had described the single thus: *"Cat still goes for the off-beat, but there is something I find mildly disappointing about this one. Parts seem that bit square, then it suddenly perks up into an explosion of sound. He's definitely an ideas man rather than an instantly distinctive singer, but a talent to commend."* I tend to disagree about Cat's distinctiveness; surely his voice is highly unusual which often lifts the ordinary and the repetitive material, but also makes his best work stand out.

It was around this time that Cat began to be interested in matters of spirituality and Eastern religion. In between all this activity, Cat contracted tuberculosis and a collapsed lung. His time in hospital gave him time to draw and start thinking more philosophically and spiritually, reading about Buddhism and practising yoga.

In October 1968 'Here Comes My Wife' was released. This was produced by Cat himself and more orchestral pop, arranged by Mike Vickers. *Record Mirror*: "*Fanfare-type intro on this welcome back Cat single. He sings with his usual flair and attack and the song has a catchy melodic content which should comfortably restore him to the charts. All rather loud and smart and slick, yet with a good atmosphere. The simplicity of the lyric line comes through well. Ambitious backing wise.*"

'Where Are You' in June 1969 saw a change of style. *Record Mirror* again: "*Self-penned, of course, back with Mike Hurst on production ... this is much more simple. Trouble is that it isn't directly melodic. Builds well with orchestral strings and the second half is well in a commercial style. But it must be that bit doubtful for the charts.*" *Shindig* called it: "*a lovely tale of loneliness sung in a noticeably deeper, growlier voice, yet it sounded like Cat had been wheeled directly from hospital to deliver it.*" The single starts with Cat's solo voice accompanied by acoustic guitar, somewhat predicting his future recordings on Island Records.

The following year Cat signed to Island. His hair had grown and he gave another haunting performance with 'Lady D'Arbanville'. Gone were the Mike Hurst production and strings, replaced with a new "honest" singer-songwriter image and a sympathetic second guitarist in Alun Davies. Stevens appeared alongside his labelmates on the Island samplers *Bumpers* and *El Pea*, effectively reinventing himself for the new decade. 'Lady D'Arbanville' was a big hit, reaching No. 7 but its parent album, *Mona Bone Jakon*, rose no higher than No. 60.

Cat Stevens performed 'Father And Son' on *Top of the Pops* in October 1970; it was taken from his second Island album, *Tea For The Tillerman*. *NME*: "*a slow ballad but with an insistent beat, particularly the more forceful chorus – it has a haunting melody that takes a few spins to register to the full. There's some delicious and sensitive guitar playing and a delightful reprise chorus featuring vocal counter-harmonies behind Cat. A supreme example of quality pop.*" This time the single failed to chart, but the *Tillerman* album went Top Twenty and stayed in the charts for nearly 40 weeks. Clearly, Cat Stevens was now regarded as an album artist.

'Father And Son' has become something of a standard these days; Boyzone's cover went to No. 2 in 1995 and went Platinum, while nearly a decade later the group's singer Ronan Keating duetted with the composer (now known as Yusuf Islam) and this version also went to No. 2. There is also a dreadful version by Rod Stewart.

Three singles were released from Cat's next album, *Teaser And The Firecat*, but they had varied success. 'Moonshadow' reached No. 22 and the old hymn, 'Morning Has Broken' with words by Eleanor Farjeon, went Top Ten. Rick Wakeman was employed to play the piano part. Here, his input was as crucial as it was to be later in the year when he played on David Bowie's 'Life On Mars'. I am assuming that Rick was just paid the standard session fee, as agreed by the Musicians Union, for his work. 'Tuesday's Dead' was a lot more rhythmic but went nowhere. *Teaser And The Firecat* was a huge success, peaking at No. 3 and staying in the UK album charts for 93 weeks. Cat Stevens had truly arrived.

Cat's subsequent albums did not match *Teaser*'s appeal or success. *Catch Bull At Four* produced just one hit with 'Can't Keep It In' which reached No. 13 in winter 1972 and stayed in the charts for nearly three months. Follow-up hit singles were problematic.

'The Hurt' was released in July 1973 at the same time as its parent album, *Foreigner*. *NME*: "*Some pretty volume pedal steel guitar leads into the long single from (Cat Stevens). It's typical Stevens – all jerky, gasping vocals and words that mean little ... Not his best stuff.*" *Record Mirror* had another point of view: "*it's a success, though perhaps short on that instant commercial appeal. But his voice fairly whips through it, producing power and style, and the story-line song builds with some delicious bridging moments from back-up voices and from bass and rhythm. It's an off-beat, chattering sort of busy recording. Quite outstanding.*" Cat's commercial appeal had peaked; the *Foreigner* album reached No. 3, but was only in the album charts for ten weeks, suggesting that his fan base had purchased the record, but it had not crossed over in the way that the *Teaser* album did. 'The Hurt' flopped. I confess to not hearing this song at the time.

'Oh Very Young' came from Cat's next album, *Buddha And The Chocolate Box*. I remember that it was played a lot on the radio. *Record Mirror*: "*Cat putting on his high-set and lilting, slightly quavering with emotion voice. There's a strange old-world sort of charm to it, yet at the same time, it's very much today. Girlie team behind do well but unobtrusively. May not be a smash hit single, as such, but it's very good Cat. Very good."* NME's reviewer disagreed: *"the horrid thing ... skips along like a demented sheep with Cat creaking slightly less than usual."* The single flopped in the UK, but went to No. 10 in the USA.

A revival of Sam Cooke's 'Another Saturday Night' hit No. 19 in late summer 1974, but was Cat's last Top Twenty hit of the 1970s. There were a number of Sam Cooke covers around this time. Rod Stewart recorded a medley of 'Bring It On Home' and 'You Send Me' on his *Smiler* album which was also the B-side of his single, 'Farewell'. Dr Hook covered 'Only Sixteen'. 'Another Saturday Night' was the title track of Charlie Gillett's Oval compilation of cajun pop and R&B from Louisiana that was released in 1974.

'Two Fine People' was a new track and included on Cat's 1975 *Greatest Hits* compilation album as a marketing tool, I suppose. This rather irritating ploy became more and more common. *Record Mirror*: *"Typical Cat Stevens — jerky rhythms and funny phrasing. The arrangement is attractive and there are ladies' voices in there doing nice things, but the tune isn't one of Cat's best."* The album reached No. 2, but 'Two Fine People' was a total flop. It was a three year gap before Cat's next chart placing – his last of the 1970s. '(Remember The Days Of) The Old School Yard' staggered to No. 44 in the 1977 Summer of Punk.

During all this time Cat Stevens continued to sell albums, but none did as well as *Teaser And The Firecat*. Perhaps it was a case of diminishing returns or did the general record buyer only "need" one Cat Stevens album?

Rod Stewart

I have had to really scrape the barrel to find a Rod Stewart flop. After 'Maggie May' in 1971, Stewart's chart success had been pretty consistent. In the 1970s Rod had five British chart-toppers, along with eight Top Ten hits, as well as four hits with The Faces. However, in 1979 the title track of *Blondes Have More Fun* was finally released as as single. Its parent album had been released in late 1978 and had reached No.3. The album included Rod's chart-topper 'Do Ya Think I'm Sexy' and 'Ain't Love A Bitch'. Fans clearly felt that extracting a third single from a best-selling album was a step too far and the single stalled outside the Top Fifty.

The Who

The Who's singles history was complicated by the band leaving the Brunswick label and recording for Reaction. Brunswick kept releasing old material to try and undermine the band's new releases. So, after three classic Top Ten hits on Brunswick – 'I Can't Explain', 'Anyway, Anyhow, Anywhere' and 'My Generation', the band signed to Reaction and immediately had a fourth Top Ten hit with 'Substitute'. Two weeks later, 'A Legal Matter' on Brunswick entered the charts and peaked at No. 32. In the autumn of 1966 'I'm A Boy' was released on Reaction and soared to No. 2; Brunswick, meanwhile released 'The Kids Are Alright' and it peaked at No. 41, dropped out of the charts and then reappeared reaching No. 48. *Record Mirror*'s singles reviewer was dismissive: *"Couple of LP tracks on Who's old label. But it should sell, this teen-slanted top deck. Good and full vocal effects with tough-sounding guitar behind."*

In 1967 The Who then signed to Track Records, a new label set up by their managers, Kit Lambert and Chris Stamp. The first release on the label was 'Purple Haze' by The Jimi Hendrix Experience, closely followed by The Who's own 'Pictures Of Lily'. Track went on to be one of the most successful smaller labels.

One flop that is worth discussing was released by The Who in 1967 in order to support The Rolling Stones. It was a cover of 'The Last Time' and 'Under My Thumb'. An advertisement in the music press stated, *"The Who consider Mick Jagger and Keith Richards have been treated as scapegoats for the drug problem and as a protest against the savage sentence imposed on them at Chichester yesterday, The Who are issuing today the first of a series of Jagger/Richards songs to keep their work before the public until they are again free to record themselves."* The single had been recorded quickly and bass player John Entwistle was unavailable for the recording session so Pete Townshend over-dubbed the bass part. *NME: "This isn't intended* as The Who's follow-up to 'Pictures Of Lily', but a tribute to the composers of the two titles, Mick Jagger and Keith Richard. Because of the rushed nature of the recording, the group hasn't attempted its own individual conception, but has relied mainly on the original Stones' stylings. This will doubtless prove a handicap chart-wise, but the disc generates plenty of excitement, and one fully appreciates The Who's gesture." It reached No. 44.

Three years later, 'Summertime Blues' fared a little better. The single was extracted from their *Live At Leeds* album. *Record Mirror*: "*it should still make single chart progress. It's a very unusual reading of the Eddie Cochran oldie, with strident guitar beatings and off-beat vocal interjections. Typical tough Who.*" This single reached No. 38.

The Who previewed 'Long Live Rock' on *The Old Grey Whistle Test* in 1973 and Bob Harris announced that the song would be on the band's next double album. This did not happen, but Billy Fury, as 'Stormy Tempest', performed the song in the film, *That'll Be The Day*, with a backing group including Keith Moon. The song was written specifically about a gig at London's Rainbow Theatre, but the melody – by Pete Townshend's standards – is a little dull to my ears. Townshend sings the first verse, while Daltrey takes the second one. The track was first available on the 1974 *Odds And Sods* album, but not released as a single until 1979, reaching No. 48.

THE YARDBIRDS

The Yardbirds released a string of memorable singles in the mid-1960s, no less than three of them written by Graham Gouldman: 'For Your Love', 'Heart Full Of Soul' and 'Evil Hearted You'. 'For Your Love' made good use of harpsichord and bongos. After Clapton's departure, Jeff Beck's extraordinary guitar was central to 'Heart Full Of Soul', 'Evil Hearted You' and 'Over Under Sideways Down'. After five Top Ten singles, The Yardbirds' final chart entry, 'Happenings 10 Years Time Ago' was a flop, going no higher than No. 43. *NME*: "*It has a pronounced Eastern flavour, a stormy rhythm, some really startling reverberating guitar and some of the weirdest sounds on disc. It's hypnotic, wild and different.*" Brian Hogg wrote in *Bam Balam*: " *'Happenings 10 Years Time Ago' may always be 2 years ahead of its time. A driving riff, a middle organised for the bizarre and a deliberate studio excellence."* A live performance on Germany's *Beat Club* programme is worth checking out with Jimmy Page highly effective on guitar. Alan Clayson, as usual, is helpful: *"the psychedelic single 'Happenings Ten Years Time Ago', which some consider an aural nightmare, while others share Tom Hibbert's view that it was 'the greatest 45 ever released'. It sold well in the States but its comparative failure at home precipitated the Yardbirds' most depressing strategy when, at Page's suggestion, they enlisted the services of Mickie Most."*

'Little Games' was reviewed in *NME*: *"Gee Whiz what a shattering beat from The Yardbirds! A heavy-handed walloping drive all the way – and then coupled with the twangy and sitar effect, creates a completely insidious and nagging wall of sound. Psychedelic it may well be but not of a distasteful mixture. The lyric is simple but absorbing and topical, and the melody is little more than a riff phrase repeated over and over. I found it compulsive and intriguing, and it should do better than The Yardbirds' last one."*

8 – Tales Of The Brothers Gibb

THE BEE GEES ARE DIFFICULT TO WRITE ABOUT without mentioning the fraternal tensions. Several books focus more on this than their wonderful catalogue, but the most recent, by Bob Stanley, happily focusses on the actual music. The sheer length of The Bee Gees' career and its ups and downs are hard to summarise easily. Between 1967 and 2001 they released over fifty singles in the UK with no less than five chart-toppers.

Their first British hit, 'New York Mining Disaster 1941' was released just six months after the 1966 Aberfan tragedy in South Wales which killed 116 children and 28 adults. As a ten-year-old (about the same age as most of the children who died), even I thought that the line about "*somebody's digging underground*" was scary.

The follow-up was 'To Love Somebody'. Barry and Robin wrote this song for Otis Redding as he supposedly asked Barry to write a song for him. Sadly, Redding died in December 1967 before he could record it. Strangely, this song, one of the very best in the Gibb brothers' incredibly rich songbook, only reached No. 41 in Britain, but reached No. 27 in the US. Cover versions abound, from Janis Joplin to The Flying Burrito Brothers, take your pick. In 1969 Nina Simone's version reached No. 5 in the UK. More recently, both Michael Bolton and Jimmy Somerville have had huge hits with the same song. *NME*'s 1967 review said "*Totally different in conception from their Mining Disaster disc. This is an uncomplicated love lyric, featuring a soulful heart-cry of a vocal by the lead singer — and the rest of the boys joining in on the pulsating throbbing chorus.*" As I write this, the song is being used in a commercial for Pandora on British television, sung by Chloe and Halle Bailey.

Penny Valentine in *Disc & Music Echo* elaborated: "*Of course, after 'New York Mining Disaster' I was bound to be a little disappointed by The Bee Gees' follow up record, which bears none of the remarkable hit-you-straight-between-the-eyes distinction and none of the strong story line. But in its way this record is a far more commercial proposition and equally as good. What I particularly like about it is the lead singer's voice. He sounds as though he's carving and cracking his way through the lyrics meaning every little bit ... Like the record very much indeed."*

In *The History Of Rock*, Steve Turner writes: *"Throughout the rest of the decade, they scored regularly with UK Top Ten singles: 'World', 'Words', 'I Gotta Get A Message To You', 'First Of May', 'Don't Forget To Remember', all of them safely within their ballad limitations. The one time they did try and step the rhythm up with 'Jumbo' [they] flopped."* Turner's whole entry for the group is far from fawning, but even the mere mention of those song titles reminds us of the sheer brilliance of the melodies in each one. Most groups would have loved to have had even one song of that quality.

Brother Robin left the group in early 1969 and had a big solo hit with 'Saved By The Bell' which reached No. 2. The follow-up, 'August October' fared less well, reaching only No. 45. Barry and Maurice continued as The Bee Gees and also reached No. 2 in autumn 1969 with 'Don't Forget To Remember'.

In March 1970 'I.O.I.O.' was released and was the group's worst chart placing since they signed to Polydor; it reached an embarrassing No. 49. Maurice is quoted in the sleeve notes to *The Tales Of The Brothers Gibb* boxed set: *"Barry's African jaunt brought this song about, we finished it together in a small studio off Marble Arch. Fun times."* The African style chorus and percussion start the song off, but then mostly disappear during the verses.

Later that year Maurice and Barry released solo singles and both were promoted through front page advertisements in *NME*. Maurice previewed his single, 'Railroad', on *Top of the Pops*; the song was a pleasant but unexceptional piece of Americana. Barry's 'I'll Kiss Your Memory' followed in the country style of 'Don't Forget To Remember Me'. Both singles failed to chart and Maurice and Barry's solo albums were subsequently abandoned.

The three brothers' reunion in late 1970 produced their first two biggest hits in America, 'Lonely Days' and 'How Can You Mend A Broken Heart'. The former was performed on *Top of the Pops* and received plenty of airplay on Radio One, but did not rise above Number 33 in Britain. Bob Stanley: *"an oddly underdeveloped recording, with a gorgeous Maurice piano line allied to some very sloppy handclaps, a lyrically monotonous chorus and a full orchestral flourish that suggested something exciting was just around the corner – though it only occurred around five seconds before the song rapidly faded.*" The far more sophisticated follow-up was 'How Can You Mend A Broken Heart'. *Record Mirror*: "*this should put them back into the charts. It's a sensitive wee song, full of vibrato and harmonies, with a catchy, if remotely corny, chorus line. They get one helluva sound going, full-blooded and simple.*" *NME*: "*a pleasantly melodic number, soothing and relaxing. So far as its chart potential is concerned, this could be a drawback, in that it lacks punch ... and [is] perhaps even a trifle dated.*" Unfortunately, this was the first actual Bee Gees flop since they arrived in Britain and signed to Polydor. The Bee Gees gained their first American No.1 with this single.

Some of The Bee Gees' best records, including 'Broken Heart', are a mix of Barry's confident, almost mid-Atlantic vocals with Robin's quavering tones. Quite often, as on 'I Gotta Get A Message To You' and 'My World' for example, the first verse is sung by Robin and then Barry tackles the second. Just compare the different way that the two brothers sing on 'My World': "*Don't shed a tear for me, it's not your style.*" The song is not even one of the group's finest compositions, but was their first Top Twenty British hit in over two years. 'Run To Me', later in 1972, was even bigger in Britain, reaching Number 9. Even Robin admits in the sleeve notes to the box set: "*it still boasts a rather infectious chorus, don't you think?*"

The sleeve notes that accompanied their boxed set are something of a rarity amongst major artists; the brothers actually admit their large number of consecutive flops in the 1970s and comment on them. If only other artists were as brutally honest. The three years between 'Run To Me' and 'Jive Talkin'' saw the group perform in cabaret at such venues as Batley Variety Club and The Golden Garter in Wythenshawe. They even had one album – *A Kick In The Head Is Worth Eight In The Pants* – rejected by the record company.

'Alive' was something of a showcase for Barry and even on the choruses Robin's vocals were indistinguishable. The song has a tremendous melody and chorus. Simon Frith remarked on the song's "*quavering romanticism*" in *Let It Rock*. This was previewed on *Top of the Pops* in November 1972 but failed to chart in Britain. After the success of 'Run To Me', 'Alive' should or could have been a hit. It was easily as good as its predecessor.

The follow-up, 'Saw A New Morning' had a different feel; it was recorded at LA's Record Plant and felt simpler and more contemporary. Interestingly, Robin's voice is once more prominent. *Record Mirror*: *"it has all the usual ingredients of a Bee Gees hit. Fact is that they made these beautiful sounds, and you take the mickey out of the vibrato work and so on at your own risk. This soars upwards and upwards, and it's got a staccato touch and it works like a dream. They have this mixture of urgency and sheer professional, musical style."* *NME*, predictably, were more patronising; *"a classic wide-screen high-budget epic with a cast of thousands, acoustic guitars and what sounds like every string player in the Western Hemisphere behind a Robin Gibb vocal."*

The Bee Gees returned to *Top of the Pops* in July 1973 in order to promote 'Wouldn't I Be Someone'. *Record Mirror*: *"Straight down to business on this one ... that is the Bee Gee vocal trademark, and a backing of utmost simplicity. Gradually the lungs expand, string players emerge from behind the pillars and the volume increases definitely if not defiantly. Meaningful instrumental touch comes then, Robin has a go – it's softly sentimental vibrato-ish pop."* Bob Stanley: *"Its pace is super-sluggish but it was lifted up by Robin's cameo on the second verse — 'Midnight stars are shining on my shoeshine'."* Although this single was a good two minutes shorter than the album version, perhaps it was the long chorus that did not appeal. This song was also recorded at the Record Plant and was released to coincide with the group's *Best Of Volume 2* album. A British tour was subsequently cancelled, presumably because of poor ticket sales, with only a night at the Royal Festival Hall in London saved. This was the group's last British concert appearance for many years.

'Mr Natural' was produced and arranged by Arif Mardin and released in the summer of 1974. Robin sings the first verse and all three brothers join in on the chorus. Barry sings the second verse, following the pattern of previous singles and Robin's hook of *"Well I cry cry cry cry"* is incredibly effective. *Record Mirror*: *"Back to simplicity for The Bee Gees who continually make good singles but do not, alas, continually make the charts. This one is somewhat bare ... that is, voices and lyrics are in no way obscured by massive orchestral touches ... So we're on basics here, and I think the song has grow-on-you appeal."* Bob Stanley stated: *"It had a groove ... The easy shuffle of 'Mr Natural' was definitely blue-eyed soul."*

'Charade' was also released as a single from the *Mr Natural* album. It is is a very smooth and dream-like track, dominated by electric piano and strings. The song is a showcase for Barry Gibb until Robin sings on the chorus. A potentially incongruous clarinet solo seems to blend in well. I cannot remember 'Charade' receiving any airplay on Radio One.

We probably all know the oft-told story behind 'Jive Talkin'' — the sound of the car going over the bridge in Miami, the lack of name on the advance promo copies of the single and so on. Colin Irwin commented in *Melody Maker*: "*It's nice to see them stepping beyond the seemingly never-ending trail of woeful anguished ballads.*" 'Jive Talkin'' reached No. 5 in 1975 and was The Bee Gees' first British hit in three years and their highest chart placing since 1969.

It seems strange to label 'Nights On Broadway' as a flop, but the only entry for the song in the *Guinness Book Of Hit Singles* is a cover version by Candi Staton in 1977. I am puzzled by the lack of British success for The Bee Gees' original, especially as this was the follow-up to the Top Five position of 'Jive Talkin''. The single is unmistakeable Bee Gees with the unique blend of Barry and Robin sharing the verses. The first use of falsetto by the group in the final choruses of 'Night On Broadway' was encouraged by producer Arif Mardin. Robin: "*this is one of my all time favourites ... it enabled (us) to get back to (our) R&B/Soul roots.*" Unfortunately, the song's slow middle eight, although artistically effective and justifiable, did not help on the dance floor. I understand that copies for clubs and radio stations edited this part of the song out. *Record Mirror*: "*The opening is underpinned by good punchy rhythm, which are soon joined by a thin strand of strings and then around the halfway mark, the whole thing gives way to a delightful lyrical passage before reverting to the opening and building to a climax.*"

'Fanny (Be Tender With My Love)' was the third single from the *Main Course* album. In the boxed set liner notes, Maurice says: "*Without a doubt one of the best R & B songs we ever wrote. I love Arif Mardin's production and his understanding from three brothers who love R&B.*" Keyboard player Blue Weaver has said that Mardin's production of Hall & Oates' single 'She's Gone' may have influenced this song with its "*escalating melody and key changes.*" Bob Stanley again: "*The interweaving falsetto and* natural harmonies of 'Fanny' would become The Bee Gees trademark sound for the next few years." It is one of the group's finest songs and performances and deserved to be a British hit. Perhaps the title – inspired by the housekeeper of 461 Ocean Boulevard named Fanny Cummings, was the problem? As British-born, surely the writers knew the problems of using this word? Comparisons were also made with the Player hit, 'Baby Come Back'. But for me, 'Fanny' is in a class of its own.

The next year, 1976 saw the release of 'You Should Be Dancing' and its parent album, *Children Of The World*. 'You Should Be Dancing' equalled the No. 5 peak of 'Jive Talkin'' in the UK, but – almost predictably – the second single taken from the album, 'Love So Right' was less successful and went no higher than No. 41 in Britain. The song was a showcase for Barry's new-found falsetto range and, as he has admitted, was very much in the style of The Delfonics. All three brothers sing the chorus in falsetto harmony and the effect is sublime. *Record Mirror*: "*More high-pitched soul from the brothers Gibb, but this time round a slow smoocher for the other side of the disco appeal. Not as instantly likeable as the last hit, but a grower.*"

It would be nearly a year until The Bee Gees were in the British charts again. A double live album, *Here At Last – The Bee Gees Live*, was released in the summer of 1977. It contained a mixture of their "old stuff" and the newer R & B songs. The live version of 'Edge Of The Universe', a track from *Main Course* released as a single in Britain, did nothing except help promote the album. The autumn of 1977 brought us 'How Deep Is Your Love' which peaked at No. 3. The best was yet to come with 1978's *Saturday Night Fever*. Maurice Gibb died in 2003, followed by his twin Robin in 2012.

Andy Gibb

Andy Gibb deserves a mention, too. We have all heard of, if probably not heard, the siblings of various stars. I think immediately of James Taylor's clan (Kate, Livingstone, Alex), Chris Jagger, Jim Rafferty, David Knopfler to name a few, but Andy Gibb was in a different league. He was the first male solo artist to have three American chart-toppers with his first three single releases. The youngest Gibb brother clearly had an advantage, but also much to prove, by being in the same family of three of the world's finest and most successful songwriters. For me, Andy both looked and sounded like a younger version of his eldest brother, Barry. On The Bee Gees' four disc *Mythology* collection, Andy has his own disc and this is the best place to hear his work. His first British hit was 'I Just Wanna Be You Everything' which reached No. 26 in 1977 but was a chart-topper in the USA.

Nearly a year later, 'Shadow Dancing' was the second American No.1 for the youngest Gibb brother, but only reached No. 42 in the UK, staying in the charts for six weeks. In *NME* Nick Kent stated " *(the) sorely underrated 'Shadow Dancing' cut all the Sylvesters and Chics right out of the running for the numero uno disco 45 of '78 as far as these ears are concerned.*" I agree with him; 'Shadow Dancing' is among the best records released by the whole family with a great melody and mood. The follow-up, 'An Everlasting Love', did far better in the UK, reaching No. 10 and was Andy Gibb's only Top Ten single here.

Andy's next single, 'Why', sounds like a typical late 1970s Bee Gees track. Barry's vocals are clearly heard on the refrain and chorus. Andy explained: "*I wrote all the melody and I took it to Barry, pretty devastated with it saying 'I just can't put lyrics to this song', and I was just on the verge of throwing it over my shoulder and going for another one. Barry put lyrics to it and now it's turned out as his favourite song on the album.*" Unfortunately 'Why' was a flop in the UK. Andy's final hit, '(Our Love) Don't Throw It Away' peaked at No. 32 and was another fine record. The Bee Gees originally recorded the track in 1977 during their *Saturday Night Fever* sessions but it was not released until 1979 when it appeared on a greatest hits compilation album. Andy released a different version after elder brother Barry had reworked the song, adding a middle eight that was not on the group's original. The song became more poignant after Andy's premature death in 1988 and his surviving elder brothers performed the song as a tribute to him on tour.

9- Session Stars

BLUE MINK

From late 1969 to the mid-1970s, Blue Mink seemed to be omnipresent on British television. They were the cream of British session musicians: Roger Coulam on keyboards, Herbie Flowers on bass, Alan Parker on guitar and Barry Morgan on drums. Featured singers were Roger Cook (who had been half of David And Jonathan — 'Lovers Of The World Unite' — and wrote hits for various acts, usually with Roger Greenaway) and Madeline Bell who had been one of Dusty Springfield's backing singers, as well as a solo act. Many of the musicians were also in CCS (see below).

After three hits on Philips: 'Melting Pot' (No. 3), 'Good Morning Freedom' (No. 10) and 'Our World' (No. 17) which suggested diminishing returns, the fourth single 'Time For Winning' did not even trouble the charts. The song was used in the film *The Raging Moon* which starred Malcolm McDowell and Nanette Newman playing a disabled couple. I cannot remember ever hearing the song or seeing the film.

A move to EMI's Regal Zonophone label brought Blue Mink back into the Top Ten with 'The Banner Man' reaching No. 3. This brass band backed march-along was very popular. There was discussion recently at a book festival I attended of Blue Mink's influence on Abba. The Swedish quartet's early recording, 'People Need Love', was cited. Apparently Benny listened to Blue Mink and admired the interaction of the male and female lead vocals and the songs' themes of racial and neighbourly harmony.

'Sunday' was the follow-up to 'The Banner Man'. *NME*: "*it makes an adequate follow up to 'Banner Man' in that it has the same jaunty approach and carefree feel. Maddy Bell and Roger Cook indulge in their usual vocal exchange bit and the melody is catchy and whistleable.*" It was the first of three consecutive flops, the others being 'Count Me In' and 'Wacky Wacky Wacky'.

In *Disc & Music Echo*, David Hughes reviewed 'Count Me In' and expressed his frustration with Blue Mink. "*Whenever I hate one of their songs (viz. 'Banner Man'), it jumps into the Top Five and when I like one ('Sunday') it zonks with virtually not a play. ('Count Me In' is) ... basically ... a 'pinch' of the old Cascades hit 'Rhythm Of The Rain', but without the original sparkle ... overall it's pretty dull and boring. Seems to have the 'power to the people' message saying that we could do better than you at sorting out the world's problems. They could also do a lot better at putting their message across. Another miss, lady and gents, I'm afraid.*" NME: "*Very strange indeed. Their songs have often hit me as unappealing, but still commercial numbers. This is a busy mid-tempo socially-conscious composition that could be liked by lots of people.*"

'Count Me In' received a completely different reaction in *Record Mirror*: "*This ... although written by Jeff Banks and Herbie Flowers, is considerably different from any of their previous singles. I find both the performance and material completely absorbing. It's a social comment lyric with vocals again shared between Madeline Bell and Roger Cook. A beat ballad building to a pulsating climax with walloping drums punctuating every phrase of the chorus. My only criticism is of the extremely slow passage in the middle which, although adding colour and atmosphere, does tend to detract from commerciality. All the same, I give it a better-than-average chance.*"

'Wacky Wacky Wacky' was written by Herbie Flowers, along with Roger Cook and Roger Greenaway. The song is a plodding novelty track with Flowers on tuba. There are nonsense words and a ghastly refrain of "*golly, golly, golly I feel so melancholy.*" One wonders why such a poor quality track was released.

The group returned to the charts in late 1972 with 'Stay With Me' which reached No. 11. In the first half of 1973 Blue Mink had chart success with 'By The Devil (I Was Tempted)' peaking at No. 26 and 'Randy' squeezing just into the Top Ten at No. 9. This was the end of Blue Mink's chart career.

More flops followed. 'Quackers' was described in *Record Mirror* as "*curious quacking noise ... over a basic rhythmic riff ... organ sounds, guitar, staccato drum beat a shuddering sort of tempo.*" Michael Bjorn described the song in *Shindig* as: "*(an) admittedly strange single*" while Roger Cook described it as: "*my unfavourite track. We were probably very high at the time.*"

'Get Up' had funky piano and guitar, but doesn't really go anywhere. *NME* commented: "*as always, a good tight sound.*" The chorus is simple, even banal with its count down of "*7-6-5-4-3-2-1.*" 'Another "Without You" Day' impressed *Record Mirror*'s reviewer: "*Hurray ... after the recent departures from their usual style, Blue Mink have come up with a goodie. Very singalong melody line, nice Madeleine Bell vocals, this record should re-establish Blue Mink in the charts.*"

In an interview with *Record Collector* an octogenarian Madeline Bell sounded a little bitter about the end of Blue Mink in 1974: "*We were being ripped off and we'd had enough. Plus, because we did the station idents for Capital Radio, the BBC stopped playing our music. We'd had four-and-a-half years and weren't having hits because we weren't getting played on radio.*" Actually, by 1974 the "session style" of British pop was out of date and groups like Blue Mink, Brotherhood Of Man and White Plains were just no longer fashionable. 'Melting Pot' and 'Good Morning Freedom' were quite unusual and appealing at the turn of the 1960s; subsequent singles – apart from, arguably, 'The Banner Man', just did not have the same appeal. Sometimes, singles were flops for good reason.

BROTHERHOOD OF MAN

Brotherhood Of Man have existed in some shape or form since 1969. Throughout this time producer and composer Tony Hiller has been at the centre of things. The original Brotherhood Of Man line-up were signed to Deram and hit the charts twice in 1970 with 'United We Stand' and 'Where Are You Going To My Love'. The original line-up included session singer-king, Tony Burrows, Roger Greenaway (both also in White Plains at the beginning — it gets confusing!), sisters Sue and Sunny (Yvonne and Heather Wheatman) and John Goodison. 'United We Stand' became something of a gay liberation anthem in the US.

Follow-ups to these two hits were unable to replicate their success. These include 'This Boy' which was reviewed in *NME*: "*A very sombre and moody offering from the Brotherhood, in contrast to its previous singles ... treated as a dramatic beat-ballad with swirling strings and rumbling tympani, it again features that ear-catching vocal blend for which this group is renowned. There's also *a tuneful and hummable hook chorus in which you can easily join."*

The follow-up, 'Reach Out Your Hand' fools most people when they first hear it. *NME* loved it: *"It's an up-beat swinger with a blockbusting rhythm emphasised by tambourine and conga drum. The impassioned male soloist is egged on by beseeching close-harmony support ... and the whole routine exudes a mid-American feel — somewhere between Detroit and Philadelphia. A disc that's guaranteed to go a bomb in the discos."* As did *Record Mirror*: *"Fast-shuffling rhythm and a change of style and approach. Lead voice almost does a Tamla thing seems to me. The basic Tony Hiller chorus certainly hits the target and it's all fairly ambitious ... Should do well."* The Tamla reference was spot on because a few years later 'Reach Out Your Hand' became a Northern soul favourite. A lot of Northern soul records are in a similar style to Tamla Motown, but were on smaller American record labels and generally less successful. The track appears on the *Decca Originals* compilation CD *The Northern Soul Scene* and is described as *"this fairly authentic modern soul number. Don't let the artist put you off — this is very good, and, if heard 'blind' you wouldn't guess the artist in a million years."*

'You And I' followed 'Reach Out Your Hand' — *Record Mirror*: *"Gospel-tinged with duet between girl and boy, and the usual fulsome chorus bit. It's a pretty powerful and commercial song, taken all round, with some tight drumming pushing and some whimsy strings helping."* *NME* agreed: *"this rhythmic ballad ... could re-establish the outfit in the Charts."* Another flop.

I remember hearing 'California Sunday Morning' on Radio One. *Record Mirror*: *"Girl-inspired vocal line-up on a gentle, wispy, wistful little song. Melodically, it seems strong enough for the charts, even if short on pow-type impact."* *NME* was more positive: *"a very pretty song. It's hauntingly melodic, gently lilting and set to one of those lush scores in which arranger Keith Mansfield specialises. The vocal blend is unimpeachable — rich golden pungent. And whilst the Brotherhood has been lacking in chart honours lately, this return to their original slow and potent style could well provide them with a hit. Because the material is clinging and hummable and the performance is of a very high standard indeed."*

'Say A Prayer' was released next. *NME* were unimpressed: *"It's been a long time since the Brotherhood has taken over the charts and I don't think this will change things ... This one ... starts off just plain mediocre then grows to epic proportions with an over-dose of strings making the final fatal blow."*

There was a different line-up of Brotherhood Of Man in 1974 on the Dawn label. 'When Love Catches up With You' was reviewed in *Record Mirror*: *"girl lead, a slow-building intro which eventually leads into a well-constructed, string-backed, chorus and hook. Could be, though, that it takes too long to get into chart-worthy form."*

Two years later, the new line-up represented the UK in Eurovision. In the 1970s Eurovision was still taken quite seriously. This was before the likes of Terry Wogan and Graham Norton started adding their facetious commentary and certainly before the contest became merely an exercise in camp. Abba's victory in 1974 had seen a flood of groups entering the contest and Brotherhood Of Man's two female, two male line-up was seen as ideal. 'Save Your Kisses For Me' not only won the contest, but also reached No.1 in the UK, selling a million copies. This was the UK's first Eurovision winner since Lulu in 1969 and the first UK Eurovision entry to reach the US Top Forty.

The follow-up, 'My Sweet Rosalie' just scraped into the Top Thirty and 'Oh Boy (The Mood I'm In)', for once written by Tony Romeo and not the usual team, saw the group return to the Top Ten, followed by two more chart-toppers, namely 'Angelo' and 'Figaro', both clearly influenced by Abba's 'Fernando'.

Amazingly, stuck between these two chart-toppers was a complete flop, 'Highwayman', was released in October 1977. Written as usual by the team of Hiller, Sheridan and Lee, this was the group's most blatant Abba copy. The two females even stood together and turned by 90 degrees in 'Mamma Mia' — video style. A full page advertisement in *Record Mirror* did not help and was undermined by a sneering review in the same publication: *"Another set of individuals keeping to the same standards. You know what to expect so I won't slag it off."* The public were unimpressed, even by a *Top of the Pops* appearance. Despite the group returning to No. 1 with 'Figaro', after this we see the predictable diminishing returns. There was something unlikeable about this Brotherhood Of Man line-up. Even for a so-called Eurovision group, they lacked the charm of their Swedish influencers. Sometimes their pure unoriginality gave them the nickname of "Brotherhood Of Abba" (sic).

The next single, 'Middle Of The Night', was neither memorable nor attractive; even an appearance on *Top of the Pops* could not push the single any higher than No. 41. *Record Mirror*: *"Probably sounds great* when you're sleeping but it's positively dreadful when you're awake." The song was included on the group's *Twenty Greatest* album, a joint release by their label, Pye and K-Tel which reached No. 6.

The same writing team of Hiller, Sheridan and Lee wrote 'Goodbye Goodbye'. This was probably not the best title for a group on a downward spiral. The single, again, was previewed on *Top of the Pops* in January 1979, but by then there was just so much excellent pop music being released by the likes of Abba, Bee Gees and Blondie that Brotherhood Of Man did not stand a chance.

CCS

CCS (short for Collective Consciousness Society) brought together the contrasting voices of Alexis Korner and Peter Thorup with the orchestrations of John Cameron and a huge bunch of top session musicians, some of whom were also in Blue Mink. CCS were far too large to be able to tour, but they did play the Royal Albert Hall on one occasion. They provided the version of 'Whole Lotta Love' which was used as the theme tune to *Top of the Pops* for several years. Two Top Ten singles followed; 'Walkin'' and 'Tap Turns On The Water'. The next release, 'Brother', reached No. 25 and was also used as a theme tune, this time for Tom Browne's *Solid Gold Sixty* which briefly replaced *Pick of the Pops* on Radio One. 'The Band Played Boogie' was CCS's final chart entry, reaching only No. 36. *Record Mirror*: "*The piano to the fore and those incisive bursts of brass, and lots of left hand down on the keyboard, and dated vocal line and a bit more nostalgia.*"

'Boom Boom' was originally performed by John Lee Hooker and covered by many British rhythm and blues groups. *NME* liked CCS's version: "*A razzle dazzler of a disc ... there's a sizzling John Cameron orchestral scoring ... the scorching beat is in the hands of no less than four drummers ... it's an exciting, tingling, electrifying sound.*"

'Sixteen Tons' was also reviewed in *NME*: "*Alexis Korner and Peter Thorup put together a soulful version of the oldie. The big brass and punchy beat decorate the slick Mickie Most production. After a couple of misses, I think this one will get them back in the chart.*" *Record Mirror*'s reviewer agreed: "*Gradually the sound builds up, with different orchestral sections moving in, and it's all over some persistent percussion. The brass bites, the atmosphere heightens. Sounds like a hit to me."*

Korner and Thorup continued to work together and teamed up with former members of King Crimson as Snape to record the album, *Accidentally Born In New Orleans*.

WHITE PLAINS

White Plains were also signed to Deram and included former members of The Flowerpot Men. Their first releases featured Tony Burrows and Roger Greenaway (who were also, confusingly in the first Brotherhood Of Man line-up). The quintet had hits with 'My Baby Loves Lovin'' and 'I've Got You On My Mind' in early 1970. Pete Nelson, another ex-Flowerpot Man, became the lead singer.

'Lovin' You Baby' — *NME*: *"Third single, another Cook-Greenaway composition and that should be sufficient to give Plains a head start in their quest for a chart hat trick ... up-beat, finger-popping instantly commercial teenybopper material. Delicious counter-harmonies weave around Peter Nelson's lead vocal. And the tune? Perhaps not so immediately catchy as the last two but very definitely a song to register fairly quickly. And another hit!"* Record Mirror (sort of) agreed: *"Usual formula ... That means orchestral build-up ... and then a jolly old chorus song which doesn't have much to say for itself but is performed with big-rising harmonies and with a strangest, sharp, single-minded commercial sound. Actually I liked it a lot and it'll do well."*

After the flop of 'Lovin' You Baby', White Plains returned with their biggest hit ever, 'Julie Do Ya Love Me'. This had been a big American hit for Bobby Sherman and was overtaken on its release in the UK by White Plains' version. Sherman's version peaked at No. 28 in the UK charts, while White Plains' rival rendition reached twenty places higher at No. 8.

'Every Little Move She Makes' was reviewed in *NME*: *"It's a bright happy-go-lucky item with a catchy hook chorus. There's a bustling orchestral backing with dancing strings and shrill woodwind prominent, plus tambourines accentuating the irresistible rhythm. Add to this some colourful harmonic exchanges by the boys and you've got the makings of a hit."* The reviewer hinted at the possibility that the record is a *"typical, even predictable, disc by White Plains"* which has always been a challenge for such singles acts. It is one of the group's better singles with a strong melody and big production.

The sublime 'When You Are A King' saw White Plains return to the Top Twenty. Written by John and Roger Hill, this single had an unusual use of a concertina in its instrumentation. It reached No. 13. The (pre-disco) Nolans, no less, recorded this song and released it as a single in 1976. Significantly, the producer was songwriter Roger Greenaway who had been involved with White Plains in their early days. It should have been a hit. There is a great clip of the Nolans performing the song on a *Morecambe and Wise Christmas Show*.

'Gonna Miss Her Mississippi' was reviewed in *NME*: "*This is a beat ballad — fairly slow, but sung with verve and spirit, and benefiting from a solid wallop beat and swirling orchestral scoring.. it's certainly an impeccably-produced and well-performed mainstream pop routine.*" I remember liking this single when it was released and being surprised at its failure to get in the charts.

'I Can't Stop' — *NME*: "*A clean, melodic mid-tempo number which will do well if it gets enough exposure. The only thing it really lacks is a little added drive behind the chorus, otherwise, they're in there.*" This is a gentle song with a repeated hook: "*I can't stop thinking about you, I won't try living without you.*"

1972's 'Dad You Saved The World' was also written by John and Roger Hill, but is miles away from the quality of 'When You Are A King'. It is as maudlin as the title suggests and probably White Plains' weakest single. We are very much in the territory of 'The Living Years'. Yes, it is that bad.

White Plains returned to the charts in 1973 with 'Step Into A Dream' which reached No. 21. This had been used as a television advertisement for Butlins with the title 'Butlinland'. Written by Roger Cook and Roger Greenaway, the words were changed and re-recorded. Cook and Greenaway had, of course, had done the same with 'I'd Like To Teach The World To Sing'.

A few years later, some members of White Plains were seen in another session group, First Class, who had a massive hit with 'Beach Baby'. Once a session singer, always a session singer.

10- The Regions

Dave Berry

Dave Berry was a minor phenomenon. In the film, *Don't Look Back*, Alan Price performs a parody of Berry's 'Little Things' in front of Bob Dylan and his entourage. Dylan, of course, does not know who Price is ridiculing. Price imitates the way that Dave Berry held his microphone and then goes over to the dressing room piano and sings and plays a bluesy performance of 'Little Things'. Price's female companion supplies the interspersed notes from the recorded version.

'This Strange Effect' was written by Ray Davies who said: *"I wrote (This Strange Effect) in Melbourne ... But I had it in mind for Dave Berry. Such a great look. And he had a really good stage presence. I wrote that with him in mind."* This was Davies' first major songwriting success outside The Kinks. The single was a huge hit in Holland and Belgium and led to a lengthy career for Berry in Europe, but only reached No. 35 in the UK. Berry later covered Pete Dello's gentle 'Do I Still Figure In Your Life' but, like the original by Dello's group, Honeybus, it failed to trouble the charts. The song is a lost classic and deserves reviving. Among the umpteen covers, Joe Cocker's rendition is probably the most famous.

Eric Burdon And The Animals

Through all their trials, tribulations, and changes of line-up and record label, The Animals (later Eric Burdon And The Animals) were incredibly consistent makers of hit singles. Chart-topper 'House Of The Rising Sun' – like 'Layla', 'Albatross' and 'All Right Now' – returned to the charts more than once as each new generation of singles buyers added it to their collections. Despite the departure of Alan Price, The Animals had a run of six Top Ten hits on Columbia, followed by three Top Twenty hits on Decca. The last of these – 'Help

Me Girl' – was the first to be billed as Eric Burdon And The Animals.

'When I Was Young' was Eric Burdon and The Animals' first single on MGM. It was a Top Twenty hit in the USA, but reached only No. 45 in Britain. Cat Stevens, no less, reviewed it in *Disc & Music Echo*; "*A lovely Eastern sort of sound from Eric ... he's talking about his youth and he sounds as if he really means what he's saying. It's a bit of disappointment to me really – the song seems to be showing off the group more than letting us hear Eric. The middle eight is good – should have been longer.*" *Shindig* was keener: "*the stunning, autobiographical 'When I Was Young'. A self-penned tale of misspent youth ... with raga guitar from (Vic) Briggs and eerie violin from (John) Weider, it radiated tension but was sung by Burdon with an air of beatific calm.*"

A move to the USA was the start of Mr Burdon's infatuation with that country, especially the West Coast. Songs like 'San Franciscan Nights' and 'Gratefully Dead' have not worn as well as the original band's recordings for Mickie Most or their next phase on Decca. *Shindig* commented upon: "*Eric Burdon's earnestness with which he embraced the West Coast's psychedelic culture.*" Photographs of Burdon at the Monterey Pop Festival show the short and stocky Geordie in a kaftan. He wore a different kaftan for the 1968 Animals reunion at Newcastle City Hall, still looking fairly ridiculous.

Shindig also commented on 'Sky Pilot': "*[it is] scathing ... a seven-minute tour de force aimed at the pep-talking army padres who blessed bombs and sent young men to die. It had flanged drums, acid rock guitar, strings and a terrifying montage of sound effects — even bagpipes.*" 'Sky Pilot' lasted nearly seven and a half minutes and was split over two sides of a single. Animals biographer, Sean Egan, called the song: "*a brave and ambitious anti-war protest*". Again, and understandably, the single went Top Twenty in the USA but reached only No. 40 in the UK.

Another single, 'Monterey', was in the same vein as 'San Francisco Nights' and was explicitly about the 1967 pop festival, captured on film by D.E. Pennebaker in *Monterey Pop*. *NME*: "*an up-beat number with sizzling brass, twangs and Eric at his most vital ... it's fascinating but singularly lacking in melody.*" I find Burdon's festival tale rather plodding and workmanlike with such lines as: "*the people came and listened*". Burdon lists some of the festival's artists with little music samples including Ravi Shankar (sitar) and Hugh Maskela (trumpet). At the end of the song he quotes from The Byrds' song, 'Renaissance Fair': "*I think that maybe I'm dreaming.*" Both The Byrds' track and Joni Mitchell's Woodstock anthem feel understated and haunting while Burdon's song is heavy-handed and lacks depth. Interestingly, Sean Egan felt the opposite: "'*Monterey*' ... *in its celebratory enthusiasm, captures the giddy atmosphere of the festival more successfully than Joni Mitchell's calm, considered take on a later, more famous hippy festival, Woodstock.*"

Worse was to come. A succession of unnecessary cover versions were released as singles. *NME* hailed Burdon's cover of 'River Deep Mountain High' with the headline "*Dynamic Eric tops Ike and Tina's original*", going onto say: "*completely different from the original version, though hard as it may seem to believe, with even more excitement ... really storms along with Eric giving one of his most dynamic performances to date.*" I beg to differ and feel that this cover adds nothing to the Phil Spector-produced classic and sounds the sort of thing that Tom Jones would have tackled on his television series.

The next single, 'Ring Of Fire', co-written by June Carter, wife of Johnny Cash, a strange song choice for even an over-stimulated Eric Burdon to tackle. *NME*: "*The Animals' most commercial single since 'San Francisco Nights'. Eric Burdon sounds more hoarse and throaty than ever before, handles the quieter passages with intensity and sensitivity, supported by sighing organ and rippling guitar. Catchy and hummable as there's also a la-la chorus.*" I remain unconvinced about the single's effectiveness; the military drumming feels incongruous at the start of this acoustic ballad. Burdon's vocals are first overblown, but then become gentler. There is a funky bass part and mass vocals. 'Ring Of Fire' reached No. 35.

SPENCER DAVIS GROUP

After the departure of Stevie Winwood (and his bassist brother Muff) from The Spencer Davis Group in Spring 1967, there was understandably a huge void to fill. Stevie had been the lead singer on all the group's hit singles and most of the album tracks, as well as playing lead guitar, piano and organ. Once Stevie left the group to form Traffic, it was clear that Spencer would be unlikely to replicate the success without his precociously talented colleague. 'Time Seller' was the group's first release with the new line-up and reached No. 30 and was the group's last release on Fontana. This doomy-sounding song was dominated by strings and a complete contrast to the Winwood hits. The group then signed to United Artists and were featured in the film, *Here We Go Round The Mulberry Bush*. The group provide several songs for the soundtrack and are seen playing in a youth club while stars Barry Evans and Sheila White are dancing. New lead singer Eddie Hardin had a fine voice and was an accomplished musician, but something was missing.

I remember buying the new line-up's album *With Their New Face On* in 1974 in Hime And Addison in Manchester for less than a quid. The record has one of the worst front covers of the 1960s, and there are plenty of contenders for that dubious honour. There are seven photographs of the group on the front cover — but none of Eddie Hardin. Considering Hardin is lead singer on most tracks, co-wrote the whole album and is featured throughout on organ and piano, this seems an unwise decision. As well as the dated look to the front cover, the album's back cover has sleeve notes from *Melody Maker*'s Chris Welch, straight out of the Tony Barrow school of prose writing on early Beatles albums.

'Mr Second Class' was the follow-up to 'Time Seller' and reached No. 35. This single is from the post- 'Nowhere Man'/'Well Respected Man' school of social comment. *Record Mirror*: "*Good song idea, distinctive instrumental intro, perhaps a shade too long, then the lyrics are handled in a fiercely aggressive sort of way.*" While *NME*'s headline was: "*Basic Tune Missing From Spencer Disc*," elaborating: "*a straight forward and extremely commercial pop record. The beat's forceful, compelling and exhilarating and the sound generated by the SDG is vibrant, full and urgent. Add to this is an absorbing lyric plus some colourful harmony work embellishing the lead vocal and you're almost there. Almost, but not quite! Because what this disc lacks is a basic tune that will register in the fans' minds. This one stumbling block will prevent it from being an enormous hit, but performance-wise it's amply good enough to do pretty well.*" Spencer Davis himself commented: "*Ray Davies used to invent characters and that's what I was doing with 'Mr Second Class'* ". Unfortunately, the only thing Spencer and Ray shared was a similar surname.

The group's next single, 'After Tea', was previewed on *Top of the*

Pops in March 1968 but did not even chart as David Wells has pointed out: *"the first Spencer Davis Group single not to reach the UK Top Fifty since their 1964 debut disc 'Dimples'."* Andy Morten wrote in *Shindig*: *"(an) admittedly commercial song probably sounded a tad passe ... with its singalong toytown theme and sitar and flute accompaniment."* I agree; it is a standard British psychedelic single, but still far better than its two predecessors. Eddie Hardin had an excellent voice; he was far more than merely a replacement for Steve Winwood.

In the 1970s, Spencer re-formed The Spencer Davis Group bringing back Eddie Hardin, Pete York and Ray Fenwick and recruiting Charlie McCracken on bass. One single, 'Catch You On The Rebop', picked up positive reviews and some airplay but did not chart.

ELECTRIC LIGHT ORCHESTRA/ELO

ELO had originally started as an extension of The Move, allowing Roy Wood and Jeff Lynne to take pop music – in their own words — beyond 'I Am The Walrus'. The first ELO album was a revelation, scraping cellos, plaintive woodwind and unusual vocal effects. Wood and Lynne each had their own songs, but arguably it was the latter who had the upper hand with '10538 Overture', both the album's opener and hit single, along with 'Mr Radio' and 'Queen Of The Hours'. Apart from the sublime 'Whisper In The Night', Roy Wood's songs were more experimental and certainly less commercial. The band had problems trying to reproduce their sound for live concerts and their first tour was delayed. Granada Television managed to capture these early days for their *Set Of Six* programme. The departure of Roy Wood from his own project surprised many people in the summer of 1972, but it seems that manager Don Arden encouraged the split, knowing that two bands were more lucrative than just one.

The band's witty version of 'Roll Over Beethoven' with its juxtaposition of Chuck Berry and Beethoven's Fifth Symphony was released in January 1973. The single peaked at No. 6, three places higher than '10538 Overture'. Even after Roy Wood went off to form Wizzard, the early ELO were often a bizarre-sounding band, far removed from their smooth, vocoder-dominated big hits of the later years. A gig at Brunel University was filmed and we see the band scraping their way through the lengthy tracks from their second album. This is not always easy listening. 'Showdown' was the band's third single and, despite starting like 'I Heard It Through The Grapevine', was actually a fine track. The rockier 'Ma-Ma-Ma-Belle' was the band's first single on Warners and reached No. 22 in 1974. However, its parent album, *On The Third Day*, was the first of three ELO albums to flop in the UK.

ELO's two finest singles were flops in the UK when first released. 'Can't Get It Out Of My Head' was taken from the band's fourth album, *Eldorado*. The record featured a 30-piece orchestra and was a lot smoother than previous releases. *Record Mirror*: "*this is a huge success in the States. It's a downtempo number that's best described as insidious – watch out 'cos it'll creep up on you after a couple of listens. Should do very well.*" The single was the band's first big hit in the USA. Ian Moss nominates 'Can't Get It Out Of My Head' as: "*probably Lynne's finest composition, yearning and gorgeous, in fact quite sublime.*"

ELO were slowly, but noticeably, changing. Jeff Lynne's hair was trimmed and tamed, his beard shaped into a goatee and he started wearing aviator sunglasses. 'Evil Woman' had reached No. 10 at the beginning of 1976 and was the band's first British hit single for nearly two years. Both of the two follow-ups, also from the band's fifth album, *Face The Music*, 'Night Rider' and 'Strange Magic', failed to reach the Top Thirty. *NME* commented on 'Night Rider': "*filtered through the inspiration of The Beatles. Good pop music that leaves me cold and in need of attention.*" *Record Mirror*, predictably, were kinder: "*Doesn't grab you on first hearing, but by the third spin, it's very catchy. Lots of strings, obviously, but some good changes of tempo and pace. Solid sound that should do very well.*"

Of 'Strange Magic' *Record Mirror* opined: "*Following the non-appearance in the charts of 'Night Rider', here's another one from the* Face The Music *album. Very similar in sound, especially the string arrangements and looks set to follow the way of its predecessor.*" Actually, 'Strange Magic' was nothing like 'Night Rider'. It was a slower, more sombre and subtle song which Jeff Lynne revived in his most recent touring version of ELO. It peaked at No. 38.

From 'Livin' Thing' onwards, ELO would have non-stop hit

singles and albums in the UK until 1983. 'Can't Get It Out Of My Head' and 'Strange Magic' were reissued, along with 'Evil Woman' and 'Ma-Ma-Ma-Belle' on the *ELO* (EP) just before Christmas 1978 but only reached No. 38. ELO's rise under Jeff Lynne's leadership was concurrent with the decline of Roy Wood's fortunes.

Bryan Ferry

Roxy Music's lead singer, Bryan Ferry, began his solo career in 1973 with the *These Foolish Things* album and its extracted single, 'A Hard Rain's Gonna Fall'. Both went Top Ten and Ferry's next two singles, covers of 'The In Crowd' and 'Smoke Gets In Your Eyes', both went Top Twenty.

'You Go To My Head' was a flop, peaking at No. 33. The song was written by J. Fred Coots and Haven Gllespie in 1938 and was subsequently covered by many of the big names who sang the Great American Songbook. Perhaps Ferry was trying to recreate the positive reaction when he covered 'These Foolish Things' and 'Smoke Gets In Your Eyes', but clearly his fans were not that interested. *Record Mirror* was positive: "*Bryan's interpretations of old songs generally have little to do with what has gone before. I adore this... The vocal's superb and the arrangement even better ... and some heavenly brass coming in later..*"

Ferry bounced back in 1976 with two Top Ten hits, 'Let's Stick Together' and *Extended Play* E.P. whose lead track was 'Price Of Love'. The next year saw two more Top Twenty singles, now on the Polydor label, the self-penned 'This Is Tomorrow' and 'Tokyo Joe'. Ferry's 1978 cover of Lou Reed's Velvet Underground song, 'What Goes On', reached an embarrassing No. 67. The follow-up, 'Sign Of The Times', did a little better, reaching No. 37. Roxy Music's successful reunion in 1979 must have been a relief to both Ferry and his fans.

Wayne Fontana

Wayne left The Mindbenders in 1965 and carried on as a solo act. The group's final single together, 'She Needs Love' was written by Clint Ballard Jr. *Record Mirror*: "*a powerhouse instrumental opening. Then it settles into a swing-along beat-ballad, with Wayne veering towards the falsetto in this big-ranged melody. A good simple sound behind him.. Song is melodically tricky, building well mid-way. Should be a goodly hit.*" The single peaked at No. 32.

Wayne's chart career continued to be something of a yo-yo effect. His first release, 'It Was Easier To Hurt Her', peaked at No. 36. *Record Mirror*: "*Originally a hit for Garnett Mimms ... Great arrangement from Les Reed with percussion, strings and girlie choir. Surprisingly well sung.*" The follow-up, 'Come On Home', did better, reaching the Top Twenty. Despite a big orchestra, again arranged by Les Reed, the very dramatic 'Goodbye Bluebird' was a flop, peaking at No. 49. A cover of a Graham Gouldman song, 'Pamela Pamela' brought Wayne to just outside the Top Ten, peaking at No. 11. This was his final chart entry.

'Storybook Children' was reviewed in *Record Mirror*: "*this is a rather lovely song, with the verse coming first, then exploding into a very commercial chorus ballad. Wayne sings well over a lavish-sounding backing. Still not his actual best, but good enough I'm sure to put him back in the chart.*"

Penny Valentine reviewed '24 Sycamore' in *Disc & Music Echo*: "*Now this is an odd record. It's very well sung, in fact the best Wayne's done, with much control and handling of difficult phrasing. It is a pretty tune. It has an adequate, if not exactly inspired, arrangement and I wouldn't be at all surprised to see it go into the chart.*" '24 Sycamore' was not a hit for Wayne, but Gene Pitney covered the song in 1973 when it reached No. 34, his penultimate British solo hit.

1968's 'Never An Everyday Thing' was a big orchestral pop single with former Manfred, Mike Vickers, as the musical director. A couple of years later, I remember a version by Eli Bonaparte being regularly played on Radio One. Neither version was a hit.

GEORDIE

Geordie featured the voice of Brian Johnson, whose singing later dominated AC/DC for so many years. 1973 was Geordie's peak and brought them two Top Twenty hits; 'All Because Of You' and 'Can You Do It' and a headlining concert at London's Rainbow Theatre. Successful follow-ups were problematic. 'Electric Lady' reached No. 32 and that was pretty much it. *Disc* reviewed the single: "*This one whirs* and turns and twists and rebels ... it's got that old-style Geordie crash bang, with a shortage of musical finesse. What gets this band going is a sheer determination not to let anyone go to sleep while they're on. Their old fashioned approach is deliberate and almost ponderous, but the lads, good luck to 'em, get material which is so much to the point that it clicks right away." *NME*'s reviewer's analysis went deeper: "If Geordie genuinely mean to ditch the 'poor man's Slade' tag they'd better recall this single instantly ... Despite all that, and even forgiving the simple-minded lyric, it is not without appeal. A robust guitar riff and square-bashing drum-work lubricate the way for unswerving verse/chorus/verse melody line that's 60 per cent Slade and 10 per cent Sweet. They risk all on a mildly intoxicating tag."

'Black Cat Woman' followed and was something else. There are screeching vocals from Brian Johnson: "*Get back, Black Cat!*" along with a great riff and interesting chords. The song is somewhat spoiled by an awful interlude, similar to the ones performed by Steve Priest in some of Sweet's singles. The follow-up 'She's A Teaser' has uninspired lyrics: "*If you want me, come and get me, come and get me, if you want me.*" One review said: "*Keith Richards chords, Geno Washington brass, usually silly vocals, and a Gary Glitter chorus of 'Come on, come on's.*"

'Ride On Baby' was released in November 1974. *Record Mirror*: "*It's been quite a time since Geordie graced the British charts, but they've obviously decided to have a good bash with this release. Very commercial, hard drumming beating the whole thing into shape, similar beat to some of the Glitter Band/Hello releases, and they've not done badly. Could be a bit too frantic.*"

Johnson's phenomenal success as lead singer of AC/DC took him from Geordieland to decades of international touring and millions of record sales. I like the guy ... until he starts singing.

The Hollies

Unlike so many of their contemporaries, The Hollies kept going through the challenges of the years after the hits had stopped a-coming, even turning their backs on cabaret and 1960s revival tours. The Hollies' hits started as far back as May 1963 with '(Ain't That) Just Like Me', an unbroken run for over a decade, despite the temporary absence of lead singer Allan Clarke.

The group signed to Polydor in 1971 and recruited Michael

Rikfors to replace Clarke. They reached No. 26 with 'The Baby', their lowest chart placing so far. The follow-up, 'Magic Woman Touch' was reviewed in *NME*: "*There's an electric sitar sound with acoustic guitars against a 2/4 beat. It's considerably more laid back than the pop things which made their reputation. Michael Rikfors has a confident voice, but I don't think this one will hit it for them.*" After the melodrama of 'The Baby', this follow-up is rather ordinary and wasn't a British hit.

The next chapter of The Hollies' long career is a little complicated. 'Long Cool Woman In A Black Dress' – an impressive John Fogerty pastiche, recorded before Clarke's departure – went Top Ten in the USA. EMI issued the single in the UK and it peaked at No. 32. Within a year, Allan Clarke returned to the Hollies and they released more faux Americana with the rather ordinary 'The Day That Curly Billy Shot Down Crazy Sam McGhee' which, despite sounding a little too much like 'Long Cool Woman', reached No. 24.

The group's next single was an exquisite cover of Albert Hammond and Mike Hazlewood's 'The Air That I Breathe'. Once again, The Hollies successfully reinvented themselves with a well chosen song (as they had done with 'He Ain't Heavy' back in 1969). This single reached No. 2 and stayed in the charts for 13 weeks. The problem then, of course, was how to follow such a tremendous artistic and commercial achievement.

'Son Of A Rotten Gambler' had been a hit in the USA for Anne Murray. Drummer Bobby Elliott explained the choice of this song in his informative memoir: "*...we needed a follow-up, Allan's 'Don't Let Me Down' seemed tailor-made, until Chip Taylor, the writer of two of our previous successes, 'The Baby' and 'I Can't Let Go', walked into the studio. He played a song entitled 'Son Of A Rotten Gambler'. Foolishly, egged on by our mentor (producer Ron Richards), we recorded Chip's song and it became our new single, but I don't think Allan was convinced it was the right decision. And he was right. 'Son Of A Rotten Gambler' didn't make the UK charts and managed a few desultory Top 100 places elsewhere.*" Andrew Darlington states: "*more than a passing nod to Don Gibson's 'Sea Of Heartbreak' ... taken at a country-slow pace ... sweetened by tasteful strings, it rises into hallmark Hollies mid-section harmonies*". Steve Millward said: "*A creditable version of Chip Taylor's 'Son Of A Rotten Gambler' condemned them to chart oblivion for six years.*" *NME* disagreed:

"*Song-writer Chip Taylor must writhe in embarrassment every time he hears this synthetic treatment.*"

'I'm Down' was penned in-house by Allan Clarke, Tony Hicks and Terry Sylvester. *Record Mirror*: "*The Hollies have stuck to the same basic rhythm of their previous hit ('The Air That I Breathe'), fairly slow with heavy strings in the background, but there's a few changes of tempo which break it up.*" Bobby Elliott wrote: "*Listening today, I hear a sombre masterpiece.. The ballad was brilliant in its own way*". It must have been hard for the group to follow 'The Air That I Breathe'. 'I'm Down' deserved to be a hit. The chorus is brilliant, displaying the writers' three part harmonies, but I find the middle eight a little plodding and over-earnest. Elliott concludes: "*Maybe those heart-rending songs were a device created by our frontman to try and release the heartache he was experiencing at the time.*"

The follow-up 'Sandy (4th July Asbury Park)' was from the pen of Bruce Springsteen and also from the group's *Another Night* album. Of all The Hollies' many British chart flops, this is the one that should have been a hit. 'Sandy' went top ten in Holland and Germany, but nowhere in the UK. It is certainly more listenable than the Springsteen original to my ears. Interestingly, both 'I'm Down' and 'Sandy' appeared on *Live Hits* which reached No. 4 in the British album charts in 1977. The success of this live album – recorded on a tour of New Zealand — prompted EMI to follow their best selling Shadows and Beach Boys *20 Golden Greats* series with a volume for The Hollies in 1978. Subtitled "20 great sounds that grew out of the North", this compilation reached No. 2 in the British album charts.

Four Hollies singles were issued in 1976, the first was the most interesting, an enthusiastic cover of Emmylou Harris's 'Boulder To Birmingham'. This rather personal song of loss by the American country singer was a highlight of her *Pieces Of the Sky* album. It was also covered by Scott Walker around the same time. The Hollies, inevitably, make it their own, producing almost a gospel feel in the final choruses.

The next single, 'Star', despite the presence of no less than Rod Argent on keyboards, is rather ordinary. 'Daddy Don't Mind' was reviewed in *Record Mirror*: "*A self-composed rocker ... with biting guitar breaks and quasi-harmonised choruses. Excellently produced and arranged with plenty of musical climaxes.*" Darlington adds: "*A kind of steamy, swampy Southern feel, punctuated by Wally Smith's trombone."*

I feel that the group's next single, 'Wiggle That Wotsit', plunged new depths. Why on earth would the Hollies attempt a disco track? *Record Mirror*: *"no way does this sound like anything The Hollies have done before. Funky, pacey – what is the world coming to? Could be a hit."* Darlington sees it as *"a fun dance-craze pastiche."* I disagree. Some British acts tried to go "disco", possibly looking enviously at The Bee Gees' successful reinvention and total mastery of this American genre. As 'Wiggle' demonstrates, these attempts were almost all unsuccessful.

Darlington also comments on 1977's 'Hello Romance', penned by the writers in the group: *"a smooth blending of Hollies-branded harmonies with expansive MOR sweep."* The Hollies' next single was another cover of an American song. This time, it was 'Love Is The Sweetest Amnesty' by Denny Douma which had been recorded by former Byrd, Chris Hillman. Shortened to just 'Amnesty', the group released the record in July 1977. 'Something to Live For' was released in spring 1979. *NME* were unimpressed: *"more of a comedown than a comeback."* Things were not looking good.

The 1980s saw The Hollies return to the singles charts with the 'Holliedaze' medley in 1981. Graham Nash returned for one album in 1983. Thanks to a Miller Lite beer advertisement, 'He Ain't Heavy, He's My Brother' went to the top of the charts in 1988, nearly twenty years since it was first a hit. Lead singer Allan Clarke retired in 2000 and was replaced by former Move frontman, Carl Wayne. Wayne died in 2004 and was replaced by Peter Howarth who is still the group's lead singer.

LIEUTENANT PIGEON

Lieutenant Pigeon were two-hit wonders, contrary to inaccurate generalisations in some recent books. The group kept churning out singles, but there were no more hits after 'Desperate Dan', the follow-up to 'Mouldy Old Dough'. 'Dan' was followed by 'And The Fun Goes On', next were 'Oxford Bags' and 'I'll Take You Home, Kathleen'. The latter was reviewed in *Record Mirror*: *"It's a typically happy instrumental with that pounding piano ... An old traditional air, now reconstructed as a foot-*

tapping base for a good old sing-song." The review is nearly correct; the single starts with a burst of 'The Irish Washerwoman' on tin whistle and then merges into a speeded-up version of 'Kathleen', previously recorded by everyone from Joseph Locke to Elvis Presley, usually at funereal-slow pace. The drumming is unusually effective (less moronic than on the two hits) and the tin whistle reappears between each verse. The group previewed the single on The Bay City Rollers' *Shang-A-Lang* television show. Apparently, the Aussies rather liked this single which went to No. 3 down under. Other flops followed including 'You Are My Heart's Delight', 'The Blue Danube' and 'Rockabilly Hot Pot'. Cherry Red Records have usefully compiled the group's singles on CD. For fans only.

THE MINDBENDERS

After parting with Wayne Fontana, The Mindbenders went on to hits of their own, notably 'Groovy Kind Of Love' which reached No. 2 in early 1966. Later the group appeared in *To Sir With Love*, memorably backing Lulu in the finale scene when she sang the film's title song to Sidney Poitier. The group had two other Top Thirty hits: 'Can't Live With You, Can't Live Without You' and 'Ashes to Ashes' (the latter was written by Toni Wine who had penned 'Groovy').

'I Want Her, She Wants Me' was written by Rod Argent of The Zombies. This song had none of the class and mystique of that group's best work. There is a bouncy beat and a rather banal chorus, sounding a little old-fashioned for late 1966. 'We'll Talk About It Tomorrow' was released in April 1967 and reviewed by Penny Valentine in *Disc & Music Echo*: *"For ages The Mindbenders have been looking for a song in the 'Groovy Kind Of Love' vein and they may well have found it here, though whether the chart want it again is another question ... (it) has the same warm consoling sound about it as their first hit. They do it very nicely ... and it's a very lulling record. It would be nice if it were a hit."*

Graham Gouldman wrote The Mindbenders' 1967 single, 'Schoolgirl', five years ahead of his link up with Eric Stewart in 10cc. The song concerned a schoolgirl pregnancy and has something of the harsh taste of 10cc's most satirical songs. Penny Valentine: *"There are* songs that are lyrically clever, bitter things with good production and well done but they just don't do anything commercially. This, I'm afraid, has all the markings of one of them. A very bright little record with cynical words and a lot of lines that will have the BBC reaching for the blue pencil, well done by The Mindbenders with a brilliant school song chorus. I admire it all but can't see it as a hit." It flopped.

The Mindbenders covered The Box Tops' American hit, 'The Letter', as Paul Hanley says: "*they hastily recorded a version with Graham Gouldman producing in the hope of beating the original to a UK hit. It didn't work.*" The Box Tops' single peaked at No. 5 in the UK, while the cover version stalled at No. 42.

Gouldman went on to join The Mindbenders in early 1968 and wrote another single for the group, 'Uncle Joe, The Ice Cream Man'. The song is included on David Wells' *Climb Aboard My Roundabout – The British Toytown Pop Sound 1967-74* compilation. Wells himself admits that 'toytown' is a "*pseudo-genre*" but the three CD set is great fun. The 'Uncle Joe' single has prominent acoustic guitar and an orchestral arrangement by John Paul Jones. If you like such 'toytown' classics as 'Penny Lane' and 'Excerpt From A Teenage Opera', you might enjoy this lost Mindbenders' single, while Hanley says that the song is "*risible*". Each to his own.

THE MOODY BLUES

The Moodies' career falls into two sections: before Justin Hayward and with Justin Hayward. Before Hayward joined, the Moodies had Denny Laine as lead singer and guitarist. The group's cover of Bessie Banks' 'Go Now' topped the UK singles charts in 1965. 'From The Bottom Of My Heart' was their only other Top Thirty hit with this line-up.

'Boulevard de la Madeleine' provoked a shocked *NME* review: "*Unbelievable! Here are The Moody Blues, of all people, with a tango! Has a decided Parisian feeling, accentuated by accordion. And the vocal is almost Vaudeville Band-ish. But on the whole, this strikes me as a gimmick disc, that's so odd and unexpected that it could happen.*" The tango rhythm soon palls and the paradiddle drums begin to irritate. It didn't chart.

'Life's Not Life' was the final single released with Laine as lead singer. Penny Valentine wrote in *Disc and Music Echo*: "*I have always* admired Denny Laine's painfully hurt voice. I also admire (the group) for sticking to a very individual style of music which is not commercially sound. Brave. But, while it satisfies people like me to sit and listen to odd half notes and strange key changes, it isn't bringing them any chart success. A problem indeed." I tend to agree with Penny's points. The song is disjointed and hard to sit and relax to. But things were soon to happen. Denny Laine went solo and two new group members arrived.

'Fly Me High' was released in May 1967 and was the first Moody Blues release to feature new members Justin Hayward (guitar/vocals) and John Lodge (bass/vocals). It does not have the over-familiarity of 'Nights In White Satin' and Hayward sounds so young. *NME* strangely don't mention the line-up change: *"Pity this has been released in such a congested week, as it's one of the best Moody Blues discs for some time. Handclaps, acoustic guitars and tambourine lead a folk-beat flavour. Mainly soloed with ensemble vocal in the catchy chorus, it also has a fascinating lyric and an invigorating sound in the backing."* Disc & Music Echo: *"Much much better than I expected now the Moodies are without the individual voice of Denny Laine, one of the best arranged records I've heard for ages, beautifully precise holding back dead sound, super production."* There is historic footage of the Moodies performing this single live on French television.

'Love And Beauty' was released in September 1967. This Mike Pinder composition has jaunty piano contrasting with the doom-sounding Mellotron – heard for the first time on their recordings – and a rather complicated vocal arrangement. The single did not trouble the charts. Finally, the new line-up's third single release in December of that year was a success. 'Nights In White Satin' entered the charts just after Christmas and reached No.19. Two re-releases in the following decade fared better: No. 9 in 1972 and No. 14 seven years later. Only a few classic singles were able to generate sales on each reissue – 'House Of The Rising Sun', 'All Right Now' and 'Albatross' spring to mind.

The Moodies appeared to be having some success in the singles charts, but it was pretty erratic: 'Voices In The Sky' (from the *In Search Of The Lost Chord* album) reached No. 27. 'Ride My See-Saw' from the same album was the follow-up. Record Mirror: *"Already a big hit in the States, this must be equally big here. Starts with a persistent sort of rhythm, then the voices come in, adamantly urgent. It's got style and professionalism, but it's also built on very commercial lines. Never lets up. Chart certainty."* The single managed only a week in the Top Fifty, staggering to No. 42, despite the group's energetic performance on BBC2's *Colour Me Pop*.

'Never Comes The Day' was lauded in *NME*: *"this is sheer poetry in music ... a delightful record. Opens quietly with just an acoustic guitar accompaniment, builds gradually as tempo increases and the beat is unleashed then tails off into the delicate realms of fantasy once again. The classically-styled scoring is both piquant and tasteful, the lyric is intriguing, and the beat penetrative."*

The Moodies' *On The Threshold Of A Dream* had reached the top spot in the British album charts and stayed in the listings for an incredible 73 weeks. 'Watching And Waiting' was featured on the group's album, *To Our Children's Children's Children*. *NME*: *"it's a sombre ballad that's both moody and blues-tinged. But the sighing organ and classically-scored strings supply a touch of refinement, almost elegance. Don't know whether it's quite the thing for the singles charts."* Record Mirror agreed: *"Predictably high standard here on this track ... A lovely big, sensitive, slow-building atmosphere and lyrics gives a haunting promotion. Not sure about its single chances but is a magnificent preview of the LP."*

To Our Children's Children's Children reached No. 2 and stayed in the charts for 44 weeks. Clearly, Moody Blues fans were now album buyers. However, 'Question's second position in 1970 gave the group their biggest hit single since 'Go Now'.

According to bassist John Lodge, 'I'm Just A Singer (In A Rock 'N' Roll Band)' was written in response to the worrying numbers of Moody Blues fans who saw the band as visionary seers and idols. It was the second single released from *Seventh Sojourn* and only reached No. 38. The band's career was put on hold for five years while all the members released solo (or duo) albums. The Moodies reconvened in 1978 with the *Octave* album. 'Steppin' In A Slide Zone' was taken from the album and released as a single. It was savaged in *Record Mirror*: *"The mercenary Moodies continue to parody themselves to the best of their ability. They sounded silly enough at the time, but 10 years on they sound downright ludicrous. The words still as meaningless as ever."*

THE MOVE

The Move's run of hit singles started with 'Night Of Fear' at the start of 1967, but was interrupted by 'Wild Tiger Woman' in 1968. *NME*'s review was headlined "*Wild Move Worth The Long Wait*", going on to say: "*the group's uninhibited treatment of this Roy Wood number is British r-and-b at its best. It drives along at a frantic pace with a spirited vocal and several incredible guitar breaks. It's an absolute scorcher, pulsating with energy and vitality ... not nearly as commercial as The Move's last one ('Fire Brigade') or 'Flowers In The Rain' because the melodic content has been swept overboard in favour of out-and-out blues, it may not have the mass appeal necessary for a huge hit.*" Half a century later, James R. Turner agreed: "*The track really rocks, with some great riffing from Roy (Wood), the band powering along, via some risque lyrics and fantastic harmony vocals. The song takes the band's existing sound and ramps up the rock element ... it also sounds fresh and potent with a wonderful piano work from Nicky Hopkins. However, it bombed completely, failing to reach the hit parade, making it a rare commercial misstep from (Roy) Wood.*" The follow-up, the more tuneful 'Blackberry Way', reached No. 1.

After Carl Wayne left The Move in 1970, the band's sound became heavier. Jeff Lynne from The Idle Race joined and Roy Wood became even more the focus of the band. 'Brontosaurus' reached No. 7, but its follow-up, 'When Alice Comes Back To The Farm', was a flop, despite being previewed on both *Top of the Pops* and *Lift Off With Ayshea*. *Disc & Music Echo*: "*The Move in their most energetic mood. Roy Wood-inspired high gymnastics, with that tremendously tough sound occasionally splattered into comparative quietitude by cellos. Vocally, it's not quite as full-sounding as some of the earlier stuff. There's a piano going near-beserk.*" While *NME* stated: "*it's a juddering, penetrating sound and the fact that it's been recorded on echo seems to intensify the earthiness ... a gutsy workout, made all the more exciting by the injection of a super-charged rock beat.*" James R. Turner described the single as, "*another sax driven hard rock track with some powerhouse drumming from Bevan ... cello breaks and woodwind clearly signpost the future of The Move's music.*"

Soon, The Move signed to Harvest and had three more hit singles. 'Tonight' and 'Chinatown' were more radio-friendly than 'Alice', being simpler songs with tuneful choruses. 'Tonight' reached No. 11, while 'Chinatown' rose no higher than No. 23. 'California Man' was something different; a brilliant rock 'n' roll pastiche with Jerry Lee Lewis-type piano and honking saxophones, possibly hinting that Wood already had the Wizzard sound in his head. This last ever Move single was their most successful in the UK since 'Brontosaurus', matching the latter's No. 7 position in the charts. Two months later, the first Electric Light Orchestra single was released. Wood, Jeff Lynne and Bev Bevan had been planning and recording this new project while continuing as The Move.

Paper Lace

Paper Lace came to fame after winning television talent show, *Opportunity Knocks*, for five weeks in a row. The group recorded a Mitch Murray/Peter Callender song, 'Billy Don't Be A Hero', which went to No.1. Paper Lace wore American Civil War uniforms on *Top of the Pops*. The single never appealed to me, but the use of a plaintive female voice was highly effective: *"keep your pretty head low"*, recalling similar moments in John Leyton's 'Johnny Remember Me' and Love Affair's 'Rainbow Valley'.

The follow-up, 'The Night Chicago Died' was more Americana (about Al Capone's gang) with the group wearing gangster suits in publicity shots and on television appearances. This reached a very respectable No. 3. The group's third single, 'The Black Eyed Boys', reached No. 11 and the group wore T-shirts emblazoned with a giant black eye!

Paper Lace's next single, 'Hitchin' A Ride '75', was a flop. *Record Mirror*: *"previously a hit for Vanity Fare. Light and bouncy, it doesn't have a lot of depth, but maybe people fancy something a little on the flighty side."* Vanity Fare's original had only been a hit five years earlier and even with a new introduction — more faux Americana, rhyming *"Louisiana"* with *"Rosanna"* — Paper Lace did not improve on it.

The follow-up, 'So What If I Am' was reviewed in *Record Mirror*: *"This is a good Murray/Callender song which allows Paper Lace to change direction without poaching on anyone's territory. The best parts are its solid rhythm, above average lyric, strong title line and cheeky Moog work. It may not be one of the* year's best singles but it could easily prove to be one of its best remembered." This single sank without trace.

I once helped a friend review the singles for his column in a local newspaper back in the late 1980s. The task took all Sunday afternoon and evening and was an exhausting and mind-numbing experience. Trying to find something interesting, helpful and original to say about a couple of dozen new singles is quite a challenge. Remember that singles reviewers like Penny Valentine and James Hamilton achieved this week after week for several years. One can see now why *NME* rotated the task of singles reviewer in the 1970s. The weekly music press in those days could receive up to 100 different singles a week.

SHOWADDYWADDY

Showaddywaddy won ITV's *New Faces* show in late 1973 and were runners-up on the Christmas all-winners show. The group were soon signed by Bell Records, where they were alongside such hit-makers as The Bay City Rollers and David Cassidy. The group's singles success was immediate with the self-penned 'Hey Rock 'N' Roll' reaching No. 2, followed by three more Top Twenty hits. In 1975 a cover of Eddie Cochran's 'Three Steps To Heaven' also reached No. 2 and was followed by the group's version of Buddy Holly's 'Heartbeat' where they replaced the guitar figure with an amusing *"I hear a heartbeat"* refrain. Holly's original had been a British hit a month before his premature death in February 1959 and reached No. 30. Nick Berry's rendition of the song was used as the theme tune for the *Heartbeat* ITV drama series and reached No. 2 in 1992. The British singles charts has never been about justice. Remember that Cilla Black's version of 'You've Lost That Lovin' Feeling' was about to eclipse the much superior Righteous Brothers' original until Andrew Loog Oldham intervened with his own press adverts, praising Phil Spector's production of the latter.

In autumn 1975 two more group compositions were less successful for Showaddywaddy. 'Heavenly' reached only No. 34, sounding like a mixture of 'Three Steps To Heaven' and 'Summertime Blues'. 'Trocadero' was released next and reviewed in *Record Mirror*: *"Finally breaking away from the Eddie Cochran/Buddy Holly type vocals, Showaddywaddy have come up with something more original, despite The Ventures' guitar break in the middle, this one should do very well. I like the shades of 10cc on the chorus."* NME were harsher: *"At least Showaddywaddy are no longer exhuming the dead absolutely note for note in the Mike Yarwood Graverobbing Cup. Their weedy re-creation of the lame shifty-eyed element of 50s rock almost assumes an identity of its own on this song."* This rather disjointed single peaked at No. 32.

A third consecutive self-penned single, 'Take Me In Your Arms', did not even chart. This single was quite impressive with brilliantly precise acoustic guitars even if the vocals are rather dull. *Record Mirror*: *"Doo wop wop double take back-up vocals and acoustic guitar on a medium paced number written by the group. Not as blatantly time-warped as usual but then it is following a minor hit."*

Having learned the hard way, Showaddywaddy resumed their covers policy, resulting in a chart-topper with their revival of Curtis Lee's 'Under The Moon Of Love'. This was followed by eight more Top Twenty hits, all covers of rock 'n' roll oldies, steaming their way through punk, power pop and disco. The group's singles were generally credited to all eight members, but it is claimed that only singer Dave Bartram and guitarist Trevor Oakes were the actual songwriters.

'A Night At Daddy Gees' broke the group's sequence of nine Top Twenty hits in 1979. This was written by Tommy Boyce and had been a Curtis Lee B-side back in 1962. Despite an appearance on *Top of the Pops*, this rather ordinary rocker went no higher than No. 39.

SLADE

Slade had a magnificent chart career in the 1970s. The band had no fewer than seventeen consecutive Top Twenty hits from 'Get Down And Get With It' in 1971 to 1976's 'Let's Call It Quits'. These included half a dozen chart-toppers, three No. 2 singles and two more peaking at No. 3. Slade's chart record easily exceeded those of any of their contemporaries at the time. Because of this, the band 's decline was more remarkable and noticeable. Fortunately, a recently published biography by Daryl Easlea covers the band's entire career in great detail, allowing us to learn of every step of Slade's downward path.

The more sensitive 'How Does It Feel' peaked at No. 15, the

band's first single not to reach the Top Ten for nearly four years. After the follow-up, 'Thanks For The Memory' reached No. 7, the next two singles – 'I For A Penny' and 'Let's Call It Quits' – both went no higher than No. 11. The band's next single in April 1976 was 'Nobody's Fool'. Supposedly inspired by the music of Queen, bassist Jim Lea originally intended the song to be a *"twenty minute extravaganza with everything thrown in"*. The idea was scrapped, but the single did sound a little different to the usual Slade style because of the female backing vocals by Tasha Thomas. The review in *Record Mirror & Disc* was positive: *"Title track from their latest album ... this is one of the best singles Slade have released for ages. Very catchy, from the first hearing. Bright and bouncy, and Slade at their best. Instant hit."* For me 'Nobody's Fool' sounds a bit laboured and predictable. Easlea is kinder: *"(it) is sweet and cheery ... infectious, nimble yet still punchy."* Despite widespread advertising with the photographs of the band sporting red noses, this single flopped. Surprisingly, the parent album with a near identical name, *Nobody's Fools*, reached No. 14, but only stayed in the charts for four weeks, suggesting that the band's loyal fanbase was getting smaller.

'Gypsy Roadhog' was (unbelievably) previewed on *Blue Peter* on BBC1 with the band performing in a cut-out car! Clearly inspired by Slade's lengthy spell in the USA, the song name-checks lots of American states, rhyming *"Alabama"* with *"Indiana"*. After this television appearance, there were complaints about the song's lyrics leading to the single being removed from the Radio One playlist. Despite the song being about a cocaine dealer, Noddy Holder maintained it was actually anti-drugs. *NME* commented: *"just the latest step in their continuing irrelevance."* Guitarist Dave Hill elaborates: *"the single 'Gypsy Roadhog' only reached No. 48, and the album,* Whatever Happened To Slade? *didn't chart at all. It was America all over again, only this time at home ... We released a string of non-album singles to try and spark something off, but nothing took off, even though we tried the serious stuff and we tried the daft stuff because both have always been valid parts of what Slade's about."*

'Burning In The Heat Of Love' was the follow-up to 'Gypsy Roadhog' and was a rather dull heavy rock track. There are dreadful pseudo-erotic lyrics that would have fallen flat on their young fans. *Record Mirror*: *"Slade are Okay. But they're gone. 3 stars for the 'You Really Got*

Me' riff." Again, Easlea is positive, seeing the song as *"polished AOR"*. The single was not even previewed on British television.

Noddy explained the band's dilemma in his autobiography: *"We continued to write and record, but we had stopped getting any big hits. The problem was that we couldn't get our songs played on the radio. We were considered old hat. Through 1978 and 1979, our hits petered off and our radio play dried up. The best we could manage was the occasional minor hit and the odd appearance on Top of the Pops. Most of our records got nowhere near the Top Twenty."*

Later in 1977, Slade combined 'My Baby Left Me' and 'That's Alright' in a tribute to the recently deceased Elvis Presley. Noddy's voice is on fine echoey form here and the two songs work well together with a great guitar solo by Dave Hill. The backing vocals sing *"that's alright"* as a refrain to Noddy singing *"my baby left me"* and there is an insistent excitement about the record. The single still only reached No. 32. Worse was to come as Hill had indicated.

There were further indignities; 'Give Us A Goal' was in a genre where many bands tried and failed – football songs (see Status Quo, Paper Lace, etc). Slade previewed the single on ITV's *Get It Together* in March 1978. Noddy looked ridiculous in a black and yellow woolly hat, Dave Hill was in his shaven head phase and looked either scary or ill. Even the children in the television studio looked bored. *Record Mirror*: *"I'd like to see the oldies make it again ... I always loved their gigs just for the atmosphere. I think that's what they must have been thinking about when they wrote this song, because it recaptures the football fervour they used to build up. That's why it's a bit sad because I don't think it worked. I think they're groping in the dark, looking backwards for their future. The song's getting plenty of guts. The typical rasping vocals, all that stuff but it's missed the goal."*

The next single was 'Rock 'N' Roll Bolero'. *Record Mirror*: *"A more mellow Slade here: gone are the raucous Noddy Holder vocals and the crashing guitars. The fact remains that they're in dire need of a hit and this could be the one."* It wasn't to be.

'Ginny Ginny' was taken from Slade's *Return To Base* album and was yet another flop. The lyrics are predictable and archaic with lines like: *"on Tuesdays she's washing her hair"*. The chorus is typical brash Slade of their heyday, but the verses listing the days of the week are dire. *Melody Maker* was scathing: *"Slade's record comes on piss yellow vinyl: the drive's still there, but not the sense of direction."*

'Sign Of The Times' showed a softer and more melodic side to Slade and featured Jim Lea on piano. The lyrics are trying a little too hard to be modern: *"Big Brother"*, *"turn on your radio"* (rhyming with *"stereo"*) *"computer age"* and *"all systems go"*. The band's overuse use of diminished chords was just becoming a little predictable too. *Melody Maker* sounded sympathetic: *"Poor old Slade. Banished by the fickle finger of public taste, they've been hovering in a sort of no-mans land for ages. This one won't recapture an audience, even though they're clearly aiming for the ELO sector. Echoed vocals, lots of bombast and the odd 'electronic' gimmick do not make a great single. Only when Noddy Holder recaptures his perfect John Lennon irritation will they rise from the ashes."*

I suppose 'Okey Cokey' counts as what Hill called *"daft stuff"*. Surely this should be left to Black Lace or Chas & Dave? Peter Checksfield rightly deems the single: *"the very nadir of their career."* By now Slade were not even making *Top of the Pops* but condemned to appear on such children's programmes as *Get It Together*.

Slade's revival has been well-documented. The band made a triumphant appearance at 1980's Reading Festival and 1981 saw them return to the Top Ten with 'We'll Bring The House Down'. 'My Oh My' and 'Run Runaway' also went Top Ten in the early 1980s. Sometimes the flops stop and an act starts having hits again, but these occasions are rare.

10cc

I first heard 10cc's debut single, 'Donna', on Radio One and was surprised to see the three members of Hotlegs appear on *Top of the Pops* under their new name. I must confess that 50 years ago, I did not know much about Graham Gouldman except I knew that he had not been in Hotlegs. I would have heard singles such as 'For Your Love', 'Bus Stop' and 'No Milk Today' loads of times, but I did not know it was Gouldman who wrote these brilliant hit singles for The Yardbirds, The Hollies and Herman's Hermits.

'Donna' reached No. 2 and there were high hopes for its similarly styled follow-up 'Johnny Don't Do It'. But whereas 'Donna' was attractive, catchy and witty, the satirical pastiche of 1960s 'death disc' records in 'Johnny Don't Do It' left many people cold and the single flopped. *NME*: *"sticking to the rockaballad formula of their hit 'Donna', this follow-up lacks the melodical content of their smash. The intriguing falsetto is still there, as is the dumb-guy background vocals. The difference is, this one is a death song."* Simon Reynolds called the single *"(a) loving parody of the motorbike-death song."* Some have said that the release of 'Johnny Don't Do It' coincided with a successful reissue of The Shangri-Las' 'Leader Of The Pack' and people had enough of such novelty records. Chart statistics tell a different story; 'Donna' had entered the British charts in late September 1972 with the reissue of 'Leader Of The Pack' following in mid-October. Both singles stayed in the charts for three months. 'Johnny Don't Do It' was released in December 1972 and was not an ideal choice for the Christmas market.

The follow-up was 'Rubber Bullets'. The single's success must have caused a massive sigh of relief for band, record company and management when it went to No.1 in June 1973. Another single about American culture, this time about high school rather than prisons, 'The Dean And I', was a successful follow-up, reaching No. 10.

'The Worst Band In the World' was released in early 1974. This single was too self-deprecating and witty for the charts. *Record Mirror*: *"there have been a few discreet changes in the lyrics of this very clever newie from the highly professional team ... changes persuaded upon them by BBC requirements. You get the original, friends. Gaps and missing rhymes and all. And you also get some inventive work by an excellent band trying hard to kick in sounds as from the worst band. Maybe the melodic content isn't so instant, but the production is first rate."* *NME*: *"(it) lacks the density of say, 'Rubber Bullets', but more than compensates by its intriguing arrangement and tongue-in-cheek lyrics. In the long haul, a hit of quite awesome proportions."* When the single flopped, Simon Frith in *Let It Rock* was curious: *"Mystery of the month: whatever happened to 10cc's 'Worst Band In The World'? It was released in January, a witty comment on making records, and got a lot of airplay. Since then? Nothing."*

By 1977 10cc became a duo after Godley and Creme left to develop their Gizmo invention. This instrument can be heard on The Scaffold's final hit, 'Liverpool Lou'. Remaining members Graham Gouldman and Eric Stewart continued having Top Ten hits with 'The Things We

Do For Love' and 'Good Morning Judge'. I was unaware of 'People In Love', the band's third single to be taken from their album, *Deceptive Bends*. This is a piano ballad with Eric Stewart singing lead, perhaps hoping to repeat the success of 'I'm Not In Love'. *Record Mirror*: *"It's sad when good groups with talent go soft and that's what happened to 10cc. This is so soppy."* The song is rather dreary and lacks the band's usual wit and originality. Another flop.

Within a year 10cc were back at the top of the charts with 'Dreadlock Holiday'. Again, there was a problem with following-up a chart-topping single. 'Reds In My Bed' was co-written by Eric Stewart and Stuart Tosh, thus lacking the Graham Gouldman input. *Record Mirror*: *"Nice clean sound, well scrubbed production. Lots of tricky little effects with a faint echo of Queen-like arrangement."* The single disappeared without trace.

The Troggs

The Troggs had a good run in the British singles charts. Starting with 'Wild Thing' in 1966, the group had six consecutive Top Twenty singles, including a chart-topper ('With A Girl Like You') and two in the second position ('Wild Thing' and 'I Can't Control Myself').

'Hi Hi Hazel' broke the group's run of hits reaching only No. 42. The single was taken from the group's first album. The lacklustre track was released by label boss/producer Larry Page without the band's permission. The Troggs were soon back in the charts with 'Love Is All Around' which peaked at No. 5. Written by lead singer Reg Presley, the song was covered three decades later by Wet Wet Wet and featured in the film, *Four Weddings And A Funeral*. Presley earned vast royalties which he allegedly spent on crop circle research.

'Little Girl' was released in February 1968. *Record Mirror*: *"They haven't 'arf quietened down, these Troggs. All is gentleness and lightness here with Reg singing his own song with a deft and very commercial styling. All very controlled and subdued but building gradually. I think that it'll do very much okay even if it's not my idea of Trogg-perfection."* Penny Valentine enthused in *Disc & Music Echo*: *"this is very pleasant and if it were a West Coast group all the cynics would be leaping around going mad. As it is, hey just sing under a nice woodwind warm* backing. It isn't an immediate record but one that will insinuate itself upon you." The Troggs had built upon the style of 'Love Is All Around' and made a more sophisticated record. 'Little Girl' peaked at No. 37 and this was the end of The Troggs' chart entries in the UK.

'Surprise Surprise' was a complete contrast to 'Little Girl'. The *NME* review was headlined "*Frenzied Rocker — The Troggs have decided to climb aboard the rock 'n' roll bandwagon ... this is an uninhibited wildie which doesn't let up from the word 'go' to the fine frenzied fade-out. Walloping drums, twangy guitars, a spirited Reg Presley vocal complete with screams, an electrifying atmosphere. Plus a rolling clanking piano ... It's exciting, all right, but hardly very distinctive. Nevertheless I imagine the group's popularity will carry it.*" Record Mirror seemed to feel the same: "*The Troggs here revert to their old-time power ... It fairly rushes along ... at a fiery pace and all the Reginald raucosity is there in the lead voice position.*"

'You Can Cry If You Want To' from the summer of 1968 was a fine record. Brian Hogg: "*a lovely song. It's sentiment as only The Troggs could do it, with those Rolling Stones' 'As Tears Go By' strings in the backing.*" This single is not usually included on the group's compilation albums and deserves wider hearing.

Penny Valentine was less impressed with the single 'Hip Hip Hooray', a Geoff Stephens composition: "*Here come The Troggs sounding like Ohio Express. I fear the impression is intentional. Especially as they follow it with a song which in its dire simplicity could be another 'Yummy Yummy'. It's very short and the sort of record I could well do without.*" Penny, as always, was spot on; this could have come out of the Kasenetz-Katz bubblegum factory and maybe should have stayed there.

'Evil Woman' was reviewed in *NME*: "*this disc reverts to the style of 'Wild Thing'. It's mean, Bluesy and sultry with a curled-up Reg Presley snarling the lyric to the accompaniment of reverberating twangs and a heavy plod.*" Record Mirror: "*Grunted-groaned voice from Reg ... with walking-bass and extremely tough work from lead guitar and drums. All very sexy, and pretty easy to hold in the mind.*" I find this single slow and menacing, but a little pedestrian. I agree that the guitar is a little weird.

Next was 'Easy Loving'. *Record Mirror* said: "*Softer than of yore, this. Almost murmured, indeed, with woodwindy backing sounds. It builds, of course, and there's a sound enough melodic hook. Improves with a few plays, actually.*

Might miss — horrid-like, but there's a commercial air of earnestness here."

'Everything's Funny' was released in 1972 on the Pye label. *NME*: *"The group somehow has managed to stay together, even after they were considered 'uncool'. This song has a distinct rock 'n' roll feel with a dash of strings and brass in the right places. The pace is very similar to the ever-up-tempo beat which was so prominent in English groups from '64 to '66."* A year later, 'Listen To The Man' was released. *Record Mirror*: *"Very much different from the old Troggs who had hits galore. Guitar intro at gentle, leisurely pace, it's miles away from the old 'Wild Thing' stuff, and it works for the lads."*

'Good Vibrations' was about the most unlikely song for a Troggs cover version, but actually happened. *Record Mirror*: *"Well I suppose only Reg Presley could make this Beach Boys classic sound like a surfin' version of 'Wild Thing', and that's what he's done. Beat slowed down to a walking pace, breathy notes — someone in the office said most unkindly that it sounded like Pinky and Perky on a bad day."*

WIZZARD

Everyone agrees that Roy Wood is a pop genius, as a singer, songwriter, multi-instrumentalist and producer. Wizzard's first three singles still sound extraordinary. 'Ballpark Incident' remains a favourite with its sheer "oomph" of piano and saxes. 'See My Baby Jive' and 'Angel Fingers' both reached No. 1, two rare occasions when the best records of an era deservedly reached the top of the charts. The band's fourth single, 'I Wish It Could Be Christmas Everyday', was beaten by Slade for the 1973 Christmas No. 1. Wizzard left the Harvest label and signed to Warners. Releasing 'Rock 'N' Roll Winter' in the spring of 1974 was a 'clever-clever' idea, but the single peaked at No. 6, suggesting a decline in popularity. Chris Welch in *Melody Maker* articulated some people's thoughts: *"A nice song from Roy Wood although the tune reminds me of something else he wrote. Oh yes, 'I wish it could be Christmas every day!' But I hate Christmas — especially in the summer!"* There was a slight air of contrivance now and the feeling that the public were beginning to get tired of such a full sound.

'This Is The Story Of My Love' was Wizzard's first single not to reach the Top Ten, breaking their run of massive hits and scraping at No. 34. Despite the usual brilliant arrangement, even at the time I felt that the song was somewhat plaintive and downbeat. The band's sound was becoming samey. *NME*: "*Roy Wood's essay in neo-Spector ... it doesn't exude quite the same teenage charm as one of his earlier efforts in the genre.*" James R.Turner disagreed: "*full of lush orchestration and instrumentation, this is Roy at his most melodic ... a big old rock 'n' roll ballad in the mould of 'Angel Fingers'. It has a full-on wall of sound production!*" Wizzard returned to the Top Ten over Christmas 1974 with a clever Bill Haley pastiche, 'Are You Ready To Rock'. The single was ruined by a self-indulgent bagpipe break towards the end of the song.

At this point the Wizzard and Roy Wood stories converge and I am grateful to James R. Turner for clarifying the rather confusing next couple of years. 'Rattlesnake Roll' was previewed – like so many mid-1970s flops – on ITV's *Supersonic* where the studio audience always seemed to be too far away to be truly involved in the performances. This single was not as strong as 'California Man' or even 'Are You Ready To Rock'. There is a lot of honky-tonk piano with plenty of saxes, but the song and performance are charmless, being almost a case of self-sabotage, designed to alienate the group's fanbase. *Record Mirror*: "*Haley-esque rock-a-boogie clearly intended as an early contender in the festive Christmas market.*"

March 1976 saw the release of 'Indiana Rainbow', billed as Roy Wood and Wizzard. Despite an archetypal Wood vocal and melody, the instrumentation sounds like a weedy dance band playing to a shuffle beat. The effect is lacklustre and underwhelming. Again, I ponder about Wood's motives; clearly he was bored with the Wizzard hit 'sound' and wanted to widen his style of music. *NME* were not impressed either: "*Wizzard chug mindlessly in the style of early Move, revelling in the fairground organ arrangement. Music would have progressed from Doris Day to this by now without the intervention of Elvis Presley.*" *Record Mirror* agreed: "*Whilst ELO seem set for another hit, poor Roy Wood and friends seem set for another miss. Despite his many talents, Roy Wood just doesn't seem to know what to do in the way of records, and this is a totally confused sound, with a strange semi-Latin drum rhythm.*"

Unbelievably, worse was to come. Approach the Wizzo Band with caution. I still remember their appearance on a BBC television/radio show called *Sight And Sound*. The TV viewer was encouraged to place their stereo speakers either side of their television to receive the FM radio signal. I was repelled by this unattractive mixture of rock and big band music.

Roy Wood

Wood's solo career started with 'When Grandma Plays The Banjo' which received some airplay but saw no chart action. The plaintive 'Dear Elaine' was his first solo success, entering the charts just three weeks before Wizzard's 'Angel Fingers' did. Even for a workaholic like Roy Wood, the timing of the solo and group singles releases is mystifying (all were issued by the same record company – Harvest). Couldn't these releases have been spaced out more evenly throughout the year so as not to compete with each other for record buyers' attention and their purses and wallets?

The same thing occurred with Wood's next solo single, 'Forever'. The song entered the charts just one week before Wizzard's 'I Wish It Could Be Christmas Every Day'. Wood's performances of the single on *Top of the Pops* were without make-up, a less outrageous hair style (with a side-parting) and no antics. 'Forever' was Wood's most successful solo single, reaching No. 8, and remains his finest recording.

Wood's next two solo single releases – 'Goin' Down The Road' (subtitled 'a Scottish reggae song') and 'Oh What A Shame' both reached a respectable No. 13. 'Oh What A Shame' in the summer of 1975 saw his final chart appearance of the 1970s. It was the culmination of an extraordinary chart career – ten hits with The Move (including one chart-topper with 'Blackberry Way'), one hit with ELO before he left to form Wizzard, seven chart appearances with Wizzard (with two chart-toppers) and the three aforementioned solo hits.

'Look Thru The Eyes Of A Fool' was the lead single from Wood's solo album, *Mustard*. James R. Turner again: "*(it) has a peppy, bouncing rhythm, resplendent with wonderful sax breaks, terrific piano and pounding drums ... Roy's vocals are on fine form.*" By late 1975, the record buying public were clearly tiring of Wood's big productions. Six months later, a second single from *Mustard*, 'Any Old Time Would Do' was released. Turner:

"With its piano-driven riff and sax, this is peerless Wood ... an honest love song. The way he blends the guitars, the pianos, the backing vocals and charming lyrics makes this a lost classic. It's also a shame that when this was released as a single, it disappeared without trace."

'(We're) Back On The Road Again' appeared on the Automatic label in 1979. *Record Mirror:* "*Yes, the same Roy Wood – now doing a goodly amount of work, what with the Darts, his own forthcoming band, Roy Wood's Rock Brigade, and this. In the days when he had solo hits, this would have been just another one for the list. Now he just stands a glimmer of hope. But it's good to hear him back, and in this case it's good that he sounds just like he did way back then..*"

11 – Liverpool Sunset

AFTER 1966, FEW OF THE ORIGINAL LIVERPOOL groups had hits. Listing all the groups' flops would take a book of its own and would become tedious and repetitive. Alan Clayson's books, *Call Up The Groups* and *Beat Merchants* carefully trace the fate of The Fourmost, Gerry And The Pacemakers, Billy J. Kramer, Swinging Blue Jeans et al. I am including here some of the acts that interested me.

GERRY AND THE PACEMAKERS

I know that Gerry Marsden and his group made the top spot with their first three singles, but I found them a little naff, even as a seven-year-old pop fan. 'I Like It' seemed corny and I have always been resistant to 'You'll Never Walk Alone', being neither a football fan nor admirer of one of Rodgers and Hammerstein's simpler songs. Autumn 1964's 'It's Gonna Be Alright' reached no higher than No. 24. The more impressive follow-up, 'Ferry 'Cross The Mersey', was written by Gerry and has lasted well, even surviving repeated plays on the local ferry boats. The song was covered by Frankie Goes To Hollywood two decades later which must have brought welcome royalties for the composer. Gerry And The Pacemakers' final British chart entry was 'Walk Hand In Hand' in late 1965, just getting into the Top Thirty.

The Gerry-penned 'La La La' was the group's first flop. Despite some interesting riffs on a 12-string guitar, this is a very ordinary Merseybeat number. The single shows that Gerry had not progressed at the same rate as fellow Liverpudlians The Beatles or The Searchers. The next release, 'Girl On A Swing' was written by Ralph Miranda. There is strummed acoustic guitar and an orchestra. It is quite a good record with wistful lyrics and had potential to become an anthem. Another flop.

Gerry went on to be an all-round entertainer, appearing in the *Charlie Girl* musical in London's West End. Later he would front new line-ups of The Pacemakers and play in nostalgia tours and cabaret. In the 1980s, Gerry was involved when two of his hits were used for charity records; 'You'll Never Walk Alone' was recorded by The Crowd in aid of the Bradford City F.C. fire victims in 1985. Four years later, 'Ferry 'Cross The Mersey' was recorded for the Hillsborough disaster victims which saw Gerry joined by fellow Scousers, Paul McCartney, the Christians and Holly Johnson.

LIVERPOOL EXPRESS

Liverpool Express was led by Billy Kinsley, formerly of The Merseys and Rockin' Horse. The group reached No. 11 in the hot summer of 1976 with the rather weedy but memorable 'You Are My Love'. The follow-up, 'Hold Tight', was less successful, peaking at No. 46. *Record Mirror*: "*Pilot-sounding follow-up aimed at the teenybop market complete with a little John Miles guitar run and handclaps. Unoriginal of the week.*"

Liverpool Express bounced back with the melodramatic 'Every Man Must Have A Dream' which went Top Twenty. The group's next single, Dreamin', only just reached the Top Forty. *Record Mirror*: "*McCartney like vocals and then the train gets stuck halfway down the tunnel.*"

THE REAL THING

The Real Thing had a wealth of experience before they emerged in 1976 with 'You To Me Are Everything' which went to No.1. The Liverpudlian quartet had an authenticity without resorting to trying to sound American or 'cool'. Lead singer Chris Amoo had a relaxed and convincing vocal style which was clearly appreciated by pop fans. The follow-up, 'Can't Get Back Without You', reached No. 2 later in the year. The group had set themselves a very high standard with these two singles.

'Love's Such A Wonderful Thing' has a Philadelphia feel with a great string arrangement. The melody is excellent and the words infectiously optimistic. The single peaked at No. 33. The follow-up,

'Lightning Strikes Again' was reviewed in *Record Mirror*: *"Potentially Britain's first thinking man's soul band. It contains another good sax break but the song's little more than ordinary."* The song is a little bland, but there is a funky intro and good strings in the arrangement. It did not chart.

'Let's Go Disco' was featured in the Joan Collins and Oliver Tobias film, *The Stud*. Pressure from DJs and journalists resulted in the song being issued as a single. The song starts with 'Car Wash' type clapping and we hear funky guitar. *Record Mirror*: *"this untypical clapping disco bubbler could just be the tonic they need between stereotyped 'official' releases."* This release is a little derivative and apparently the group hated it. The single reached No. 39. 'Rainin' Through My Sunshine' came next. *Record Mirror*: *"Not as exciting as some of their earlier stuff, but could take off just the same. There's something terribly feeble about 'rainin' through my sunshine' for a hook line that makes me wince."* This single peaked at No. 40.

1979 saw a boost in The Real Thing's fortunes. 'Can You Feel The Force?' had no formal connection with *Star Wars* but clearly benefited by using the film's catchphrase, reaching No. 5. The follow-up 'Boogie Down (Get Funky Now)' peaked at No. 33.

The Real Thing's two biggest hits were re-mixed and released in 1986 and both went into the Top Ten. These were followed by a re-mix of 'Can You Feel The Force?' which peaked at No. 24.

The Scaffold

The Scaffold were an unlikely singles chart act. Comprising singer Mike McGear, poet Roger McGough and funny man John Gorman, the group's stage act always included music, poetry and humour. It was harder to capture such moments on record and it is no coincidence that the group's most enjoyable albums were recorded live. 'Thank U Very Much' was The Scaffold's first hit, reaching No. 4. The catchy single made the trio household names. The record was, reportedly, Harold Wilson's favourite song. However, behind the catchy ditty were subtleties of satire (the first, and possibly only, pop record to mention 'napalm') and originality; everyone wanted to know what on earth was an *"Aintree iron"*.

The follow-up, 'Do You Remember', was described by McGear as *"the gentle summer satire"*. In his autobiography he elaborates: *"Not that we didn't try the more esoteric, arty, farty, satirical records ... we did, but they just boomeranged back in our faces (the mass public it seems don't like clever clever songs, they prefer it from the heart)"*. McGough added: *"But following the success of 'Thank U Very Much', the pressure was on the group to provide a follow-up ... deciding on 'Do You Remember', a summer-of-love kind of toe tapper. Although they were very much like myself, naïve and sentimental, I still retain a fondness for the lyrics, which prescribed the tempo and almost wrote the music. Mike crooned the verses save one, which I voiced in the manner of a lovelorn poet, and into the middle eight we introduced a soft-shoe shuffle for John to perform on stage, for whenever we made a record it was always with the theatre performance in mind, not a sound policy, as it turned out, because although Mike looked like a singer, I could pass for a poet and John was hilarious hoofing about on stage, we weren't visible on record and 'Do You Remember' became only a minor hit. The pressure was on."*

NME commented: *"this displays the more serious side of The Scaffold's nature. The lyric is nostalgic, almost sentimental, while the tune is simply constructed and very quick to register. There are several obvious gimmick attractions — such as in the way in which the word 'do' is repeated five times on every occasion the title phrase crops up. Then there's the cute shuffle beat sand dance passage in the middle and the chugging lilt beat that permeates the rest of the disc ... it's catchy and entertaining. Doesn't have the immediate impact of the last one, but the group's popularity should carry it."* 'Do You Remember' reached No. 34. Peter Asher, by then working with McGear's elder brother, Paul McCartney at Apple Records, allegedly said that the single was *"a hit in every way except sales!"*

The Scaffold's next single was '1-2-3'; NME: *"a novel; roundelay that's based upon the repetition of sequences of numbers ... it's very catchy at the outset when the boys are supported by a thump beat. But then it goes off on a tangent with a massive symphonic styling, swirling organ and even a sitar solo and the basic simplicity's lost."* McGear: *"(this) was The Scaffold's answer to 'A Day In The Life' but not quite as popular (except for John's operatic solo, that is). The track sums up the hopeful, Carnaby Street, meditation, flower power, fun era of the much maligned 'Swingin' 60s'."* This release did not chart at all. I always enjoyed the lines, *"I was born in Liverpool 8"* and *"no-one seems to like my face,"* sung by John Gorman.

'Lily The Pink' gave the group a Christmas No. 1 in 1968 and leapt back to the top spot in the second week of January 1969. Again, following-up such a popular single presented a problem. 'Charity Bubbles' was described in *NME* as *"rather appealing ... the gimmickry isn't as pronounced as 'Lily' and 'Thank U Very Much' and the chorus isn't as catchy. Sung by Mike McGear with his romantic face on, it's about a Salvation Army girl who gives away her love and affection to charity."*

The trio returned to *Top of the Pops* at the end of 1969 to reprise 'Lily The Pink' and decided to have some fun. McGough: *"we came up with the concept of looking as if we hadn't worked for a year. We dirtied up some old white suits, frayed the cuffs and pulled off buttons, and John (Gorman) unstitched a sleeve that was to come off during the final chorus ... BBC top brass ... were not amused and the show's producer nailed us in the bar afterwards and accused us of sending up the programme, the jewel in the Corporation's popular music crown. Not the programme, we countered, but ourselves. But he'd have none of it and our copybook had been well and truly blotted."* The Scaffold did not appear again on *TOTP* for four years and their hits dried up for the same length of time.

'All The Way Up' was written by Howard Blake as the title song for the 1970 Warren Mitchell comedy film; neither record nor film were successful. Mitchell was somewhat typecast with a reprise of his Alf Garnett persona from the BBC television series, *Til Death Us Do Part*. The single release of the song is livelier than the one used in the film's opening titles. The latter has rather cheesey organ from Brian Auger no less and longer instrumental breaks.

'Gin Gan Goolie' is a gibberish song known to millions as a Boy Scout anthem which I remember learning when I was a cub scout. The song was adopted by scouts in Scandinavia before spreading around the world, no doubt at international jamborees. This was a strange choice for a Scaffold single, perpetuating the trio's family appeal. McGough added lyrics which were not his most inspired or witty. The single reached No. 38 and stayed in the lower reaches of the charts for eleven weeks. The B-side was 'Liver Birds', the theme song for Carla Lane's television comedy series. This would have been a better choice for the A-side.

The next single, 'Busdreams', used the words from 'Busseductress', one of Roger McGough's funniest poems. Unfortunately, the song has a rather dull melody. The poet's tale of a nymphomaniac bus conductress was hardly suitable for a family audience and this was at the heart of The Scaffold's dilemma. On television their hit records, white suits, *Score With The Scaffold* children's series and *Decimal Five* information slots were misleading. Here was a trio with a unique and complementary blend of music, humour and poetry whose live appearances were extremely entertaining. Check out the trio's first album *Live At The Elizabeth Hall* and Side 2 of their *L. The P.* album, recorded in front of an audience of London University students. The Scaffold's sketches were too satirical to be family entertainment.

McGear explains 1971 single 'Do The Albert': "*commissioned by the BBC for a TV extravaganza to celebrate the centenary of the lovely old Albert Hall. Alongside Sir John Gielgud and Sir John Betjeman, the London Philharmonic Orchestra and giant size video blow ups of ourselves we performed this song which featured, amongst others, Neil Innes on piano, Les (Harvey of Stone The Crows) on guitar solo, Viv Stanshall on deep throat and Keith Moon (on drums).*" *NME*: "*it's a blatant rocker. It is therefore a little dated in concept – though, within its TV context, it had the effect of lifting the show out of the stodge into which it was in danger of falling. Whether or not it will have the same effect on the Chart remains to be seen.*"

There were no Scaffold singles for three years; a spell with Island Records saw the release of one album, *Fresh Liver*, produced by Tim Rice. The early 1970s saw The Scaffold team up with former Bonzos Neil Innes and Viv Stanshall, former Liverpool Scene members Adrian Henri and Andy Roberts, poet Brian Patten and several musicians including Zoot Money and Mike Kellie. The collective were called GRIMMS, initials formed from the names Gorman, Roberts, Innes, McGear, McGough and Stanshall. Their shows were a delightful mixture of songs, sketches and humour. I saw them live twice, after both Adrian Henri and Viv Stanshall had left, but before the departure of McGear.

The Scaffold had their final hit in 1974 when they signed to Warner Bros. The trio reached No. 7 with their cover of the Dominic Behan folk song, 'Liverpool Lou', which was recorded at Strawberry Studios in Stockport and produced by Paul McCartney. The record is enhanced by the "Gizmo", a harmonising device invented by Lol

Creme and Kevin Godley of 10cc. The parent album, *Sold Out*, was unlike previous Scaffold albums with little poetry or humour. There were some folk songs including 'Lord Of The Dance', 'Mingulay Boating Song' and 'Leaving Of Liverpool'. The latter was released as a single and flopped, despite being praised in *Record Mirror*: *"Scaffold have bounced back with an updated and up-tempo version of a traditional folk song. Nice one to sing along to and get happy."* The song would be well known to the public through famous recordings and live performances by the Clancy Brothers, The Spinners and The Dubliners.

'Mummy Won't Be Home For Christmas' was another unsuccessful single; this was meant to be a pastiche of an American country ballad, but is not particularly amusing. A child's mawkish monologue towards the end of the song recited in a Scouse accent does not help.

The Searchers

The Searchers, unlike their labelmates, The Kinks, did not have a gifted songwriter in their ranks so were very much reliant on finding the right song from outside writers. The group had three chart-toppers in 1963 and 1964, along with six more Top Twenty hits. They were the first British group to have hits written by such American writers as Jackie de Shannon, Malvina Reynolds and P.F. Sloan. The quartet's first self-written A-side, 'He's Got No Love', reached an encouraging No. 12, but this was their penultimate Top Twenty placing.

Fortunately for us, The Searchers' long-time bass player Frank Allen (who replaced Tony Jackson in 1964) has published an entertaining, informative, honest and well written memoir, *The Searchers And Me*. If only even a few of his peers had written such equally helpful works! I am truly indebted to Allen's comments on his group's ups and downs.

Drummer Chris Curtis had found a copy of Bobby Darin's 'When I Get Home' in the USA and decided that it would be an ideal single for The Searchers. Bassist Frank Allen told Peter Doggett: *"it would have been a good album track, nothing more"*. In his memoir, Allen bravely quotes both Derek Johnson in *NME*: *"an exhilarating and stimulating disc ... moves along at a fast pace ... distinctive and ear-catching guitar sounds in which the band specialises"*, and Norman Jopling's less enthusiastic review in *Record*

Mirror: "*... not exactly the best thing they have done ...*" The group performed the single on *Sunday Night At The London Palladium* and footage of their spot is on YouTube. This was the group's first flop, reaching no higher than No. 35.

Just two months later, The Searchers were back in the Top Twenty with 'Take Me For What I'm Worth' which was penned by 'Eve Of Destruction' songwriter P.F. Sloan. For me, this was the group's finest recording and remained a highlight of their concerts throughout the decades. But the single only just scraped in at No. 20 and Allen admitted: "*we were on the slide, so it didn't have as big an impact as we'd hoped.*"

'Take It Or Leave It' was a Jagger/Richards composition that the group had learned from the composers during an Australian tour. The single reached No. 31. I have always felt that The Searchers actually improve the Stones' song which appears on the latter's *Aftermath* album. The group certainly sing it better than Mick 'n' Keef and the echoey production enhances what Steve Appleford calls: "*like any number of the early, easily forgotten Jagger/Richards originals under orders from Andrew Oldham ... a shapeless misfire.*" I have always liked this single's clever arrangement, combining acoustic and electric guitars. *NME*: "*great sound ... all credit to The Searchers for adapting it to their own style instead of trying to emulate the Stones ... rather unusual number, fractionally under mid-tempo ... not particularly strong melody-wise but the group's interpretation is highly colourful and they have got some great sounds going.*" *Record Mirror*: "*A smooth, very smooth production.*"

The follow-up, 'Have You Ever Loved Somebody' was also from the pen of a British pop group, The Hollies, but did not stop the steady decline of The Searchers' chart career. A rival version by Paul and Barry Ryan was produced by the group's former drummer Chris Curtis. Neither single did well; The Searchers reached No. 48, while the Ryan twins got to one place lower. It is a fast, almost frantic song, but has a memorable chorus. Bassist Frank Allen told Peter Doggett: "*it was a very catchy record and if it had followed 'Goodbye My Love', it could have been a smash.*"

'Popcorn Double Feature' was previewed on *Top of the Pops* in January 1967. Frank Allen: "*We began 1967 with yet another futile stab at the charts (it) was an interesting departure for us, almost a foray into the realms of psychedelia with lyrics full of allegory and innuendo as opposed to the more* direct and non-threatening happy-clappy words that constituted the major part of our normal repertoire". Record Mirror: "a lack of immediate distinctiveness but it's a good strong song and the presentation is commercial." Bob Stanley wrote in the group's *Pye Anthology* sleeve-notes: "*The spooked Luddite protest song that started the year. was one of their best singles. From its arresting spangly intro through its melancholy, Graham Gouldman-like chorus hook ... sounded like a huge hit but oddly failed to chart anywhere.*" Frank Allen: "*that was probably our last good single on Pye.*"

'Western Union' was a cover of a single by The Five Americans and released in April 1967. *Disc*'s Penny Valentine commented: "*Good version of a pleasant song ... not over-great but quite nice.*" Allen's memoir is merciless and, again, admirably honest: "'*Western Union' was a dog when we made it and did not improve with age or benefit when viewed through the rose-tinted blinkers of nostalgia.*"

The Searchers' final single on Pye, 'Secondhand Dealer', was written in-house by guitarist Mike Pender and bassist Frank Allen and released in November 1967. Penny Valentine: "*It's a pity that such a talented group as the Searchers has lapsed into semi-obscurity. Their vocal sound is just as distinctive as ever and I found this tale of the trials and tribulations of a rag-and-bone man both gripping and poignant.*" Bob Stanley thought this single: "*had a suitably haunted, lonely atmosphere. As the band describe the decline and eventual death of the poor chap.*" Again, Frank Allen was blunt: "*Our disc was stillborn.*"

Around this time The Searchers found employment in cabaret clubs throughout the country and developed a highly polished act. The group were next signed to Liberty Records and released two singles, 'Umbrella Man' and 'Kinky Kathy Abernathy' in 1969, both written by Kenny Young who went on to work with Clodagh Rodgers. These singles – as Allen states: "*sank without trace.*"

The beginning of the next decade saw The Searchers without a recording contract but they were soon signed to RCA. I can just about remember two of their singles on this label. 'Desdemona' – not the John's Children song – was quite distinctive with an unusual melody. Allen: "*It was catchy and up-tempo although not a typical Searchers sound by any means.*" I must have heard this single no more than twice on the radio when it was released, but the hook of the chorus has stayed with me over half a century! I listened to the song again on some website and it was just as catchy.

The Searchers were persuaded by RCA to re-record some of their Pye hits, releasing a maxi-single which included 'Needles And Pins' and 'When You Walk In The Room' and an album called *Second Take*. The front cover of the album showed the group in early 1970s clothes, surrounded by a collage of vintage press cuttings. This was not a good look or sound. Re-recordings are the bane of a music historian's life; often in exceedingly small print one can read words to the effect of "these are not the original recordings".

The Searchers' final release for RCA was a cover of the Neil Sedaka song 'Solitaire'. Sedaka was enjoying something of a renaissance thanks to teaming up with members of 10cc at their Strawberry Studios in Stockport and recording an impressive new repertoire, far removed from his Brill Building pop of the previous decade. Allen: "*We immediately honed in on the emotive ballad 'Solitaire'. Everything about it screamed 'quality' and quite possibly 'hit'. This was excellent material with a superb tune and meaningful lyrics that tugged at the emotions.*" Again, I remember hearing the single on Radio One at least once, but clearly it did not reach enough listeners nor attract buyers. Allen: "*Six months later Andy Williams released his version of the song. (It) shot to number four and our stay at RCA was at an end.*"

The Searchers released no new material for over six years but right at the end of the 1970s, the group were signed to Seymour Stein's Sire label. They made some excellent recordings at Rockfield Studios in South Wales, previously used by Dave Edmunds, The Flamin' Groovies, Queen and others. Allen: "*the first tune to be taken was 'Hearts In Her Eyes', an up-tempo number very much in the old style we were used to but with more punch. Written by Will Birch and John Wicks of a group called The Records, it had it all as far as we were concerned. Rhythm, a catchy melody with simple yet interesting lyrics and a guitar riff that could have been tailor-made for us.*" Despite excellent reviews for both the single and album, sales were disappointing. Allen: "*If press coverage had been easy to come by, radio and television were different matters entirely. Disc jockeys who had keenly courted our company when we were riding high were not so enthusiastic about forging associations with a past from which they were forever trying to distance themselves.*"

Frank Allen makes a pertinent point here; many of the flops described in this book were unsuccessful singles because disc jockeys were scared of appearing unhip or "out of time" if they were playing them on their programmes. Ironically many of these artists produced their finest work after the high point of their chart career.

In 1983 I saw The Searchers in cabaret at Sour Hall, a remote venue on the Lancashire/Yorkshire border. The Searchers dutifully played all their hits and managed to sneak in some of the new Sire recordings including Alex Chilton's 'September Gurls' and Micky Jupp's 'Switchboard Susan'. They displayed the confidence and craftsmanship of a group with an established line-up. Bass player Frank Allan had become the quartet's front man. I remember him encouraging us to clap along to the choruses of 'Take Me For What I'm Worth'. Twenty-five years later the same man has written one of the finest pop memoirs.

12- Good Clean Fun

Tony Christie

Tony Christie had been performing for many years before his single, 'Las Vegas', written by hit songwriters, Mitch Murray and Peter Callander, entered the charts in 1971, reaching No. 21. His strong voice was similar to Tom Jones, but distinct enough to attract a following. The melodramatic follow-up, 'I Did What I Did For Maria', reached No. 2. Maria was also name checked in the less violent 'Is This The Way To Amarillo' which was written by Neil Sedaka and Howard Greenfield. This song was revived four decades later by Peter Kay for Comic Relief with a celebrity-packed video. When Sedaka performs his own version of 'Amarillo' in Britain, he now has to mention the Kay connection.

Yet another slice of Americana, 'Don't Go Down To Reno' was previewed on *Top of the Pops* in June 1972 and *NME* stated: *"He'll probably retain his chart success with this big production number."*. However 'Reno' failed to chart. The follow-up, 'My Love Song', was also reviewed in *NME*: *"With his operatic voice and orchestra, this one's bound to please the mums. Suddenly half-way through, a 'pop' beat is introduced and then sacked in preference to a 'Zorba The Greek' treatment. O jeeze, it's all too much for me."* This single also flopped.

Christie's theme song to *The Protectors* series on ITV, 'Avenues And Alleyways', was widely heard, but reached a disappointing No. 37 in 1973. Next released was yet another Murray and Callander song, 'Love And Rainy Weather' which was featured in *The Lovers* film. This flopped, as did the same team's 'You Just Don't Have The Magic Anymore'. Clearly, Murray and Callander's magic was not working and Christie's next singles were penned by other writers.

Barry Mason and Roger Greenaway's 'Happy Birthday Baby' attracted some interest but failed to chart. The song starts with melodramatic strings in a minor key, but soon becomes a big, brash singalong. I am surprised that this single failed as I can imagine hearing it at pubs and parties. Two later 'Happy Birthday' songs – very different to each other– by Altered Images and Stevie Wonder both reached No. 2 in 1981. Perhaps Peter Kay could revive Christie's single?

In 1976, 'Drive Safely Darlin'' peaked at No. 35. Christie performed the song on *Top of the Pops*. This mawkish song's chorus goes, "*drive safely darlin', mind how you go.*" The song's storyline recalls the worst type of Nashville melodrama dross: "*outside a storm was blowing ... there's a long long road ahead ... that godforsaken night.*" The song reminded me of the tasteless American singles that Kenny Everett compiled for his *World's Worst Records* album.

Christie sang the part of Magaldi on the *Evita* studio cast album in 1976 and a re-recorded version of his featured song, 'On The Night Of A Thousand Stars' was later released as a single. Despite being produced by the song's writers – Andrew Lloyd Webber and Tim Rice – this failed to chart.

Guys 'N' Dolls

Guys 'N' Dolls are better known these days as spawning the hit duo Dollar – David van Day and Thereze Bazar – who left the group in 1978 and went on to far greater success. The original group comprised three pairs of males and females. They reached No. 2 with 'There's A Whole Lot Of Loving Going On' in spring 1975. Next was 'Here I Go Again'. *Record Mirror*: "*Hasty (very) follow-up to their current hit, and unfortunately without that certain something that was so apparent then. This one's a boy-girl number, sweet harmonies and all, but somehow I don't think so.*" It was a flop, peaking at No. 33.

Worse was to come with 'Let's All Get Together'. *Record Mirror* again: "*Having learned that one smash hit isn't automatically followed by another, Guys 'N' Dolls are obviously hoping that this will redress the balance. Simple singalong Summer Holiday-type number, it's an improvement on their last song, but still not as strong as the first. Its fate is definitely in the lap of the air-play gods.*" This single did not even enter the charts.

Guys 'N' Dolls were signed to the Magnet label who had had a great run of hits by Alvin Stardust and two Top Five hits by Peter Shelley. The ups, and more often downs, of Guys 'N' Dolls must have been frustrating for both label and group. The sextet bounced back with their own version of 'You Don't Have To Say You Love Me' which reached No. 5. The song had been a chart-topper for Dusty Springfield's definitive version in 1966 and a Top Twenty place for Elvis Presley just five years later.

'Stoney Ground' was released in November 1976 and previewed on *Top of the Pops*. *Record Mirror*: "*Well, they might have broken away from the sweeter sound but what they've come up with instead is mediocre nothingness I'm afraid.*" The single peaked at No. 38. Next up was 'Mamacita', a Cynthia Weill and Barry Mann composition, produced this time by Jonathan King and arranged by his long-time collaborator Johnny Arthey. *Record Mirror* was merciless: "*Bland sugary pop, usual harmonies and non-harmonies. Okay if you like this sort of thing. I don't.*" Another complete flop. The follow-up, 'Let's Make Love', displeased the publication even more: "*total lack of inspiration, overbearing wetness, utter irrelevance ... where do they get them from?*"

'Only Loving Does It' was a last gasp and staggered to No. 42 in 1978, probably thanks to a *Top of the Pops* appearance. *Record Mirror*: "*From hereinafter known as the theme music from the OXO advert ... MOR juvenile jigsaw song.*"

Meanwhile Dollar had signed to the Carrere label and had no less than four Top Twenty hits within a year. The duo's success continued in the early 1980s once they signed to WEA and worked with Trevor Horn.

Engelbert Humperdinck

The former Arnold Gerald Dorsey had an extraordinary start to his UK chart career. 'Release Me' kept The Beatles' double A-side, 'Penny Lane/Strawberry Fields Forever' off the top spot at the beginning of 1967. The million-selling single stayed in the UK charts for 56 weeks and the two follow-ups, 'There Goes My Everything' and 'The Last Waltz', were almost as successful; the former reached the second spot and the latter was another chart-topping million seller.

'My Marie' broke Engelbert's run of Top Twenty hits in 1970 by only reaching No. 31. A Tony Macaulay and Barry Mason composition, the song sounds very old fashioned even by Engelbert's standards. There is gentle piano at the start but we soon are bombarded with another big ballad. *"Oh Marie, I can't bear to see the children without bread."*

Engelbert's next single was a cover of The Bee Gees' 'Sweetheart', a country-style ballad that had been the B-side of the group's 'I.O.I.O' single. This did the trick for Engelbert, bringing him back into the charts and reaching No. 22. This was followed by no fewer than three complete flops.

'Santa Lija (Sogno D'Amore)' was described by *NME* as *"a romantic ballad with a throbbing beat and captivating Latin lilt ... a colourful arrangement of heavenly voices and cascading strings. It lacks one of those repetitive sing-a-long hooks which have been the hallmark of so many Engelbert discs and it's possible that this may prevent it being a super hit."*

Next was 'When There's No You', written by Les Reed and Jackie Rae, who borrowed the song's melody from Ruggero Leoncavallo's opera, *Pagliacci*. The single went nowhere in the UK, but topped the American Easy Listening charts. Understandably, the song is very melodramatic and operatic, but also sounds predictable and dull.

'Our Love Will Rise Again' was reviewed in *Record Mirror*: *"Great simplicity, a pacey tempo and I'd say the most commercially direct single from Engelbert in a heck of a time. It's instantly catchy and he punches home the lyrics and the arrangement is strictly uncluttered and everything falls into place."*

Two Top Twenty hits followed. 'Another Time, Another Place' written by Mike Leander and Eddie Seago, reached No. 13. It was the title track of Engelbert's album which was released at the same time. 'Too Beautiful To Last' was the theme to the 1971 film *Nicholas And Alexandra* which starred Michael Jayston and Janet Suzman in the title roles. The song was written by Richard Rodney Bennett and Paul Francis Webster. Bennett was nominated for an Oscar for his score, but he did not win.

This was pretty much the end of Engelbert's 1970s chart career. 'In Time' was released in June 1972, followed by 'I'm Leaving You' which was released in March 1973. *Record Mirror* commented on the latter: "*Provided this gets the radio plays it should make a romantic way into the charts. It's one of those lost-love, gawd-I'm-forlorn sort of songs, constructed to suit Engel's flowing tones. He's a good balladeer, no arguments, and this is an exciting gem for the easy listening millions.*"

Engelbert reached his peak in the very first year of his chart career and had been on a downward trend ever since then. His fans had basically stopped buying singles in large quantities and Engelbert's albums had not reached the Top Twenty since *We Made It Happen* in 1970. A Greatest Hits collection in 1974 gave Engelbert his first, and only, chart-topping album which stayed in the charts for thirty-four weeks.

'Love Is All' was Engelbert's last chart entry for twenty-six years, reaching no higher than No. 44. *NME* commented: "*If you don't mind me saying so, Engelly, this sounds awfully like 'Release Me'* ... *However we should all give him credit for handling these ballads with flair, sensitivity, style and monotonous regularity. A professional performance – tell your Mum.*" 'Free As The Wind' was released in March 1974 — *Record Mirror*: "*Beautiful creamy ballady sound on this, which is the theme from the movie* Papillon. *It lilts along. Engel in vocal top form* ...*Could well become a movie-theme classic that's after Mr Humperdinck has had a first bite at the charts with it.*"

A quarter of a century later, Engelbert briefly returned to the UK charts with his version of 'Quando Quando Quando' in 1999.

Tom Jones

It is hard not to lapse into cliches about Thomas Jones Woodward and his incredible ability to not only sing so heartily, but survive and reinvent himself and abandon the rather naff cabaret image of which his colleague and rival Engelbert Humperdinck has struggled to rid himself. After years of singing around the working men's clubs in his native South Wales, Tom went to No. 1 with his very first hit single, 'It's Not Unusual'. This was the beginning of a decade-long relationship with Decca Records.

Phil Hardy and Dave Laing summed up the situation: "*Over the next two years Jones had more flops than hits, but then found his true audience on TV and in cabaret and never looked back.*" Tom's follow-up to 'It's Not Unusual' was

'Once Upon A Time' which staggered to No 32. Written by Gordon Mills (who had co-written 'It's Not Unusual' with Les Reed), the song is not much more than a sequel to that first hit. The single has the same beat and a similar tune and arrangement. In consecutive verses Tom sings about Adam and Eve in Eden and then Delilah, no less. Now the latter woman might make the subject of a song on her own.

Curiously, Tom's James Bond theme, 'Thunderball', only reached No. 35 in early 1966. His previous film theme, 'What's New Pussycat?', had peaked at No. 11 the previous summer. 'Thunderball' is not the best of the 1960s Bond themes and pales into comparison with 'From Russia With Love', 'Goldfinger' and 'You Only Live Twice'.

Tom performed 'Stop Breakin' My Heart' on *Top of the Pops* in March of the same year. This track appeared three decades later on Decca's *The Northern Soul Scene* CD. In the sleeve-notes, John Reed says: *"An awesome powerhouse vocal by Tom on this ... flop single which barely grazed the charts back in 1966. A 100mph stormer if ever there was one ... even gains grudging respect from the 'true' soul connoisseurs."* Reed is correct; this is a real Northern stomper with lively brass and female backing vocals, truly an exciting single. If only Tom had recorded a whole album of this sort of material.

Another flop, 'This And That', peaked at No. 44 in August 1966, but was followed three months later by 'Green Green Grass Of Home'. The latter, a Jerry Lee Lewis album track, was a sentimental country ballad which gave Tom his second chart-topper, staying at No. 1 for seven weeks over the Christmas period. 'Green Green Grass Of Home' was followed by a dozen Top Twenty hits (eight of which went Top Ten). 'Puppet Man' sneaked into the Top Fifty, peaking at No. 49. Tom returned with the melodramatic 'Till' which took him back to No. 2. There were so many flops for Tom in the 1970s that I will only describe a selection.

'Letter To Lucille' was slammed in *NME* in 1973: *"Tom sings pretty good, but the song is so impossibly dire that it makes you wince ... If Tom Jones hadn't gone cabaret and had fronted a nice, tough little six-piece band, he'd probably be one of the funkiest singers in the world, and maybe one of the poorest."* *Record Mirror*'s reviewer disagreed: *"This has a bright bouncy basic beat, and Tom does his business-like job on it. Got a touch of the old prison-discipline about it, a story of yearning and hope, and urgency."* 'Lucille' stalled at No. 31.

'Golden Days' was released in November 1973 and previewed on *Top of the Pops*. It is one of Tom's worst singles with intrusive female backing vocals. The lyrics are dire: *"golden day, come and play"* and *"catch a girl, kiss a girl."* A deserved flop.

'Today I Started Loving You Again' was written by American country singer-songwriter, Merle Haggard. *NME*'s reviewer compared the single to 'Green Green Grass Of Home': *"where 'Grass' was eager and dynamic, this is a perfunctory performance. Uninspired boogie guitar and workmanlike electric piano are joined by simpering strings ... Most unremarkable."* Clearly both Tom and the record company had misjudged the British public's appetite for country music. Haggard was a talented writer and many American acts had successfully covered the same song. Interestingly, Scott Walker also went through a country music phase around this time, covering unlikely songs which were also met with indifference from the public.

'La La La (Just Having You Here)' was released in February 1974. *Record Mirror: "Tom singing out with a soulful intensity on a bluesy sort of item. The blend of his voice, well out in front, and the soul-sister routine behind ... sounds certainly good enough to crack the charts, despite his recent somewhat in-and-out form in the Top Fifty."*

Tom's rendition of 'Something 'Bout You Baby I Like' was quite energetic and reached No. 36 in 1974. Seven years later, Status Quo got as high as No. 9 with their version. 'Pledging My Love' failed to impress *Record Mirror*: *"This is Mr Jones Mark 2 – the slow ballad singer.. Actually I found this slow to the point of boring."* The same publication was also unimpressed with 1975's 'I Get Your Number': *"Pseudo-soulful backing with odd bits of* Shaft, *inspired by unusually tame vocal from Tom, who admittedly hasn't got much to work with. Back to the big ballads, boyo."*

Tom's 1970s UK singles chart career ended in 1977 with 'Say You'll Stay Until Tomorrow' which reached No. 40. There were several years in the artistic wilderness before Tom's talent was truly appreciated. His own son took over management duties and steered Tom's career away from naffness and into emphasising the blues and gospel roots of Jones The Voice. But this was way in the future and more mediocrity was to come.

Matt Monro

Matt Monro just slips into this book because he had two Top Thirty hits in the UK between 1965 and 1979, namely his cover of 'Yesterday' (which reached No. 8, the same position that The Beatles' original reached in 1976 when EMI began their big reissue campaign) and 'And You Smiled', No. 28 in 1973. The latter was a vocal version of Simon Park's 'Eye Level' theme for the television series, *Van Der Valk*. Monro's heyday was in the first half of the 1960s. He had Top Ten hits with 'Portrait Of My Love', 'My Kind Of Girl' and 'Walk Away'. Surprisingly, his Bond theme, 'From Russia With Love' (written by Lionel Bart) only reached No. 20, while Monro's Oscar winning song, 'Born Free' (written by Don Black and John Barry) did not chart on either side of the Atlantic. Vic Reeves, no less, had the British chart success with 'Born Free', reaching No. 6 in 1991. Chartland is a strange world.

Another Matt Monro flop is worth mentioning; 1970s 'We're Gonna Change The World' was an unusual record. The song was written by Tim Harris and David Matthews as the latter explained to Jon Kutner: *"the idea was to take a whimsical look at what was happening in the streets in the mid-sixties in the way of protest marches."* Apparently, lyricist Tim Harris used the names of two of his exes and his own wife as the three characters in the song – Shirley Wood, Margaret Beatty and Annie Harris. The single was played a lot on Radio One, earning that term "turntable hit". I remember 'We're Gonna Change The World' very well; the hook *"Come with us, run with us..."* More recently I heard Robert Elms praising this song.

The New Seekers

As the name suggests, there is a real link between The Seekers and The New Seekers. Keith Potger, guitarist and vocalist with the original Seekers, used his name and patronage to launch the new group. The group's first releases did not chart, but a cover of Melanie's 'Look What They've Done To My Song, Ma' was previewed on *Top of the Pops* in summer 1970 but only reached No. 44. A lively cover of Delaney &

Bonnie's 'Never Ending Song Of Love' reached No. 2 the following year, establishing The New Seekers as a chart act. I must confess that I did not know the origin of this single at the time.

The group's next single was another uptempo sing-along called 'Good Old Fashioned Music'. *NME*: "*A sort of country sing-along complete with all the trappings of the idiom – banjo, fiddles and brass bass, it features the boys and girls in a perky vocal exchange. Leading up to the inevitable rousing join-in chorus which we've come to expect from The New Seekers' discs ... but now that the outfit is fully established in Britain, it's bound to be a thundering hit.*" There is a lively version from the group's 1972 Royal Albert Hall concert which can be viewed on YouTube. Banjo and washboard give the song a skiffle feel. Despite a *Top of the Pops* appearance in October 1971 and being sandwiched between their No. 2 hit and the chart-topper, 'I'd Like To Teach The World To Sing', it seemed that the British record-buying public did not care for 'Good Old Fashioned Music': it was a total flop.

Coca-Cola brought the group back to the top of the charts with 'I'd Like To Teach The World To Sing (In Perfect Harmony)' which stayed at No. 1 in January 1972 for four weeks. The group's Eurovision entry, 'Beg, Steal Or Borrow', went to No. 2 and three more Top Twenty singles followed in the next twelve months.

The next year started badly for The New Seekers with three of their singles not reaching even the Top Thirty. Eve Graham was featured on 'Nevertheless (I'm In Love With You)', a song written in 1931 and re-launched in an MGM Fred Astaire musical from the fifties. The same song was covered by Harry Nilsson on his album, *A Touch Of Schmilsson In The Night*, which was released a couple of months later. The New Seekers' version is very M.O.R., perhaps hinting at the group's future direction. *NME*'s reviewer was unimpressed: "*This toon is a real load of baloney. Sun-stroked strings and an entire thirties-type approach as Eve Graham adapts a Bette Midler stance. Strictly middle of the road stuff.*" 'Nevertheless' peaked at No. 34.

The follow-up, 'Goodbye Is Just Another Word', was reviewed in *Record Mirror*: "*Back to the roots – that's one way of putting it. A fine melody (by Lobo) with Eve Graham singing in an authoritative voice and the right amount of sadness coming through ... This will become a much-requested family favourite as well as a top three single.*" This single reached No. 36.

Worse was to follow, 'We've Got To Do It Now' certainly eluded me at the time. This was another Cook and Greenaway composition and was part of the Keep Britain Tidy campaign. The single was a big bouncy orchestral number telling us to save the earth as *"we can't go on forever"*. Predictably, *NME* were harsh: *"The New Seekers look pretty damn stupid singing about cleaning rivers and so on when it's such a poor song ... there's the usual jolly good time harmonies, carried with some conviction."* Eve was again the lead singer.

Such a string of flops usually demand a rethink from the record company and, just two months later, the retro-sounding 'You Won't Find Another Fool Like Me', written by Tony Macaulay and Geoff Stephens, gave the group their second chart-topper. The single – and its Top Five follow-up, 'I Get A Little Sentimental Over You' – both featured Lyn Paul as lead singer and this MOR change of style was clearly the right commercial move. The group began to splinter but 'Sing Hallelujah' followed — *Record Mirror*: *"They may technically be dead but they won't lie down. This is another instantly commercial biggie with Lyn doing the lead vocal, as she has on the last couple. It's not for me as commercial as 'Sentimental', to shorten a huge hit, but it's still the thing that roars straight to the top of the charts."*

A new line-up of the group were then signed to CBS. 'It's So Nice To Have You Home' was reviewed in *Record Mirror*: *"Action replay with The New Seekers. Back with a swinger, not unlike the sort of record football clubs bring out for the supporters to sway to on a Saturday afternoon. Clean cut, loyal all that sort of thing. I'll be surprised if it misses."* Despite a *Top of the Pops* appearance, the single only reached No. 44. 'It's So Nice' is actually not that bad a record and certainly better than its follow-ups..

'I Wanna Go Back' saw a return to the Top Thirty, peaking at No. 25 and 'Anthem (One Day In Every Week)' benefited from a *Top of the Pops* appearance and reached No. 21. Next was 'Flashback' which flopped — *Record Mirror*: *"Sounds impossible but they're even worse than Brotherhood Of Man."* This was the group's final chart appearance. Worse was to follow. 'Love Is A Song' was released in 1979 — *Record Mirror*: *"Another hit from the reserve squad, but the cracks are beginning to show. No matter how bouncy they seem The New Seekers are slowly being drowned out by a top-heavy wall of sound. Buy, it won't last long."*

GILBERT O'SULLIVAN

Once Gilbert O'Sullivan signed to Gordon Mills' MAM label, the hits started and kept on coming. There were a couple of flops along the way. His second single on MAM, 'Underneath The Blanket Go', reached No. 40. I did not like this song when it was first released; the words felt ambiguous and slightly disturbing. The line: *"I've even wrote to Marjorie Proops"* (then the *Daily Mirror*'s famous agony aunt) was not funny even in 1971. The song has not worn well. This lowly chart placing was a solitary blip in a run of eleven Top Twenty hits (including two chart-toppers with 'Clair' and 'Get Down').

For every classic Gilbert single such as 'We Will' and 'Alone Again (Naturally)', there were monstrosities such as 'Oooh-Wakka-Doo-Wakka-Day' and 'A Woman's Place'. The latter deservedly only went as high as No. 42. By 1974, chauvinist views on women's lib were still widespread, but this surely was not a wise marketing move by an artist who principally appealed to females. If Gilbert was trying to be ironic, he failed spectacularly. The song is not even witty or shocking, just mediocre and dull. One line says: *"I'm all for a woman, who can make it on her own, But I believe, a woman's place is in the home."* He told *Shindig*: *"yes, the lyric was a loser... I paid a heavy price for that, but I don't regret it. The lyric may be old fashioned, but I did believe a woman's place was in the home because I was brought up by my mother, not my father. So everything about being at home looking after children, I saw. So I put that into the song."* *NME* disagreed: *"this 'un possesses more balls than anything the Hermit of Tin Pan Alley has put out since 'Get Down' ... but the tune ain't really strong enough to take it higher than the twenties."* On Gilbert's debut album, *Himself*, there is an even worse set of lyrics in 'Permissive Twit' which was another unfunny misogynist ditty.

The dreary 'Christmas Song' restored Gilbert to the Top Twenty, but was followed by 'You Are You'. *Record Mirror*: *"lines like 'You're like Dr Kissinger on a peace mission for two' or 'you're like a tin of soup by Warhol'. There's that same sing-along bouncy beat, and everything's lovely but the sentiment or rather the way it's expressed leaves me cold."* 'You Are You' is another "list" song, but Gilbert does not have the wit of Cole Porter to carry this off. Unsurprisingly, it flopped. The next single was 'I Don't Love You But I Think I Like You'. This was Gilbert's final hit of the 1970s, reaching No. 14.

'I'll Believe It When I See It' was released in 1975 and previewed on *Top of the Pops*. I can remember hearing the song's marvellous melody. Despite the female backing singers and overblown orchestral arrangement, this is one of Gilbert's finest singles. The tale of the cuckolded narrator in the song is genuinely moving as he observes that his partner is "*to spend the weekend with another man.*" *Record Mirror*'s review quoted the MAM press release, "*much more of a soulful ballad.*" and then sneered saying the song is "*sounding about as soulful as Vera Lynn.*" calling it "*schmaltz.*". Perhaps the backing singers are too dominant towards the end of the song, but at least Gilbert improvises over them in counterpoint. Unfortunately, 'I'll Believe It When I See It' was the first of seven more flops for O'Sullivan on MAM.

'You Never Listen To Reason' was slammed in *Record Mirror*: "*Indifferent and badly-mixed uptempo number that is way below Gilbert's best. What little life there is in it is all thanks to the tambourine and sax.*" Next up was 'Doing What I Know'. This single was dismissed in *Record Mirror & Disc*: "*I'm afraid there's nothing in this song to recommend it, boring lyrics, monotonous beat. Back to the drawing board.*" The same publication dealt with 'To Each His Own' with just three words: "*Little boy lost.*"

In Barry Scott's book *We Had Joy We Had Fun*, Gilbert states, "*the records were tailing off as they do for most artists. It was a bad period. The result was that through 1976 and 1977, I broke up with Gordon (Mills).*" The details of this sad episode is described by Simon Garfield in *Expensive Habits*. "*The hits dried up in the mid-seventies. The singles came out as before, but airplay was slight and sales small. The songs in themselves didn't change that much, and perhaps that was the problem. After four great years, O'Sullivan was now something of a man out of time.*" There was a lengthy court case over under-paid royalties which O'Sullivan eventually won. However, his career was on hold for several years and never properly recovered.

Pickettywitch

Pickettywitch emerged in 1970 with three Top Thirty hits in a row, namely 'That Same Old Feeling', '(It's Like A) Sad Old Kinda Movie' and 'Baby I Won't Let You Down'. That 'Same Old Feeling' and 'Sad Old Kinda Movie' were both written by John MacLeod and Tony Macaulay, while 'Baby I Won't Let You Down' was written by Les Reed and Geoff Stephens. All three were produced, arranged and even conducted by John MacLeod. This was harmless chart pop on the Pye label, which has actually lasted better than many songs from that era.

Follow-ups were trickier and unsuccessful. The first was 'Waldo P. Emerson Jones', originally written for the American cartoon group, The Archies, by Andy Kim and Jeff Barry. The song concerns a Walter Mitty character who went "*backstage at Woodstock.*" It is not Jeff Barry's finest hour, nothing like the quality of the many classics that he wrote with Ellie Greenwich. There is footage of Pickettywitch performing 'Summertime Feeling' on a Roger Whittaker television show. This single, co-written by MacLeod, sounds a bit too much like 'Same Old Feeling'.

There is colour film footage of the group miming their next release 'Bring A Little Light Into My World' in a garden. This is probably Pickettywitch's best single and should have been a hit. The song has a great melody with plenty of hooks and was again written by MacLeod and Macaulay. MacLeod also handled arrangement and production duties.

When television critic Clive James reviewed the 1974 Eurovision Song Contest, he described Abba's song 'Waterloo' as "*built on a T. Rex riff and delivered in a Pickettywitch style that pointed up the cretinous lyric with ruthless perfection.*" I wonder if Polly Brown was aware of this comparison as she returned in the summer of 1974 in the duo Sweet Dreams with a cover version of 'Honey Honey', one of Abba's few flops. This reached No. 10. The same year Polly had a minor solo hit with 'Up In A Puff Of Smoke'.

Cliff Richard

Cliff's chart career is, to use that frequently misused word, unique. He has been having hit singles since 1958 and remains a constant presence in the UK singles charts. Cliff managed to maintain his popularity and chart career throughout the 1960s. The 1970s were trickier times for him and the erratic nature of Cliff's chart positions suggested that his record company's A & R department were not concentrating. There were clearly problems with quality control. Generally, Cliff's flops were usually deserved.

1971's 'Flying Machine' peaked just outside the Top Thirty at No. 31. It was written by Georg Hultgreen, a former member of Eclection and later known as Georg Kajanus when he led Sailor. The song was used in the title sequence of the television programme *Get Away With Cliff* which featured the singer in a fairground in, you have already guessed, a flying machine. Norrie Paramour arranged, conducted and produced this old-fashioned sounding record which could have been made at any time in the previous five years. Kajanus/Hultgreen wrote many memorable songs for Sailor; it was disappointing that 'Flying Machine' was so unremarkable.

Cliff's follow-up, 'Sing A Song Of Freedom', was written by Doug Flett and Guy Fletcher and fared better, reaching No. 13. Next was another step backwards: in 1972 'Jesus' scraped to No. 35 and predictably alienated Cliff's non-Christian fans. The song had been a big hit in Europe when it was recorded by Helmut Grabher under the name of Jeremy Faith. *NME*: *"This is Cliff singing to his main man, asking him to come back to Earth and save us from the filth and scum we live in. The song isn't exactly heavy-weight, but that won't stop the mums and vicars from buying it."* Many decades later, Andrew Ure wrote in *Shindig* magazine: *"(Cliff's first religion themed single) opens with a phased drumbeat and quickly settles into a laidback groove. A gospel choir joins in a fuzzy guitar solo appears ... lyrics like 'Jesus come back to earth (and) 'save us from Satan' were always going to be a tough sell to the average record buyer. 'Jesus' flopped becoming his worst selling single to date. Despite the commercial failure though Cliff said he 'was really quite pleased with the recording' as well he should have been, because it's a damn good one."* Perhaps a less obvious song title could have helped?

Cliff previewed 'A Brand New Song' on *Top of the Pops* in November 1972. *NME* liked it; "*This one ... is another good pop song in a light vein well done. He's got good control – albeit a bit too clear at times for my tastes.*" Then the unthinkable happened – it was a flop. Simon Frith in *Let It Rock* summed up the problem: "*I must have heard Cliff Richard's 'Brand New Song' at least thirty times and I can't remember a thing about it.*"

Spring 1973 saw Eurovision and Cliff was representing the UK for the second time. 'Power To All Our Friends' brought him back into the Top Five again. More hits followed until the release of 'It's Only Me You Left Behind'. This was a Hank Marvin and John Farrar composition with Bruce Welch joining the writers for production duties. *Record Mirror*: "*The song isn't the most inspired thing Cliff's ever done, a sort of mid-tempo ballad with a few hand-claps at the chorus.*" Once again, Cliff performed the song on *Top of the Pops* as a new release. It did not reach the singles charts.

'Honky Tonk Angel' had been a Country No. 1 in the USA for Conway Twitty. Bruce Welch of The Shadows had heard the song and thought it would make a good comeback single after Cliff's disappointing chart performances since his second Eurovision attempt. The track was produced by Hank Marvin, Bruce Welch and John Farrar and was arranged by the latter. In *Let It Rock*, John Peel sneered: "*a dreary country-up, lacking in character, humour and/or balls should continue the series of failures.*" Peel was correct, but failed to mention that the term 'honky tonk angel' was an American slang for a woman of ill-repute. Once Cliff was informed of this, the single was quickly withdrawn. He said in the press: "*I hope it's a flop. I never want to hear it again and I hope most of the public never hear it. I knew honky-tonks were something to do with bars, but I completely misconstrued the meaning. Okay, some people might say I'm naïve – obviously it's very embarrassing for me. Now I know what I've been singing about. I've taken steps to do all I can to make it a flop. I hope no-one buys it. If the record is a hit and I'm asked to sing it, I will refuse unless the words are changed.*"

Cliff had a much better year in 1976. 'Devil Woman' brought him back to the Top Ten for the first time since 'Power To All Our Friends', three years earlier. This single gave Cliff a more modern image and saw the parent album, *I'm Nearly Famous*, reach No. 5 in the album charts, his highest position since 1969. The follow-up to 'Devil Woman' was the genuinely innovative 'I Can't Ask For Anything More Than You' which showcased Cliff's falsetto voice and reached No. 17.

The next single was 'Hey Mr. Dream Maker'. The song suggests that composers Bruce Welch and Alan Tarney had been making notes from both the lyrics of Lindisfarne's 'Meet Me On The Corner' (*"Hey Mr Dream Seller"*) but also the tune of Dr Hook's 'Sylvia's Mother'. There was a prominent acoustic guitar while Cliff sang softly about how he *"ain't got no Josie no more."* That's a lot of negatives! Thanks to a *Top of the Pops* appearance, the single reached No. 31 in 1976.

Cliff came back with the lively 'My Kinda Life' which reached No. 15, but it would be his last Top Thirty hit for over two years. Up next was 'When Two Worlds Drift Apart' which featured Elton John-style piano and was elegiac and slow. The strings come in the second verse. *Record Mirror* agreed: *"This one is a bit slow to be a real biggie in the summertime perhaps."* The single scraped to No. 46.

'Can't Take The Hurt Anymore' by Laurie Andrew is a slow ballad with strummed acoustic guitar. Steel guitar comes in and there is a dramatic instrumental break. The chorus is merely the song title repeated ad nauseum. 'Yes He Lives', written by Terry Britton, was another gospel number. *Record Mirror* were under-whelmed: *"Unmemorable splash in the disco pool."*

Cliff had a hitless year in 1978: 'Please Remember Me' was written by Dave Loggins and Bruce Woodley and previewed on *Top of the Pops* in August. It is all rather American sounding with phrases like *"weather report"*. *Record Mirror* liked it: *"This is a cracking single, he's caught a bit of the West Coast sound without wallowing in the soppy blandness that usually comes with it."* The following year, 'Green Light' was released as a single in February 1979. This was the title track of Cliff's album from the previous year. We hear funky guitar and keyboards, the hook *"searching for a green light"* and a guitar solo, but the song does not really go anywhere. Despite being penned by hit songwriter, Alan Tarney and an energetic *Top of the Pops* appearance, 'Green Light' only staggered to No. 57.

There was relief for all concerned when 'We Don't Talk Anymore' went to No. 1 in the summer of 1979. This single was Cliff's first chart-topper since 1968's 'Congratulations' and thoroughly deserved its success. Again written by Alan Tarney and produced by Bruce Welch, the song brought out the best in Cliff. The instrumental backing is unusual and effective. I remember critics at the time championing the song's clever fade-outs of the keyboards. This was genuinely an original sounding pop record and Cliff's voice was noticeably more expressive and distinct.

Unfortunately, Cliff finished the 1970s at a low point with 'Hot Shot' that scraped in at No. 46. It was written by Terry Britton and B. A. Robertson. *Record Mirror*: *"a big brassy sound classily produced ... Cliff's ol' vocal chords are in great shape as usual..Yet another hit without a doubt."* The record company were quick learners and brought in Alan Tarney to work again with Cliff over the next two albums.

The Seekers

The Seekers had an impressive run of hits, nearly all written and produced by Tom Springfield. This Australian quartet had a formula, but it was both original and successful. They had two British chart-toppers 'I'll Never Find Another You' and the million-selling 'The Carnival Is Over'. One of my strongest memories of 1960s pop was hearing Judith Durham's distinctive voice on the group's many hits, especially when she often sang a descant part on the songs' final choruses.

'Emerald City' was released in time for the Christmas market in 1967. It was the group's final chart single, reaching only No. 50 for just one week. *NME*: *"(I) don't think it will do as well as 'Morningtown Ride' ... but it's an obvious chart-buster. The melody is based upon the last movement of Beethoven's Symphony No. 9 but it's become an enchanting ballad with a lovely fairy-tale lyric admirably suited to Judith Durham's crystal-clear voice. There's a kiddies' choir joining in on the chorus and a rippling accompaniment. It's hummable, undemanding and refreshingly uncomplicated."*

EMI kept releasing singles after the flop of 'Emerald City', not realising that The Seekers' appeal now was to adults who generally purchased albums not singles. 'Days Of My Life' was released in the last week of April 1968 as 'by The Seekers featuring Judith Durham' and was previewed on *Top of the Pops* the following week. *NME*: *"this is a*

Mickie Most production — and that's usually the stamp of success. A very nice disc it is too. The group sings in ensemble — though as usual Judith Durham's crystal-clear tones rise way above the boys' voices and she takes a solo passage midway through. The song is faintly folksy, and has a wistful yearning quality." Record Mirror predicted: "a number which will go straight into their list of evergreens" and *Melody Maker*'s reviewer agreed: "*I fail to see how their folksy choice of material can miss ... this is certainly going to go right to the top.*" This time even Mickie Most's golden touch did not work.

Later in the year the group toured Britain concluding with a cabaret stint at the Talk Of The Town in London in July. Their set was recorded and released as The Seekers' farewell album, effectively a greatest hits collection. Sales were excellent with the album reaching No. 2. 'Love Is Kind, Love Is Wine' was billed as '*Seekers Farewell Single*'. *NME*: "*A track written by Bruce Woodley. Typical folk-beat material of the kind we shall long associate with this group. It's exhilarating and bouncy and makes an ideal vehicle for The Seekers' unmistakeable vocal sound.*" Another flop.

EMI realised that The Seekers' audience were clearly keen album buyers. Just two months later, *The Best Of The Seekers* was rush-released; all the hits were included and there was also room for 'Emerald City' and 'Island Of Dreams'. The album's front cover was a very formal photograph of the men in matching jackets and trousers, while Judith Durham has her hair "up" and is wearing a full length dress with a high neckline and far too many ruffles. All four are unsmiling and look ill at ease. They needn't have worried. The album went to No.1 and stayed in the charts for an astonishing 125 weeks, a feat bettered in the 1960s only by *The Black And White Minstrel Show*, *The Sound Of Music*, *Sergeant Pepper* and *The Best Of The Beach Boys*. The Seekers no longer needed hit singles.

'Island Of Dreams' was released as as single at about the same time as it appeared on *The Best Of The Seekers*. Penny Valentine: "*I often think it's rather odd how things go full circle. Here are The Seekers who no longer exist here, with a track from one of their albums. It happens to be a Tom Springfield number that Dusty, he and Mike had their first hit ever as The Springfields and it happens that Dusty first discovered The Seekers in Australia. Ah well – the song sounds as good as usual.*" The Springfields' original version had reached No. 5 in 1962 and stayed in the charts for six months. The Seekers' version had appeared on their 1966 album, *Come The Day*, so this was a rather pointless release for a single.

This, however, did not stop EMI releasing another single, 'Colours Of My Life', as late as August 1969. I love Penny Valentine's scathing comments: *"They might have broken up, but it's doubtful if EMI Records will ever let us forget The Seekers were once alive and well and a commercial proposition. Not that it really matters because they make a very sweet pleasant sound and, of its type, this is very very nice. Very charming and undemanding, it will probably do exceptionally well."* *NME* was kinder: *"vintage material ... a rhythmic ballad in folk beat style with a commercial gloss provided by added strings. It's a showcase for Judith's crystal-clear tones ... not perhaps one of the strongest songs the group have ever waxed, an effective showcase for the quartet's distinctive style."* I can only agree with Penny Valentine; it felt like EMI were milking The Seekers catalogue dry.

THE SHADOWS

The Shadows had an extraordinary chart career starting with their first hit 'Apache' in 1960, the first of five chart-toppers for them in the early 1960s. The group's two attempts at vocal singles in 1965, 'Mary Ann' and 'Don't Make My Baby Blue', both went Top Twenty. This must have encouraged the group to do more of the same as their instrumental singles were faring less and less well. The Shadows' vocals were always tuneful, avoiding nasal delivery or affectation, but were also fairly characterless. I feel that both Bruce Welch and Hank Marvin sound a little like Cliff himself, but there are many worse singers to copy.

'The Dreams I Dream' was a Hank Marvin composition. *NME*: *"A very pretty mid-tempo ballad with the most intricate vocal harmonies we'd heard from The Shadows on disc. Hank leads with Bruce joining in some passages, and others weaving an underlying harmonic pattern. There's a steady beat with clanking piano, a plaintive feel to the lyric and the jog-trotting rhythm is a bit Good-Time-ish. Very relaxing."* At No. 42, it was the Shads' lowest chart placing so far.

'Maroc 7' was the group's last instrumental hit of the 1960s. Like 1966's 'A Place In The Sun', it only reached No. 24. 'Tomorrow's

Cancelled', a Hank Marvin and Brian Bennett composition, was released in September 1967. Campbell: "*This release was a brave departure from the group's usual sound and totally different from their previous disc. It's a gentle, dreamy sort of number, which jogs along at a steady relaxed pace. Hank's reflective guitar gives way to vibraphone and ethereal wordless voices, which double up the melody in some places.*" Maurice Woodcraft of *Bungleflint* (sic!) adds: "*It was largely a jazz/pop piece, excellent in its own way, but probably uncommercial in the light of The Beatles' movement into psychedelic music.*" *NME* were also generous: "*Gentle, easy to listen to and with a very catchy melody .. should get a lot of airplay. Would be nice to see them back in the singles chart.*" Penny Valentine was more perceptive: "*In a funny way, now that the Pirates are gone, I expect The Shadows to come leaping back into the chart ... again. After all, it's going to be the consistent old-timers who are going to have all the breaks now ... This is one of their all-playing pieces that reminded me of 'The In Crowd' with wobbly guitars. I am not impressed.*"

'I Met A Girl' was another vocal number with Hank singing lead — *NME*: "*a happy-go-lucky bouncer with a strong country flavour. It's very much a Hank Marvin showcase. Snappy medium-fast pace ... and a fairly catchy tune.*" *Disc & Music Echo* thought that the single had: "*a fairly catchy tune ... But with so many vocal groups around, I don't think it will be a big hit.*"

'Dear Old Mrs Bell' was The Shadows' first single in six months. It was given a thoughtful critique by Penny Valentine: "*This is a very pretty record, very well produced and very well sung but I still don't like it very much. The main reason being that somehow I feel songs about people like this sound so dated these days, and however sweet she is, does one's heart really go out to 'Mrs Bell' as it did to 'Eleanor Rigby'? As far as I'm concerned it doesn't.*" According to *NME*, the record was: "*a pretty little song about the isolated life of an old-age pensioner ... Hank and Bruce handle the lyric – harmonising attractively in the chorus and taking solo passages in the verses ... The tune is hummable and melodic, and the lyric is highly sentimental.*" I agree; 'Dear Old Mrs Bell' was contrived and patronising, whereas the Beatles' song, 'Eleanor Rigby', eighteen months earlier, had been both original and deeply moving.

The Shadows' cover of 'Slaughter On Tenth Avenue' was the group's final single of the 1960s. This song was from a ballet sequence in Rodgers and Hart's 1936 Broadway musical, *On Your Toes*. The tune had been covered many times already, including by The Ventures in

1964. *Record Mirror*: "*Simple, straightforward Hank B. Marvin-led reading of the Richard Rodgers standard ... Ever so musicianly natch, and the melody is treated with reverence. Hard to see just how far it will go, but it's a fine arrangement.*" At the end of the following decade, The Shadows could only get hits with cover versions and their albums were also dominated by them covering other people's hits.

After a couple of years as Marvin, Welch and Farrar with Australian singer-songwriter, John Farrar, Hank and Bruce realised that they could not escape their Shadows legacy and trademark. Even when this very effective vocal trio performed live, the audience expected and requested old Shadows songs, especially as encores. The two Marvin, Welch and Farrar albums are worth hearing and may surprise listeners.

Hank and Bruce reunited with drummer Brian Bennett as The Shadows and released 'Turn Around And Touch Me' in 1973. This was the group's first single in four years. *NME*: "*Ahhh welcome back. This little hummola brings back memories of 'Wonderful Land' and Jeff Beck's extravaganza version of 'Love Is Blue', so by all accepted criteria it has to be great and so it is bedad. Hank Marvin's still doin' it like he used to, so all you nostalgists, get down, get set — wallow!*" Record Mirror agreed: "*the decisive lead guitar figure of Hank, the powering percussion, the simple melodic line – all there all over again.*" Campbell, inevitably, is fairer: "*a slow wistful number highlighting Hank's brilliant phrasing and that cantabile tone of his as he melted the notes in the finest Shadows tradition.. Clean, uncluttered production work.*"

The Eurovision Song Contest in 1975 brought the group back into the charts with 'Let Me Be The One', but follow-ups were unsuccessful. 'It'll Be Me Babe' was written by John Farrar and Hank Marvin and is in that ersatz funky style of Fox that was briefly popular in the mid-1970s. Bruce Welch and Hank Marvin are duetting and the performance sounds nothing like the Shads. The single was reviewed in *NME*: "*although this is lightweight, it's startlingly funky. Hank Marvin cuts up with some of the, um, wilder guitar work of his last 10 years.*"

'Run Baby Run' displayed a frequent trait of flops; when artists simply tried to copy the style of a previous hit. Campbell: "*the problem was that the song was too similar to 'Let Me Be The One', but was inferior in every respect, a caricature, in fact..*" Rhythm guitarist Bruce Welch allegedly referred to the track as '*Let Me Be The Two*'.

A carefully compiled *20 Golden Greats* album was released by EMI in 1977 and was one of the first TV advertised albums by a single artist (K-Tel, Ronco and Arcade had been releasing TV advertised various artists albums since the early 1970s). The album went to No. 1 just as a Beach Boys' compilation, with the same title, had done a year before. This was The Shadows' first chart-topping album since 1962, staying at No. 1 for six weeks. Both these two *20 Golden Greats* albums avoided having a picture of either group on their front cover. The Beach Boys' album had just a painting of a surfer, while the Shads' album sleeve merely featured three guitar machine heads on a plain yellow background. This was a trick used many years later for the million-selling *Abba Gold* CD.

'Another Night', a group composition with Alan Tarney, was released while *20 Golden Greats* was doing well in the album charts. This is an old-fashioned instrumental and quite dramatic and enjoyable. Campbell: *"'Another Night' exudes class, a superb melody bolstered by powerful percussive effects and a robust bass line."* 'Another Night' and another flop!

'Love Deluxe' was written by Tom Shapiro and was released in August 1978. The single has uncharacteristic fuzz guitar and piano. The lyrics — *"too bad you never asked her name"* and *"cats eyes ... cat-like walk"* — feel archaic for that time. Campbell sees 'Love Deluxe' as: *"a disco-flavoured song ... with fine synth accompaniment from Adrian Lee ... The lead vocal was taken by Bruce himself and the single was far removed from the sound associated with the group."*

Later in the year The Shadows returned to the singles chart for the first time since Eurovision with an instrumental version of 'Don't Cry For Me Argentina'. The single did exceedingly well in the run up to Christmas, peaking at No. 5. This was the group's highest instrumental single chart placing since 1964's 'The Rise And Fall Of Flingel Bunt'. There was clearly a market for The Shadows to perform their own versions of well-known songs and this formula did very well for many years. 'Theme From The Deer Hunter' (Cavatina) brought the group back into the Top Twenty in Spring 1979. The problem for me was that The Shadows' instrumental hits of the 1960s still sound interesting, modern and unpredictable, whereas the late 1970s tracks have not lasted as well.

Peter Skellern

Skellern's first hit, 'You're A Lady', established a style which was original and became instantly recognisable. Here we heard the mild Lancashire accent, high tenor voice, swooping choir, muted brass band and clever arrangements. The choir became a favourite effect for Skellern in the studio; it was achieved by recording the voices at a slower speed and making them sound faster and higher when played back at normal speed. 'You're A Lady' became something of a standard with cover versions by Johnny Mathis and many others. It can be difficult for an artist to follow-up a huge hit.

The follow-up, previewed on a Harry Secombe television show, was 'Our Jackie's Getting Married'. This release was a serious error, being a little too gimmicky; from the title's Northern style and Skellern's affected voice to the brief burst of Mendelsohn's 'Wedding March'. The song still sounds rather twee to these ears with its out of tune piano and brass band in waltz time. Whereas 'You're A Lady' had considerable charm and originality, this follow-up felt too self-conscious and contrived. *Record Mirror* called it: "*a jolly little romp about an old fashioned pastime known as courting.*" Skellern himself told the same publication his honest feelings about the single being a flop: "*I wasn't really upset about 'Jackie' not making it ... I didn't really want it released. We (Skellern and his producer Paul Sammes) were going to do another song but the mixing went wrong so 'Jackie' was put out as a sort of stop-gap by the record company.*" I wonder what Skellern's opinion would have been had 'Jackie' been a hit?

Even worse was the third single on Decca. 'Roll Away' is hard to describe. The record is very slow with organ, a big choir and orchestra. This release was clearly a big mistake for both artist and record company. A television performance is curiously unappealing, too. *Record Mirror*, unusually, has their critical antennae out of order: "*he is surely one of the most important and significant figures to emerge in the last year or so. This is a softly-sensitive song, with some truly splendid arrangements mixing voices and instruments, and organ and atmosphere.*" The same year, 1972, saw the breakthrough of David Bowie, Roxy Music, Hawkwind, Lindisfarne, Lynsey de Paul and Stealers Wheel, and *Record Mirror* puts

Peter Skellern up there?

Derek Taylor produced Skellern's *Not Without A Friend* album; this L.P. mixed ballads and ragtime tunes but was not successful. 'Still Magic' was released as a single — *Record Mirror*: *"The smokey and slightly wavering voice, and the intensity which never gets out of hand, and the semi-religious touches, and the piano. It's Peter back in 'You're A Lady' mood of not long ago. A sensitive performance and song, and no expense has been spared on the arrangement with strings all over the place. Quality pop music this."*

The next hit surfaced in 1975. 'Hold On To Love' saw a change of approach. Perhaps the line: *"it pays to wait"* was a dig by Skellern at his record company's inability to get him a follow-up hit to 'You're A Lady' for over two years? This single reached No. 14.

Skellern left Decca and signed with Island. 'Oh What A Night For Love' was reviewed in *Record Mirror*: *"The man-most-likely takes laid-back slow shuffling reggae as summer offering. Killer intro eases into cracked up vocal style but too much emphasis on production, methinks."* I purchased the follow-up, 'Hard Times', on its release, attracted by the witty lyrics and and clever arrangement, the latter reminding me of a Captain and Tennille single. *"She asks me round to have a bite to to eat, when I get there, she's invited the street, she gives me hard times."*

'Now That I Need You' was released in November 1975. *Record Mirror* summed it up well: *"This is a jaunty Gilbert O'Sullivan-ish type song and Gilbert, if he got his hand on it, would no doubt get himself a big hit with it. The trouble with Peter Skellern's voice is that when he tackles uptempo numbers his foggy vocals tend to get swamped by the arrangement and relegated to the minor and unmemorable role which is exactly what's happened here."*

HURRICANE SMITH

Hurricane Smith was a one-off; an EMI producer and engineer who had worked with Pink Floyd and The Pretty Things. He wrote a song, 'Don't Let It Die', which he wanted John Lennon to sing, and played it to fellow producer, Mickie Most. Most encouraged Smith to record the song himself. The single was released in 1971 and unbelievably reached No. 2. Smith's voice was very distinctive (described as a *"croak"* in *NME*) but the song – with its ecological theme – connected with the record-buying public. The follow-up, 'Write The Music, Sing Your Song' was tipped for the charts by *NME*: *"opens with a lush and lilting orchestral intro ... utterly commercial ... I don't think it can miss."* The record sank without trace. The following spring, Smith came back with 'Oh Babe What Would You Say', a bouncier song with a ragtime feel which reached No. 4. A cover version of Gilbert O'Sullivan's 'Who Was It' went Top Thirty in the autumn and that was it.

'Beautiful Day, Beautiful Night' was reviewed in *Record Mirror*: *"That honky tenor sax, that old-style instrumental lead in, then that voice that is fast becoming a cult sound in the States and elsewhere. There's a kind of trad-jazz feel in the way he phrases through the instantly commercial song ... all throaty, and strained and plaintive. An absolute giant smash arranged, conducted, produced and sung by Hurricane."* *NME*'s reviewer was also impressed: *"Own up time. I like Hurricane Smith's records, and that hokey '30s feel mixes so nicely with his ragged, down-at-heel voice ... it's just like all the other ones."*

But before long, Hurricane's voice began to lose appeal. 'My Mother Was Her Name' did not impress *NME*: *"Hurricane could have another monster hit on his hands but I don't like it one bit. It plays on a corny empathy for the mother who can do no wrong. Yech, it's too much. Really sickening. Sweet strings and Hurricane's warbling I can do without."* Smith was releasing singles as late as 1973. 'Bye Bye' was also slated in *NME*: *"one of his stilted, moony ballads with the vocals double-tracked. Not one of his better efforts as the bass, drums, piano setting are replaced with an overworked string section."*

13 – Glam

Barry Blue

I remember seeing Barry Blue (formerly Barry Green) in the resident band on *Lift Off* on Granada TV. Later, Barry turned up as a songwriter and performer on Bell Records. He reached No. 2 with '(Dancing) On A Saturday Night' and No. 7 with 'Do You Wanna Dance'. The former unusually featured a balalaika. Then we got the inevitable diminishing returns; 'School Love' reached No. 11, 'Miss Hit And Run' No. 26 and three places higher – No. 23 for 'Hot Shot'.

'You Make Me Happy (When I'm Feeling Blue)' was arranged and produced by Gene Page, the man behind Barry White's wonderful string scores. *Record Mirror*'s reviewer was most unimpressed: "*The orchestra on this almost drowns out Barry's voice altogether and after that the vocal continues to fight for its life all the way. Apart from a few neat touches of brass, this one is jolly boring and can hope to give Barry nothing but a big flop.*" Unfortunately correct on all counts.

The follow-up, 'If I Saw You I Can Dance', saw Barry redeem himself with the same publication: "*Barry returns to his original teenybop neo-Greek style with this release ... packed with balalaikas and ruthless teeny-rock rhythms. Some pleasant vocal harmonies help to hold the listener's attention. A very obvious commercial sound, far more hit-worthy than the previous release.*" This was also a flop.

'A Lover Lovin' You' was released on Private Stock. *Record Mirror*: "*Another wet ballad from the man with the silliest name in the music biz.*" I am not sure if the latter comment is fair, as the next entry is clearly sillier.

Gary Glitter

I was initially reluctant to write about Gary Glitter, as his recent convictions have overshadowed a phenomenal chart career. He had no less than eleven Top Ten singles in a row, including three chart-toppers – 'I'm The Leader Of the Gang', 'I Love You Love Me Love' and 'Always Yours'; four other singles reached No. 2. Glitter's last big hit was 1975's 'Doing Alright With The Boys' which reached No. 6. After this, like other glam acts, his descent was speedy.

The Rivingtons' 'Papa Oom Mow Mow' was a novelty record and later covered by The Beach Boys. Gary Glitter's attempt was described by Peter Checksfield as *"a dreadful version of a weak song"* which went no higher than No. 38. The single broke Glitter's run of Top Ten singles. A female chorus repeat the title endlessly and the song does not really go anywhere. The verses alternate with the nonsensical chorus. Cover versions of novelty songs suggest a certain desperation, despite an energetic performance on the 1975 *Saturday Scene* Awards show at Wembley Empire Pool. At this event, alongside much younger acts such as The Bay City Rollers and Guys 'N' Dolls, Glitter was beginning to look truly bizarre. His wig looked precarious, his eye make-up rather strange and his silver lame trousers just embarrassing. It is very easy in hindsight to see both the ridiculous and sinister elements of Glitter's act, but he was genuinely popular with young audiences for several years. *NME* writer Nick Kent wrote a very critical piece about Glitter in March 1974 called A Whole Hunka Human He-Man. Kent also attended one of Glitter's Rainbow concerts a year before and his review makes fascinating reading.

'You Belong To Me' went no higher than No. 40. Checksfield calls it *"a tremendous single"*. I am not sure I agree. There is a "funky" keyboard introduction and a chorus of *"can't keep us apart"*, becoming what I can only describe as pseudo-anthemic but sounds and feels tired and dated. A performance on *Supersonic* reunited Glitter with the Glitter Band. Perhaps the lack of a plug on *Top of the Pops* ruined its chances.

'A Little Boogie Woogie In The Back Of My Mind' was advertised as: *"Back with a bang Gary Glitter does it again with his powerful new single echoing the sound that first brought him fame. Already receiving extensive airplay and bound to be another success for this dynamic performer."* Record Mirror was unimpressed: *"Tedious, monotonous, repetitive. Seems he's a shade stuck for ideas, torn between cabaret, middle of the road and rock. This really is a nothing single.*" It peaked at Number 31 and was Glitter's last chart appearance in the 1970s. 'Boogie Woogie' was covered by Shakin' Stevens in 1987 when it reached No. 12.

Glitter moved to Arista like many of his Bell labelmates (e.g. Showaddywaddy, Bay City Rollers) and 1977's 'I Dare You To Lay One On Me' was his first complete flop. There is an old-style Glitter Band guitar riff with added saxophone and rock 'n' roll piano. Glitter's voice is higher in pitch and in an Elvis style. This was followed by 'Oh What A Fool I've Been' (clearly Glitter was being ironic or refreshingly honest). A move to the GTO label later in 1977 saw the release of an old recording, 'Baby Please Don't Go', from the early 1970s. It is vintage Gary Glitter with the insistent beat of the two drummers. This, incidentally, was the year Glitter went bankrupt.

'Superhero' was a characterless disco track, bringing the decade to an end. The 1980s saw Glitter briefly return to the Top Ten with 'Another Rock 'N' Roll Christmas'.

The Glitter Band

The Glitter Band were recruited to be Gary Glitter's backing group and originally called The Glittermen. Their recording career in their own right started well; they had five consecutive Top Ten singles while the sixth release, 'Love In The Sun', peaked at No. 15. As the band's star rose, their boss's seemed to fall; The Glitter Band did not appear to need Gary's endorsement. 'Alone Again' was released in November 1975 and broke the band's successful run of hit singles. *Record Mirror*: "*Different sound from The Glitter Band this time, opting for a semi-Christmas/Spector sound behind the vocals. Might take you a while to get into it because it is so different, but should be one of the festive season's biggies.*" This single did not chart. Slowly the band seemed to be distancing themselves from both Glitter the man and glitter the costume and image.

In 1976 the band briefly changed their name to The G Band and released 'Don't Make Promises (You Can't Keep)'. This was a group composition by Gerry Shepherd and John Springate. It was another lead vocal by the latter. *Record Mirror*: "*Another change of style for the Glitter mob resulting in top class pop with two hooks (no less)."* A performance on *The Arrows* ITV series shows guitarist, Gerry Shepherd, wielding a banjo for almost a country song with a complete absence of saxes and thumping drums. The single went nowhere and a simultaneous *Greatest Hits* album release only managed a week just outside the Top Fifty.

The following February saw another G Band release, 'Look What You've Been Missing', on the CBS label. I have no recollection of these final releases, but have to disagree with the usual reliable *Record Mirror* who said: *"Good old fashioned pop ... The G Band has always been good at turning out good pop singles and this is one of their best ... straightforward, competent."* Inevitably, the band appeared on *Supersonic*. All I can hear are weak vocals and an ordinary chorus.

STEVE HARLEY & COCKNEY REBEL

Cockney Rebel's first release, 'Sebastian', was probably the band's greatest moment; a grandiose, over-the-top and lengthy performance with choir and orchestra. Despite much press coverage and success in Europe, the single did not chart in the UK. The more radio-friendly 'Judy Teen' started off the band's British chart career and there was a further hit single with 'Mr Soft'.

'Big Big Big Deal' was released in November 1974 as a Steve Harley solo single just before he formed the second line-up of Cockney Rebel. Harley plays all the instruments – except drums – himself on the track. He told *Record Mirror*: *"I don't want anyone thinking it's my new group playing on it because it isn't."* The same publication reviewed the single: *"I don't think it's as good as the material he produces with the band, with the exception of the last minute or so when he goes into a semi-la-la hook line. The rest of the single just doesn't have the force normally associated with him."*

The band was now known as Steve Harley & Cockney Rebel with Jim Cregan on guitar, George Ford on bass and Duncan Mackay on keyboards. Only drummer Stuart Elliott remained from the original line-up. Whereas Cockney Rebel's first line-up had an extraordinary image — as clearly shown on the cover of *The Human Menagerie* album, the second line-up looked to me (and others) like a bunch of session men drafted in to back the "star". The chart-topping 'Make Me Smile

(Come Up And See Me)' was a bitter "dig" at his former bandmates. The split had occurred at the end of a British tour when allegedly the other original band members told Harley that they wanted to record their own songs, and not just his. Opinion was very much divided on Steve Harley. An interview with Nick Kent in *NME* in 1974 makes fascinating reading. A former journalist himself, Harley seemed to over-react to criticism in the press.

In 1976 the band's fourth album, *Timeless Flight*, reached No. 18, but the two singles taken from it did less well. By now guitarist Jim Cregan, whose solo on 'Make Me Smile' was a highlight, had left Harley to join Rod Stewart's band. 'Black And White' was supposedly inspired by T.S. Eliot's poem, 'The Hollow Men'. There is a ten-piece choir, ten cellos and ten violas. Harley told *Record Mirror*: "*I knew it was either going to be massive — top three — or a complete stiff. It turned out to be a stiff. They didn't get it in the right shops at the right time and promote it properly.*" 'Black And White' also failed to get a plug on on *Top of the Pops*, but there was an appearance on ITV's *Supersonic*.

'White, White Dove' was the second single released from the *Timeless Flight* album and came out in February 1976. *Record Mirror*, again: "*not ... one of Steve's strongest songs, but the funky little guitar patterns, Harley's well-paced vocal and sterling production all help to make it man enough for the job of chart breaching.*" The single was another flop.

'(I Believe) Love's A Prima Donna' was the title track of Harley's fifth album and released as a single in October 1976. *Record Mirror*: "*lots of changes of rhythm and tempo (plus a burst of Queen type backing). It's fairly complex and that might put its chances at risk.*" It reached No. 41, while the parent album reached No. 28.

Harley was totally absent from the British singles charts in 1977 and 1978. 'Best Years Of Our Lives' was released in September 1977. *Record Mirror*: "*This one is live and it's a cracker ... easily the best track on* Face To Face *and though I don't know how valid it is as a single, it's a worthwhile buy for any hard-up fans who can't afford the fancy double album package.*"

'Roll The Dice' saw a different approach — *Record Mirror*: "*This single is strongly Americanised: very smooth, very polished with Harley's voice less distinctive than usual. It's got a hook line which I can't stop singing and which you should give a listen to.*" I had always thought that the whole point of Cockney Rebel *was* Steve Harley's unusual and highly distinctive voice. His voice may not have been to everyone's taste (I dislike the band's version of 'Here Comes The Sun', but clearly many thousands disagreed as it went Top Ten in the drought summer of 1976), but we always knew it was Steve Harley.

Harley's final chart entry of the 1970s was 'Freedom's Prisoner' which only reached No. 58. *Record Mirror*, again: "*The hook comes before the vocals, with a call out melody. Downhill from there, but Harley's return may still be timely.*" A further review elaborated: "*Corny but fun, Dr Zhivago-style Russian chorus and danceable melody clicks very nicely thank you. That instant hook is just what Mr Harley needs to get himself noticed again.*"

The 1980s saw a return to the charts for Harley. A Mike Batt song, 'Ballerina (Prima Donna)', reached No. 51 in 1983. The 12 inch version featured 'Sebastian' on the B-side, which may have helped sales. However, 1986 saw Harley's first Top Ten hit in a decade – a dramatic duet with Sarah Brightman no less, of the title song from *The Phantom Of The Opera* which reached No. 7. Unlike Brightman, Harley did not go on to perform the song on stage in the West End. Would he have been more effective than Michael Crawford?

Within another decade, 'Make Me Smile' was used in *The Full Monty* film and clearly found a new audience, no doubt helped over the years by several high profile cover versions by the likes of Duran Duran, Erasure and The Wedding Present.

HELLO

Hello were part of the Mike Leander Rock Artists Management stable and, like The Glitter Band, signed to Bell Records. In *Shock And Awe*, Simon Reynolds noted: "*Hello were that rare thing in glitter pop: 'actual teenagers.'*" The group entered the charts in late 1974 with a confident version of Billie Davis' 1963 hit, 'Tell Him'. The American original by The Exciters had lost out to Davis in the UK and reached No. 46.

The follow-up, 'Games Up', was co-written by two members of The Glitter Band. Record Mirror: "*Good old skinbasher number that trips along with a beat you can't miss. Sometimes the vocals slow down over the drumming, and slipping the title phrase into the middle of each verse makes it just that bit different."*

A cover of 'Bend Me Shape Me' (a British hit for Amen Corner in 1968) was also unsuccessful and it took Russ Ballard's 'New York Groove' to bring Hello into the charts again. This excellent pop record used the riff from Hamilton Bohannon's 'Disco Stomp' to good effect and reached No. 9. Another Ballard composition, 'Star Studded Sham', was the follow-up but flopped. *Record Mirror*: *"New York Groove showed that Hello had at last got a style of their own and this confirms it. It's got a good beat with handclap effects helping out. Bob Bradbury's vocal is really excellent and the back up voices are most skilfully employed. The chorus isn't as good as 'New York Groove', but no matter - this will be a hit."* I quite like 'Star Studded Sham'. The verses are melodic and the singer sounds a bit Dylanesque.

1976 saw Hello back on *Top of the Pops* plugging the inferior 'Love Stealer'. The single has a funky guitar opening and the hook is *"she's got her eye on you."* There is a terrible telephone bit: *"better come quick"* from the bass player. After the chorus and the second verse, the telephone gimmick returns. *Record Mirror*: *"Change of producer and songwriters for Hello – those slots now taken over by Phil Wainman, ex-Mud, ex-Rollers etc. It's a very different sound for the band, with strong pounding bass beat and powerful vocals, but despite the change in direction, I think it's touch and go whether it'll make it or not."* It didn't.

Mott The Hoople

Mott The Hoople's second phase started when they moved from Island Records to CBS. David Bowie's song, 'All The Young Dudes', gave the band a Top Three hit and a new and younger audience. Four more Top Twenty hits followed; all had wit, musical variety and style. 'Foxy Foxy' was the follow-up to 'Golden Age Of Rock 'N' Roll' but only reached No. 33. Simon Reynolds described the song as *"replicating The Ronettes"* as the 'Be My Baby' drum beat is the dominant sound of the song. *NME* enthused: *"Mott's de luxe brand of rock 'n' roll gets increasingly better with each consecutive outing. Seems that Hunter and the Hooplettes have been checkin' out a whole bunch of those timeless Phil Spector classics ... not to the extent that they can be publicly numbered as rip-off merchants. To Mott's credit, they've been able to adapt those pounding grand piano triplets, sheets of saxes, thunderstorm percussion backbeat and the sensuous 'sha-la-la-laing' of the ladies of the chorus to fit most comfortably into wide-screen Mottarama."* I felt that Ian Hunter's voice sounded tired. After promoting 'Foxy Foxy' on *Top of the Pops*, the band played at the Palace Lido in Douglas on the Isle of Man. This was guitarist Ariel Bender's last gig with Mott. Further dates were cancelled.

The band's final single was the autobiographical 'Saturday Gigs', the only band A-side to feature new guitarist Mick Ronson. Dave Laing's review in *Let It Rock* was blunt: *"It's bizarro punk-rock that would have seemed monstrous even in the golden age of LA garage bands. The attraction lies precisely in the record's total lack of redeeming artistic value. It's awful – but I kinda like it."* Record Mirror merely noted: *"The delivery's slow and easy with everyone joining in for the chorus."* Simon Reynolds is damning: *"a valedictory song that ran through Mott's entire career verse by verse ... Mott's inspiration had exhausted itself. And they'd exhausted the public's interest."* I find myself disagreeing with all these snipers above; it is my favourite Mott track with its wonderful chorus and touchingly nostalgic verses. It was disappointing to see 'Saturday Gigs' fare even worse than 'Foxy Foxy', reaching only No. 41 in late 1974.

Mud

Mud had formed in the mid-1960s and were an experienced live act. They had eight consecutive Top Ten hits, with no fewer than ten Top Twenty hits in a row between 1973 and 1975 including three chart-toppers with 'Tiger Feet', 'Lonely This Christmas' and 'Oh Boy'. There was an almost universal goodwill towards the band, fostered by their frequent and often amusing *Top of the Pops* appearances.

Before Mud starting releasing singles on their new label, Private Stock, RAK continued to issue singles. 'Moonshine Sally' was clearly an old recording, but the group still promoted it on *Top of the Pops*. It reached No.10 – their lowest chart placing since 'Hypnosis' in summer 1973. The follow-up was a cover of 'One Night' which had been a hit first for Smiley Lewis in 1956 in the USA and later for Elvis Presley. Whereas several Mud singles had featured Les Gray's Elvis impression on new songs, Mud's version of 'One Night' was less of a pastiche and more a pure imitation of the King and only reached No. 32.

The move to Private Stock saw the band break away from songwriters Nicky Chinn and Mike Chapman, intending to write their own material, as well as having a more lucrative recording contract. For a while, this move seemed successful with a rocker ('L-L-Lucy') and a ballad ('Show Me You're A Woman') both reaching the Top Ten in autumn 1975.

The following year saw two Top Twenty hits, the untypical 'Shake It Down' and a cover of Bill Withers' classic, 'Lean On Me'. 'Nite On The Tiles', however, was a flop. Written by bassist Ray Stiles and guitarist Rob Davis, the song has frenetic guitar, harmonies and unison vocals, as well as a soft middle eight with acoustic guitar. *Record Mirror*: "*Searing faster than ever, Mud give you something entirely different and more ambitious. Harmonies and good guitar work make you say 'Thank You'*". *Shindig* wrote: "*It's jam-packed with muscular riffs, multi-tracked vari-speed guitars and vocals and unexpected changes, in mood and tempo (including a melodic middle eight reminiscent of* Parachute-*era Pretty Things).*"

Mud's final single on Private Stock was 'Beating Around The Bush' which *Record Mirror* disliked: "*it's no more than a too often repeated chorus built around a fair to middling Acme Mud riff.*"

The group left the struggling Private Stock label and signed to RCA in 1977. 'Slow Talking Boy' was written by John Kongos and Peter Leroy. Untypically for Mud, the song is mainly acoustic with an Italianate mandolin but awful synthesiser, sounding like a Euro-pop song. *Record Mirror*: "*Strangely low-key release for Mud. I don't know if people will be able to handle such a dramatic change of style in one leap, but it creeps up on you. Could do it, but it might take a while.*" There was a performance on *Top of the Pops*, but the single did not reach the charts.

Three months later was 'Just Try (A Little Tenderness)', written by two members of the group. *Record Mirror*: "*Not the great Stax track (perhaps as well) but a brassy bouncealong bit of Mudpop which sounds like a pretty desperate measure to get Mud back in the chart. Hardly a sellout perhaps, but hardly to their credit either.*"

'Cut Across Shorty' was previewed on *Top of the Pops* at the end of March 1978. This old rocker had been the B-side of Eddie Cochran's

'Three Steps To Heaven'. Curiously, singer Les Gray refrained from employing his Elvis voice here. The single sounds as if Mud are busking a skiffle version of the song. There is not much to enjoy here.

The last years of Mud were rather disappointing and, later, tragic. Les Gray's solo version of 'A Groovy Kind Of Love' had made No. 32 in spring 1977. Later he left the group and was briefly replaced by a female singer called Margo Buchanan. Mud finally broke up in 1979. Guitarist Rob Davis later went on to write hits for Sophie Ellis Bextor, Kylie Minogue and others. Bass player Ray Stiles joined The Hollies and has been with them for decades. Gray later formed a new line-up of the group and toured as Les Gray's Mud — never a good sign. He died in 2004 and, two years later, drummer Dave Mount passed away.

ROXY MUSIC

Roxy Music had a string of memorable hit singles starting with their finest one, 'Virginia Plain', a single that had no chorus and a set of lyrics that everyone at school could recite without exactly knowing their meaning. Who was Baby Jane and why was she in Acapulco? It was all in Bryan Ferry's stylised voice (later "borrowed" by several others). 'Virginia Plain' reached No. 4, 'Pyjamarama' peaked at No. 10, 'Street Life' went one place higher, 'All I Want Is You' reached No. 12, 'Love Is The Drug' just missed the top spot and 'Both Ends Burning' peaked at No. 25. The band split up in 1976 and a stop gap re-release of 'Virginia Plain' reached No. 11 in 1977.

Following the success of the reissue of 'Virginia Plain', which had coincided with the release of Roxy Music's *Greatest Hits* album, Island released 'Do The Strand' as a single in January 1978. The track had already been released as a single outside the UK, but was only previously available as a track on *For Your Pleasure*. The single was an edit of the album track, 45 seconds shorter. It flopped.

'Trash' was the comeback single in 1979 for Roxy Music after a gap of three years. This was a strange choice as the first single to be taken from their new album, *Manifesto*. There is a guitar riff and a rather weedy organ that reminds me of the Sir Douglas Quintet. The lyrics are not up to Bryan Ferry's usual standard: *"Are you customised or ready made?"* and the refrain of *"only seventeen"* feels dated. The B-side, 'Trash 2', is a heavier and slightly slower version of the song with more prominent drumming and guitar. Played alongside Roxy's glorious parade of hit singles, 'Trash' is definitely their weakest release.

Just two months later, 'Dance Away' was the second track released as a single from *Manifesto*. This was far more memorable and effective and brought the band back into the Top Ten, equalling 'Love Is The Drug''s second position. Seven Top Twenty singles followed including a chart-topper with Roxy's cover of John Lennon's 'Jealous Guy'.

Alvin Stardust

Top of the Pops viewers of a certain age might have recognised A.S. when he first appeared on their screens in late 1973. *"Isn't that Shane Fenton with dyed hair?"* was muttered by some. The answer being, *"yes."* Alvin Stardust was a new pseudonym for Bernard Jewry and a highly successful one. He had six Top Twenty hit singles (including a chart-topper, 'Jealous Mind' and 'My Coo-Ca-Choo' in second position) among the Magnet label's first twenty or so releases. This put the label alongside RAK or Apple Records in terms of successful hit to release ratio. A young Pete Waterman worked as the label's A & R man. But good things (including high chart positions) often come to an end.

Both 'My Coo-Ca-Choo' and 'Jealous Mind' were well-crafted pop singles with memorable melodies and hooks. Alvin's next four releases all went Top Twenty but he was already on a downward path. 'Tell Me Why' peaked at No. 16, although its follow-up went five places higher.

'Sweet Cheating Rita' staggered to No. 37 and was Alvin's last hit on Magnet. Significantly, it was Alvin's first single not masterminded by Peter Shelley. *Record Mirror*: *"The song written by Roger Greenaway and Geoff Stephens doesn't give Alvin one of his strongest records."* These two highly successful and respected songwriters had clearly had an off day. The rhyming is dire at times: *"I'll never tame her and I won't blame her."* We have the usual guitar riff and Alvin's echoey vocals and a reference to *"the local hop"*, but this is a sub-standard song.

John Peel reviewed Alvin's next release, 'Move It' in *Let It Rock*: *"Alvin Stardust has just released a 'Move It' which isn't in the same league as Cliff*

Richard's punk original." *Record Mirror* gave greater detail: "*The old Cliff hit given a new lease of life by Alvin whereas Cliff's was a real rocker, Alvin's slowed things right down – with the exception of a break in the middle where it becomes more lively. Certainly better than his last offering.*" Slowing down a song like 'Move It' was not a good idea and plenty of artists had done a better job. The funky electric piano and finger clicks just sound incongruous. I wonder if the label was trying to replicate David Essex's work with Jeff Wayne. Alvin promoted the single on *Top of the Pops* and *Supersonic*, but it was his first flop on Magnet.

'Move It' was closely followed by the equally unsuccessful 'Angel From Hamburger Heaven'. *Record Mirror*: "*Poor old Alvin hasn't had too much success with singles of late and I'm not too sure about this one, although it is a bit better than the last two and has a fairly catchy chorus line.*" I wonder if the title would have put off both disc jockeys and record buyers. If it was meant to be retro or camp, then other artists, such as Mud and Wizzard, were far better at doing this. The song's guitar sounds like a poor Joe Meek imitation. The song is as bad as its title.

'It's Better To Be Cruel Than Kind' was released in 1976. *Record Mirror & Disc*: "*Mr Stardust has lost a few sequins recently with a pretty disappointing track record as far as the charts are concerned. This one, methinks, ain't going to do much to change things. A bit like Les Gray's Elvis impressions, this is a ballad fit to bust the heart strings.*" With its saxophone and predictable chord sequence, the song sounds like one of Billy Fury's weaker performances. By now Alvin was not even getting on *Top of the Pops* and appearances on *Sez Les* and *The Arrows* show did not help the single's chart chances.

Next was 'The Word Is Out', penned by the 'Hamburger Heaven' team of veteran (and highly respected and successful) songwriters Barry Mason and Roger Greenaway. *Record Mirror*: "*Piano-based pseudo reggae shuffler with back echo vocals from nice guy Alvin gives him his strongest contender for some time.*" The guitar sounds weedy and the vocals are echoey as usual but not as strong as in Alvin's early hits. The rot had set in; teenage record buyers had moved on and were simply not interested any more.

Alvin, unbelievably, made two comebacks in the next decade, first on the Stiff label and then with Chrysalis. Clearly, he was a survivor, having first entered the charts as far back as 1961 as Shane Fenton with 'I'm A Moody Guy'. He died in 2014.

The Sweet

Like their contemporaries and inevitable rivals, Mud, The Sweet had had years of touring experience behind them. Their four-part harmonies were perhaps the band's secret weapon. Group-penned B-sides revealed a different side to Sweet. John Peel once played one such track and asked listeners to write in and guess who they thought it was. Many felt that it was a lost Led Zep song!

'Alexander Graham Bell' was the follow-up to the bubblegum hit, 'Co-Co', which had reached the No. 2 position in summer 1971. *NME*: "*Pounds along with a solid beat, is lustily sung by The Sweet and has a rip-roaring orchestral scoring. It lacks the teenybopper hook chorus of 'Funny Funny' and 'Co-Co' ... but still boasts a catchy refrain with which it's easy to sing-along. A very commercial disc – not quite as twee as the last two, but still loaded with instant appeal and clearly destined to complete Sweet's chart hat-trick.*" I quite liked this record which was much better than the group's previous hits – or its safe successor, 'Poppa Joe', a mere retread of 'Co-Co'. It only reached No. 33.

'Turn It Down' was the group's last single with Nicky Chinn and Mike Chapman. It reached No. 41, breaking a run of seven Top Ten hit singles. The beginning sounds a bit like 'Born To Be Wild', but doesn't really go anywhere. Bassist Steve Priest's predictable camp bit (e.g. "*we just haven't got a clue what to do*") is replaced by a sort of rap spoken in a faux American accent. Earlier in 1974, Sweet's lead singer Brian Connolly was viciously attacked outside a pub in Staines. "*He got kicked in the throat,*" noted Steve Priest in *Shindig* magazine. "*He never sung quite the same afterwards.*" It appeared that Connolly now "*had a more limited range*". Simon Frith: "*but Sweet's total failure with 'Turn It Down' is really quite astonishing. It's not Sweet's best record, but it's more aggressive than usual.*" *NME*'s reviewer was also unimpressed: "*this is The Sweet doing what they do best and most often, although more than the glitter has worn off by now. To make it worse, 'Turn It Down' comes straight from the bottom of the Chinn Chapman barrel.*" *Record Mirror* were hopeful: "*a heavy rocker that'll stand out a mile in the charts amongst those softer soul ballads that are there at the moment."* A performance of 'Turn It Down' on Tyne-Tees' *The Geordie Scene* has a "live" feel to it and the band look, and sound, like a heavy rock band. Steve Priest sports sunglasses and the glam look has disappeared. The line, *"I can take no more of that godawful sound so turn it down"* seemed to sum up many pop fans' attitude to the single. This was a justified flop.

The Sweet followed the failure of 'Turn It Down' with their own song, 'Fox On The Run', which leapt to No. 2 in spring 1975; in the summer the follow-up, 'Action', went Top Twenty and it seemed that the band could cope without Chinn and Chapman. The next release, 'Lost Angels', was also both written and produced by the band. *Record Mirror*: *"Sweet return with a mini-opus full of tempo changes, instrumental breaks and Queen-like phrasing. Not quite sure how wide its appeal as a single but it sort of grows on you."* 'Lost Angels' did not chart.

'Lies In Your Eyes' reached no higher than No. 35. The single was another group composition and production. Bass player Steve Priest told *Shindig*: *"'Action' didn't do too bad but 'The Lies In Your Eyes' was a flop ... it was hopeless. We didn't know what to write any more, 'cos nothing was working. The record company wasn't behind us."* *Record Mirror* were quite impressed: *"Pounding rhythm from Sweet introduce their new single which might have you singing 'Fox On the Run' at the chorus break by mistake, as the two songs are very similar at some points. That said, after a couple of hearings, you won't remember 'Fox' and you will buy this one.."*

'Stairway To The Stars' was released in July 1977, the summer of punk. *Record Mirror* stated the obvious: *"Consistently delivering the goods, but not too many folk seem that interested any more."*

Unbelievably, The Sweet returned in 1978 on a new label with a Top Ten hit with 'Love Is Like Oxygen'. It looked like a major comeback but it was the band's final hit of the decade.

Of the four original group members, only guitarist Andy Scott is still alive. He is fronting a touring version of Sweet. Brian Connolly died in 1997, followed by drummer Mick Tucker in 2002 and bassist Steve Priest in 2020.

T. Rex

T. Rex's chart history is well-chronicled. The band's story is, like so many other artists in this book, one of diminishing returns. This is especially noticeable if you listen to their hit singles in order of release. 'Ride A White Swan' still sounds fun and innocent. Both 'Hot Love' and 'Get It On' are showcases for Bolan and backing singers, Flo & Eddie (actually former Turtles Howard Kaylan and Mark Volman) and sound magnificent. Tony Visconti's production does wonders for Bolan's limited skills. Both reached No. 1. in 1971. The next year saw two more chart-toppers, 'Telegram Sam' and 'Metal Guru'. At the time I felt that the rot began to start with the former; 'Telegram Sam' always sounded too much like 'Get It On' for me. In addition, the band's own record company, T. Rex Wax Company, was centred around a picture of Marc Bolan's face on the record label and advertisements. The focus on Bolan was not only misleading but simply unfair. T. Rex were not a one-man band but relied on other musicians, backing singers and, most crucially, on producer and arranger Tony Visconti.

T. Rex's chart-toppers were followed by four Top Five singles with 'The Groover' being Bolan's last time in the Top Ten. On this single, the speeded-up guitar and chanted "T-R-E-X" did not bode well. 'Truck On Tyke' (No. 12) and 'Teenage Dream' (No. 13) were the last great T. Rex singles. Worse, and much worse, was to come. Paul du Noyer wrote in *Word* magazine: "*the sound was getting repetitive.*" Tony Visconti told du Noyer in the same publication: "*The last album I did was Zinc Alloy, which was good but very ragged. It was the end of T.Rextasy in the sense that Marc was very formulaic, he wouldn't listen to reason. I was secretly looking to Marc to branch out. People's taste in rock was getting more sophisticated. But he wouldn't listen to any of that.*"

'Zip Gun Boogie' was the title track of T. Rex's sixth album but only reached No. 41. Simon Frith commented: "*I'm not surprised that Marc Bolan's tedious 'Zip Gun Boogie' hasn't caused queues in Boots.*" *NME* was just as harsh: "*Well, whatever happened to Marc Bolan's imagination? Here he seems totally at a loss for a good idea and once more sticks to a basic blues/rock 'n' roll structure which isn't such a bad thing in itself, other than the fact he's been doing it for a long time now, and doing it badly at that. The instrumentation, in which* clavinet and organ are dominant, is ugly and the lyric content is exceptionally banal, even by Bolan's standards. It isn't even played particularly well, and the addition of a heavy riff which crops up on the introduction and at subsequent intervals throughout the song has all the panache of Uriah Heep. Hasn't he cottoned on to he fact that his records are not selling anymore?" Significantly, this was Bolan's first record without Tony Visconti producing and it showed.

'London Boys' was released in March 1976 and *Record Mirror* seemed to like it: *"this is one of the best things he's done in ages. Lots of rhythm and action with a very solid vocal chorus."* This was another non-album single, originally intended for one of Marc's rock operas, either *The London Opera* or *Billy Super Duper* and reached No. 40. The song was rather repetitive.

'Laser Love' was the follow-up to 'I Love To Boogie' (which had reached No. 13). *Record Mirror & Disc*: *"Stones riff marks the ultimate punky pop song from Marc. It's got two hooks, unbelievable lyrics and the chance of being his biggest in years."* I found the backing vocals on this single a little too loud. This one went no higher than No. 41.

'The Soul Of My Suit' was praised in *NME*: *"(it) shows Marc's voice is as good as ever and his guitar playing, while missing the strangulated sparkle of yore, is more assured than ever."* The single was previewed on *Top of the Pops*, *Supersonic* and *Get It Together*. We hear uncharacteristic organ and saxes and even a guitar solo. It was Bolan's last chart single before his untimely death later in the year, reaching No. 42.

'Dandy In The Underworld' was the third single released from the album of the same name. It was remixed and partially re-recorded for single release with new lead vocals and added guitar and strings. Steve Harley was featured on both harmonies and backing vocals. The song feels like the old style T. Rex. Despite the first 25,000 copies coming in a picture sleeve, 'Dandy' did not enter the charts.

'Celebrate Summer' was Bolan's final release in his lifetime. *Record Mirror* said: *"Bolan returns to his former glories. A sound reminiscent of his early days,"* while *Sounds* detected: *"(a) strong punk influence."* *NME* was almost enthusiastic: *"For one golden instant I thought Marc had finally pulled off the unalloyed pop triumph that he needs as a convincing follow-up to 'Get It On'. This isn't it, but it's certainly the most likeable single he's made for a very long time, even though it borrows the melody and chord sequence of The Deviants' 'Let's Loot The*

Supermarket'.'" Within just six weeks, Marc Bolan was dead, only thirty.

14 – Harmony Constant

ARRIVAL

Hailing from Liverpool, Arrival had two Top Twenty hits on Decca in 1970: 'Friends' (No. 8) and 'I Will Survive' (No. 16). Both featured the strong lead vocals of the late Dyan Birch. There were three other singers in the group, Carroll Carter, Frank Collins and Paddy McHugh. Arrival appeared at the 1970 Isle Of Wight Festival, although they do not appear in the *Message Of Love* film of the event. The group's performance impressed the Friday afternoon audience at Afton Down, particularly with their rendition of a gospel song, 'See The Lord'.

'Love Song' was the group's first single on CBS; this Jimmy Webb song had been featured on the composer's *Words And Music* album. Arrival's version is quite similar to the original but with stronger lead vocals from Dyan and confident backing vocals from her bandmates. Again, the orchestral arrangements were by Paul Buckmaster who did so much work with Elton John. I remember purchasing a Pop-Ex copy of this.

The follow-up was more interesting. 'Family Tree' has an annoyingly lengthy subtitle ('We'll Shake It, And Break It, Cos' We're Going To Make It Alone'). There is a simpler early version of the song recorded at a BBC session in September 1969. *Record Mirror*: "*Long time off the chart scene, but the distinctive blend of voices is still there ... in fact it seems fuller than ever right now. Lovely girl lead, a thundering piano, careful deliberation on the build up ... best single of the week. Lovely amounts of what sounds like anguish.*" This is a lost classic which is worth tracking down. A mimed performance on German television is essential viewing. The young seated audience are waving their arms in the air as the strong hook "Alone" is heard. British pop music is rarely as good as this! If only 'Family Tree' had been a hit.

'The Theme From *The Heartbreak Kid* (You're Going Far)' was released in June 1973. *Record Mirror*: *"Well-performed treatment, particularly on the vocal arrangement, but not predictably one of those hit movie-themes."* This song was taken from the 1972 version of the Neil Simon comedy, *The Heartbreak Kid*, which starred Charles Grodin and Cybil Shepherd, the more recent remake starring Ben Stiller is better known. The song starts with 'My Sweet Lord'-style slide guitar and has a clear and confident lead vocal by Birch. As usual, there is a superb group vocal arrangement but I feel that their performance is better than the actual song. It is another lost treasure, though.

'He's Misstra Know It All' was a key track on Stevie Wonder's 1973 *Innervisions* album; it is one of his most beautiful songs. Arrival covered the song and released it as a single. *Record Mirror*: *"This is a strikingly laid down single; good vocal work, some scarily high backing sounds, gospelly feel. Really a first-rate single. Try it."* It went nowhere, despite its undoubted quality. This was Arrival's final single. Stevie's original version was released as a single the following year and reached No. 10.

Arrival split and three of the singers, Dyan Birch, Frank Collins and Paddy McHugh, later formed Kokomo, one of the most popular of the "pub rock" bands of the mid-1970s. Kokomo appeared on the *Naughty Rhythms* Tour in early 1975, alongside Dr Feelgood and Chilli Willi And The Red Hot Peppers. Some of you may remember the diminutive figure of Collins singing behind Terence Trent D'Arby on *Top of the Pops* in the late 1980s.

THE FORTUNES

The Fortunes had three Top Twenty hits in the mid-sixties including the Cook-Greenaway composition, 'You've Got Your Troubles'. Their single, 'Caroline', was effectively used by the pirate radio station of the same name but was not a hit. The record remains a powerful and vital sound, reminding me of the sheer ubiquity of Radio Caroline North in my childhood when it seemed that everyone was tuned into this station whether at home, in shops, garages or cars.

A five-year absence from the British charts followed. 'Is It Really Worth Your While' was one of the flops. *NME*: *"An excellent performance from The Fortunes in this rhythmic ballad. Verses are quiet and tender but in the* chorus the whole thing erupts into a walloping shaker beat with crashing drums, pounding tympani and cascading strings. The boys give it all they've got in a powerful yet controlled, styling embellished by a rich Les Reed backing."

'The Idol' was a complete change of style and arguably one of the finest 1960s singles to be a flop. Written by group members Rod Allen and Barry Pritchard, this 1967 single was performed on Germany's *Beat Club* programme. One can see the group's quiet confidence in the quality of the song. They know that it is excellent, but they never seem smug. The song is a clever commentary on the superficiality of success. This is never an easy topic for a song, but 'The Idol' is a superb record. NME: "*Thoroughly intriguing lyric about the false cardboard world of a pop star, in which money is by no means everything. Bounds along at a steady toe-tapping pace and features some colourful harmonies and excellent guitar work. There's an ear-catchy fade-out too – switching to slower tempo, and punctuated with deep sighs.*"

It is hard to imagine a time when 'Seasons In The Sun' was a new and shocking song. Syruppy chart-topping renditions by Terry Jacks in 1974 and Westlife in 1999 have made the song over familiar. 'Seasons In The Sun' was a translation by Rod McKuen of Jacques Brel's 'Le Moribond'. An early 1960s television performance by McKuen shows how close he kept to Brel's original brisk Gallic style. Accompanied only by guitar and double bass, the song is revealed as sardonic and mocking. The first popular version to be released was probably by The Kingston Trio in 1962 on their album, *Time To Think*. The trio very much follow Rod McKuen's approach.

The Fortunes covered 'Seasons In The Sun' in 1968; the recording was arranged and produced by Mike D'Abo of Manfred Mann. The group's version stays close to the McKuen and Kingston Trio ones, but the beat is less strident and lead singer Rod Allen has made the melody softer, emphasising the wistfulness of the lyrics. The Fortunes were probably the first British group to cover the song. Penny Valentine in *Disc & Music Echo* was impressed: "*Continuing their policy of bringing us well-recorded, well-produced and very well sung records come The Fortunes. It's time they had a hit and I'd love to see them get it with this really beautiful record ... the group does a lovely vocal job, sliding into each verse with melancholy voices really feeling the lyrics – which are lovely by the way. I shall play it a lot.*"

Disappointingly, the single was another flop, except in the Netherlands where it reached No. 4.

'Seasons In The Sun' was just waiting to be a hit in the UK and the USA. In 1970 Terry Jacks (then of The Poppy Family) attempted to produce a version with The Beach Boys, but it was not officially released for half a century. Carl Wilson – arguably one of the greatest white pop voices ever – sings lead with conviction. All versions to this point retained the French word "Adieu" throughout. Jacks' own version went to No. 1 on both sides of the Atlantic. He replaces "Adieu" with just "Goodbye" and effectively censors the song's lyrics, removing the central adultery theme.

'Here Comes That Rainy Day Feeling Again' echoed the group's 1965 hit 'Here It Comes Again' but went nowhere in the UK. It was a Top Twenty hit in the USA. Two singles in the early 1970s saw the Fortunes return to the Top Ten in the UK; 'Freedom Come, Freedom Go' – with its slightly anti-permissive society lyrics, reached No. 6 and stayed in the charts for seventeen weeks. 1972 saw 'Storm In A Teacup', co-written by Lynsey De Paul and Ron Roker, reach No. 7. Follow-ups did not chart; 'Baby By The Way' was reviewed in *NME*: "*The Fortunes are one chart group that always seem to arrest my interest no matter how trivial the song ... the lead singer's voice always appeals to me. This is snappy and idiotical, but I love it. Should be a smash.*"

'Whenever It's A Sunday' was released in June 1973. *Record Mirror*: "*Written by Cook and Greenaway and produced by the same team. It's a fair old showcase for one of the best harmony teams in the business, but the reggae-calypso-hoedown-Latin mixture tend to confuse the ability to stretch out big ballady sounds. Catchy though, well drummed, probably a minor hit.*"

The Ivy League

The Ivy League did not just have an American-themed name, they had a gift for melody and harmony that rivalled pretty much any vocal act in the USA. They truly were that good. 'Funny How Love Can Be' be reached No. 8 in early 1965, 'That's Why I'm Crying' peaked at No. 22 and 'Tossing And Turning' fared even better and got to No. 3. Subsequent releases failed to reach the British Top Thirty, but are all worth hearing.

'Our Love Is Slipping Away' was the follow-up to 'Tossing And Turning'. *NME* stated: "*a really beautiful slow rockaballad, reflective and intense with a well-constructed melody. The trio harmonise most attractively ... a pleasant melody, delightfully handled.*" This single is simply sublime with delicate piano and faultless harmonies. The mournful flavour of the song is reinforced in the hook-line: "*don't let it go.*" A lost classic.

'Running Around In Circles' was more up-tempo — *NME*: "*The trio's distinctive falsetto harmonies blend with a pounding wallop beat, accentuated by organ. The boys' performance of the lyric is both ear-catching and stimulating ... I don't rate it as one of their best, but it's stamped with their highly individual trademark and should register. Not a huge hit.*"

'Willow Tree' — *NME*: "*The League's best for several months. Despite the change of personnel, the lads retain their distinctive falsetto harmonies in this folk-flavoured number. Set at a snappy pace, with a double-time shuffle backing, tambourine and 12 string guitar. A thoroughly infectious sound and a well constructed lyric.*" It scraped in to No. 50.

'My World Fell Down' was another flop for The Ivy League. Written by John Carter and Geoff Stephens, this extraordinary song fell into obscurity in Britain. However, it was picked up by American producer Gary Usher for his studio-based group Sagittarius which featured Glen Campbell on lead vocals. This version later appeared on Lenny Kaye's *Nuggets* compilation where it reached a wider audience.

THE ROCKIN' BERRIES

I always feel frustrated — and even a little sad — at the career of The Rockin' Berries. With Geoff Turton they had one of the best falsetto voices in British pop and lead singer Clive Lea also had a strong voice. Their first big hit featured Turton's vocals on 'He's In Town', a cover of The Tokens' American hit, written by Gerry Goffin and Carole King. Nearly six decades after its release, the record still transfixes the listener; it is basically faultless.

The group's next big hit, 'Poor Man's Son', used both singers' voices effectively. This song had been recorded in the US by The Reflections. Unfortunately, Lea could also impersonate a few famous people (notably Norman Wisdom) and the group drifted into summer seasons, pantomime and cabaret. This tended to obscure the group's brilliant harmony showcases such as 'You're My Girl'. *NME*: "*(they) latch on to a Goffin-King composition ... The leader dual-tracks, supported by that intriguing high register work. It's very tuneful, as you would expect from that songwriting team and the tempo's a finger clicking medium pace. Harmonica well to the fore. Reckon this'll be a big one.*" *Record Mirror* was also impressed: "*it's high-pitched, falsetto-laden, and darned easy on the ear. Highly commercial and there's plenty of vibrancy in the Berries' voices. Backing is marvellously controlled. Should be a hit.*" This lost classic only reached No. 40.

I was alerted to The Rockin' Berries' hidden gems by the excellent *Ripples* series of British sunshine pop compilations, taken from the Pye label vaults. I subsequently bought the group's double CD collection, *They're In Town*. The "comedy" tracks have to be skilfully avoided. 'The Water Is Over My Head', stands out; it has a great lead vocal by (a very serious) Clive Lea. The single reached just No. 43. *NME*: "*Apart from the introductory passage, the Berries have again abandoned their falsetto style on this beaty ballad. Features some attractive counter-harmonies, and a solid medium-paced rhythm, but the most absorbing aspect is the lyric which really holds the attention.*"

'I Could Make You Fall In Love' was released in April 1966 and had previously been the B-side of The Ivy League's 'Our Love Is Slipping Away'. *Record Mirror*: "*some high-pitched vocal lines from the boys. But the main thing is the infectious beat and drive, good enough to make the charts. It has a lilting arrangement, nice guitar work.*" The next single was 'Midnight Mary' — *NME*: "*A thumping beat, accentuated by tambourine, and a volume of sound in the backing – including sweeping strings and background chanting gives this Rockin' Berries' disc quite a kick. It's a happy little tune.*"

'Sometimes' was reviewed by Penny Valentine in *Disc & Music Echo*: "*Improvement: The Rockin' Berries are beginning to sound like Jay And The Americans. Now they need to get their hands on a better song than 'Sometimes' and they really could do nice things.*"

The song 'Smile' was from Charlie Chaplin's film, *Modern Times*, and co-written by the multi-talented Chaplin. The Rockin' Berries' single in July 1967 was obviously inspired by The Lettermen's 1962 version. *NME*: "*No doubt cashing in on the success of 'This Is My Song', The Rockin' Berries revive one of Chaplin's earlier hits. It is, of course, a lovely melody and I must say the boys handle it exceptionally well. An ear-catchy vocal blend, acoustic guitars and an unobtrusive beat make it a thoroughly enjoyable disc. But as it's accepted as a standard, it may be too well-known to register in the chart."* 'This Is My Song' had been written by Charlie Chaplin for his film *The Countess Of Hong Kong* and had been a chart-topper for Petula Clark.

'Dawn (Go Away)' was a cover of a Four Seasons single. Many other artists had great success in the UK with songs by either The Four Seasons or Frankie Valli such as 'Silence Is Golden' (The Tremeloes), 'The Sun Ain't Gonna Shine Anymore' (Walker Brothers), 'Can't Take My Eyes Off You' (Andy Williams), 'Bye Bye Baby' (Bay City Rollers), 'Working My Way Back To You' (Detroit Spinners). Sadly 'Dawn' went away and did not join this list.

1968 saw the group release a Macaulay/Macleod song, 'When I Reach The Top'. *Record Mirror*: *"The Berries, literally as ever, make the best of the song and get fine harmonies going."*

Over the years The Rockin' Berries had changes of personnel. Clive Lea joined The Black Abbotts, replacing Russ Abbott. Geoff Turton briefly became known as Jefferson and had a hit with 'Colour Of My Love' in the UK and 'Baby Take Me In Your Arms' in the USA. After spending time across the Atlantic, Turton rejoined his old group.

I heard the Berries' 'Rock-A-Bye Nursery Rhyme' on Radio One when it was released in 1974. I never owned a copy, but remembered enjoying it. The group perform a series of (mainly glam rock) parodies with nursery rhyme lyrics. This single has more ingenuity than most of The Barron Knights' spoofs. We start with a Gary Glitter impression in the title/chorus and segues into 'Street Life' by Roxy Music with the words of 'Higgledy Piggledy My Black Hen'. There is another Glitter chorus and we hear a Rubettes' parody about Humpty Dumpty. In place of the spoken bit in 'Sugar Baby Love', we hear an Alan Freeman impersonation with Fluff's catchphrases *"pop pickers"* and *"stay bright"*, pleading *"let's put Humpty together again"*. The guitar intro to 'Move It' tells us Cliff Richard is the next target who replaces Glitter on the chorus. Next up is 'Little Miss Muffet' to the tune of Cockney Rebel's 'Judy Teen'. Harley's voice is difficult to copy but the singer captures his ridiculous intonation perfectly. The phrase *"curds and whey"* from

'Little Miss Muffet' is repeated in another Glitter parody which then becomes 'Ring A Ring A Roses'. Next up is 'Little Jack Horner'. The final chorus is in a Quo style.

'Black Gold' was released in February 1975. *Record Mirror*: *"Topical little ditty from The Rockin' Berries about Abdul and his oil. It's presented in an almost serious way — except for the odd Turkish Delight musical bits here and there and I'm sure all us paid up members of the Save-It brigade applaud the sentiments expressed. But a hit, it ain't!"*

'Lovely Summer' was released in the hot days of August 1975. *Record Mirror*: *"Not immediately obvious, this is another of those blue-eyed soulsters that seem to appeal to me so much these days. Delicately constructed with Jefferson's (Geoff Turton) Four Seasons voice working well, it's a light and airy gentle clopper."*

15- Mixed Bag

The Equals

The Equals were another act with a wildly erratic chart career. 'Baby Come Back' was a two-year-old track which finally took off in the UK having been a hit in Germany and the Netherlands. The single reached No. 1 in July 1968, staying there for three weeks. The group's three big chart successes were interspersed with a series of flops. 'Laurel And Hardy' was the follow-up but only reached No. 35. 'Softly Softly' fared worse, reaching No. 48 in late 1968.

'Viva Bobby Joe' reached No. 6 in the summer of 1969. The follow-up was 'Rub A Dub Dub' — *Record Mirror*: "*Pretty much on a reggae-calypso sort of style, dead straight and simple. By no means their best, sometimes just monotonous.*"

'Help Me Simone' was reviewed in *NME*: "*a wonderfully happy record that's instantly commercial – it's a blend of samba, calypso, blue beat and r-and-b. The tune is simple, repetitive and catchy. A thumping great hit … It's another of those slap-happy fast-moving pieces with lusty singalong chanting from the other boys to support Eddie's solo. Very much in the 'Viva Bobby Joe' style, it has an irresistible join-in compulsion. Dancing strings have been added to the lads' own rhythm section and the whole routine emerges as uplifting and stimulating.*

I remember hearing 'Happy Birthday Girl' on Radio One; it was used as a jingle for the inevitable request slots on the daytime programmes. *NME*: "*unadulterated rock 'n' roll with some fine rolling boogie piano … a lusty vocal with a catchy hook line and a segment of raucous guitar twanging.*" 'Stand Up And Be Counted' was released in 1972 but *NME* were unimpressed: "*This must be chapter 112 in the Sly Syndrome, with the worst load of crap conceivable as lyrics.*"

'Honey Bee' was released on CBS in 1973 — *NME*: "*This newie, the first for some time, is disappointing and starts out with the 'Baby Come Back' riff turned upside down and played on either a fuzz guitar or synthesizer. It then develops into trivia of the highest degree with a repeated chorus which usually denotes a record's fade-out starting about mid-way through and never stopping until the end."*

Eddie Grant went on to a very successful solo career where he had complete control over recording, production, pressing and distribution.

THE FOUNDATIONS

The Foundations were, arguably, the first multi-racial pop group to top the charts in the UK. 'Baby Now That I've Found You' was their first hit and went to No.1. It was probably the group's finest moment. Three decades later, American bluegrass singer, Alison Krauss, covered the song and introduced it to a much different and wider audience.

'Any Old Time You're Lonely And Sad' was reviewed by Penny Valentine: *"A third record after two hits is always a dodgy thing. Here The Foundations try a slightly different sound after their past successes, and I hate to say it but I don't think it works. A nice song by Macaulay and MacLeod but it's taken at a rather dull pace and isn't helped by the tambourine being ON the beat rather than slightly off it. It all sounds a bit bogged down although after a few plays it does improve."* It reached No. 48.

The Foundations decided to return to their old sound and the plan worked. 'Build Me Up Buttercup' reached No.2 and was quickly followed by 'In The Bad Bad Old Days (Before You Loved Me)' which peaked at No. 8. After these Top Ten hits, later releases were less successful. 'Born To Live, Born To Die' was reviewed in *Melody Maker*: *"The Foundations promised a complete change for the first single they have written and produced themselves. They weren't kidding. This Eric Allendale song gets completely away from their previous soul formula. The group is augmented with strings, bells, the lot. The results is a very commercial song and sound – and an answer to all those who thought the group was in a rut."* The group's hits stopped at the end of the 1960s.

Film companies realised that using pop songs at the cinema made the films seem potentially more appealing to a younger audience. In the 1960s, *Here We Go Round The Mulberry Bush* and *Up The Junction* were two films to have a pop soundtrack. Many more films used a song over the opening credits. *Take A Girl Like You* was based on the Kingsley

Amis novel and starred Hayley Mills, Oliver Reed and Noel Harrison. The Foundations recorded a song of the same title, written by Bill Martin and Phil Coulter. This is one of the group's better songs and has a wonderful hook and should have been a hit.

Fox

Fox were an unusual act. Fronted by the alluring Noosha Fox, the group were put together by songwriter Kenny Young who had worked with Clodagh Rodgers. 'Only You Can' had reached No. 3 in 1975 and was swiftly followed by 'Imagine You, Imagine Me' which peaked at No. 15.

'He's Got Magic' was the group's next single; it's sort of plodding funk (almost a thumping Euro-beat) with an overdubbed child-like voice and just not as impressive as the hits. The follow-up, 'Strange Ships', was reviewed in *Record Mirror*: "*Easily Fox's best yet. At times Noosha's unworldly vocal puts one in mid of Julie Driscoll on 'This Wheel's On Fire'. The arrangement's good 'n' punchy with lots of special effects. Top five.*" I hear odd keyboard sounds and funky guitar and a repeated phrase of "*we never saw our friends again*". This was a flop.

Fox returned to the singles charts in 1976 with 'S-S-S-Single Bed' which reached No. 4. Eighteen or so months later Noosha reached No. 31 with 'Georgina Bailey'. The following year Young's new group, Yellow Dog, reached No. 8 with 'Just One More Night', their only Top Thirty hit from six single releases on Virgin Records.

Hudson Ford

Richard Hudson and John Ford were the rhythm section in The Strawbs for four albums from *Just A Collection Of Antiques And Curios* to *Bursting At The Seams*. They were responsible for the band's atypical but biggest hit 'Part Of The Union'. Hudson and Ford had originally recorded the track as a novelty single under the moniker of The Brothers, but their record company persuaded them to release the song as The Strawbs. 'Part Of The Union' reached No. 2 but confused and alienated long-term Strawbs fans who were used to the voice of Dave Cousins as lead singer.

Hudson and Ford left The Strawbs in 1973 after an American tour and formed their own band. Their first single, 'Pick Up The Pieces', reached No. 8 and featured Hudson's slide guitar and unison falsetto vocals on the verses. Ford joined in on the chorus.

The follow-up single, 'Take It Down', was an acoustic singalong with electric guitar riffs and boogie piano and was surprisingly a flop. *NME*: "'*Pick Up The Pieces' had that weird interval in the first line which even dogged repetition throughout the record's duration didn't quite kill off. 'Take It Back' has nothing comparable and will surprise me if it achieves similar success. A flat, loose turgid tune that sounds like an album track rushed out to capitalise on early conquests.*" Record Mirror was kinder: "*it's got an infectious spirit about it, nothing too hectic ... and the odd vocal riff which makes it stick first hearing. Could be another Top Tenner. Chart Cert.*" Were these critics listening to the same record?

Ford's Lennonesque voice had been heard on such Strawbs tracks as 'Thirty Days' and 'Heavy Disguise' and was the lead on the band's next hit, 'Burn Baby Burn'. Hopes were high for the band, who were headlining a major UK tour. For a while, Hudson Ford were more successful in the UK than The Strawbs. *Record Mirror* had had mixed feelings initially about 'Floating In The Wind': "*I now realise it's really a stronger, nicer, more together single (than 'Burn Baby Burn') after all, so it's going straight into the (top) twenty, possibly the (Top) Five. It's gentle, lilting, and the lyrics are good and the arrangement is just right ... nothing over-played.*" Despite plenty of airplay on Radio One, the single peaked at No. 35 and that was the band's final chart entry.

Hudson Ford changed labels to CBS which saw the team of Rupert Holmes and Jeffrey Lesser, fresh from their success with Sailor, brought in as arranger and producer respectively. This team saw the release of yet two more flops — 'Sold On Love' and '95 In The Shade'. *Record Mirror* reviewed the latter: "*Clever top production on an honest medium pacer that hasn't got anything but a lethargic hook.*" A follow-up was produced by Hudson Ford themselves and finally, Robin Geoffrey Cable was brought in to produce the band. Cable had worked with Elton John, Lindisfarne and many others. There was a surprise appearance on *Top of the Pops* in September 1977 with a disco record, 'Are You Dancing?'

There is funky guitar and disco strings, but unlike The Bee Gees, this reinvention was neither successful nor satisfying. Hudson Ford later re-emerged as The Monks with the catchy but unfunny 'Nice Legs Shame About The Face'.

Manfred Mann's Earth Band

After the comparative lack of success of his jazz rock band, Chapter Three, Manfred Mann initially seemed to return to pop music. Two singles on Philips in 1971 were actually credited to Manfred Mann (the group); but they soon became Manfred Mann's Earth Band who, after a short time on Philips and Vertigo, moved to the Bronze label. Their first hit 'Joybringer' was based on Holst's *Planet Suite* but was followed by three years of flops. I remember hearing 'Be Not Too Hard' on the radio, but hardly anyone bought it. *Record Mirror*: *"in a completely different way has the same catchy sound to it that 'Joybringer' had. Nice organ playing and vocal harmonies. Don't know if it'll be a hit."*

The band's covers of Dylan ('Father Of Day, Father Of Night') and Springsteen ('Spirits In The Night') did not bother the UK singles charts. *Disc* reviewed the latter: *"Earthy Manfred and his trusty team make a valiant go of this classy Bruce Springsteen composition. It opens with a tardy riff and a few hisses. It's a fairly basic low-profile melody with some tongue-twisting lyrics. The emphasis is on atmosphere and tension rather than on tune."*

Yet it was another Springsteen cover, 'Blinded By The Light', that brought the Earth Band back to the singles charts in 1976. Over in the US the record reached the top of the charts. By now, the band had a new lead singer in Chris Thompson who we were later to hear in Jeff Wayne's *War Of The Worlds*. Follow-up success was again a problem. Another classical adaptation, this time from Schubert, called 'Questions' was the next release. *Record Mirror*: *"this one started off OK, but what happened to the chorus? It just didn't happen did it?"*

'California' received some airplay when it was released in 1977 but did not chart. I remember hearing it at the time, but missing the song being performed on *Top of the Pops*. The flops continued – another Dylan cover, 'You Angel You' (which reached No. 54) and Mike Heron's 'Don't Kill It Carol', both in 1979.

McGuinness Flint

McGuinness Flint seemed to come from nowhere in 1970, despite the familiar sight of Tom McGuinness, veteran of Manfred Mann. McGuinness was now sporting a massive beard, suggesting that the band were perhaps a British equivalent of The Band. Drummer Hughie Flint had played with John Mayall, notably on the *Bluesbreaker* album with Eric Clapton. Despite the band's name, it was the songwriting team of Benny Gallagher and Graham Lyle who were behind the band's two hit singles. 'When I'm Dead And Gone' reached No. 2 and would have been a chart-topper if Dave Edmunds hadn't been hearing you knocking for so long. The song's unusual use of a mandolin helped make the record stand out, as did the use of kazoos towards the end. The follow-up, 'Malt And Barley Blues', reached No. 5 and featured a banjo with a piano accordion filling out the sound. The song was a wry commentary on how the two songwriters were treated in their home town of Largs once they had had success. Both singles still sound great.

Hopes were high for the band's third single, 'Happy Birthday Ruthy Baby' — a tribute to Tom McGuinness's then wife — which was previewed on *Top of the Pops* in mid-August 1971. The single featured session king, Nicky Hopkins' unmistakeable piano and an ocarina solo. *NME*: "*this is another easy going item with a jogging rhythm and a strong country-blues feel ... Rolling piano supports the vocal and there's an immensely catchy chorus which I feel will soon be on everyone's lips.*" Surprisingly, the single flopped.

Later in the year Gallagher and Lyle left and the band lost its principal songwriters and singers. While the duo would eventually become a successful singles and album act, McGuinness Flint never recovered, going through line-up and label changes. They released a single about the Troubles in Northern Ireland, 'Let My People Go' in 1972, which was reviewed in *NME*: "*it gets better with each play. It chucks along with a nice groove, with lyrics pertaining to the current crisis in Ireland. With references to the 'grocer', I doubt whether the BBC believe in their music to play it.*" Along with Wings' 'Give Ireland Back To The Irish', the single was banned by the BBC. Wings reached No. 16. 'Let My People Go' flopped.

A new line-up of (Dennis) Coulson, (Dixie) Dean, McGuinness

and Flint released *Lo And Behold*, an album of unreleased Bob Dylan songs on DJM which was well received. Their single, 'Lay Down Your Weary Tune' received some airplay and deserved success. Later the band were signed to Bronze and released 'Ride On My Rainbow' in 1973. *NME*: "*a useless song, a plodding rhythm, and more of that infernal slide guitar.*" A final single, 'C'est La Vie', was released in July 1974. At the end of the decade McGuinness and Flint reunited and formed part of The Blues Band with Paul Jones, Dave Kelly and Gary Fletcher.

John Miles

John Miles hailed from Tyneside and had been in bands since leaving school in the mid-1960s. He appeared unstoppable when he first had hit singles in 1975. 'Highfly' sounded a bit too much like Pilot but still reached No. 17. The follow-up, 'Music', was something else, being a multi-sectioned song in the grand tradition of 'MacArthur Park', 'Eloise' and 'Bohemian Rhapsody'. The single featured Miles on vocals, grand piano and guitar and had a Pearl and Dean-type flourish. Production was by Alan Parsons and Andrew Powell was behind the orchestration. 'Music' reached No. 3 and set Miles a peak which he never saw again. *Melody Maker* named him: "*the brightest, freshest face in British rock.*"

Following up an epic such as 'Music' would be a challenge to anyone. Miles released 'Remember Yesterday' and *Record Mirror* was positive: "*Fluid crystalline romancer portraying the young Miles in a more sentimental mood. The newie is a lot simpler than his previous epic but still exudes the same classy texture. Miles of magic.*" The single stalled at No. 32.

'Slow Down' was completely different; Miles now had shorter hair and the song was a frenetic white funk composition, taken from his *Stranger In The City* album. There was another impressive *Top of the Pops* performance and 'Slow Down' reached No. 10.

I wonder if 1978's 'No Hard Feelings' was a dig at Decca's promotion team. *Record Mirror*: "*Another change of image. It's charisma that's missing. This effort sounds Beatlish. Pleasant enough – should be a minor hit.*" It wasn't. Ian Gilbey in *Electronics & Music Maker* wrote: "*In the world of Rock music, there can be no greater travesty than the way John Miles' music has* been ignored, especially by the weekly music press. Musical skill has never been high on their list of pre-requisites for stardom and as soon as John's fifteen minutes of fame had terminated in the mid-Seventies, the shutters came down with a resounding bang. 'Passée' and 'old-fashioned' were the usual glib diatribes flung insultingly in Mr. Miles' direction with every subsequent record release, yet to those prepared to listen, each and every album contained material that consolidated his status as an exceptional songwriting talent."

Miles went on to work with The Alan Parsons Project for several albums and toured with Jimmy Page and Tina Turner. Later he wrote musicals as well as appearing for many years in European pop/classical concerts known as *A Night At The Proms*. He died in 2021.

Mungo Jerry

Mungo Jerry broke through at 1970's Hollywood Festival which was actually held in Staffordshire. Their first single 'In The Summertime' sold seven million copies and topped the charts in the UK. This was very much the song of summer 1970, full of hooks, attractive gimmicks and witty lyrics. The follow-up, 'Baby Jump', also reached No. 1, but was a total contrast. In hindsight, 'Baby Jump' is one of the most bizarre and manic sounding chart-toppers of the last 50 years. After this there was the predictable diminishing returns: the tuneful 'Lady Rose' went Top Five, 'You Don't Have To Be In The Army' went Top Twenty and the slightly creepy 'Open Up' peaked at No. 21.

I cannot remember 'Open Up''s follow-up, 'My Girl And Me', from 1972. The band's website states: *"(it) received virtually no airplay in the UK."* There is phased guitar at the start with distorted vocals and a simple repeated guitar pattern. The song doesn't sound like Mungo Jerry nor go anywhere interesting.

After this Mungo Jerry made a strong comeback with 'Alright, Alright, Alright' which reached No. 3, and was followed by 'Wild Love'. *Record Mirror*: *"What this one does is stamp along. Ray Dorset doing his wild-animalistic noises and vocal refrains out front. It's full of riffs, hey-hos, repeated title phrases and talking bits … It'll hit the charts in a big way, but for me doesn't have the instant appeal of 'Alright, Alright, Alright'."* I found the song rather predictable and not witty. It peaked at No. 32. 'Long Legged

Woman Dressed In Black' echoed the repetition of earlier hits and reached No. 13. This was the end of Mungo Jerry's time in the UK charts.

1974's *All Dressed Up And No Place To Go* was an E.P.; clearly the term "maxi-single" was now out of favour. There is a powerful bass riff and something of a rock 'n' roll pastiche with boogie piano in the style of Little Richard and Jerry Lee Lewis.

By 1975 the band were on the Polydor label. 'Can't Get Over Loving You' was reviewed in *Disc*: "*Pretty lightweight stuff ... Ray Dorset seems to be struggling badly to come up with something that will hold everybody's interest, almost as if he's lost his old touch ... For your money you get a lukewarm but perky song with a too-simple-by-far hook-line and some pretty mundane lyrics. Repetitive to the point of overkill. Not a chart sound.*" It's more rock 'n' roll pastiche and faux nostalgia, better than Showaddywaddy, but not that much better.

'Hello Nadine' was also released in 1975 and condemned in *NME* as: "'*In The Summertime Part 36*'". Actually, the song sounds more like their 1971 hit, 'Lady Rose', with its mandolin riffs. The words are nostalgic — "*I remember when the days were young.*" We even hear the word "*summertime*"!

Don Partridge

Partridge emerged in 1968 from the London busking scene. This one-man-band act with guitar, harmonica, kazoo and bass drum operated by his knee was immediately appealing to both record company and television producers. In those days of just three television channels, a single TV appearance could transform the life and fortunes of performers, Esther and Abi Ofarim being perhaps the other best example. Signed to Columbia, Partridge had two Top Five hits – 'Rosie' and 'Blue Eyes' – in quick succession. He even performed at that year's *NME* Pollwinners Concert at Wembley Empire Pool.

Follow-ups were problematic. Partridge's whole image and success had been built around the simplicity and honesty of his one-man-band set-up. Surely, buskers are not accompanied by orchestras? 'Top Man' was arranged by Joe Moretti. *Record Mirror*: "*Harmonica-wailed intro, then a very catchy instant rhythm and into a Kerr-Maitland song again ... a happy sort of song with Don working over strings and other orchestral bits 'n' pieces. This will be a biggie. Start whistling right now."* It wasn't even a smallie.

In 1969 Partridge hired the Royal Albert Hall for a *Buskers' Concert* which featured many of his fellow street performers who would share the profits equally. This led to a ten-date Buskers' Tour where the performers travelled around the country in an old London Transport bus. The line-up included a young Dave Brock (pre-Hawkwind) and singer/guitarist Gordon Giltrap.

'Breakfast On Pluto' brought Partridge back into the charts at the beginning of 1969, but the single peaked at a disappointing No. 26. His fifteen minutes of fame were clearly over. 'Colour My World' (not the Tony Hatch song) was released next. *Record Mirror*: *"A very pleasant song with sentimental lyrics.. Don's voice gets a fair break in the middle of a big orchestral arrangement. Gentle mid-tempo stuff with moments on fire on the main chorus line, plus guitar at the base. A very nice record."* Penny Valentine: *"This has such a very pop chorus it might well get away. The song (is) a new thing with a rather undistinguished verse and on which Don sounds sadly lacking on a few notes. But never mind, the chorus, where he's double-tracked and sounds a lot better for it, makes up for that. Not a great record by any means. But pleasant."*

'Going To Germany' appeared later in the year. This single was back to Partridge's busking style and is in a bluesy jug band vein. We hear honky tonk piano and, towards the end, his blues harmonica and kazoo (which were so loved on his big hits). He sings: *"go away from my window"* which may have been inspired by Dylan's 'It Ain't Me Babe' and then *"stop knocking on my door"*. If this had been released after 'Blue Eyes', it surely would have been a hit. By this time though Partridge's time in the spotlight was over. He went back to busking, living for a while in Scandinavia.

THE RUBETTES

The Rubettes were quickly put together to provide a group to mime to 'Sugar Baby Love' on *Top of the Pops*. The falsetto vocal had been provided by one Paul Da Vinci who subsequently reached No. 20 under his own name with 'Your Baby Ain't Your Baby Anymore'.

'Sugar Baby Love', whatever you think of it, is some sort of classic (selling three million copies, no less) and was featured decades later in *Muriel's Wedding* to provide just the right mood of the slightly naff 1970s revival. On *Top of the Pops*, some may have recognised the lead singer and the drummer when they were known as Baskin and Copperfield from 1970 when they performed 'I Never See The Sun'. With their matching caps and suits, The Rubettes were never going to be a fashionable act, but they achieved seven consecutive Top Thirty hits in just eighteen months. 'Under One Roof' – with its same sex couple storyline – was less successful, peaking at No. 40. *Record Mirror* did not even comment on the storyline: "*Complete change of style heralds Yankee sounding slow wispy folk tune with especially good harmonies. The lilt ain't that catchy but it's quality stuff.*"

Their 1977 single, 'Baby I Know', was a complete change of style with a different lead singer. This was gentle country pop, but highly successful, reaching No. 10. Follow-ups fared worse. *Record Mirror's* review of 'Ladies Of Laredo' was both damning and patronising: "*A bit long and drawn out, but at least they are adventurous enough to try something different. Probably a grower.*" The same paper's reviewer dealt with the next single, 'Come On Over', even more harshly: "*This is their new laid-back country image and they sound very smooth but ultimately boring.*"

'Somewhere In Oldchurch' was reviewed in *Record Mirror* in January 1978: "*A very pretty song featuring slide guitar makes them sound like an American West Coast band – but they've got that bit of extra push in their vocals to keep them out of that rut. A good pop song which deserves to make it.*"

Barry Ryan

The twin son of singer Marion Ryan, Barry Ryan was originally a double act with brother Paul. They had four Top Thirty hits between 1965 and 1967 on Decca which are largely forgotten these days. Paul then decided to focus on writing and late 1968 saw his twin's solo triumph 'Eloise' just miss out on the top spot, peaking at No. 2. It was, and still is, an extraordinary, melodramatic record, setting the bar impossibly high for both writer and singer. It sold over three million copies worldwide and was No. 1 in many countries. Unlike so many 1960s "classics", 'Eloise' does not suffer from over-familiarity, partly, I believe, because it does not easily fit into a golden oldies radio format. Eighteen years later, The Damned released an almost identical cover version which reached No. 3. The follow-up, 'Love Is Love', just scraped into the Top Thirty, peaking at No 25 and therefore allowing me to include Ryan here.

Ryan's next few singles were all interesting and far removed from most of the other releases of the time. Even the songs' titles were unusual; no-one else was releasing songs with titles like 'The Hunt', 'Magical Spiel' or 'Kitsch'. Ryan had his feet in two camps – a solo pop performer, but (because of his brother's songs style) completely out of step with his apparent peers such as Cliff, Tom and Engelbert. The songs' elaborate orchestral arrangements would have meant that live performances would be challenging to replicate. In the next decade, a performer like Ryan could have made special live appearances with an orchestra — like Barclay James Harvest and Procol Harum successfully did. No wonder the Germans loved him; perhaps the songs' arrangements reminded them no less of Beethoven or even Wagner? If an artist's first success is a huge triumphal hit – sundry other examples could include the likes of Sparks and Thunderclap Newman — it is very hard to match such an achievement and the only way in chart terms is, unfortunately, down. There will inevitably be pressure from the record company and management, along with expectation from both critics and fans. All these parties will demand and expect similar-sounding releases, while the critics will then eagerly pounce on artists who deliver the same sort of thing time and again. I have limited sympathy for true "one hit wonders". The vast majority of acts do not have even one hit record. The real geniuses of pop constantly reinvent themselves so that their hits don't sound the same.

Ryan's melodramatic records continued. 'The Hunt' was his first single on Polydor, rather than MGM. You must try and hear this with its shouts of *"Tally ho!"* and the insistent, repeated *"I'm on my way."* Record Mirror: *"though there are signs of yet another massive production, in fact it is a much simpler sort of sound ... no expense is spared in making his singles 'complete productions'. Once this gets over the first over-done bit, it's a jogging impacting piece."* NME felt the same: *"it is in much the same expansive style as*

'Eloise' and lacking the melodic content ... (it) is an incredible dynamic performance by Barry, a scorching up-tempo pace; and a magnificently-scored arrangement that's almost over-powering in its impact." The single was clearly too overpowering as it stalled at No. 34 but deserved better. How many other songs have been written about a fox hunt?

'Magical Spiel' was an extraordinary record with Ryan spelling out the letters of the title — "*M is for Magdalene, A is for Alchemist.*" etc and shouting out "*Lucifer*", "*Talisman*" and "*Ouija Board*"! Record Mirror: "A good strained exuberant mood here. Barry, despite the constant knockers, does make good-class pop records – lots of thought, plenty of ability. This is a less ambitious production, but there is still a helluva lot happening. It really does push along." Despite a *Top of the Pops* appearance and wide airplay, 'Magical Spiel' only reached No. 49.

I remember hearing 'Kitsch' on the radio and seeing music press advertisements. Ryan performed the song on *Top of the Pops* in April 1970. This was – and remains – one of the strangest pop records of the 1970s. "*Kitsch, it's a beautiful word, it's a beautiful lullaby.*" The single peaked at a disappointing No. 37.

Less than a year later, Ryan was back on *Top of the Pops* promoting 'It Is Written'. The song starts slowly with piano backing, but true to form, soon speeds up. He sings "*I've been down so long*" and soon a female chorus and orchestra come in. Ryan shouts "*C'mon!*" and the song feels almost Biblical in its theme. This single is more jaunty than melodramatic and becomes something of a singalong but was a complete flop.

'Can't Let You Go' received much airplay and yet another preview on *Top of the Pops* when released in December 1971. Record Mirror: "A Russ Ballard song this time. Brisk piano intro, fair old tempo and Barry doing a much less cluttered vocal job over a basic boogie beat. His voice seems set a shade higher, but the energy is still there. The odd gimmick up in the falsetto range comes in, but it's much less contrived than some of those early ones. Sounds like a hit to me." 'Can't Let You Go' entered the charts in mid January 1972 and stayed for five weeks, peaking at only No. 32. This was Ryan's final chart entry in the UK.

NME reviewed Ryan's next single, 'From My Head To Toe': "*This kinda record, with busy orchestral buzzings, fast shake beat and spiralling hook* chorus, would have been a gigantic hit three years ago with the nation's Saturday night Mecca Ballroom jet-setters. *If that crowd are still buying this kinda record, then it could be a hit ... know what I mean?"*

'I'm Sorry Susan' was another Paul Ryan composition, but produced and directed by Wayne Bickerton who went on to work with The Rubettes a couple of years later. The song is less melodramatic and more introspective than earlier Paul Ryan compositions and has a great chorus and touching words — *"I'm sorry Susan that I made you cry, that I said goodbye"*. The production is less ambitious and has a lovely string arrangement.

Unfortunately, by 1972, Ryan's orchestral pop was unfairly seen as old hat and linked to MOR performers and cabaret appearances. Brother Paul died in 1992 and Barry died in 2021, having become an acclaimed photographer.

Sailor

Sailor hated being called a glam rock band so I will respect their wishes by not placing them in that chapter! I always admired Georg Kajanus' single-minded vision of the subject matter of the group's songs. After the huge success of 'A Glass Of Champagne' and 'Girls, Girls, Girls' in the UK and all over Europe (especially Germany), the group struggled to find a successful follow-up. 'Stiletto Heels' was released in late 1976. *Record Mirror*: *"As blatantly Roxy as 'Champagne' but totally infectious with the nickelodeon grinding away throughout. Whistles and clicking heels."* NME liked it too and made it their single of the week, proclaiming the song *"irresistible dance-wise and a sure hit."* It flopped.

'One Drink Too Many' may have continued the alcohol theme of their biggest hit but was sufficiently different to reach No. 35 in early 1977. The single benefited from the band's appearances on *Top of the Pops* and ITV's *Supersonic*, but was Sailor's final chart entry.

Worse – much worse – was to come. The band's fourth album was produced by former Beach Boy Bruce Johnston and songwriter, Curt Boechter. I interviewed lead singer George Kajanus 30 years ago and he was scathing about the production team; *"My God! That was quite a horrendous task. We were lumbered with another American team. We had a lot of problems. The sound was absolutely dreadful there was no warmth."*

'Down By The Docks', despite keeping the maritime theme of the band's first three albums, was something else. *Record Mirror*: *"This is awful – Sailor going disco if you can imagine it, and in the process losing all their old charm and eccentricity. Now they just sound like another band off the assembly line."* The reviewer is correct, the song is dire. Producer Bruce Johnstone said: *"Curt and I tried to direct Sailor to the 'radio' once again but I guess we missed! We even thought that those nice blonde German Sailor fans would love hanging out in the discos of 1977-1978 groovin' to 'Down By The Docks', but we were wrong!"* A year or so later, Johnstone and Boechter revived an old Beach Boys track, 'Here Comes The Night', and successfully turned it into a disco hit for Brian Wilson's group.

Sailor's follow-up, 'Romance' – also from the *Checkpoint* album – was released three months later and was much better, reverting to Sailor's usual style. The vocals were exceptional. James McGarraher: *"Bruce and the three musicians gathered around one microphone singing individual notes or harmonies. As a result, a single wall of sound was created."*

The next year was even worse for Sailor. 'All I Need Is A Girl' was released in March and was an upbeat song, but the group's sound and image was changing. Even the very loyal German fans did not make this single a big hit. The nickelodeon had virtually disappeared. The follow-up, 'The Runaway', was Sailor's first single not to be written nor sung by lead singer/guitarist Georg Kajanus. Written and sung by keyboard player Phil Pickett (later to be a co-writer and musician in Culture Club), the single was previewed on *Cheggers Plays Pop* and was an unremarkable song and performance.

Three months later 'Give Me Shakespeare' was released. McGarraher praised the song: *"(this) is the hit many people wished Georg could have written back in 1976, as a follow-up to 'A Glass Of Champagne' and 'Girls Girls Girls'. It is a tremendous piece of writing - up-beat, up-tempo and very amusing with some deliberately corny rhyming couplets. The track was an attempt to 'punk up' the Sailor sound, to make it more accessible to a wider audience."* I feel that this guitar-based song has clever lyrics but a dull tune. Incredibly, this single was also performed on *Cheggers Plays Pop*. Sailor's final single of the 1970s, 'Stay The Night', was also promoted on British children's television, this time *Crackerjack*.

Happily, Sailor's original line-up reunited in the 1990s and released two albums of new quality material, another eponymous title and its follow-up *Street Lamp*. These releases are outside the scope of this book but are well worth hearing. Some of these flop stories have a happy ending.

CRISPIAN ST PETERS

Crispian's real name was the rather more ordinary, Peter Smith, but his stage name suggested English churches, heritage, Shakespeare and more. If I remember there was some controversy (no doubt staged by a clever P.R. working with Decca Records) where Crispian claimed to be the next Elvis Presley! 'You Were On My Mind' was written by Sylvia Fricker of Ian and Sylvia fame, a Canadian couple who both wrote songs together and separately. Ian Tyson wrote 'Four Strong Winds' and 'Some Day Soon'. 'You Were On My Mind' was a big hit in the US for the We Five, but failed to take off in Britain. Crispian St Peters covered the cover, as it were, and reached No. 2 over here in 1966. His follow-up, 'Pied Piper', reached the Top Five and was covered five years later by reggae duo, Bob and Marcia.

'Changes' was reviewed in *Record Mirror*: "*A Phil Ochs composition and very well sung by Crispian. Gentle opening in the normal voice range, then he moves into the upper register, almost Orbison style, but the voice is true and distinctive. Vocal aid later on from group, and a jogging arrangement.*" The single peaked at No. 47. Penny Valentine reviewed 'Almost Persuaded': "*Crispian handles this with enough non-effort to make him sound like the very most genuine of American country and western singers in the Jim Reeves style.*"

'Free Spirit' was reviewed in *NME*: "*It's a snappy bouncer, with a very commercial catch-line, and the title phrase continually repeated in multi-track. The tune is simple and registers quickly, and the beat makes you want to dance. But for all its qualities, I can't be too optimistic about its chances.*"

Peter Sarstedt

Peter Sarstedt usually appears in articles on one-hit wonders centred around his name-dropping million seller, 'Where Do You Go To My Lovely?' I remember his *Top of the Pops* appearances and the fascinating list of names, places and products. I still don't know who Ceezy Jamere is. The single earns a place in an all-time collection of great list songs – which includes 'You're The Top', 'Let's Do It', 'You're Moving Out Today' and 'These Foolish Things'.

The follow-up to Sarstedt's massive seller, 'Frozen Orange Juice', also went Top Ten. Steve Wright used to occasionally play this on Radio 2 but the song was inevitably over-shadowed by its predecessor. Sarstedt's next single, 'As Though It Were A Movie', was the title track of his second album and was widely advertised. There were Hollywood look-alikes such as Charlie Chaplin and Mae West on the front cover. Sadly, the single did not grab the public's attention and flopped in the UK. In the next few years there would be many, many songs about Hollywood and movies; perhaps Peter's song was just mistimed.

1971's 'You're A Lady' was reviewed by Penny Valentine who had now moved to *Sounds*: *"After a long absence Peter Sarstedt comes back with not a jot of that highly identifiable voice out of place. Neither has he lost that clarity and directness of production and lyric appeal- 'You're a lady- I'm a fan of yours."*

Seven years later, Sarstedt released a single called 'Beirut' on the Ariola label. I remember hearing this at the time. Songs about war zones are problematic – I think of Boney M's 'Belfast' and the Human League's 'The Lebanon' – but I found this single quite pleasant. *Record Mirror*'s reviewer was less impressed: *"The melody itself is pleasant enough, but is weighted by Sarstedt's cumbersome lyrics."*

Leo Sayer

Leo Sayer's career on the Chrysalis label is impressive; one chart-topper, four No. 2 hits and eleven Top Ten hit singles. This was in addition to five consecutive Top Ten albums. Sayer first came to attention in December 1973, dressed as a pierrot, singing 'The Show Must Go On'. Rock scholars already knew that Sayer had co-written (with Dave Courtney) not only Roger Daltrey's solo single, 'Giving It All Away', but nearly the whole of the latter's eponymous first album. Sayer's second album was called *Just A Boy*, a line, of course, from 'Giving It All Away', and contained more hits.

In between all this early success was a cover of 'Let It Be' which was included on that dreadful *All This And World War Two* album. *Record Mirror*: "*Very glossy version ... with Leo sounding a lot like Elton John. He opens just to piano accompaniment and then the arrangement builds nicely with strings and choir making their place in the proceedings along the way. Leo displays more technique than on any of his previous singles and his excellent work should earn him another huge hit.*" This Beatle cover didn't trouble the UK singles charts.

For his fourth album, *Endless Flight*, Sayer teamed up with Richard Perry. The set contained 'When I Need You', written by Albert Hammond and Carole Bayer Sager which was No. 1 on both sides of the Atlantic. Two other tracks from the album, 'You Make Me Feel Like Dancing' and 'How Much Love', were also huge hit singles.

I cannot honestly remember Leo Sayer's flops in the late 1970s. 'There Isn't Anything I Wouldn't Do' came from the pen of John Yastano and was on the *Thunder In My Heart* album, another Richard Perry production. This is a piano-led ballad with the inevitable strings and sax solo. It feels like an attempt to replicate 'When I Need You' with rather hackneyed lyrics such as "*holding you close*", "*fly like an eagle*", "*fantasy*" and "*just like a miracle*". Sayer is quoted in Barry Scott's book: "*The sad thing was that 'There Isn't Anything' I thought could have been a Top 5 record. I really did.*" *Record Mirror*: "*Best produced and most beautifully sung cut from the* Thunder In My Heart *album. A bit reminiscent of 'When I Need You', but more hard core bluesy and soulful. Note the strong and well-arranged backing.*"

The flops continued. 'Dancing The Night Away' (1978) was another ballad, complete with a gypsy violin break and plaintive, nostalgic and romantic lyrics. *Record Mirror*: "*Nouveau Sayer West Coast type ballad. Fairly lightweight, but Richard Perry production that'll grab hold of late nighters in discos. Lyrically it's quite appalling.*" I find this one rather ordinary and predictable.

The titles of the next two single flops, 'When The Money Runs Out' and 'The World Has Changed' in hindsight seem particularly appropriate for Sayer's declining appeal. *Record Mirror* on 'Money': "*An uncharacteristic barn-stormer complete with righteous sentiments from a commercial artist with more than a fair share of suss.*"

In early 1979 Sayer's *Very Best of* compilation (which included 'Dancing The Night Away') reached No.1 so plenty of people would have heard that flop single. His next album, *Here*, staggered to No. 44; clearly the record buying public preferred familiar songs, rather than new material.

The early 1980s were kinder to Sayer with his cover of Bobby Vee's 1961 hit 'More Than I Can Say' reaching No. 2 and two other Top Twenty hits. Albums of new material also reached the Top Thirty. Leo Sayer is a survivor. A dance remix of 'Thunder In My Heart' by British D.J. Meck titled 'Thunder In My Heart Again' reached No. 1 in 2006, 29 years after Sayer's original hit.

STEELEYE SPAN

Steeleye Span released a few singles over the years, notably an acappella version of Buddy Holly's 'Rave On' which showed their not so serious side. I suppose that it is inevitable that British folk rock acts tended to only have novelty hits that would cross over to the wider record buying public. Fairport Convention's solitary hit was their Cajun rendering of Dylan's 'If You Gotta Go, Go Now' which they translated into 'Si Tu Dois Partir'.

Span's dog-Latin 'Gaudete' was (eventually) a big Christmas hit in 1973 with, if I remember rightly, the group wandering around the *Top of the Pops* studio carrying candles. This was a whole year after its first release but did not appear to revive sales of its 1972 parent album, *Below The Salt*.

A follow-up to 'Gaudete' was problematic. *Record Mirror*'s singles reviewer pinpointed the problem with 'Thomas The Rhymer': "*It's a very clever bit of singing – an arrangement which sets the voices very high, produces moments of glorious and orthodox harmony, then wanders off into the off-beat.*" In *Disc* the reviewer was more optimistic: "*Another unusual single from Steeleye. This time produced by Tull's Ian Anderson. The words are traditional and the whole feel of this record is vaguely Chaucerish. If the very thought makes you shudder, remember what a great job they did of a Latin chant. Forsooth, it will be a hit."* Thomas The Flopper.

Steeleye's gimmicks were a little hit and miss with more emphasis on the miss. On their album *Now We Are Six* the band wasted their time and talent on including 'Twinkle Twinkle Little Star' and a cover of the old Teddy Bears' hit, 'To Know Him Is To Love Him'. The latter featured no less than David Bowie guesting on saxophone. On the next album, *Commoner's Crown*, the band included their version of folk club favourite, 'New York Girls'. When extracted as a single, it did not bother the charts, despite receiving much publicity for featuring Peter Sellers guesting on ukulele. This rather simplistic song was just not chart material.

Just seven months later 'All Around My Hat', produced by Womblemeister Mike Batt, was a big hit, reaching No. 5. Sometimes a big hit can backfire for an act; they sell thousands of singles, but often then alienate – and even lose – their original fanbase. The Toy Dolls with 'Nelly The Elephant' and Chumbawamba with 'Tubthumping' are just two obvious examples, but there are many more. Steeleye Span's singer, Maddy Prior, had a different view as she told *Record Collector*: *"They (the hit singles) were the best thing that ever happened to us. They're both good songs, and that's why they did well. I always think, 'We've done Top of the Pops, done big stadiums' – I wouldn't have missed that for anything. But I wouldn't want to live there."* 'All Around My Hat' was the title track of the band's new album which helped sales. The *Hat* album reached No. 7 and stayed in the charts for 20 weeks. This was Steeleye Span's commercial peak.

'London' was released as the follow-up. *Record Mirror*: *"Has a similar driving beat to 'All Around My Hat', though less appealing. Maddy in fine voice sings about claret wine and politics ... it's all very rustic and jolly."* But the public did not buy it. Its parent album, *Rocket Cottage*, also produced by Batt, in contrast to the *All Around My Hat* album, staggered to Number 41 and was in the charts for just three weeks. 'Fighting For Strangers' was also taken from *Rocket Cottage* in time for Christmas 1976. *Record Mirror*: *"Sounds like the hymn to which we primary school rebels would sing 'To be a grim pill' to. At least they've not given us 'Gaudete' again – yet!"* As the reviewer hints, there are elements of the tune of the old hymn 'To Be

A Pilgrim' (with new words), interspersed with a folk song about the army sung by Tim Hart over quite an interesting percussion track. This doesn't really work as a single.

'Rag Doll' was released as a single in 1978. In concert, such a novelty can be quite effective, especially if the rendition is acappella or slowed down. In this case, Steeleye just sound like a cover band. Maddy Prior is an extraordinary singer, but 'Rag Doll' is essentially Frankie Valli's song. Recent productions of the musical *Jersey Boys* show how hard, nay impossible, it is to replicate his vocals. Valli's voice is not so much unique, but simply unmistakeable. *Record Mirror* was ruthless: *"This must be a bad joke. Fab Four Seasons biggie sounds utterly wretched in the hands of Span. Totally worthless effort."*

THE STRAWBS

I get sentimental about The Strawbs. They were the very first band that I saw play live and I was a loyal fan, I suppose, until 'Part Of The Union'. The band had been signed to A&M Records since 1969 and released a series of well received singles and albums, centred around leader Dave Cousins' distinctive voice. Rick Wakeman was their first keyboard player and helped transform the band from a folk rock trio to a much fuller sound, benefiting from Wakeman's extraordinary virtuosity on various keyboards. The rhythm section of Richard Hudson and John Ford saw the band become a quintet.

I was first introduced to The Strawbs by their appearance on the album spot on *Top of the Pops* performing 'The Hangman And The Papist' in summer 1971. Over a half a century later, the drama of this song still resonates, not least if you know – as I learned at the gig – that the song was about Northern Ireland. Wakeman was soon poached by Yes and replaced by Blue Weaver, formerly of Amen Corner. Within a year, acoustic guitarist Tony Hooper (who had been with Cousins for many years right back to The Strawberry Hill Boys) was replaced by Dave Lambert from The King Earle Boogie Band. Lambert was an electric guitarist and his playing dominated the band's first hit single, 'Lay Down' which reached No. 12 in late 1972. The follow-up was the uncharacteristic 'Part Of The Union' with lead vocals by bassist John

Ford which reached No. 2. People still argue whether the song was pro- or anti-trade union. I fear it was the latter.

This was followed by the departure of bassist John Ford and drummer Richard Hudson to form their own band, Hudson Ford, which also recorded for A&M Records. The new Strawbs line-up previewed their new single 'Shine On Silver Sun' on *Top of the Pops* in September 1973. The song later appeared on the band's *Hero And Heroine* album. *Record Mirror*: "*It's got that determined beat, and that almost pedantic melodic hook, and the whole thing goes with a piano-filled enthusiasm. Nothing all that different, in terms of group-style ballads, but it's just ... effective. Must be, will be a giant.*" The public, including this writer, thought otherwise and it reached no higher than No. 34. *NME* agreed: "*a tepid piece of droning nausea that must represent some kind of low point for The Strawbs,*" but worse was to follow. Unfortunately for The Strawbs, their former rhythm section had beaten them in the chart stakes, achieving a Top Ten hit with their single, 'Pick Up The Pieces'. Two more tracks from *Hero And Heroine* were released as singles, the title track and 'Hold On To Me'. They both flopped.

'Grace Darling' was taken from the band's next album, *Ghosts*. *NME*: "*It's a perfect example of production overkill, not to mention bad lyrics. A choir helps Dave Cousins out with some of the most dire lyrics I've heard for a long time ... Cathedral-type organ is prominent too.*" The follow-up was 'Lemon Pie'. *Record Mirror*: "*while not a good commercial proposition, it's delightful listening and an object lesson in how to make a classy, interesting record out of what is basically unpromising material. I like it a lot.*" Two more flops.

'I Only Want My Love To Grow In You' was featured as a record of the week on Radio One and received lots of airplay but still did not chart. Next single was 'Charmer'. *Record Mirror*: "*Another deep cut, this time a mid-tempo shuffler with good hooks, but since their last one got so much airplay and not a lot of action in the charts, what chance has this got?*" The reviewer raises an excellent point; how many times can a band follow up a flop? The number of acts who returned after a long break from the charts is quite small; The Bee Gees, Olivia Newton-John and Status Quo spring to mind. By now the band were on the Oyster label and still the flops continued.

Later releases included the execrable 'Back In The Old Routine' in 1977 which even name-checked Noel Edmonds. This singalong number had the rhythm of John Sebastian's 'Daydream', but with none of the latter's charm. Just five years after seeing the band at my first ever gig, it was a shock to see their *Top of the Pops* appearance. This did not help the single's fortunes, only Dave Cousins remained from the 1972 line-up.

Record Mirror reviewed 'Joey And Me': "*Their first single on Arista and it's catchy. There's no mistaking Dave Cousins' voice. Good but not, I feel, enough character to put Strawbs back in the charts.*" There is lots of strummed guitar and some truly uninspired lyrics; "*shoulder to shoulder*" and "*under the open skies, living in paradise.*" I found it hard to believe that this was from the same pen as the writer of such classic songs as 'The Hangman And The Papist', 'Glimpse Of Heaven' and 'Benedictus'. 'Joey' was the first of three singles taken from the *Deadlines* album. The band's penultimate single, 'New Beginnings', was praised in *Record Mirror*: "*this record is really quite nice in a soothing sort of way ... so relaxing that Radio One are bound to flog it to death which at least should give the band a much-needed, and well deserved, hit.*" Neither the airplay nor the hit happened. Finally, there was 'I Don't Want To Talk About It' which I have never heard.

That was pretty much it for The Strawbs. They disbanded later in 1978 and did not reunite until nearly a decade later. Leader Dave Cousins began a successful career in local commercial radio. I wonder if he ever programmed 'Back In The Old Routine'?

The Wombles

The Wombles' television series was in the same slot on BBC1 as *Hector's House*, *The Herbs* and *Sir Prancelot* just before the evening news. The theme tune was a surprisingly big hit, reaching No. 4 in spring 1974. The follow-up, 'Remember You're A Womble', did even better, as did 'Wombling Merry Christmas', The Wombles' fifth hit of the year! Mike Batt was clearly a superb craftsman at pastiche, ensuring that each release was a different genre but still with his unmistakeable voice.

1974 was The Wombles' peak year: no fewer than five Top Twenty singles and three Top Twenty albums. 1975 inevitably brought diminishing returns with none of The Wombles' singles entering the

Top Ten. 'Wombling White Tie And Tails' was a favourite of my friends. Even if the tune reminded some of 'Little Deuce Coupe', there was a clever arrangement and witty words. 'Let's Womble To The Party', an awkward mixture of swing – with an Andrews Sisters pastiche – and rock 'n' roll went no higher than No. 34. This was demonstrated at The *Saturday Scene* Pop Awards 1975 held at Wembley Empire Pool in November of that year. Mike Batt appears as himself, uncostumed except for a pair of furry boots, singing along to 'Let's Womble To The Party' in front of several Wombles in full costume, some wearing Teddy Boy drape jackets.

The Wombles' next single, 'The Womble Shuffle', was their first complete flop. I find the song rather monotonous. *Record Mirror*: "*another ditty with soulful harmonica blending into the chorus. Although it should make the charts, I don't think it's as strong as some of the previous Womble cuts.*" Perhaps CBS should have flipped the record and promoted the B-side, 'To Wimbledon With Love', instead. As the title suggests, this was a clever pastiche of a Bond movie theme. Mike Batt – with his background in arranging and conducting – succeeds brilliantly here. This sublime song is an affectionate and respectful tribute to John Barry.

The Wombles' record career ended quite suddenly after an unfortunate episode of franchising. Mike Batt told *Record Collector*'s Nick Dalton: "*Bill Kenwright got the Wombles' copyright holders to let him put on stage shows simultaneously in nine cities and they were terrible. People complained and there was a lot of bad feeling when people saw that The Wombles weren't a real group ... Record sales plummeted. That was the point when I decided that they had to be killed off. We'd had eight hits, a pretty good run.*" I remember reading about the disappointed family audiences at Christmas being faced with rather lean looking animal costume wearers miming to records.

Mike Batt had just one hit single under his own name; billed as Mike Batt with The New Edition, 'Summertime City' was the theme tune to BBC1's *Summertime Special* series and reached No. 4 in 1975. Over the next few years Batt penned huge hits such as 'Bright Eyes' for Art Garfunkel and 'A Winter's Tale' for David Essex. More recently he has guided the career of Katie Melua. Happily, Batt revived The Wombles at Glastonbury in 2011 where they were a huge success. Batt recalled: "*We had the biggest crowd for our time slot.*" His memoirs are well worth reading, if only for their unusual honesty about his financial and artistic ups and downs.

16 – Celtic Connections

Junior Campbell

Campbell was lead guitarist and songwriter for Marmalade, co-writing 'My Little One', 'Rainbow' and 'Reflections Of My Life' with singer Dean Ford. He left the group in early 1971, wanting to study musical arrangement and enrolled at the Royal College of Music. Campbell later had two Top Twenty hits with fairly enjoyable white soul songs, 'Hallelujah Freedom' and 'Sweet Illusion'. Later in 1973 '(Reach Out And) Help Your Fellow Man' was released. *Record Mirror*: "*Personally I'd have pruned the intro a bit and got down to the highly successful Campbell plus chorus mix ... Junior's determined American-sounding voice gets to grips with this one ... Chart Cert.*" This one didn't chart. 'Sweet Lady Love' was reviewed in *Record Mirror*: "*Piano introed, sturdy basic beat. Junior's voice at its lightest, but that's not to say weakest. There's a rolling, almost gospel feel to this once it gets under way. It'll be a hit, because it has excitement and a strong all-round vocal arrangement, and also because it never lets up. Could turn out to be Junior's biggest yet.*" This wasn't to be.

Campbell was branching out as a songwriter, penning the excellent 'Carolina Days' for Clodagh Rodgers. He also worked as an arranger for many artists. 'Carabino Lady' was released on Elton John's Rocket label. *NME*: "*Jolly, jumping reggae routine from Junior, a British pioneer of blue-eyed soul.*" I quite like this; it is a busy white reggae record and far far better than the likes of 'Dreadlock Holiday'.

In 1976 Campbell produced and arranged Barbara Dickson's first album for RSO. As late as 1978 he released a single on Private Stock. *Record Mirror* reviewed 'Highland Girl': "*Here's a change ... with a clean ballad. Make that really clean – no slush at all. In fact, the backing's original enough to give Junior a comeback chance.*"

In recent years Campbell has written the music for *Thomas The Tank Engine* and other television series. He is clearly a survivor, knowing when to change career. There is a fascinating interview with Campbell on the *Strange Brew* podcast series. I was impressed with his honesty, intelligence and modesty.

Dave Edmunds

Edmunds seems to have had as many contrasting phases in his career as The Bee Gees. After a Top Five hit in 1968 with Love Sculpture's frenetic version of 'Sabre Dance', Edmunds seemed to disappear for a couple of years. He returned with his cover of Smiley Lewis's 'I Hear You Knocking', the first release on Gordon Mills' MAM label. The record, deservedly, reached the top of the charts, staying there for six weeks including the whole of December. This was one of the very few Christmas chart-toppers not to be a seasonal nor novelty record. With Edmunds' echoey vocals and crisp guitars, the single rivalled Creedence Clearwater Revival for sheer sonic quality.

Edmunds moved to Regal Zonophone where he made three attempts at repeating the success of his big hit. 'I'm Coming Home' was previewed on *Top of the Pops* in April 1971. NME liked it: "*a rip-roaring rocker, in similar style to his previous single. The singing is spirited, the beat is very compelling and infectious – and there's some brilliant reverberating guitar plucking. A very commercial sound indeed.*" The single failed to chart. Next was Edmunds' version of Fats Domino's 'Blue Monday'. *NME*: "*This latest release is obviously a very important disc for Dave because, if he is to consolidate his star status, he must secure another hit quickly … the approach, the treatment, the sound and even, to some extent, the song are all very similar to Dave's chart-topper. Perhaps even too similar for many potential buyers!*" This, essentially, was the challenge for Edmunds in trying to have a hit follow-up to 'I Hear You Knocking'. Radio One's Stuart Henry would use the line, "*Oh, Saturday morning*" (in a tape loop) from 'Blue Monday' for his weekend programme.

'Down Down Down' was released next. *NME*: "*this is a great choice for a single. Hopefully the bopping rhythm will give Dave his long-awaited follow-up hit to 'I Hear You Knockin'. His voice is tinged with echo while the rhythm guitar pumps and churns with the same drive that Chuck Berry's best songs feature.*" This song had a faster pace than Edmunds' previous solo singles and flopped. A few years later Edmunds would produce a very similar-sounding version by The Flamin' Groovies for their second Sire album.

Edmunds would not return to the UK singles charts for three more years. Hidden away in Rockfield Studios in South Wales, he widened his repertoire from rock 'n' roll to girl group pop with majestic versions of 'Baby I Love You' and 'Born To Be With You' which both went Top Ten in 1973. There were a couple of flops in 1974, but this did not matter as Edmunds was busy in charge of The Stray Cats' music in the David Essex film *Stardust*. One of the flop singles, 'Need A Shot Of Rhythm And Blues' was included in the film and appeared on the original soundtrack album. He also appeared on screen as a member of The Stray Cats, alongside Keith Moon, Karl Bowmer and Peter Duncan. *Record Mirror* praised the single: *"This is an old Mersey-beat era favourite, driving rhythm and all ... could do well."*

'I Ain't Never' was released in 1975. *Record Mirror*: *"As with all Dave Edmunds' releases, the production is fabulous, but the song isn't as strong as his last single. That died without trace, so this probably will fare likewise."*

By 1976 Edmunds had signed to Led Zeppelin's Swansong label. Initial releases did not chart. 'Here Comes The Weekend' was a joint composition with Nick Lowe, 'Where Or When' was reviewed in *Record Mirror*: *"Surf's up as Mr Edmunds sings Rodgers and Hart a la Beach Boys. He's a rocker at heart, but since his belters don't sell well, here he sings at the wrong speed. At least he keeps trying."* Edmunds eventually reached No. 26 with another Nick Lowe song, 'I Knew The Bride' which I had always thought did better than that. Again, follow-ups were problematic. Yet another Lowe composition 'Television' flopped as did an Edmunds collaboration with Will Birch, 'A1 On The Jukebox'. 'Juju Man' was praised in *Record Mirror*: *"A rocking accordion!? Yes, and more. Delicious flavour and cherry centre. Edmunds production – discipline, subtlety in a word – class. Five stars."* I imagine that being on Led Zeppelin's label took some of the financial pressure off Edmunds, but I would hate to imagine how their manager Peter Grant would have reacted to so many flops.

'Deborah' was released in 1978 and *Record Mirror* enthused: *"How does he manage to be such a genius? Apart from his truly wonderful singing and playing, the drumming on the single is fantastic. The bass playing ain't bad either. It's like a super speedo Everly Brothers song."*

Edmunds reached the Top Ten in 1979 for the first time in six years. He completely transformed Elvis Costello's 'Girls Talk' with an incredibly crisp and vital performance and production. The follow-up, a cover of country song 'Queen Of Hearts', reached No. 11 but another cover – this time the Graham Parker song, 'Crawling From The Wreckage' only staggered to No. 59.

Andy Fairweather Low

The story of Andy Fairweather Low (or AFL) is like something out of a Hollywood script proposal: from singer of a late 1960s "teenybopper" group to playing lead guitar with Eric Clapton! It is a highly unusual tale. If you check out footage of Eric Clapton *Unplugged*, the *Concert For George* and the more recent Mick Fleetwood celebration of the music of Peter Green, you will spot in the centre of the music making as MD, guitarist and backing vocalist Andy Fairweather Low. Just watch his focus, modesty and incredible musicianship. In between there were solo albums, stints with Pink Floyd and much else. Low's solo career had its ups and downs, to put it mildly. His first solo album was *Spider Jiving* and one track, 'Reggae Tune', reached No. 10 in 1974.

La Booga Rooga's title track was issued as the album's first single. *Record Mirror*: "*the one where Andy really gets down to it. Without being heavy, it's the kind of stomping sound that comes over well ... a good advert for the album.*" This was later covered by The Surprise Sisters who had Tony Visconti as their producer. Unfortunately, that female group is outside the remit of this book.

The only hit from the *La Booga Rooga* album was the extraordinary 'Wide-Eyed And Legless' which peaked at No. 6. Having such a big hit single would have helped Low shift several thousand copies of the parent album which was much admired at the time

Low's next album also had an unusual title: *Be Bop 'N' Holla*. The first single taken from the album was 'Travellin' Light' which was released in August 1976. This was a rendition of Cliff Richard and The Shadows' 1959 rather inconsequential chart-topper and probably not worth covering by someone of Low's talent. *Record Mirror*: "*When he's good, he's very good, when he's bad ... This is too mellow and thin and meanders on and on."* The album's title track was also released as a single and was previewed on *Top of the Pops* and flopped.

GALLAGHER AND LYLE

Benny Gallagher and Graham Lyle hailed from Largs in Scotland and were originally signed as songwriters to Apple. Mary Hopkin later recorded two of their songs. Soon they joined McGuinness Flint, writing that band's two hits, 'When I'm Dead And Gone' and 'Malt And Barley Blues'. Gallagher and Lyle left McGuinness Flint after the unsuccessful single and album, *Happy Birthday Ruthy Baby* and remained with Capitol Records as a duo.

A move to A&M Records was not initially successful. Like labelmates Supertramp, Gallagher and Lyle took several years before they started selling many records. They even spent time in Ronnie Lane's Slim Chance, contributing to the 'How Come' single. After half a dozen unsuccessful singles and three unsuccessful albums, 1976 finally saw chart success for the duo with 'I Wanna Stay With You' and 'Heart On My Sleeve', both reaching No. 6. A new producer, David Kershenbaum, seemed to do the trick. The parent album, *Breakaway*, also reached No. 6 and was in the charts for a respectable 35 weeks. However, when the title track was released as a single, it staggered to No. 35. A cover version by Art Garfunkel, who also used the song as the title track of his 1975 album, will have brought in welcome royalties.

A new single, 'Every Little Teardrop', halted just outside the Top Thirty at No. 32 in 1977 and this was the end of Gallagher and Lyle's singles success as performers. There are simply too many unsuccessful follow-ups for me to adequately comment upon. 'Runaway' (not the most original choice for a song title), 'Had To Fall In Love', 'Showdown' and 'You're The One' appeared over the next two years, before the end of their A&M contract. I cannot confess that I was aware of any of these at the time. The *"funkyish"* (according to *Record Mirror*) 'Showdown' was performed on *Top of the Pops*.

NME reviewed 'You're The One': *"an anaemic ditty which nevertheless manages to be so sickly sweet that they should consider calling themselves Tate &*

Lyle." A cheap shot, I admit but one that I had never thought of using myself!

Graham Lyle went on to be a highly-successful songwriter, penning 'What's Love Got To Do With It' and 'We Don't Need Another Hero' for Tina Turner.

Middle Of The Road

I am going to be generous to Middle Of The Road. Originally signed to RCA's Italian division, the group had a couple of unique-selling points (at the time). Their blonde, photogenic lead singer, Sally Carr, had a clear and powerful voice and their songs were repetitive and catchy. But, certainly in the UK, it was all over in just over a year. 'Chirpy Chirpy Cheep Cheep' and 'Tweedle Dee Tweedle Dum' notched up an amazing 51 weeks in the British charts but soon became irritants. 'Soley Soley' was better, showing Carr's voice to better effect, but neither 'Sacramento' nor 'Samson And Delilah' made the Top Twenty. Bob Stanley explored the more obscure side of Middle Of The Road's releases in a *Record Collector* column. I will focus on the more well-known British releases after the hits stopped coming for Carr and the lads.

'Talk Of All The USA' was the group's first real flop — *Record Mirror*: "*This one has already been a big hit on the Continent. It has got some hefty piano rolling along behind the voices and the main arrangement is in a straight commercial style. Less reliance on Sally Carr's distinctive solo voice this time. Could well do nicely.*" It didn't.

'Bottoms Up' was worse. The chorus, "*Bottoms up, good people, sit you down*" tended to irritate. A lively performance on a European pop show reveals an audience happy to clap along. *NME*: "*This sounds like 'Soley Soley' played at 33 ... It's the same old light riff only a bit slower than usual.*" Simon Frith again: "*I've always liked Middle Of the Road but they seemed to have reached the end of it with 'Bottoms Up', even THEY don't enjoy THIS song.*"

'Union Silver' was reviewed in *Record Mirror*: "*Things quietened down for the Sally Carr-led team after that string of giant hits. Maybe because they weren't varying the style much. But this is a pretty drastic change ... piano-styled* start, with Sally singing almost breathlessly. Not so much of the wavering stuff, and the main melodic theme is slow and determined. Strings swirl around amiably. Not instant commercialism, but nice tuneful pop."

Pilot

Pilot were an unlikely pop group. Two of their members had been in an early version of The Bay City Rollers, but one would never have guessed. David Paton had a distinctive high register voice that made the group's singles stand out on the radio and television. 'Magic' reached No. 11 and stayed in the charts for eleven weeks in the winter of 1974/75. The song is still heard in advertisements. The New Year brought the appropriately-named single 'January', which went to the top of the charts at the start of the next month where it stayed for three weeks. Former Floyd engineer Alan Parsons was producing and all seemed well. Sadly, the Easter time follow-up, 'Call Me Round', crept to No. 34, despite being very much in the same style as their previous releases.

In September a new version of the group's debut single, 'Just A Smile' was reissued. *Record Mirror*: "*This song was ... their first single. They've now re-recorded it and added strings to fill out the sound.*" David Paton told Sean Egan: "*The single had an orchestra added to it. That's the only difference. That was just fashionable in those days.*" This was the group's finest hour as far as I was concerned; a lost classic. I even bought the single at the time. Paton sings the first verse an octave lower than expected and it was more effective. This gave the wonderfully higher pitched chorus more dynamism. The second verse was also in a higher register. Disappointingly, 'Just A Smile' only did slightly better than 'Call Me Round', reaching No. 31.

Parsons' final single with Pilot was 'Lady Luck'. This was a distinct change of style. I cannot remember hearing it at the time. *Record Mirror*: "*This should quickly mend Pilot's ailing fortunes. The song's a simple affair that the arrangement does wonders for. It's laden with lots of vaudevillian style brass, which occasionally gives way to sweeping strings and there are a couple of great bursts to give the main theme a rest for a few seconds. A good one.*" There are female voices that remind me of 'Johnny Remember Me' and then a thumping 4/4 beat. The backing vocals start to be intrusive. A falsetto middle eight, *"why did God make these girls so goddamn pretty?"* grates a little. In the second verse there are more strings followed by a guitar solo. 'Lady Luck' flopped.

A rethink was needed and the group set off to Morin Heights in Canada with new producer Roy Thomas Baker as Parsons was unavailable. The remote recording studio gave Pilot the title of their third album. Paton describes the experience in his fascinating memoir, *Magic*. The first single taken from the album was 'Running Water', written by lead guitarist Ian Bairnson. *Record Mirror*: *"The promised new sound from Pilot doesn't sound very promising to my ears on first hearing ... very dreary sound."* This was another uncharacteristic single which record buyers ignored, despite being played on Radio One. Almost finally, the group returned with 'Canada'; this was the old Pilot sound: *"Ooh, California, ... gonna warn ya, here comes Canada."* *Record Mirror*: *"The three man line-up has reverted somewhat to their old harmony sound. Catchy and a chance for Pilot to get another crack at the charts."* I thought that a *Top of the Pops* appearance would help. Some wag called it "February", but the single still did not chart.

Paton describes the effect of being in a pop group on both his health and his finances. A third single, 'Penny In My Pocket', was taken from *Morin Heights* and Paton was forced to promote the song on television. Paton: *"I had no option but to do the show. I've watched that performance on YouTube and I certainly don't look like I'm happy to be there. It was ironic to be appearing on that Arrows TV show singing 'Penny In My Pocket' a song about not having the money for a tube train or taxi to the studio."*

Paton later joined The Alan Parsons Project and played on no less than nine of their albums, finding both financial and spiritual security. He also appeared on Kate Bush's first album, *The Kick Inside*. Paton has worked with many other artists including Elton John, Chris Rea, Jimmy Page and Paul McCartney. Like Andy Fairweather Low, Paton is a highly-talented survivor who reinvented himself after his pop career ended.

Gerry Rafferty

After Stealers Wheel broke up, due to management and contractual problems, legal proceedings prevented Rafferty releasing any new solo recordings for three years. He signed to United Artists and released the *City To City* album in 1978. The first single taken from the album, 'Baker Street', reached No. 3. Follow-ups were problematic; 'Whatever's Written In Your Heart' was reviewed in *NME*: *"This isn't a single, really, it's an album track they haven't even bothered editing it down from a cumbersome five and a quarter minutes. Sure enough, Gerry does some more soul-searching but without a sax solo, it's no 'Baker Street'."*

The single unsurprisingly flopped and was followed by 'Right Down The Line'. *Record Mirror*: *"this is a more confident release (than its predecessor). It's no 'Baker Street' but like that classic it is at once commercial and unreachable. He's outstanding at this sort of aloof love song."* This single also flopped in the UK but was a big hit in the USA, reaching No. 12 in *Billboard* and No. 8 in *Cash Box* and even reached No. 1 in the adult contemporary chart over there.

'Night Owl', the title track of Rafferty's next album, reached No. 5 and was followed-up by 'Get It Right Next Time' which reached No. 30. The 1980s saw further albums, but only *Snakes And Ladders* reached the Top Twenty. Rafferty's shyness and drink problems affected his career. He died in 2011, aged just sixty three.

The Sensational Alex Harvey Band

A veteran of the Scottish music scene, Alex Harvey was noticeably older than his peers. He was in the band at a London theatre production of the *Hair* musical, but wanted to return to rock music. Harvey linked up with the band Teargas to form The Sensational Alex Harvey Band (SAHB). The band toured constantly and were signed to progressive label, Vertigo. A live cover of the old Tom Jones hit, 'Delilah' reached No. 7 in the summer of 1975, but follow-ups were not as successful. 'Gamblin' Bar Room Blues' was an old Jimmie Rodgers song and taken from *The Penthouse Tapes* album. This album was mostly covers with versions of 'Crazy Horses', 'Runaway', 'Cheek To Cheek' and

'School's Out' and reached No. 14. 'Gamblin' Bar Room Blue's peaked at No. 38.

'Runaway' was released as a single in March 1976. *Record Mirror*: "*The band have been doing Del Shannon's old hit onstage for years, but this is a new recording of it and a very good one it is too. The whole timing of it is very tongue-in-cheek and Alex's vocal is delightfully gauche. This will be one of the SAHB's biggest hits.*" The record buyers didn't think so.

SAHB returned to the singles charts with 'The Boston Tea Party' which peaked at No. 13. I can see why the band were such a popular live attraction (although I never saw them in concert), I just found this an unremarkable single. By now the band were signed to the Mountain label. 'Amos Moses', like 'The Boston Tea Party', was taken from the *SAHB Stories* album. Originally written and recorded by Jerry Reed and a million seller in the USA, this was the only cover version on the album and did not chart.

'Mrs Blackhouse' was released in September 1977. It was clearly a dig at morality campaigner, Mary Whitehouse (geddit?). *Record Mirror*: "*Some might say over the top — Alex's lyrics do tend to lack a certain subtlety ... done as a jolly singalong number — just the thing for encores at (their) gigs. And just think of the fun and games there'll be if it makes the charts.*" We will never know.

Alex Harvey died in 1982.

STEALERS WHEEL

Stealers Wheel featured Scotsmen Gerry Rafferty and Joe Egan. Rafferty had been in — believe it or not — a folk duo with Billy Connolly called The Humblebums. He then recorded a solo album for Transatlantic on which Egan had sung harmonies. Fellow Scots singer-songwriter, Rab Noakes, had been in an early line-up of Stealers Wheel but had left to pursue a solo career. The band was signed to A&M and was the first British act to be produced by legendary songwriters and producers, Leiber and Stoller. Stealers Wheel's eponymous first album was a minor classic. The first single, 'Late Again', was probably too slow to be a hit single. A reviewer complimented the band on "*a very fine song with Beatle-ish harmonies*".

'Stuck In The Middle With You' will be known by everyone, especially after its use in the film, *Reservoir Dogs*. It was originally released in October 1972 but did not break through. The single eventually reached No. 8 in spring 1973. During this time Gerry Rafferty had quit the band, but was persuaded to return once 'Stuck In The Middle With You' was a hit. Between its release and its appearance in the charts, a third single, 'You Put Something Better Inside Of Me', had been taken off the first album. This was another slow song which flopped.

There can often be problems following up a huge hit single. People outside an artist's loyal fanbase will usually want something quite similar sounding to the big hit. Unfortunately, this then creates the criticism that the artist's output is too samey.

Later in 1973 most of the band quit, leaving Gerry Rafferty and Joe Egan remaining as a duo. Stealers Wheel's second album, *Ferguslie Park*, was named after a district of their home town of Paisley. The first single taken from it was 'Everything'll Turn Out Fine' which just failed to get into the Top Thirty — *Disc*: "*Oh dear. The harmonies are pristine, of course, but apart from a neat almost early-Stones type passage ... the melody's too much like a variation of 'Stuck In The Middle With You', which is a shame because I thought they had more ability than that.*"

The follow-up, 'Star', (written by Egan) was more successful and reached No. 25. Its strummed guitars and infectious refrain, "*Oh, tell me...*" clearly appealed to both record buyers and – like me – aspiring singer/guitarists.

A third album, *Right Or Wrong*, followed in 1975. By then Stealers Wheel were just the duo of Rafferty and Egan, backed by session musicians, and had stopped touring. I can't really remember the title track which was the first single taken from the album, but the repetitiveness of the second sing, 'Found My Way', was memorable.

Gerry Rafferty went on to great success with 'Baker Street' three years later and is discussed elsewhere. Joe Egan never recaptured his fame with Stealers Wheel, left the music business and worked in publishing. He died in 2024.

Them

It is easy in hindsight to write about Them purely in terms of their lead singer, Van Morrison, and his subsequent lengthy and successful solo career. Them had two Top Ten hits in 1965 with 'Baby Please Don't Go' and 'Here Comes The Night'; the latter reached the No. 2 position. I remember seeing Morrison in concert in the early 1980s and he performed both these songs early on in the set, strapping a guitar on and rushing through them.

Follow-ups were interesting but not successful. Alan Clayson named them: *"a hat trick of flop A-sides."* First was '(It Won't Hurt) Half As Much' — *NME*: *"Very slow bluesy beat-ballad from the once all-Irish group Them, has a walking guitar figure throughout. There's a pronounced r-and-b slant to the solo vocal."* Next was 'One More Time' — *NME*: *"on the evidence of their last two releases, the lead singer of Them generates more genuine soul than any of his British contemporaries. The slowly pounding beat ballad 'One More Time' is sung with intense feeling and heart searching to the accompaniment of an insidious compulsive riff."*

'Mystic Eyes' was the third of the hat-trick — *NME*: *"a frantic r-and-b raver with a really wild rhythm, wailing harmonies takes the first chorus carried on by that stormy shattering beat then lead guitar takes over. Plenty of excitement generated by Them on this disc. Vocal doesn't start until halfway through and it's more of a semi-spoken, semi-shouted pronouncement."* Alan Clayson commented: *"The most surprising failure ... which though an atypical neo-instrumental was an exciting streamlining of Them's R-and-B passion."* The follow-up was 'Call My Name' — *NME*: *" strident guitar work, tambourine and organ support the lead singer who throws himself into the lyric in Burdon-like style. Basically a mid-tempo number, but with sudden and highly effective pauses."* Brian Hogg knew better: *"an empty, unfinished demo with more steals ('Don't Let Me Be Misunderstood')."*

Perhaps Decca should have released the group's rendition of 'It's All Over Now Now Baby Blue' as a single. The track's haunting keyboard part was later sampled by Beck on 'Jack Ass' in the 1990s. Joan Baez had reached No. 22 in summer 1965 with her own cover of this classic Bob Dylan song, but surely the British record buyers would have loved to own Them's version? Van Morrison must have known that their version was excellent, he included it on the second volume of his *Best Of* compilations. The performance stands out amidst Van's later solo work.

'Richard Cory' — *NME* : "A bouncy beat, a predominant r-and-b style, an attention-seeking lyric soloed in semi-shout style, startling breaks in tempo and some superb guitar work. Those are the ingredients for this Paul Simon song, though I'm not convinced it's the right treatment." Nor were the record buyers and the single did not chart.

17 – The Kid's A Punk

I WAS UNSURE WHETHER TO INCLUDE ANY BRITISH punk or "new wave" acts in this book. A quick thumb through the *Guinness Book of Hit Singles* reveals some surprising facts. The Clash were not big single sellers until 1979's 'London Calling'. Similarly, 'Teenage Kicks' by The Undertones stalled at No. 31. The Damned also had no chart action with their singles on Stiff and their former label-mates, The Adverts, had just one solitary Top Twenty hit.

Buzzcocks

Buzzcocks' first release, *Spiral Scratch* E.P., was the first British punk 45 on a D.I.Y. independent label. Frontman Howard Devoto soon left the band to found Magazine. Signed to United Artists, Buzzcocks' fourth single on the label, 'Ever Fallen In Love (With Someone You Shouldn't've)' finally cracked the Top Thirty, peaking at No. 12 and remains the band's most famous and most successful single. A cover version by Fine Young Cannibals in 1987 did better reaching No. 9. Two more Top Thirty hits followed, 'Promises' and (my favourite) 'Everybody's Happy Nowadays' which had a wonderful chorus and plenty of hooks.

'Harmony In My Head' was the first Buzzcocks A-side to be written and sung by Steve Diggle. A much heavier sound than its predecessors, 'Harmony' peaked at No. 32. This is probably the weakest of all the late 1970s singles by the band. A *Top of the Pops* performance emphasised the weak lead vocals by Diggle on the verses, almost as if he was trying too hard to be "punk". The chorus and title hook are a bit more tuneful. Pete Shelley stands back in a supportive role and does not join in on the chorus until near the end. A reissue of *Spiral Scratch* with former Buzzcock member Howard Devoto's name added to the front cover reached one place higher at No. 31.

Less than three months after 'Harmony In My Head', the band's next single, 'You Say You Don't Love Me', saw Pete Shelley back in charge, but it did not chart. *Record Mirror*: *"A love song that is also a pop song is a formula established by The Beatles fifteen years ago. The technique here is more sophisticated, the lyrics more eloquent ... but the guts of the song are, to its loss, firmly rooted in a well known rut. It's a different kind of Buzzcocks we're hearing now, the tougher edge worn away. "*

The Clash

The Clash's chart history is difficult to discuss. Neither 'White Riot' nor 'Remote Control' reached the Top Thirty ('Remote Control' was not even a minor hit) and several of the band's key singles were not big hits. No doubt, the band's refusal to appear on *Top of the Pops* did not help. I remember Legs And Co dancing to 'Bankrobber', wearing bandanas over their mouths! *Top of the Pops* did not handle punk very well. Regular viewers, who did not listen to John Peel or read the weekly music press, would have been confused about which punk bands really mattered.

'Complete Control' was The Clash's response to CBS releasing 'Remote Control' without their permission and was the band's first Top Thirty hit, peaking at No. 28. The follow-up, 'Clash City Rockers', went no higher than No. 35. *Record Mirror*: *"Tough cover, tough lyrics. Angry words that have made The Clash and the vast majority of the others a worn out cliché."* I must confess that I am no great fan of Joe Strummer's vocal style, but 'Clash City Rockers' is one of his worst performances. I can hardly make out most of the words in the song.

'(White Man) In Hammersmith Palais' had a fascinating backstory. Strummer went to see some reggae acts at the aforementioned London venue but was disappointed by their image and performances. The guest reviewer in *Record Mirror* sums it up better than I could: *"The Clash go reggae and it's not very inspiring ... you can't hear the words, so what's the point?"* Garry Mulholland explains the scenario: *"The single as gig review is a relatively small sub-genre, and for good reason. But, once Strummer gets a disappointing reggae night out at the Palais out of his system, he makes a leap of logic, faith and intellect that took The Clash to a new plateau."*

Mulholland argues that Strummer knows that punk rock cannot change politics and *"the game was up."* Strummer sneers at *"the new groups"* in their *"Burton suits"*, concluding: *"You think it's funny? Turning rebellion into money."* Hmm, I wonder if being signed to a major American record company and going on to name an album after a Nicaraguan liberation group isn't the same thing.. This single stalled at No. 32.

After this, The Clash's singles went on to have greater chart success; 'Tommy Gun' was their first time in the Top Twenty and 'English Civil War', the band's updating of 'When Johnny Comes Marching Home', reached No. 25. 'London Calling' entered the charts in the last month of the 1970s and would eventually reach No. 11, the band's highest ever chart placing during its lifetime ('Should I Stay Or Should I Go' went to No.1 in 1991). 'London Calling' benefited from an atmospheric video, filmed at night time overlooking the River Thames, allowing the band to stay out of the *Top of the Pops* studio.

Generation X

Unlike The Clash, Generation X were not too proud to appear on *Top of the Pops*. The more that I think about it, The Clash's "stance" on boycotting the top British television pop programme seems pointless and counter-productive. On paper, The Boomtown Rats were probably the most successful British or Irish singles act to come out of punk and new wave. They had nine consecutive Top Twenty singles, two of which were chart-toppers ('Rat Trap' and 'I Don't Like Mondays') and five were in the Top Ten. But the Rats are generally sidelined in histories of the era, except in interviews with Bob Geldof.

Generation X's first two singles, 'Your Generation' and 'Ready Steady Go', did not penetrate the Top Thirty but appearances on television helped establish them beyond their fan base. 1979's 'King Rocker' went as high as No. 11, no doubt helped by its *Top of the Pops* appearances. A swift follow-up, 'Valley Of The Dolls', reached No. 23. 'Friday's Angels' was also taken from the band's *Valley Of the Dolls* album but was a flop, peaking at a lowly No. 62. Lead singer Billy Idol then went on to a highly successful solo career, while guitarist Tony James eventually formed Sigue Sigue Sputnik.

THE JAM

The Jam's first single, 'In The City', peaked at No. 40 and was quickly followed by 'All Around The World' which reached No. 13. This was the first of three Jam singles which ended with the word "world", almost designed to confuse pop quiz participants.

The follow-up 'The Modern World', despite being part of the band's second album title, *This Is The Modern World* – peaked at No. 36. The line *"I don't give two fucks about your review"* was replaced by *"I don't give a damn."* Record Mirror: *"Third single up and it's disappointing. More of a formula re-run than a dynamic new pressing for a rock band about to devour the world. Then again they've come a long way in a hurry and not everything can be gold dust."*

In the 1980s, The Jam crossed over to a much larger fan-base and achieved eight Top Ten hits and no fewer than four chart-toppers. Unusually for a band, they quit at the top and have never had a reunion.

PUBLIC IMAGE LIMITED

In 1978 Johnny Rotten was keen to dissociate himself from the whole Sex Pistols story. He reverted to his own name, John Lydon, and teamed up with Keith Levene and Jah Wobble. Public Image Limited's first two singles – 'Public Image' and 'Death Disco' – both went Top Twenty. They were both extraordinary and challenging records.

P.I.L.'s third single was 'Memories'. *Record Mirror* was not impressed: *"The vague ramblings of a geriatric ex-punk. When will he finally shut up?"* Gary Mulholland was more positive: *"'Memories' is mutant Arabic speed-disco-gone-flamenco, a deep warm, sleek ride, another mean Wobble bassline, more virtuoso Keith Levine guitar and Lydon raving furiously this time about nostalgia. It's a beautiful record, almost perfect in its wilfully obscure way. But ironically, Lydon's obsession with burying the past fell on deaf ears. His public had already moved on."* The single peaked at a miserable No. 60.

Tom Robinson Band

Tom Robinson was always regarded as part of the punk movement, despite his age and the tunefulness of some of his songs. At the time, his unashamed gay identity was something of a novelty. Remember this was several years before the likes of Bronski Beat hit the charts. '2-4-6-8 Motorway' was the band's first hit, reaching the Top Five. I never really understood this song. Was it a 'life on the road' song? Some say, inevitably, that it has a gay subtext. 'Don't Take No For An Answer' was the lead track on the live *Rising Free* E.P. which also contained the songs 'Martin', 'Glad To Be Gay' and 'Right On Sister'. The E.P. reached No. 18, but follow-ups were less successful.

'Up Against The Wall' was released in May 1978. The song has typical punk guitar and vocals and sounds rather dated to these ears. It is very angry with lines like: "*Teenage guerillas on the tarmac!*" The picture sleeve's front cover has a black schoolboy standing "up against" a graffitied wall. Despite an enthusiastic *Top of the Pops* appearance, the single stalled at No. 33.

'Too Good To Be True' was reviewed in *Record Mirror*: "*It has none of the raunch of the campaigning one's earlier efforts. The song moves along at a pedestrian pace whilst Tom's others accelerate like a grey Cortina. Not even a blistering guitar solo rescues it. Fine as an album track, not as a single.*" I always felt that the song's verses were a little similar to Van Morrison's 'Moondance'. Despite Radio One airplay and a *Top of the Pops* appearance, 'Too Good To Be True' did not bother the charts.

Tom went on to work with some unlikely and "unpunk" musicians and producers. 'Bully For You' was co-written by Tom and Peter Gabriel. It was taken from the *TRB2* album which was produced by Todd Rundgren. It starts with a Kinks-style riff and we are straight into more angry lyrics. This one peaked at No. 68.

'Never Gonna Fall In Love Again' was co-written by Tom and Elton John, and was billed as Tom Robinson with The Voice Squad. The late 1970s were not the best of times for Elton John (see Chapter 7) as he had stopped working with his long-time lyricist Bernie Taupin and producer Gus Dudgeon. 'Never Gonna Fall In Love Again' is an unremarkable attempt at disco, but lacking in style or imagination and did not reach the charts.

Sham 69

Jimmy Pursey was another charismatic frontman, again, not too proud to appear on *Top of the Pops* where television proved to be an ideal medium for him. The band's first five hits all went Top Twenty, three of which made the Top Ten. The band's highest chart position was 'Hersham Boys' No. 6 place.

The follow-up to 'Hersham Boys' was a complete contrast. 'You're A Better Man Than I' had been a Yardbirds B-side, written by brothers Mike and Brian Hugg. Mike Hugg had been the drummer with Manfred Mann but was also a proficient keyboard player. The song had been covered by some American bands such as Terry Knight and the Pack and New Colony Six. *Record Mirror* reviewed Sham 69's version: *"They're dead but they won't lie down, or something like that ... an almost folky, certainly quiet and acoustic number. Anyway, something different from Sham, for which much thanks."*

Siouxsie And The Banshees

The Banshees peaked early with their first single, 'Hong Kong Garden' which reached No. 7. They would not return to the Top Ten for five years when their cover of John Lennon's 'Dear Prudence' reached No. 3. The band's only flop of the 1970s was 'Mittageisen (Metal Postcard)', a double A-side with 'Love In A Void'. The latter track appeared on the *Once Upon A Time* singles compilation. *Record Mirror* reviewed 'Mittageisen': *"By popular request ... that foreign animal. I find Siouxsie intensely depressing in English, but in German the sky's the limit. But it slots into place in their row of hits and has biggish heaps of aggression."* This single peaked at No. 47.

The Stranglers

After a brilliant first single – 'Grip' (which went no higher than No. 44) – the Stranglers had a good run of Top Thirty hits; all of them but their cover of Bacharach and David's 'Walk On By' reached the Top Twenty. Their two final releases of the 1970s were flops. I must confess that I cannot remember hearing 'Nuclear Device (The Wizard Of Aus)' or the *Don't Bring Harry* E.P. at the time. The former record proves yet another rule in pop music: use puns at your peril. After the band's outdoor concert that featured female strippers on stage, many people – already aware of The Stranglers' misogynist lyrics – began to tire of them. 'Nuclear Device' sounds to these ears almost like a pastiche, as performed perhaps by the *Not The Nine O'Clock News* cast or – worse – Hazel O'Connor. *Record Mirror* was confused: "*As usual I haven't the faintest idea what they're rattling away about, and if I had I'd probably find this quite sinister. As it is, here's another action-packed Stranglers single ... less poppy than 'Duchess' with ol' Hugh (Cornwell) positively scowling vocally on the chorus.*" I find the squeaky keyboard and the vocal unconvincing, especially the way the word "device" is pronounced.

Record Mirror reviewed 'Don't Bring Harry': "*a cursory listen informs me that this – like 'The Raven' – is not one of the Strangling Ones best.*" The song is led by an interesting piano figure and Jean Jacques Burnel sings in a deep Lou Reed style voice. There is a guitar solo towards the end of the song. The band were in a sombre mood when they performed 'Harry' on *Top of the Pops*. The single peaked at No. 41. The Stranglers' flops continued into the early 1980s until 1982's 'Golden Brown' brought the men in black to No. 2 in the charts.

UK Subs

I cannot remember much about the UK Subs, except – perhaps unfairly – the comparatively advanced age of lead singer Charlie Harper. Harper was born in 1944 so was in his early 30s when punk happened. As I write this, several octogenarians are still recording and performing. The UK Subs had two Top Thirty hits in 1979 – 'Stranglehold' and 'Tomorrow's Girls'. A third release that year an

E.P, *She's Not There/Kicks*, peaked at No. 36, hence its inclusion here. The band performed 'She's Not There' on *Top of the Pops*. This, an unattractive speeded-up version of The Zombies' 1964 classic, could have been another *Not The Nine O' Clock News* parody. Yes, that bad.

X-RAY SPEX

Poly Styrene was one of the more distinctive singers of the punk movement. The band's first single, 'Oh Bondage Up Yours', surprisingly did not chart. The band's next three singles, 'The Day The World Turned Day-Glo', 'Identity' and 'Germ-Free Adolescents' all went into the Top Thirty. X-Ray Spex's album, *Germ Free Adolescents*, entered the charts in December 1978 and stayed there for fourteen weeks, peaking at No. 30. X-Ray Spex's final single was 'Highly Inflammable' which reached No. 45. *Punk 77* commented: *"the first one to go off the boil. Don't get me wrong, it's still a classic song but the lyrics are unwieldy strapped to the almost jaunty ska feel of the track."*

What About Queen?

THIS WRITER HAS TO ADMIT THAT HE ALWAYS assumed that Queen in the 1970s, like The Beatles and The Rolling Stones in the 1960s, simply did not have flops. Between 1974 and 1979, Freddie and the boys were omnipresent in the charts after their first hit, 'Seven Seas Of Rhye'. 'Rhye' peaked at No. 10 and was followed by 'Killer Queen' which reached No. 2 in autumn 1974. A year later, 'Bohemian Rhapsody' was a chart-topper, staying at No. 1 for an impressive nine weeks. Two more Top Ten hits, 'You're My Best Friend' (No. 7) and 'Somebody To Love' (No. 2) came along in 1976.

March 1977 saw the release of a second track from the *A Day At The Races* album, 'Tie Your Mother Down', a Brian May composition. Robin Smith wrote in *Record Mirror*: "*Back to their roots with some tasty hard rock. Freddie's strident vocals knife the air apart and there's the inevitable solo from Brian May.*" There's lots of guitar on this rather ordinary rocker. The title might have been a little shocking nearly half a century ago, but now it just feels boorish. It stalled just outside the Top Thirty at No.31.

Queen reached No. 2 for the third time in autumn 1977 with 'We Are The Champions' which was taken from the *News Of The World* album. 'Spread Your Wings" was the second track to become a single. This piano-dominated ballad was written by bass player, John Deacon and the verses remind me a little of Paul McCartney's 'Rocky Raccoon.' It fell to Robin Smith again in *Record Mirror* to review the single: "*Semi-raw Queen taken from the latest album of a similar nature. Bites at first before fading halfway through. Great comeback but could have done with some more heavy guitar. Very creditable.*" The song, with a rather pointless storyline, is a little dull I have to say. This peaked at No. 34.

'Love Of My Life' had first appeared on the album, *A Night At The Opera* in 1975 and became something of a concert favourite. The song was included on 1979's Live Killers set. This live version was released as a single in the summer of 1979, following 'Don't Stop Me Now' (No. 9). Lesley-Ann Jones witnessed South American audiences' response to this song: *"One special song stole the show: 'Love Of My Life'. the fans knew the song by heart. Their English was word-perfect. The throng was suddenly transformed into a sea of swaying flames as thousands pulled their lighters out."* So that's where this "sing it back" tradition might have started! The single staggered to No. 63 in the UK, but was a chart-topper in Latin America. Norma Waterson covered the song twenty years later, it is worth a listen.

Queen stormed back later in 1979 with the rockabilly 'Crazy Little Thing Called Love' which became the band's fourth single to reach No. 2. Their run of hits continued throughout the next two decades, even after Freddie Mercury's untimely death in 1991.

Afterword

THE RESEARCH AND WRITING OF THIS BOOK took over two years, but has been the result of six decades of enjoying pop music. I listened to hundreds and hundreds of songs from my own collection and found myself purchasing umpteen compilation albums to fill the gaps in my knowledge and, indeed, collection. YouTube and Spotify became essential, especially for artists who lacked comprehensive or affordable compilation albums. The whole experience has made me reassess several artists and I hope that you are encouraged to do the same. I never realised how many flops existed in virtually every artist's catalogue.

I started buying singles myself in 1970 and this continued throughout that decade. My generation was blessed with the best music from both sides of the Atlantic. There was quite a lot of pop on television, not just the music programmes such as *Lift Off*, *Colour Me Pop*, *Doing Their Thing*, *Supersonic*, *Disco 2*, *The Old Grey Whistle Test* and, of course, *Top of the Pops*, but also children's shows such as *The Basil Brush Show* and the various light entertainment programmes. There was also a choice of five or more weekly music papers.

Listening to so many flops has provided me with an alternative history of British pop between 1965 and 1979. Imagine what the charts would have been like if Procol Harum had gone Top Ten with 'A Salty Dog' and The Hollies' cover of Springsteen's 'Sandy' had done as well as 'The Air That I Breathe'! These are just pleasures – without any guilt.

Select Bibliography

Allen Frank: *The Searchers And Me — The History Of The Legendary Sixties Hitmakers* Aureus 2009

Batt Mike: *The Closest Thing To Crazy — My Life Of Musical Adventures* Nine Eight Books 2024

Black Cilla: *What's It All About?* Ebury Press 2003

Black Don: *The Sanest Guy In The Room* Constable 2021

Blackford Andy: *Wild Animals — The Story Of The Animals* Sidgwick & Jackson 1986

British Hit Singles And Albums, Guinness World Records Limited 2005

Buckley David: *David Bowie — The Complete Guide To His Music* Omnibus Press 2004

Campbell Malcolm (editor), Bradford Rob & Woosey Les: *A Pocket Guide To Shadow Music* Idmon Publications 2006

Celmins Martin: *Peter Green — The Biography* Castle Communications 1995

Checksfield Peter: *Look Wot They Dun! The Ultimate Guide To UK Glam Rock On TV In The '70s* Privately published 2019

Checksfield Peter: *Top of the Pops The Lost Years Rediscovered 1964-1975* Privately published 2022

Clayson Alan: *Beat Merchants* Blandford 1996

Clayson Alan: *Call Up The Groups* Blandford Press 1985

Darlington Andrew: *On Track...The Hollies* Sonic Bond Publishing 2021

Davis Sharon: *Every Chart-Topper Tells A Story* Mainstream Publishing 1998

Doggett Peter: *The Man Who Sold the World: David Bowie And The 1970s* Vintage 2012

Easlea Daryl: *Whatever Happened To Slade? When The World Went Crazee* Omnibus Press 2023

Egan Sean: *Animal Tracks — The Story Of The Animals: Newcastle's Rising Sons* Helter Skelter 2001

Elliott Bobby: *It Ain't Heavy, It's My Story* Omnibus Press 2021
Essex David: *A Charmed Life* Orion 2002
Frith Simon: *Music For Pleasure* Polity Press 1988
Frith Simon & Goodwin Andrew (editors): *On Record – Rock, Pop And The Written Word* Routledge 1990
Garfield Simon *Expensive Habits — The Dark Side Of The Music Industry* Faber and Faber 1986
Garner Ken: *In Session Tonight The Complete Radio 1 Recordings* BBC Books 1993
Gillett Charlie (editor): *Rock File* Pictorial Publications 1972
Gillett Charlie (editor): *Rock File 2* Panther 1974
Gillett Charlie & Frith Simon (editors): *Rock File 3* Panther 1975
Gillett Charlie & Frith Simon (editors): *Rock File 4* Panther 1976
Gillett Charlie & Frith Simon *Rock File 5* Panther 1978
Hanley Paul: *Leave The Capital — A History Of Manchester Music In 13 Recordings* Route 2024
Hardy Phil & Laing Dave: *The Encyclopedia Of Rock Volumes 1, 2, 3* Panther 1976
Harrison George: *I Me Mine* Weidenfield & Nicolson 2002
Heatley Michael (editor): *The History Of Rock Volumes 1-10* Orbis Publishing 1984
Heylin Clinton *Revolution In The Air: The Songs Of Bob Dylan Vol 1: 1957-73* Constable 2009
Hill Dave: *So Here It Is: How The Boy From Wolverhampton Rocked The World With Slade* Unbound 2018
Hinman Doug: *The Kinks – All Day And All Of the Night* Backbeat Books 2004
Hinton Brian: *Nights In Wight Satin — An Illustrated History Of The Isle Of Wight Pop Festivals* Isle Of Wight Cultural Services Department 1990
Hodkinson Mark: *As Tears Go By — Marianne Faithfull* Omnibus Press 1991
Holder Noddy with Verrico Lisa: *Who's Crazee Now? My Autobiography* Ebury Press 1999
Horn Trevor: *Adventures In Modern Recording From ABC To ZTT* Nine Eight Books 2022
Hounsome Terry: *Single File* Terry Hounsome 1990

Hughes Andrew Mon, Walters Grant & Crohan Mark: *Decades — The Bee Gees In The 1970s* Sonic Bond 2023

John Elton: *Me* Macmillan 2019

Jones Lesley-Ann: *Ride A White Swan — The Lives And Death Of Marc Bolan* Hodder & Stoughton 2012

Kon Andrea: *This Is My Song, A Biography Of Petula Clark* Comet 1984

Larkin Colin (editor in chief) : *The Virgin Encyclopedia Of Popular Music* Virgin Books 1999

Logan Nick & Woffinden Bob: *The Illustrated New Musical Express Encyclopedia Of Rock* Salamander 1977

Lulu: *I Don't Want To Fight* Sphere 2010

McCartney Mike: *Thank U Very Much — Mike McCartney's Family Album* Granada 1981

McGarraher James: *Sailor* Sarum Publishing 2004

McGough Roger: *Said And Done — The Autobiography* Century 2005

Manning Toby: *The Rough Guide To Pink Floyd* Rough Guides 2006

Meyer David N: *The Bee Gees Biography* Da Capo 2013

Millward Steve: *Fast Forward — Music And Politics In 1974* Matador 2016

Moss Ian Keith: *45 The Original Soundtrack* Empire Publications 2022

Paton David: *Magic — The David Paton Story* Sonicbond Publishing 2023

Quatro Suzi: *Unzipped* Hodder & Stoughton 2007

O'Brien Lucy: *Dusty — A Biography Of Dusty Springfield* Sidgwick & Jackson 1999

Rees Dafydd: *Star File — The Ultimate Rock Reference* Star Books 1977

Reynolds Anthony: *The Impossible Dream — The Story Of Scott Walker And The Walker Brothers* Jawbone 2009

Reynolds Simon: *Shock And Awe: Glam Rock And Its Legacy* Faber & Faber 2016

Roach Martin: *Top 100 Singles* Chrysalis Impact 2002

Roberty Marc: *The Complete Guide To The Music Of Eric Clapton* Omnibus Press 1995

Rooksby Rikky: *The Complete Guide To the Music Of Fleetwood Mac* Omnibus Press 1998

Scott Barry: *We Had Joy We had Fun — The "Lost" Recording Artists Of the Seventies* Faber and Faber 1994

Seaton Pete with Down Richard: *The Kaleidoscope British Television Music & Variety Guide II Top Pop: 1964-2006* Kaleidoscope Publishing 2007

Shaw Sandie: *The World At My Feet — A Personal Adventure* Fontana 1992

Simpson Graham: *The Judith Durham Story — Colours Of My Life* Virgin Books 2003

Stanley Bob: *The Bee Gees — Children Of The World* NineEight Books 2023

Strong Martin C: *The Great Rock Discography* Canongate Books 202

Turner James R: *On Track… Roy Wood The Move, ELO & Wizzard* Sonic Bond Publishing 2021

Visconti Tony: *The Autobiography — Bowie, Bolan And The Brooklyn Boy* Harper Collins 2007

Wale Michael: *Voxpop — Profiles Of The Pop Process* Harrap 1972

Magazines and newspapers used: *Bam Balam, Comstock Lode, Disc & Music Echo, Electronics & Music Maker, The Guardian, Let It Rock, Melody Maker, Mojo, New Musical Express, Q, Record Collector, Record Mirror, Shindig, Sounds, That Will Never Happen Again, Top Pops & Music Now, Uncut, Vox, Zigzag.*

Various sleevenotes on compilations and reissues have also been invaluable.

The most useful websites are Discogs, Seventies Sevens, 45s World and World Radio History.

All quotes from secondary sources are for study, review and critical purposes.

Acknowledgements

THANKS TO THE FOLLOWING PEOPLE FOR THEIR encouragement and support in writing this book: Keith Baxter, Gary Canning; Peter and Maria Cooper, George Dawes; Simon Frith; Marc Gleeson; Andrew Gold; Clinton Heylin; Mark Hodkinson; Mary Joy; Sara Littler; Mick Middles; Steve Millward, Hannah Ryder, Natasha Smith, Nicky Thompson, Kellie While, Andrew Willan. Thanks to the staff of Central Library, Manchester; British Library Reading Room, Boston Spa and the Sydney Jones Library, Liverpool University.

Special thanks to my sister, Sara Littler, for her thorough proofing of the manuscript. Grateful thanks to Clinton Heylin, Mick Middles and Mark Hodkinson for reading early versions of the book.

Thanks to Nicky Thompson for his cover design. I have worked with Nicky for several years on the *Discover Amazing Women by Rail* projects and he was the obvious choice for *Flops On 45*. Nicky's website is: www.nickythompsonart.co.uk

Thanks to all the singles reviewers at *Disc & Music Echo*, *Let It Rock*, *Melody Maker*, *New Musical Express*, *Record Mirror* and *Sounds* over the years, especially Simon Frith and the late Penny Valentine.

Even more thanks to Simon Frith for his introduction. Simon generously offered to write this without me even asking. To have someone whose writing and research I have admired for over half a century endorse this book is more than I could ever imagine.

Finally, thanks to all at Empire Publications who also published my first book, *Were You There? Popular Music At Manchester's Free Trade Hall 1951-1996*. Thank you for your faith and enthusiasm in this book.

Richard Lysons
June 2025

Index

10cc 158, 197, 204, **207-209**, 220, 224

Abba 48, 99, 126, 177, 181, 182, 238, 247
Abbott, Russ 274
Aberfan Disaster (1966) 170
AC/DC 192, 193
Adverts, The 314
Alan Parsons Project, The 13, 283, 308
Alderton, John 108
Alfie Darling (film) 101
Alice In Wonderland (film) 49
Allen, Frank 221, 222, 223, 225
Allen, Raymond 25
Allen, Rod 270
All Our Yesterplays (radio) 11
All The Way Up (film) 219
All This And World War Two (film) 293
Almond, Marc 50
Amen Corner **32-33**, 257, 296
American Breed, The 32
Amis, Kingsley 277
Amoo, Chris 216
A&M Records (record label) 71, 163, 296, 297, 305, 310
Anderson, Ian 78, 79, 294
Anderson, Lynn 61, 135
Andrew, Laurie 241
Andrews, Chris 131, 132, 133
Anita In Jumbleland (TV) 115
An Officer And A Gentleman (film) 72
Antony, Miki 28
Apple Records (record label) 115, 116, 117, 133, 218, 261, 305
Arcade (record label) 247
Arden, Don 108, 109, 110, 189

Argent 60, **66-67**
Argent, Rod 66, 67, 195, 197
Ariola (record label) 119, 292
Arista Records (record label) 118, 157, 159, 253, 298
Armatrading, Joan 98
Arrival **268-269**
Arthey, Johnny 34, 228
Asher, Peter 218
Ashton, Gardner & Dyke 25
Ashton, Tony 74, 82, 83
Astaire, Fred 106, 234
Atlantic Records (record label) 121
Atomic Rooster **67-68**, 78
Automatic Records (record label) 214
Aznavour, Charles 138

Bacharach and David 101, 106, 131, 136, 320
Bad Company **68**
Baez, Joan 115, 117, 312
Bailey, Chloe 170
Bailey, Halle 170
Baker, Ginger 72
Baker, Roy Thomas 308
Baldry, Long John 48
Ballard Jr, Clint 191
Ballard, Russ 60, 66, 67, 257, 288
Bam Balam (fanzine) 168, 328
Band, The 40, 281
Banks, Bessie 198
Banks, Jeff 178
Barclay James Harvest 287
Barnard, Stephen 56
Barn Records (record label) 83
Barrett, Syd 86
Barrie, JJ 26
Barron Knights, The **23-26**, 48, 274

Barrow, Tony 188
Barry, John 49, 123, 233, 299
Bart, Lionel 133, 134, 233
Bartram, Dave 204
BASCA (British Association of Songwriters) 110
Baskin and Copperfield 286
Batley Variety Club 172
Batt, Mike 119, 150, 151, 256, 295, 298, 299
Bay City Rollers, The **33-35**, 42, 136, 149, 203, 252, 274, 307
Bazar, Therese 227
Beach Boys, The 46, 71, 195, 211, 243, 247, 252, 271, 290, 303
Beat Club (TV) 10, 38, 46, 89, 160, 169, 270
Beatles, The 15, 20, 33, 40, 89, 143, 145, 146, 154, 161, 188, 190, 215, 228, 233, 245, 315
Beck 312
Beck, Jeff 168, 246
Bee Gees, The 92, 93, 134, **170-175**, 182, 196, 229, 280, 297, 302
Behan, Dominic 220
Bell, Eric 94
Bell, Madeline 38, 177, 178, 179
Bellotte, Pete 48, 153
Bell Records (record label) 118, 251, 253, 256
Bell, Thom 153
Bender, Ariel 258
Bennett, Brian 244, 246
Bennett, Hywel 155
Bennett, Richard Rodney 229
Berry, Chuck 189, 302
Berry, Dave **185**
Berry, Nick 203
Betjeman, Sir John 220
Bevan, Bev 201, 202
Bextor, Sophie Ellis 260
Bickerton, Wayne 289
Biddu 103
Billboard (magazine)
19, 20, 94, 104, 126, 138, 309
Birch, Dyan 268, 269
Birch, Will 224, 303
Birrell, Pete 27
Bjorn, Michael 178
Black Abbotts, The 274
Blackburn, Tony 11, 101
Black, Cilla 10, 98, **99-102**, 131, 132, 160, 203
Black, Don 49, 127, 233
Black, Johnny 121
Black Lace 207
Black Sabbath **68-69**, 76
Blackwell, Chris 76
Blakley, Alan 43, 44
Blanche, Carte 112
Blind Date (TV) 102
Blondie 159, 182
Blue 41
Blue, Barry 107, **251**
Blue Mink 24, 48, 141, **177-179**, 182
Blue Peter (TV) 25, 205
Bluesology 153
Blunstone, Colin 13
Bob and Marcia 291
Boechter, Curt 289, 290
Bohannon, Hamilton 257
Bolan, Marc 25, 93, 124, 141, 265, 266, 267
Bolton, Michael 170
Bonaparte, Eli 192
Boney M 292
Bonham, John 122
Bonner, Gary 105
Bonzo Dog Doo-Dah Band, The 29
Boorman, John 143
Bowie, David 47, 53, 57, 87, 108, 117, 123, **141-143**, 158, 165, 248, 257, 295
Bowmer, Karl 303
Bown, Andy 37, 38, 93
Box Tops 70, 198
Boyce, Tommy 204
Boyzone 165
Brackman, Jacob 130

INDEX

Bradbury, Bob 257
Bradford City F.C. Fire (1985) 216
Bradley's Records (record label) 28
Brecker Brothers 21
Breen, Joe 41
Brel, Jacques 49, 50, 52, 270
Brian and Michael 29
Brice, Trevor 47, 48
Briggs, Vic 186
Brightman, Sarah 256
Britton, Terry 241, 242
BRMB 26
Broaden Your Mind (TV) 28
Brock, Dave 285
Bronski Beat 318
Bronze (record label) 280, 282
Brooker, Gary 13, 89, 90
Brooke Taylor, Tim 29
Brotherhood Of Man 126, **179-182**
Brothers, The 278
Brown, Errol 57, 58, 59, 60
Browne, Tom 182
Brown, Faith 102
Brown, Joe 29
Brown, Polly 238
Bruce, Jack 72
Brunel University 190
Brunswick (record label) 167
Bryant, Boudleaux 84
Buchanan, Margo 260
Buckingham-Nicks 75
Buckmaster, Paul 268
Buck's Fizz 126
Buie and Cobb 47
Bunyan, Vashti 98
Bungleflint (magazine) 245
Burdon, Eric **185-187**, 312
Burnel, Jean Jacques 320
Burnette, Johnny 21, 125
Burrell, Boz 68
Burrows, Tony 28, 179, 183
Burton, James 125
Bush, Kate 98, **102**, 308
Buskers' Concert 285
Butlins 184

Buzzcocks **314-315**
Byrds, The 115, 187

Cable, Robin Geoffrey 279
Cagney, James 102
Caine, Michael 101
Callender, Peter 46, 202, 226
Cameron, John 99, 182
Campbell, Glen 111, 272
Campbell, Junior 40, 130, **301-302**
Capaldi, Jim 84, 96
Capital Radio 26, 179
Capone, Al 202
Captain and Tennille 249
Carrere (record label) 228
Carr, Roy 16, 18
Carr, Sally 306
Carry On Doctor (film) 114
Carter, Carroll 268
Carter, John 27, 29, 46, 272
Carter, June 187
Cascades, The 178
Cash Box (magazine) 309
Cash, Johnny 25, 187
Cason, Buzz 38
Cassidy, David 123, 137, 149, 203
Casuals, The **35-36**
CBS Records (record label) 40, 43, 45, 50, 148, 150, 235, 254, 257, 268, 276, 279, 299, 315
CCS (Collective Consciousness Society) 177, **182-183**
Chaney, Lon 102
Chaplin, Charlie 105, 273, 274, 292
Chapman, Mike 61, 62, 63, 64, 259, 263
Chapman, Roger 73, 74
Charisma (record label) 77
Charles, Tina **103**
Charlie Girl (musical) 216
Charlton, Manny 83, 84
Chas & Dave 207
Checksfield, Peter 10, 207, 252
Cheggers Plays Pop 290
Chelsea (record label) 123

333

Chicory Tip **36-37**, 48
Chilli Willi And
   The Red Hot Peppers 269
Chilton 225
Chinn, Nicky 10, 61, 62, 63, 64, 259, 263, 264
Christie, Tony **226-227**
Chrysalis (record label) 262, 292
Chumbawamba 295
Cilla's World Of Comedy (TV) 101
Citizen Smith (TV) 17
Clancy Brothers, The 221
Clapton, Eric 17, **69-70**, 71, 72, 113, 168, 281, 304
Clark, Dave 144, 146
Clarke, Allan 13, 193, 194, 195, 196
Clarke, Nobby 34
Clark, Petula 98, **103-107**, 120, 274
Clark, Roy 138
Clash, The 159, **315-316**
Clayson, Alan 76, 143, 144, 160, 169, 215, 312
Clements, Rod 80, 81
Cobell, John 39
Coburn, James 109
Coca-Cola 234
Cochran, Eddie 80, 168, 203, 259
Cocker, Joe 28, **70-72**, 90, 96, 185
Cockney Rebel **254-256**, 274
Collins, Frank 268, 269
Collins, Glenda 27
Collins, Joan 217
Collins, Larry 50
Collins, Pauline 108
Collins, Phil 78
Colour Me Pop (TV) 38, 39, 129, 200, 323
Columbia (record label) 88, 89, 120, 185, 284
Comic Relief (charity) 226
Concert for George (film) 17, 304
Confessions From A Holiday Camp (film) 31
Connolly, Billy **26**, 310
Connolly, Brian 263, 264
Cooke, Sam 166

Cook, Roger (journalist) 109
Cook, Roger (singer/songwriter) 27, 47, 49, 100, 177, 178, 183, 235, 269, 271
Coolidge, Rita 53
Coots, J. Fred 191
Cope, Julian 50
Cornwell, Hugh 320
Costello, Elvis 304
Coulam, Roger 177
Coulson, Dennis 281
Coulter, Phil 26, 34, 42, 132, 278
Countess Of Hong Kong (film) 105, 274
Country Music Association, The 126
Courtney, Dave 293
Cousins, Dave 115, 278, 296, 297, 298
Coverdale, David 73
Covington, Julie 119, 149
Cowe, Simon 81
Cox, Paul 89
Crackerjack (TV) 290
Crane, Vincent 68
Crawford, Michael 25, 256
Cream 69, **72**
Creedence Clearwater Revival 302
Cregan, Jim 119, 254, 255
Crisis (charity) 117
Croce, Jim 100
Cropper. Steve 21
Crowd, The 216
Cullum, Jamie 38
Curtis, Chris 221, 222
Cutler, Adge 30

D'Abo, Mike 160, 270
Daltrey, Roger 73, 156, 168, 293
Damned, The 287, 314
Dandelion (record label) 82
D'Arby, Terence Trent 269
Darin, Bobby 221
Darlington, Andrew 194, 195, 196
Darts **146**, 214
Dave Clark Five, The **143-146**
David And Jonathan 177

INDEX

David, F.R. 46
Davies, Alun 164
Davies, Hunter 96
Davies, Ray 47, 88, 154, 156, 157, 158, 159, 162, 185, 188
Davies, Rick 94
Davies, W.H. 75
Da Vinci, Paul 285
Davis, Billie 256
Davis, Rob 259, 260
Davis, Spencer 187, 188, 189
Dawn (record label) 25, 67, 147, 181
de Paul, Lynsey 91, 98, **107-110**, 127, 271
de Shannon, Jackie 113, 145, 221
Deadlier Than The Male (film) 51
Deacon, John 322
Dean, Dixie 281
Dean Ford And The Gaylords 40
Decca Records (record label) 28, 32, 35, 40, 77, 94, 120, 129, 141, 161, 180, 185, 186, 230, 231, 248, 249, 268, 282, 286, 291, 312
Decimal Five (TV) 220
Dee, Dave 34, 37
Dee, Kiki 12, 38, **110-113**, 123
Deep Purple **72-73**, 78
Delaney & Bonnie 32, 69, 233
Delfonics, The 175
Dello, Pete 185
Dells, The 99
Denny, Sandy 98
Denselow, Robin 15
Denver, John 125, 126
Deram (record label) 163, 179, 183
Derek And The Dominoes 69
Detroit, Marcella 70
Deviants, The 266
Devoto, Howard 314
Diamond, Neil 120
Dick and Dee Dee 27
Dickson, Barbara 119, 149, 301
Diddley, Bo 75
Difford, Chris 162, 163

Diggle, Steve 314
Disc (newspaper) 205, 223, 237
Disc & Music Echo (newspaper) 24, 35, 43, 48, 75, 89, 91, 105, 106, 114, 120, 122, 129, 142, 144, 145, 160, 170, 178, 186, 192, 197, 199, 201, 209, 245, 270, 273, 329
Dixie Flyers, The 121
DJM (record label) 46, 47, 48, 152, 282
Dodd, Ken 27
Doggett, Peter 141, 142, 143, 221, 222
Doing Their Thing (TV) 40, 44, 323
Dollar 227, 228
Domino, Fats 302
Donegan, Lonnie 23
Donovan 56, 134, 146, **146-148**
Don't Look Back (film) 185
Dorset, Ray 283, 284
Dorsey, Arnold Gerald 228
Doubleback Series 90
Douma, Denny 196
Dowd, Tom 121, 122
Downes, Geoff 138
Dr Feelgood 269
Dr Hook 114, 166, 241
Driscoll, Julie 61, 278
Dr John 21
Drury, Jim 162
Dubliners, The 221
Dudgeon, Gus 111, 318
Dummer, John 146
Duncan, Lesley 38, 125
Duncan, Peter 303
Dunn, Clive 25
Durham, Judith 242, 243
Dylan, Bob 69, 70, 71, 113, 124, 134, 135, 146, 159, 160, 185, 280, 282, 285, 294, 312

Eadon, Auguste 'Gus' 39
Easlea, Daryl 204, 205, 206
Eclection 239

Edmands, Bob 53
Edmonds, Noel 298
Edmonton Symphony Orchestra 90
Edmunds, Dave 224, 281, **302-304**
Edwards Hand 99
Egan, Joe 310, 311
Egan, Sean 186, 187, 307
Electric Light Orchestra, The (ELO) 124, **189-191**, 207, 212, 213
Electronics & Music Maker (magazine) 282
Eliot, T.S. 255
Elliman, Yvonne 106
Elliot, Mama Cass 114
Elliott, Bobby 194, 195
Elliott, Stuart 254
Ellison, Lorraine 52, 112, 150
Ellis, Steve 38
Emerson, Keith 32
EMI (record label) 39, 41, 65, 88, 101, 102, 120, 126, 177, 194, 195, 233, 242, 243, 244, 246, 249
Entwistle, John 167
Epic (record label) 45
Equals, The **276-277**
Erasure 256
Eric Burdon And The Animals **185-186**
Essex, David 112, 119, **148-151**, 262, 299, 303
Eurovision Song Contest, The 48, 74, 109, 115, 121, 125, 126, 129, 132, 181, 234, 238, 240, 246, 247
Evans, Barry 188
Everett, Betty 118
Everett, Kenny 227
Everly Brothers, The 84, 92, 303
Evita (musical) 119, 149, 227
Exciters, The 256

Faces, The 166
Fairport Convention 294
Fairweather-Low, Andy 32, 33, **304-305**

Faithfull, Marianne **113-114**
Faith, Jeremy 239
Faltskog, Agnetha 99
Family **73-74**, 77, 83
Farjeon, Eleanor 165
Farlowe, Chris 67, 68, 161
Farrar, John 125, 126, 127, 128, 240, 246
Farrell, Wes 123
Felix, Julie 10
Fenton, Shane 261, 263
Fenwick, Ray 189
Ferry, Bryan 92, **191**, 260
Fiddler, John 82, 83
Fine Young Cannibals 314
Finian's Rainbow (film) 106
First Gear (radio) 11
Fishman, Jack 106
Fitzpatrick, Rob 55
Five Americans 223
Flamin' Groovies, The 224, 303
Fleetwood Mac 72, **74-76**, 78
Fleetwood, Mick 304
Fletcher, Gary 282
Fletcher, Guy 30, 131, 239
Flett, Doug 30, 131, 239
Flint, Hughie 281
Flo & Eddie 162, 265
Flowerpot Men, The 183
Flowers, Herbie 135, 149, 177, 178
Fly/Cube (record label) 71
Flying Burrito Brothers, The 170
Follow That Camel (film) 114
Fontana (record label) 37, 87, 159, 188
Fontana, Wayne **191-192**, 197
Ford, Dean 13, 40, 41, 42, 301
Ford, George 254
Ford, John 278, 279, 296, 297
Fortunes, The **269-271**
Foundations, The 48, **277-278**
Fourmost, The 215
Four Preps, The 23
Four Seasons, The 43, 274, 275, 296
Four Tops, The 111

Index

Four Weddings And A Funeral (film) 209
Fox 130, 246, **278**
Fox, Noosha 278
Frampton, Peter 21, 37, 38, 84
Frankie Goes To Hollywood 215
Franklin, Aretha 121
Franks, Clive 112
Freberg, Stan 23
Freddie And The Dreamers **26-28**
Free 68, **76-77**
Freeman, Alan 274
Fricker, Sylvia 291
Friedman, Dean 53
Frith, Simon 7, 12, 45, 59, 62, 74, 80, 81, 82, 83, 94, 107, 155, 156, 157, 161, 172, 208, 240, 263, 265, 306, 329
Fullerton, Fiona 49
Fury, Billy 168, 262

Gabriel, Peter 77, 78, 318
Gallagher and Lyle 281, **305-306**
Gallagher, Benny 281, 305, 306
Gallagher, Noel 89
Garden, Graeme 28, 29
Garfield, Simon 237
Garfunkel, Art 299, 305
Garrity, Freddie 26, 27
Gayden, Mac 38
Gaye, Marvin 59, 109
Gee, Rosko 96
Geeson, Judy 121
Geldof, Bob 316
Generation X **316**
Genesis **77-78**
Gentrys, The 33
Geordie **192-193**
Gerry And The Pacemakers **215-216**
Get It Together (TV) 206, 207, 266
Gibb, Andy **175-176**
Gibb, Barry 57, 127, 170, 171, 172, 173, 174, 175, 176
Gibb Brothers 40, 124
Gibb, Maurice 122, 171, 174

Gibb, Robin 127, 170, 171, 172, 173, 174
Gielgud, Sir John 220
Gilbert and Sullivan 119
Gilbey, Ian 282
Gillan, Ian 73
Gillett, Charlie 166
Giltrap, Gordon 285
Glitter Band, The 95, 193, **253-254**, 256
Glitter, Gary 33, 46, 193, **251-253**, 274
Gillespie, Haven 191
Glover, Roger 73
Godley and Creme 208, 220
Godspell (musical) 148
Goffin and King 55, 64, 99, 100, 136, 272, 273
Goffin, Gerry 272
Golden Garter, The (venue) 172
Goodbye Mr Chips 106
Good Earth (record label) 117
Goodhand-Tait, Philip 38, 39, 40
Goodies, The **28-29**
Goodison, John 47, 179
Gordon, Alan 105
Gorman, John 217, 218, 219, 220
Gouldman, Graham 55, 85, 168, 192, 197, 198, 207, 208, 209, 223
Grabher, Helmut 239
Graham, Eve 234
Grammy Awards, The 125
Granada Television 40, 44, 113, 189, 251
Grant, Eddie 277
Grant, Peter 303
Gray, Les 45, 258, 259, 260, 262
Grease (film) 128
Great American Songbook, The 191
Greenaway, Roger 27, 28, 47, 49, 100, 177, 178, 179, 183, 184, 226, 235, 261, 262, 269, 271
Greenfield, Howard 48, 226
Green, Hughie 115
Green, Peter 74, 75, 304

Grey & Pink Records (shop) 11
Grimaldi, John 67
GRIMMS 220
Growth Summer Festival And Free Concert 141
GTO (record label) 53, 123, 253
Guardian, The (newspaper) 15
Guest, Reg 52
Gurvitz, Paul 123
Guys 'N' Dolls 33, **227-228**, 252

Haggard, Merle 232
Hain, Marshall 150
Hair (musical) 309
Haley, Bill 212
Hall & Oates 174
Hamilton, James 203
Hammond, Albert 27, 194, 293
Hammond, Celia 147
Hardin, Eddie 188, 189
Hardy, Francoise 116
Hardy, Phil 230
Harley, Steve 13, 93, 254, 255, 256, 266, 274
Harper, Charlie 320
Harris, Alan 42
Harris, Anita 105, **114-115**
Harris, Bob 82, 168
Harris, Emmylou 84, 195
Harrison, George **15-17**, 20, 71, 115, 124, 125
Harrison, Larry 111
Harrison, Neil 123
Harrison, Noel 278
Harris, Tim 233
Harry, Bill 58
Hartman, Dan 124
Harvest Electric (record label) 89, 201, 211, 213
Harvey, Alex 50, 309, 310
Harvey, Les 122, 220
Hatch, Tony 49, 104, 105, 106, 120, 285
Hawker, Mike 136
Hawkes, Chip 43, 44, 45, 46

Hawkwind 248, 285
Hayward, Justin 150, 198, 199
Hazlewood, Lee 25
Hazlewood, Mike 27, 194
Hazzard, Tony 159
Heartbeat (TV) 203
Heath, Ted 25
Hello 60, 193, **256-257**
Helsing, Lenny 88
Hendrix, Jimi 41, 152, 167
Henri, Adrian 220
Henry, Lenny 25
Henry, Stuart 302
Herd, The 34, **37-38**
Here We Go Round The Mulberry Bush (film) 95, 160, 188, 277
Herman's Hermits 29, **55-57**, 58, 80, 121, 207
Heron, Mike 280
Heylin, Clinton 70, 329
Hicks, Tony 195
Hill, Dave 205, 206, 207
Hiller, Sheridan and Lee 181, 182
Hiller, Tony 47, 179, 180, 181, 182
Hill, John 184
Hillman, Chris 196
Hill, Roger 184
Hillsborough Disaster (1989) 216
Hime And Addison (shop) 188
Hinsley, Harvey 59
H.M. Queen Elizabeth II 28
Hodgson, Roger 93, 94
Hogg, Brian 162, 168, 210, 312
Holder, Noddy 205, 206, 207
Hollies, The 85, **193-196**, 207, 222, 260, 323
Holly, Buddy 45, 163, 203, 294
Hollywood Festival, The 283
Holmes, Rupert 110, 279
Holst, Gustav 280
Home 124
Honeybus 185
Hooper, Tony 296
Hope Evans, Peter 82, 83

Hopkin, Mary 58, 98, **115-118**, 133, 139, 305
Hopkins, Gaynor 139
Hopkins, Nicky 201, 281
Horn, Trevor 138, 228
Horowitz, Jimmy 119
Hot Chocolate **57-60**, 65, 124
Hotlegs 207
Howard, Ken 34, 37
Howarth, Peter 196
Hudson Ford **278-280**
Hudson, Richard 278, 296, 297
Hugg, Brian 319
Hugg, Mike 160, 319
Hughes, David 178
Hughes, Glenn 73
Hull, Alan 80, 81
Hultgreen, Georg (see also Kajanus, George) 239
Human League, The 292
Humblebums, The 310
Humble Pie 38, 76
Humperdinck, Engelbert 15, 144, **228- 230**
Hunter, Ian 66, 258
Hurst, Mike 163, 164
Hynde, Chrissie 61, 156, 157

Ian and Sylvia 291
Ian Campbell Folk Group 99
Idle Race, The 201
Idol, Billy 316
Immediate (record label) 32
I'm Sorry I'll Read That Again (radio) 28
Ingham, Chris 16, 17, 19, 20
Innes, Neil 220
Irish Republican Army (IRA) 158
Islam, Yusuf (see also Stevens, Cat) 163, 165
Island Records (record label) 28, 114, 164, 220, 249, 257, 260
Isle Of Wight Festival 135, 152, 268
Ivor Novello Awards 107, 108
Ivy League, The 29, 43, 46, **271-273**

Jackson, Ray 80, 81
Jackson, Tony 221
Jacks, Terry 270, 271
Jack The Lad 81
Jagger, Chris 175
Jagger, Mick 156, 161, 167, 168, 222
Jamere, Ceezy 292
James, Clive 126, 238
James, Dick 47
James, Elmore 74
James, Jimmy 103
James, Sally 33
James, Tony 316
Jam, The 158, **317**
Japp, Mike 41, 42
Jay And The Americans 273
Jayston, Michael 229
Jefferson 274, 275
Jersey Boys (musical) 296
Jesus Christ Superstar (musical) 106
Jethro Tull 72, **78-79**
Jet Records (record label) 108
Jett, Joan 61
Jewry, Bernard (see also Stardust, Alvin) 261
Jimi Hendrix Experience, The 167
John, Elton 18, 21, 41, 110, 111, 112, 123, 124, 125, **151-153**, 241, 268, 279, 293, 301, 308, 318
Johnson, Bob 117
Johnson, Brian 192, 193
Johnson, Derek 154, 221
Johnson, Holly 216
Johnson, Richard 51
Johnston, Bruce 289, 290
Johnstone, Davey 151
Johnstons, The 116
Jones, John Paul 56, 198
Jones, Lesley-Ann 323
Jones, Paul 159, 282
Jones, Tom 11, 144, 187, 226, **230-232**, 309
Joplin, Janis 170
Jupp, Micky 225

Kajanus, George
(see also Hultgreen, Georg)
239, 289-290
Kallen, Kitty 101
Kasenetz-Katz 210
Kaye, Lenny 272
Kaylan, Howard 162, 265
Kay, Peter 226, 227
Keating, Ronan 165
Keep Britain Tidy 235
Keller, Jerry 145
Kellie, Mike 220
Kelly, Dave 282
Kelly, Stan 99
Kent, Nick 83, 96, 157, 176, 252, 255
Kerr, Bob 29, 285
Kiki Dee Band, The 111
Kim, Andy 238
King, B.B. 75
King, Ben E. 18, 67
King, Carole 55, 64, 98, 99, 100, 136, 272, 273
King Crimson 68, 183
King Earle Boogie Band 296
King, Jonathan 34, 228
Kingston Trio, The 23, 270
Kinks, The 104, **154-159**, 185, 221, 318
Kinsley, Billy 216
Kipling, Rudyard 51
Kirke, Simon 68
Kirwan, Danny 75
Kiss 66
Klein, Alan 29
Knight, Gladys 123
Knight, Graham 42
Knight, Peter (arranger) 49
Knight, Peter (Steeleye Span) 117
Knight, Terry 319
Knopfler, David 175
Kokomo 269
Kongos, John 25, 259
Kopf, Biba 52, 53
Korner, Alexis 182, 183
Kossoff, Paul 77

Kraftwerk 36
Kramer, Billy J. 215
Krauss, Alison 277
Kretzmer, Herbert 138
Kristina, Sonja 61
K-Tel (record label) 182, 247
Ku Klux Klan, The 151

Ladybirds, The 38
Laine, Cleo 10
Laine, Denny 19, 198, 199
Laing, Dave 230, 258
Lambert, Dave 296
Lambert, Dennis 111
Lambert, Kit 167
Lane, Carla 219
Lane, Ronnie 156, 305
Langford, Pete 26
La Strada (film) 38
Lauder, Andrew 11
Lazell, Barry 38
Lea, Clive 272, 273, 274
Lea, Jim 205, 207
Leander, Mike 46, 120, 229, 256
Led Zeppelin 66, 80, 87, 122, 263, 303
Lee, Curtis 204
Lee, Peggy 99, 135
Legrand, Michael 49
Leiber and Stoller 310
Leigh, Spencer 45
Lennon, John **17-18**, 21, 82, 113, 145, 156, 207, 249, 261, 319
Lennox, Annie 117, 136
Leoncavallo, Ruggero 229
Leroy, Peter 259
Lesser, Jeffrey 279
Let It Rock (magazine) 5, 6, 36, 45, 62, 74, 80, 82, 94, 107, 108, 155, 161, 172, 208, 240, 258, 261, 329
Levene, Keith 317
Levy, Marcy 70
Lewis, Jerry Lee 202, 231, 284
Lewis, Linda **118-120**

INDEX

Lewis, Smiley 258, 302
Leyton, John 95, 202
Liberty Records (record label) 11, 223
Lieutenant Pigeon **196-197**
Lift Off (TV) 38, 201, 251, 323
Lind, Bob 113
Lindisfarne **79-81**, 241, 248, 279
Little Big Time (TV) 27
Little Richard 284
Liverpool Express **216**
Liverpool Scene, The 220
Liverpool Stadium (venue) 83
Lloyd Webber, Andrew 106, 119, 149, 227
Locke, Joseph 197
Lodge, John 199, 200
Logan, Nick 81
Loggins, Dave 241
London Palladium (venue) 130
London Philharmonic Orchestra 220
Loot (film) 39
Lord, Jon 73
Loudermilk, John D. 27, 113
Louis, Arthur 70
Love Affair 35, **38-39**, 202
Love, Darlene 119
Love Sculpture 302
Lowe, Nick 303
Lulu 10, 12, 98, **120-124**, 132, 181, 197
Lydon, John 317
Lyle, Graham 281, 305, 306
Lynn, Loretta 50
Lynn, Vera 237
Lynne, Jeff 66, 189, 190, 191, 201, 202
Lynott, Phil 95
Lynyrd Skynrd 81

Macaulay, Tony 47, 229, 235, 238, 274, 277
Mackay, David 100
Mackay, Duncan 254
MacLeod, John 47, 238, 277
MacRae, Dave 28

Madison Square Garden (venue) 18
Magnet (record label) 228, 261, 262
Maharishi Mahesh Yogi 146
MAM (record label) 108, 110, 236, 237, 302
Manchester Apollo (venue) 81
Manchester University (venue) 162
Manfred Mann 101, **159-161**, 192, 270, 281, 319
Manfred Mann's Earth Band **280**
Manic Street Preachers, The 132
Mann, Barry 228
Man Of A Thousand Faces (film) 102
Mansfield, Keith 38, 39, 40, 130, 144, 180
Marble Arch (record label) 154
Mardin, Arif 21, 121, 173, 174
Margolis, Mike 114, 115
Marley, Bob 29, 69
Marmalade 35, **40-42**, 44, 301
Marriott, Steve 38, 156
Marsden, Gerry 27, 215
Martin, Bill 26, 34, 42, 132, 278
Martin, George 99, 100
Marvin, Hank 125, 127, 240, **244-246**
Marvin, Welch and Farrar 125, 246
Mason, Barry 105, 144, 226, 229, 262
Mason, Dave 95, 96
Mathis, Johnny 248
Matlock, Glen 43
Matthews, David 233
Matthew's Southern Comfort 11
Mayall, John 281
May, Brian 322
May, Chris 51
May, Phil 87
McCartney, Linda 19
McCartney, Paul **18-20**, 98, 113, 115, 156, 216, 218, 220, 308, 322
McCoy, Van 119
McCracken, Charlie 189
McCulloch, Jimmy 41
McDowell, Malcolm 177
McGarraher, James 290

McGear, Mike 217, 218, 219, 220
McGough, Roger 217, 218, 219, 220
McGuinness Flint **281-282**
McGuinness, Tom 160, 281, 305
McHugh, Paddy 268, 269
McKeown, Les 34
McKuen, Rod 270
McTell, Ralph 115, 116, 117
McVie, Christine 75, 76
Meat Loaf 139
Mecca Ballroom 289
Meck (DJ) 294
Medicine Head **82-83**
Meek, Joe 27, 262
Melanie 30, 98, 101, 233
Melody Maker (newspaper) 40, 44, 89, 92, 118, 137, 155, 156, 157, 158, 159, 174, 188, 206, 207, 211, 243, 277, 282, 328, 329
Melua, Katie 299
Mercury (record label) 81, 138, 149
Mercury, Freddie 322, 323
Merseys, The 216
Message Of Love 268
MGM (record label) 186, 234, 287
Middle Of The Road 25, **306-307**
Midler, Bette 50, 127, 234
Mike Cotton Sound, The 155
Miles, John 13, 216, **282-283**
Miller and Rost 119
Miller, Jimmy 96
Mills, Gordon 108, 110, 231, 236, 237, 302
Mills, Hayley 278
Millward, Steve 194
Mimms, Garnett 192
Mindbenders, The 191, **197-198**
Minogue, Kylie 260
Miranda, Ralph 215
Mitchell, Guy 5
Mitchell, Joni 11, 83, 98, 102, 187
Mitchell, Warren 219
Mock Turtles, The 155
Modern Times (film) 273
Money, Zoot 39, 220

Monks, The 280
Monro, Matt 113, **233**
Monster Music Mash (TV) 38
Monterey Pop Festival 186
Monterey Pop (film) 186
Montez, Chris 120
Moody Blues 158, **198-200**
Moon, Keith 168, 220, 303
Moran, Mike 109
Morecambe and Wise Christmas Show (TV) 184
Moretti, Joe 284
Morgan, Barry 177
Moroder, Giorgio 36, 48, 53
Morrissey, Steven Patrick 56, 131, 132, 134
Moss, Ian 190
Most, Mickie 55, 56, 57, 58, 59, 60, 65, 120, 121, 122, 135, 148, 169, 182, 186, 243, 249
Mott The Hoople 68, **257-258**
Mountain (record label) 310
Mount, Dave 260
Move, The 189, **201-202**, 213
Mrs Mills 36
Mud 45, 158, 257, **258-260**, 262, 263
Muldaur, Maria 109
Mulholland, Garry 315, 316, 317
Munden, Dave 44, 46
Mungo Jerry 80, 147, **283-284**
Munns, Stephen 99
Muriel's Wedding (film) 286
Murray, Anne 194
Murray, Mitch 46, 202, 226
Murray, Pauline 5
Muscle Shoals Studios 121

Naked Attraction (TV) 93
National Lampoon (film) 29
Naughty Rhythms Tour 269
Nazareth **83-85**
Neil, Christopher 150, 151
Nelson, Pete 183
Nelson, Ricky 72, 125
Newcastle City Hall (venue) 81, 186

New Faces (TV) 203
Newman, Nannette 177
Newman, Randy 160
New Musical Express (NME) (newspaper) 16, 19, 23, 24, 25, 27, 30, 32, 34, 36, 38, 40, 41, 43, 44, 45, 46, 47, 48, 51, 53, 56, 58, 67, 69, 71, 72, 73, 74, 75, 76, 77, 78, 80, 81, 83, 85, 86, 87, 88, 90, 91, 95, 96, 100, 108, 109, 113, 115, 116, 120, 121, 122, 123, 125, 132, 133, 134, 135, 136, 137, 138, 141, 143, 144, 145, 146, 147, 148, 153, 154, 155, 156, 157, 158, 159, 160, 161, 163, 164, 165, 166, 167, 168, 169, 170, 171, 172, 173, 176, 177, 178, 179, 180, 182, 183, 184, 186, 187, 188, 190, 193, 194, 196, 198, 199, 200, 201, 203, 204, 205, 208, 210, 211, 212, 218, 219, 220, 221, 222, 226, 229, 230, 231, 232, 234, 235, 236, 239, 240, 243, 244, 245, 246, 249, 250, 252, 255, 257, 263, 265, 266, 269, 270, 271, 272, 273, 276, 279, 281, 282, 284, 287, 289, 291, 297, 301, 302, 305, 306, 309, 312, 313
New Seekers, The 12, 233, **233-236**
Newton-John, Olivia **124-129**, 297
New Vaudeville Band, The **29-30**
New World **61**, 64, 135
Nice, The 32
Nicholas And Alexandra (film) 229
Nicholas, Paul 150
Nicholson, Hugh 41
Nilsson, Harry 21, 133, 160
NME Pollwinners Concert 284
Noakes, John 25
Noakes, Rab 310
Nolans, The 184
Noone, Peter **56-57**, 107
Norman, Chris **63-65**

Norton, Graham 181
Not The Nine O'Clock News (TV) 320, 321

Oakes, Trevor 204
O'Brien, Lucy 136
Ochs, Phil 291
O'Connor, Des 129
O'Connor, Hazel 320
Oddie, Bill 28, 29
Ofarim, Abi 284
Ohio Express 210
Oldfield, Mike **85-86**
Oldham, Andrew Loog 32, 161, 203, 222
Oldham, Spooner 50
Oliver In The Overworld (musical) 27
Oliver! (musical) 134
Olympic Games (1968) 24
On Your Toes (musical) 245
Open Road 147
Opportunity Knocks (TV) 61, 115, 135, 202
Orson, Anne 112
Osborne, Gary 153
Oscars, The (The Academy Awards) 229, 233
Osmond, Donny 149
O'Sullivan, Gilbert 35, 107, 108, 158, **236-237**, 249, 250
Otis, Johnny 69
O'Toole, Peter 106

Page, Gene 112, 251
Page, Jimmy 169, 283, 308
Page, Larry 47, 209
Page One (record label) 46
Pagliacci (opera) 229
Paper Lace **202-203**, 206
Paramour, Norrie 239
Parfitt, Rick 92, 93
Parker, Alan 177
Parker, Graham 304
Park, Simon 233
Parlophone (record label) 37, 39

Parsons, Alan 13, 282, 307, 308
Parsons, Gram 84
Partridge, Don **284-285**
Pat Garrett And Billy The Kid (film) 70
Paton, David 13, 307, 308
Patrick, Mick 49
Patten, Brian 220
Paul, Lyn 235
Paul McCartney and Wings 19
Pearl and Dean 282
Peebles, Andy 153
Peel, John 11, 79, 80, 82, 83, 85, 90, 240, 261, 263, 315
Penn, Dan 50
Pennebaker, D.E. 186
Penning, Les 86
Penny Farthing (record label) 24
Percy (film) 155
Perry, Richard 293
Pete Kelly's Blues (film) 99
Peter, Paul and Mary 107, 113
Petrusich, Amanda 50
Pet Shop Boys 139, 158
Petty, Tom 139
Philips (record label) 50, 110, 137, 138, 177, 280
Philips, Tim 51
Piaf, Edith 117
Piccadilly Radio 26
Pickett, Phil 290
Pickettywitch 48, **238**
Pidgeon, John 36, 74, 108
Pilot 216, 282, **307-308**
Pinder, Mike 199
Pink Floyd 66, 82, **86-87**, 249, 304
Pipkins, The 28
Pitney, Gene 160, 192
Plant, Robert 73
Plastic Ono Band 17, 160
Platters, The 21
Player 175
Poets, The 41
Poitier, Sidney 121, 197
Polydor (record label) 82, 107, 109, 131, 171, 172, 191, 193, 284, 287
Poole, Brian 43
Pop-Ex (record label) 11, 268
Poppy Family, The 271
Porter, Cole 17, 237
Potger, Keith 233
Potter, Brian 111
Powell, Andrew 282
Praetorious, Michael 86
Presley, Elvis 75, 197, 206, 212, 228, 258, 291
Presley, Reg 209, 210, 211
Preston, Billy 21, 71
Pretenders, The 158
Pretty Things, The **87-89**, 249
Price, Alan 10, 101, 120, 160, 185
Priest, Steve 193, 263, 264
Prior, Maddy 295, 296
Pritchard, Barry 270
Private Stock (record label) 251, 258, 259, 301
Procol Harum **89-91**, 287, 323
Proops, Marjorie 236
Public Image Limited **317**
Pursey, Jimmy 319
PVC-2 42
Pye Records (record label) 39, 67, 92, 104, 105, 124, 125, 131, 133, 135, 147, 154, 155, 182, 211, 223, 224, 238, 273
Quatro, Suzi 12, **61-63**
Queen 85, 205, 209, 224, 255, 264, **322-323**

Racey **63-64**
Radio Caroline 91, 111
Radio Caroline North 269
Radio City 26
Radio Four 109
Radio Luxembourg 10, 11
Radio One 10, 11, 21, 26, 33, 39, 41, 55, 56, 71, 73, 74, 78, 79, 82, 109, 115, 116, 134, 138, 142, 147, 153, 160, 171, 174, 180, 182, 192, 205, 207, 224, 233,

INDEX

274, 276, 279, 297, 298, 302, 308, 318
Radio Two 11, 28, 292
Rae, Jackie 229
Rafferty, Gerry **309**, 310, 311
Rafferty, Jim 175
Raft (record label) 118
Rainbow 60
Rainbow Theatre (venue) 168, 192, 252
RAK (record label) 55, 57, 61, 63, 64, 65, 135, 258, 261
Ralphs, Mick 68
Ramones, The 159
Rascals, The 137
Raspberries, The 158
Rave (magazine) 37
Ray, James 17
Raymonde, Ivor 136
Ray, Rita 146
RCA (record label) 130, 142, 143, 155, 157, 223, 224, 259, 306
Rea, Chris 308
Reaction (record label) 167
Reading Festival 207
Real Thing, The **216-217**
Record Collector (magazine) 11, 58, 179, 295, 299, 306
Record Mirror & Disc (newspaper) 205, 237, 262, 266
Record Mirror (newspaper) 18, 19, 21, 25, 31, 32, 34, 36, 37, 39, 41, 43, 49, 52, 53, 56, 57, 58, 59, 60, 62, 63, 64, 66, 67, 68, 69, 70, 71, 74, 78, 79, 80, 81, 83, 84, 85, 86, 88, 89, 90, 93, 94, 95, 100, 101, 102, 103, 104, 105, 106, 108, 109, 111, 112, 113, 114, 116, 117, 118, 119, 120, 121, 123, 125, 126, 127, 128, 130, 132, 133, 134, 135, 138, 139, 142, 145, 146, 147, 148, 150, 151, 152, 153, 154, 155, 156, 157, 160, 162, 163, 164, 165, 166, 167, 168, 172,

173, 174, 175, 178, 179, 180, 181, 182, 183, 188, 190, 191, 192, 193, 195, 196, 199, 200, 202, 203, 204, 206, 208, 209, 210, 211, 212, 214, 216, 217, 221, 222, 223, 227, 228, 229, 230, 231, 232, 234, 235, 236, 237, 240, 241, 242, 243, 245, 246, 248, 249, 250, 251, 252, 253, 254, 255, 256, 257, 258, 259, 261, 262, 263, 266, 268, 269, 271, 273, 274, 275, 276, 278, 279, 280, 282, 283, 284, 286, 287, 288, 289, 290, 291, 292, 293, 294, 295, 296, 297, 298, 299, 301, 303, 304, 305, 306, 307, 308, 309, 310, 315, 322
Record Plant (studio) 173
Record World (magazine) 21, 128, 129
Redding, Otis 170
Reddy, Helen 50
Red, White & Blues (film) 124
Reed, Jerry 310
Reed, Les 105, 111, 144, 192, 229, 231, 238, 270
Reed, Lou 108, 191, 320
Reed, Oliver 278
Reeves, Jim 291
Reeves, Vic 233
Reflections, The 272
Regal Zonophone (record label) 71, 117, 177, 302
Reid, Keith 90, 91
Reid, Terry 48
Relf, Keith 82
Reparata and The Delrons 130
Reservoir Dogs (film) 311
Reynolds, Anthony 51, 52
Reynolds, Malvina 221
Reynolds, Simon 9, 208, 256, 257, 258
Rice, Tim 106, 119, 149, 227
Richard, Cliff 10, 69, 126, 127, **239-242**, 244, 261, 274, 287,

304
Rich Kids, The 43
Righteous Brothers, The 203
Rikfors, Michael 193, 194
Rivingtons, The 252
Roberts, Andy 220
Robertson, B.A. 242
Roberty, Marc 70, 72
Robinson, Smokey 64
Robinson, Tom **318**
Rocket Records (record label) 41, 110, 123, 301
Rockfield Studios 224, 303
Rockin' Berries, The 154, **272-275**, 275
Rockin' Horse 216
Rocky Sharp And The Razors 146
Rodgers and Hammerstein 215
Rodgers and Hart 245, 303
Rodgers, Clodagh 98, **129-131**, 278, 301
Rodgers, Jimmie 309
Rodgers, Paul 68, 77
Rodgers, Richard 246
Roe, Tommy 159
Roker, Ron 271
Rolling Stone (magazine) 89
Rolling Stones, The 15, 76, **161**, 167, 210
Romeo, Tony 181
Ronco (record label) 247
Ronettes, The 52, 113, 257
Ronson, Mick 141, 258
Rooksby, Rikky 75
Rose, David 37
Rossi, Francis 93
Rossi, Mike 92
Rostill, John 125, 126, 128
Rotten, Johnny 317
Roulettes, The 66
Roxy Music 191, 248, **260-261**, 274, 289
Royal Albert Hall 17, 182, 234, 285
Royal College of Music 301
Royal Festival Hall 173

Rubettes, The 37, 63, 274, **285-286**, 289
Rufus 62
Rush, Tom 52
Russell, Leon 70, 71, 148
Rutherford, Mike 78
Ryan, Barry 222, 286, 287, 288
Ryan, Marion 286
Ryan, Paul 222, **286-289**

Sager, Carole Bayer 138, 293
Sagittarius 272
Sailor 239, 279, **289-291**
Sammes, Paul 248
Santana 75
Sarstedt, Peter **292**
Saturday Night Fever (film) 175, 176
Saturday Scene (TV) 33, 252, 299
Sayer, Leo **292-294**
Scaffold, The 11, 208, **217-221**
Scaggs, Boz 52
Schroeder, John 92
Schubert, Franz 280
Score With The Scaffold (TV) 220
Scott, Andy 264
Scott, Barry 237, 293
Scott, Ronnie 139
Seago, Eddie 229
Searchers, The 103, 104, 154, 215, **221-225**
Seaside Special 101, 121
Sebastian, John 134, 298
Secombe, Harry 105, 248
Sedaka, Neil 48, 224, 226
Seeger, Pete 115
Seekers, The 233, **242-244**
Seger, Bob 95
Sellers, Peter 295
Sensational Alex Harvey Band, The **309-311**
Set Of Six (TV) 189
Sez Les (TV) 262
Shadows, The 125, 127, 195, 240, **244-247**, 304
Shakespear's Sister 70

Index

Sham 69 **319**
Shane, Bob 23
Shang-A-Lang (TV) 197
Shangri-Las 208
Shankar, Ravi 186
Shapiro, Tom 247
Shaw, Greg 33
Shaw, Sandie 10, 100, 104, **131-136**
Shelley, Pete (Buzzcocks) 314, 315
Shelley, Peter (songwriter) 123, 228, 261
Shepherd, Cybil 269
Shepherd, Gerry 253, 254
Sherman, Bobby 183
Sherrill, Billy 50
Shindig (magazine) 41, 44, 88, 91, 163, 164, 178, 186, 189, 236, 263, 264
Showaddywaddy **203-204**, 253, 284
Siffre, Labi 10
Sigue Sigue Sputnik 316
Silver Dream Racer (film) 151
Silverstein, Shel 114
Simon and Garfunkel 40
Simon, Carly 110, 130
Simone, Nina 170
Sinatra, Frank 23
Sinatra, Nancy 25
Siouxsie And The Banshees **319**
Sir Douglas Quintet 64, 260
Sire (record label) 224, 225, 303
Skellern, Peter **248-249**
Slade 61, 158, 193, **204-207**, 211
Slik **42-43**
Sloan, P.F. 55, 221, 222
Small Faces 38, **161-162**
Smith, Mike (producer) 39
Smith, Mike (The Dave Clark Five) 143, 144, 145, 146
Smith, Norman 'Hurricane' 87, 88, **249-250**
Smith, Peter 291
Smith, Robin 322, 323
Smith, Tony Stratton 77
Smith, Verdelle 132

Smith, Wally 195
Smith, 'Whistling' Jack 30, 31
Smokie 61, 63, **64-65**
Snape 183
Snow, Tom 129
Solid Gold Sixty (radio) 182
Some Mothers Do 'Ave 'Em (TV) 25
Somerville, Jimmy 170
Sounds (newspaper) 26, 82, 90, 155, 266, 292, 329
Sour Hall (venue) 225
South, Joe 61, 135
Space 46
Sparks 9, 10, 287
Spector, Phil 16, 17, 119, 187, 203, 212, 253, 257
Spedding, Chris 55
Spencer Davis Group, The **187-189**
Spencer, Jeremy 74, 75
Spencer, Pete 64
Spinners 221
Springate, John 253
Springfield, Dusty 98, 110, 130, **136-139**, 177, 228, 243
Springfield, Tom 114, 242, 243
Springsteen, Bruce 33, 195, 280, 323
Squeeze **162-163**
Stamp, Chris 167
Stanley, Bob 105, 170, 171, 173, 174, 223, 306
Stanshall, Viv 29, 220
Stardust, Alvin 33, 228, **261-263**
Stardust (film) 303
Starr, Kay 117
Starr, Ringo **20-21**
Star Wars (film) 217
Staton, Candi 174
Status Quo 38, **91-93**, 94, 206, 232, 297
Stax (record label) 112, 259
Stealers Wheel 248, **310-311**
Steele, Tommy 5, 106
Steeleye Span 117, **294-296**
Steinman, Jim 139
Stein, Seymour 224

Stephens, Geoff 27, 29, 30, 210, 235, 238, 261, 272
Steve Harley and Cockney Rebel **254-256**
Stevens, Cat 43, 79, 80, 118, 119, 135, **163-166**, 186
Stevens, Shakin' 253
Stewart, Eric 197, 208, 209
Stewart, Rod 33, 80, 165, **166-167**, 255
Stiff Records (record label) 262, 314
Stiles, Ray 259, 260
Stock, Aitken and Waterman 136
Stookey, Paul 107
Stories 59
St Peters, Crispian 37, **291**
Stranglers, The **320**
Strawberry Hill Boys 296
Strawberry Studios 220, 224
Strawbs, The 278, 279, **296-298**
Streisand, Barbra 123
Strong, Martin C. 156
Strummer, Joe 315, 316
Stubbs, Mick 124
Stylistics, The 28, 153
Styrene, Poly 321
Sue and Sunny 179
Sullivan, 'Big' Jim 56
Sunday Night At The London Palladium (TV) 222
Supersonic (TV) 10, 212, 252, 254, 255, 262, 266, 289, 323
Supertramp **93-94**, 305
Surprise Surprise (TV) 102
Swansong (record label) 87, 303
Sweet, The 9, 10, 36, 40, 193, **263-264**
Swinging Blue Jeans, The 215
Swing Out Sister 137
Sylvester, Terry 13, 195

Take A Girl Like You (film) 277
Take That 124
Talk Of The Town (venue) 114, 243
Tamla Motown (record label) 64, 110, 112, 133, 180
Target (record label) 42
Tarney, Alan 241, 242, 247
Taupin, Bernie 21, 112, 151, 153, 318
Tavares 111
Taylor, Alex 175
Taylor, Chip 194
Taylor, Derek 249
Taylor, James 175
Taylor, Kate 175
Taylor, Livingstone 175
Tebb, Johnny 35
Teddy Bears, The 295
Temperance Seven, The 29
Temptations, The 59
Tennyson, Lord 15
Terry, George 70
That'll Be The Day (film) 148, 168
That Will Never Happen Again (fanzine) 129, 131
The Arrows (TV) 30, 254, 262, 308
The Basil Brush Show (TV) 94, 323
The Black And White Minstrel Show (TV) 243
The Countess Of Hong Kong (film) 274
The Des O'Connor Show (TV) 129
The Full Monty (film) 60, 256
The Geordie Scene (TV) 10, 264
The Go-Between (film) 49
The Goodies (TV) 28
The Guinness Book Of Hit Singles (book) 11, 12, 174, 314
The Heartbreak Kid (film) 268, 269
The History Of Rock (magazine) 38, 56, 58, 171
Them **312-313**
The Mad Dogs And Englishmen (tour) 71
The Man With The Golden Gun (film) 123
The Mike and Bernie Winters Show (TV) 130
The Music Of Lennon McCartney (TV) 113
The Old Grey Whistle Test (TV) 108, 118, 168, 323

INDEX

The Phantom Of The Opera (musical) 256
The Pirates Of Penzance (opera) 57
The Protectors (TV) 226
The Raging Moon (film) 177
The Record Producers (radio) 55, 62
The Sound Of Music (album) 243
The Sound Of Music (musical) 107
The Stud (film) 217
The Two Ronnies (TV) 103, 130
The World Is Full Of Married Men (film) 139
Thin Lizzy **94-95**
Thomas, Ralph 51
Thomas, Tasha 205
Thompson, Chris 280
Thompson, Danny 115, 116
Thorup, Peter 182, 183
Three City Four 99
Thunderclap Newman 41, 287
Tilbrook, Glenn 162, 163
Tobias, Oliver 217
Tomorrow 84, 124
Tom Robinson Band, The **318-319**
Top Gear (radio) 11, 85
Top of the Pops (TV) 10, 24, 25, 28, 29, 36, 38, 39, 41, 42, 43, 44, 45, 46, 47, 49, 56, 61, 62, 63, 68, 72, 73, 75, 76, 78, 82, 98, 99, 100, 101, 102, 103, 104, 105, 106, 107, 108, 111, 112, 117, 118, 119, 121, 122, 123, 125, 127, 129, 130, 131, 132, 133, 134, 135, 137, 138, 139, 143, 146, 147, 150, 154, 160, 164, 171, 172, 173, 181, 182, 188, 201, 202, 204, 206, 207, 213, 219, 222, 226, 227, 228, 231, 232, 233, 234, 235, 237, 240, 241, 242, 252, 255, 257, 258, 259, 261, 262, 266, 269, 279, 280, 281, 282, 285, 286, 288, 289, 292, 294, 295, 296, 297, 298, 302, 305, 308, 314, 315, 316, 318, 319, 320, 321, 323

Tosh, Stuart 209
To Sir With Love (film) 120, 197
Tottenham Royal Ballroom (venue) 32
Tourists, The 136
Toussaint, Allen 21, 71
Townsend, Rob 83
Townshend, Pete 24, 156, 167, 168
Toy Dolls, The 295
Track Records (record label) 167
Traffic 84, 90, **95-96**, 160, 187
Transatlantic (record label) 116, 310
Travis, Dave Lee 109
Tremeloes, The 12, **43-46**, 274
Trent, Jackie 49, 104, 105, 106
T. Rex 45, 238, **265-267**
T. Rex Wax Company 265
Troggs, The **209-211**
Tucker, Mick 264
Tucker, Tanya 50
Turner, James R. 201, 212, 213, 214
Turner, Steve 171
Turner, Tina 283, 306
Turtles, The 105, 162, 265
Turton, Geoff 272, 274, 275
Twiggy 115
Twitty, Conway 240
Tyler, Bonnie **139-140**
Tyler, Tony 16, 18, 19
Tyrannosaurus Rex 90
Tyson, Ian 291

UK Subs, The **320-321**
Ultravox 42, 54
Undertones 314
Up The Junction (film) 160, 277
Ure, Andrew 239
Ure, Midge 42, 54
Usher, Gary 272

Valentine, Penny 24, 27, 30, 43, 44, 47, 56, 82, 87, 88, 96, 105, 114, 121, 131, 132, 133, 135, 137, 141, 170, 192, 197, 198, 203, 209, 210, 223, 243, 244, 245, 270, 273, 277, 285, 291,

292, 329
Valli, Frankie 274, 296
Vance and Pockriss 132
van Day, David 227
Van Der Valk (TV) 233
Van Halen 158
Vanilla Fudge 91
Vanity Fare **46-49**, 202
Varstand, Johnny 129
Velvet Underground, The 191
Ventures, The 204, 245
Verity, John 67
Vertigo (record label) 92, 94, 280, 309
Vickers, Mike 101, 164, 192
Virgin Encyclopedia Of Popular Music (book) 18
Virgin Records (record label) 50, 85, 278
Visconti, Morgan 118
Visconti, Tony 42, 115, 116, 117, 141, 265, 266, 304
Voice Squad, The 318
Volman, Mark 162, 265

Wailers, The 29
Wainman, Phil 257
Wakeman, Rick 66, 165, 296
Wale, Michael 10
Walker Brothers, The 12, **51-54**, 150, 274
Walker, Gary 53
Walker, John 53
Walker, Johnnie (DJ) 33
Walker, Junior 81
Walker, Scott **49-51**, 53, 195, 232
Wallinger, Karl 106
Warner Bros. (record label) 108, 190, 211, 220
Warnes, Jennifer 72
Warwick, Dionne 106, 131
Washington, Geno 193
Waterman, Pete 6, 136, 261
Wayne, Carl 196, 201
Wayne, Jeff **148-150**, 262, 280
WEA (record label) 228

Weaver, Blue 32, 174, 296
Webb, Jimmy 268
Webster, Francis 229
Wedding Present, The 256
Weider, John 186
Weill, Cynthia 228
Welch, Bruce 125, 126, 128, **240-244**, 246
Welch, Chris 44, 89, 92, 188, 211
Weller, Paul 35, 158, 317
Wells, David 189, 198
Wembley Arena (venue) 33
Wembley Empire Pool (venue) 33, 252, 284, 299
Westlake, Clive 106, 130, 137
Westlife 270
West, Mae 292
West, Rick 44
West Side Story (musical) 148
Wet Wet Wet 209
Wexler, Jerry 121
What A Crazy World (film) 29
White, Barry 112, 251
Whitehead, Alan 42
Whitehouse, Mary 310
White Plains 179, **183-184**
White, Sheila 188
White & Torch 54
Whittaker, Roger 238
Whitten, Danny 85
Who, The 156, **167-168**
Wicks, John 224
Wilde, Kim 65
Wilde, Marty 35, 91
Williams, Andy 106, 224, 274
Williams, Don 70
Williams, Jimmy 111
Williams, Richard 118
Williams, Tony 21
Wilson, Brian 290
Wilson, Carl 271
Wilson, Dennis 71
Wilson, Harold 25, 217
Wilson, Jackie 146
Wilson, Margaret 58

Wilson, Nancy 111
Wilson, Tony 57, 59
Wine, Toni 197
Wingfield, Pete 128
Winwood, Muff 187
Winwood, Stevie 95, 96, 187, 188, 189
Wisdom, Norman 273
Withers, Bill 259
Wizzard 42, 158, 189, 202, **211-213**, 262
Wizzo Band, The 212
Wobble, Jah 317
Woffinden, Bob 58, 81
Wolfe, Steve 138
Wogan, Terry 181
Wombles, The 33, **298-300**
Wonder, Stevie 227, 269
Woodcraft, Maurice 245
Woodley, Bruce 241, 243
Wood, Roy 35, 108, 146, 189, 191, 201, 202, 211, 212, **213-214**
Wood, Shirley 233
Wood, Victoria 91, 108
Wooley, Bruce 138

Wright, Dougie 135
Wright, Richard 86
Wright, Steve 292
Wurzels, The **30-31**
WWA (record label) 83
Wyllie, Ross D. 57
Wynette, Tammy 26, 130

X-Ray Spex **321**

Yardbirds, The 69, 75, 82, 142, **168-169**, 207, 319
Yarwood, Mike 25, 204
Yastano, John 293
Yazz And The Plastic Population 103
Yellow Dog 130, 278
Yes **96-97**
Young, Bob 92
Young, Johnny B. 57
Young, Kenny 129, 130, 223, 278
Young, Neil 145

Zombies, The 66, 197, 321
Zoo Records (record label) 50